0   200   400   600   800

Miles

R. Tanais

R. Borysthenes

SARMATIA

Tibiscus

DACIA

Tauris

R. Danube

PONTUS EUXINUS

OESIA

Haemus Mts.

Thrace

Rhodope Mts.

Constantinople

Bosporus

ARMENIA

MEDIA

Macedonia

Bithynia

Pontus

Hellespont

Troy

R. Halys

Cappadocia

R. Tigris

Boeotia

ASIA

Phrygia

Achaia

Lydia

Cilicia

Mesopotamia

Lycia

Antioch

Syria

R. Euphrates

Cyprus

Laodicea

Phoenicia

Palmyra

Babylonia

Heliopolis

Damascus

Babylon

Crete

Baby lonia

AN   SEA

Cyrene

Palestine

Judaea

ARABIA

Marmarica

Alexandria

Y   A

Heliopolis

Memphis

EGYPT

R. Nile

RICUM

EX LIBRIS

Randy Manning

The History of the
Decline and Fall
of the Roman Empire

Edward Gibbon in 1764, the year he first conceived the idea of writing his great work

Edward Gibbon

THE HISTORY OF
THE DECLINE AND FALL
OF THE ROMAN EMPIRE

VOLUME I

THE TURN OF
THE TIDE

*Edited and with an introduction
by Betty Radice*

LONDON
THE FOLIO SOCIETY
MCMLXXXIII

The first volume of Gibbon's *History of the Decline and Fall of the Roman Empire* was published in 1776, and the history was completed in 1788. This text is reproduced by kind permission of J. M. Dent and Son Limited, from the Everyman edition, 1910.

© Introduction: The Folio Society Limited, 1983

First published by The Folio Society 1983.
Reissued with new binding 1995.
Ninth printing 1998.

Set in Lasercomp Poliphilus
at The Alden Press, Oxford.
Printed on Balmoral Book Wove paper
at The Bath Press, Bath
and bound by them in full elephanthide,
blocked with a design based on a
binding by Henry Walther, c. 1780.

CONTENTS

ILLUSTRATIONS

(Many of the pictures are reproduced by kind permission of the Trustees of the British Museum.)

INTRODUCTION

A FTER TWO HUNDRED YEARS THE REPU-
tation of *The Decline and Fall of the Roman Empire* still stands high. For
Hugh Trevor-Roper it remains 'the greatest historical work in our
language'.* The grandeur of its theme ranges over nearly fourteen
hundred years of western history, from the Antonine emperors of AD 100
to the fall of Constantinople to the Turks in 1453. Woven into its texture
are the history of the Early Church, the dispersal of the Germanic
peoples, the rise of Islam, the Dark Ages of Europe and the Crusades, all
of which Gibbon saw as elements in a continuous process of change and
development. The classical oratory of its style never fails to offer unexpected pleasures – a flash of wit, a pointed epigram worthy of Tacitus, a
touch of delicate humour, a thumb-nail portrait painted with demure
irony and a dramatic scene eloquently presented. Then there are the
notes, estimated at over eight thousand. These are not only Gibbon's
solid justification for his facts and the interpretation he puts on them, but
reveal the man himself and the wide range of his interests, his engaging
delight in information about travel and geography, natural history,
antiquities, current affairs and the oddities of men whose frailties fall
victim to his sly ridicule or whose misguided fanaticism meets with his
scorn. We have to accept his idiosyncrasies and limitations (he shows no
interest in music, art or natural beauty); but we can only admire the
clear, dispassionate intelligence which marshals the facts and presents the
historian's personal viewpoint in the manner necessary to save his great
work from being no more than a narration of events.

The Decline and Fall is a watershed between the painstaking
chroniclers and ecclesiastical antiquarians and the historians of the
Enlightenment and after, some of whom were the doctrinaire thinkers
and idealists whose purpose was to create a better world, and whose
tendency was to brush aside what did not fit in with their theories.
Voltaire had even said: *'Malheur aux détails, c'est une vermine qui tue les
grands ouvrages.'* [A curse on details; they are vermin which kill great

* H. R. Trevor-Roper, 'Edward Gibbon after Two Hundred Years', *The Listener*,
22.10.64, p. 617.

works.] Gibbon was not a philosopher in the French sense: he used the term 'philosophy' to express his humanist belief in the rational thinking by which a man can rise above bigotry and superstition and try to make sense of his experiences. So, too, the 'philosophical traveller' means one who is observant, informed and unprejudiced. Gibbon had no wish to reform society; he sought only to understand and rationalise the past. After *The Decline and Fall* the writing of history could never be the same again.

'The combination of philosophic history with the antiquarians' method of research became the aim which many of the best historians of the nineteenth century proposed to themselves. It is still the aim that many of us propose to ourselves. It means two difficult things: the constant repression of the *a priori* attitude inherent in the generalising approach of the philosophic historian and, on the other hand, the avoidance of the antiquarian mentality with its fondness for classification and for irrelevant detail.'*

Gibbon's classical model was Tacitus, the 'decisive authority' for whom his admiration was unreserved. Tacitus had set out to explain the moral decline of his own times by starting with the civil wars following the murder of Nero (*The Histories*), and then going back to Augustus (in *The Annals*) to show that the seeds of decay were sown when the one-man principate replaced the republican democracy. Gibbon too came to think that he should have chosen an earlier starting point than the Antonine Age. Both historians tended to idealise the virtues of the Roman Republic, but Gibbon is less relentlessly pessimistic than Tacitus, thanks to his Enlightenment background.

Gibbon's modern mentors were especially Bayle and Montesquieu. Bayle was the most famous exponent of the sceptical approach to history, the empirical method which denied the possibility of absolute truth. His *Dictionnaire historique et critique* of 1697 taught Gibbon to weigh the validity of facts to be used as historical evidence, not allowing them to be perverted in the interests of religion or of national or human vanity. There are over twenty references to Bayle, all appreciative of his accuracy and learning. The great political thinker Montesquieu had written his own *Considérations sur les causes de la grandeur des Romains et de leur décadence* in 1734, in which he traced the collapse of the Empire to its own immoderate growth that led to the corruption of the 'general spirit' of the Republic. This term Montesquieu defined and expanded in his major

* A. Momigliano, 'Ancient History and the Antiquarian', *Studies in Historiography* (London, 1966) p. 25.

work, *L'esprit des lois* (1748); a nation or society has a general spirit pervading all its aspects, and ideally its laws must conform with this. That is, he judged laws and institutions by reference to the social system in which they functioned, and to the geographical, economic and historical factors creating patterns of society. Montesquieu can therefore be considered the founder of the sociological approach to history. Gibbon refers to him some fifty times, and though occasionally critical of his 'lively fancy' and inaccuracy, found him an excitingly liberating influence, freeing the philosophic historian from the total scepticism of Bayle and the metaphysical explanations of the churchmen.

Gibbon left six incomplete drafts of Memoirs, from which Lord Sheffield took selections for an *Autobiography*, and which later editors have augmented and entitled *Memoirs of My Life*. They show how *The Decline and Fall* came to be written and what were the exceptional qualities which went into it: sustained concentration, retentive memory, intellectual honesty and the capacity to see a way through a wood dense with trees. Gibbon was born in Putney on 8 May 1737, the eldest child of Edward Gibbon and Judith Porten; six more children died in infancy and his mother before he was ten. He himself was so puny and sickly that he survived only through the devoted care of his mother's sister, Catherine Porten, the 'dear Aunt Kitty' on whose death he was to write: 'To her instructions I owe the first rudiments of knowledge, the first exercise of reason and a taste for books which is still the pleasure and glory of my life.'* His formal schooling was frequently interrupted, but he had freedom to read whatever captured his imagination, Pope's Homer, the Arabian Nights, Dryden's Virgil. He then moved on to anything he could find on geography and world history when he had the run of his grandfather Porten's library in Putney, and later that of his father's country seat at Buriton, near Petersfield. The future historian took shape more from the solitary boy's determined application, ill though he was, than from a succession of private tutors and two broken years at Westminster School. Then his health improved and was to remain generally good; his father decided to send him to Oxford, to Magdalen College as a gentleman commoner. There he arrived in April 1752, just before his fifteenth birthday, 'with a stock of erudition that might have puzzled a doctor, and a degree of ignorance of which a schoolboy would have been ashamed.'

Eighteenth-century Oxford was no place for a precocious scholar, and Gibbon looked back on the fourteen months spent at Magdalen as

* Letter to Lord Sheffield, 10 May 1786.

'the most idle and unprofitable of my whole life'. There was no sound teaching to improve his inadequate grammatical grounding, no stimulus to direct his eagerness to learn. Bored and lonely, still reading where he wished, his relish for religious debate which had often baffled his aunt took him to the writings of the English Jesuit Robert Parsons and of the French Jesuit Bossuet; and these brought about his intellectual conversion to the Catholic Church. His angry father promptly removed him from Oxford and packed him off to Lausanne, in Protestant French Switzerland, for instruction and reformation by the Calvinist pastor Daniel Pavilliard.

This was most fortunate for Gibbon, if not at first any happier. He knew no French, lacked money and companionship, and the Pavilliard household was austere and uncomfortable; but he was resilient. M. Pavilliard wisely made no attempt to indoctrinate him, but trusted to his intellectual honesty to bring him to the Protestant way of thinking; and this 'was principally effected by my private reflection'. From Protestantism Gibbon moved away to the rational scepticism which he retained for life. It is characteristic of him that all these changes in belief were due to no one's persuasion but to his independent logical thinking. M. Pavilliard was a sympathetic and inspiring teacher and Gibbon was only too eager to consolidate his Latin and improve his rudimentary Greek, as well as to work on a planned course of geography, modern history and the French classics. Within months his French was excellent, and he had read all the major Latin authors; he was even able to correspond in Latin on textual problems with professors in Zurich and Paris. He began to enjoy Lausanne society, developed a love for the French theatre, and made a friend for life in young Georges Deyverdun. His brief romance with Suzanne Curchod might have led to marriage if his father had not forbidden it because of his lack of prospects. It appears that Gibbon quite soon came to realise that he was better suited to a wellordered bachelor life. (Suzanne was later to marry Jacques Necker, the French Director General of Finance, and was the mother of Madame de Staël.)

In April 1758 Gibbon returned to England, at the age of nearly twentyone, after almost five years of the 'fortunate banishment' which had exchanged the 'port and prejudice' of a stagnant Oxford for a French cultural education which had been of incalculable benefit. It was to be some twelve years before he could start writing *The Decline and Fall*, but without that French education Gibbon could never have written it. European scholarship at the time was practically a French monopoly, and Gibbon's reading had taken in the best of the Age of Enlightenment at an impressionable time of his life. Many of the notes he would write refer to French authorities; the only writers in English to whom he gave more than passing reference were those of the Scottish Enlightenment, the philosopher David Hume and historian William Robertson, whose *History of England* (1754) and *History of Scotland* (1759) he admired. He says that he left Lausanne more French than English; yet there is always something in his sturdy independence which seems to hark back to his forebears – the Gibbons were an old family of not particularly dis⁄ tinguished Kentish gentry. For instance, though he 'had the satisfaction of seeing the most extraordinary man of the age' and was civilly received by Voltaire in retirement outside Geneva, he was not unduly dazzled and could later be critical of Voltaire's cavalier treatment of evidence; and though his mentors for *The Decline and Fall* were French, he shows an underlying pragmatic optimism which seems very English.

Meanwhile his first work was written in French, started at Lausanne and dedicated to Suzanne Curchod. The *Essai sur l'étude de la littérature* was published in 1761; its theme is the need to study literature as social history, to achieve a synthesis of classical learning and scientific enlight⁄ enment; its model is Montesquieu. It appeared while Gibbon's time was taken up by service as a captain under his father in the Hampshire militia, formed as a sort of Home Guard during the Seven Years War. He took his books around with him, and spent his spare time reading Cicero's philosophic works, Strabo's geography and the Iliad, while 'on every march, on every journey, Horace was always in my pocket, and often in my hand'. Again it is typical of Gibbon to be optimistic about the value of his two years' service – 'the making me an Englishman and a soldier.' He even maintained that 'the discipline and evolutions of a modern battalion gave me a clearer notion of the phalanx and the legion.'*

As soon as the war ended and his father gave funds and permission, Gibbon set out on the Grand Tour, reaching Paris on 28 January 1763. There he spent three months combining the pleasures of cultivated society with visits to the public libraries and the Academy of Medals and Coins. It was then that he began to study the works of the Benedictine scholars of Saint Maur, Montfaucon's *Palaeographia graeca* (1708) on the Greek characters, and Mabillon's *De re diplomatica* (1681) which had laid down principles for establishing the authenticity of documents and

* But see E. Badian, 'Gibbon on War', *Gibbon et Rome à la lumière de l'historiographie moderne* (Geneva, 1977), pp. 103 ff.

charters. He moved on to Lausanne to make new friends, John Baker Holroyd (later Lord Sheffield) and William Guise, and enjoy the society of the Pays de Vaud for nearly a year, while preparing himself for his first visit to Italy. He worked on 'the topography of Rome, the ancient geography of Italy and the science of medals', reading the best sources available – notably the travel books of J.B. d'Anville, 'the first of modern geographers', so often appreciatively quoted in his notes, Janus Gruter's *Inscriptiones antiquae totius orbis Romani*, and the work on coins and medals of the Swiss Ezechiel von Spanheim. He had long since decided to be a historian, and during his militia days had toyed with ideas for a subject – a life of Sir Walter Raleigh, the invasion of Italy by the French Charles VIII, Florence under the Medicis, the history of the liberty of the Swiss – but all his earlier classical reading and now his intensive studies pointed in one direction.

Years later Gibbon recalled his decision as a flash of inspiration, though now it would seem to be more a crystallisation of his thoughts. There are three versions of that famous moment, from which Lord Sheffield chose this one for the *Autobiography*:

'It was in Rome, on the 15th of October 1764, as I sat musing amidst the ruins of the Capitol, while the barefooted friars were singing vespers in the temple of Jupiter, that the idea of writing the decline and fall of the city first started to my mind.'*

The planned tour was cut short when Gibbon was recalled to cope with his father's failing health and mismanagement of his finances. The next five years, until his father's death in 1770, were 'the portion of my life which I passed with the least enjoyment', and it took another two to disentangle the family affairs and save what he could of his encumbered inheritance. He could not settle to any long-term project: 'the Decline and Fall of Rome I still contemplated at an awful distance.' He started on the History of the Swiss, helped by Georges Deyverdun with the German sources, but soon gave it up. Fortunately he sent the first chapters to Hume, who gave the sound advice that he should stop writing in French. He published a few learned articles and extended his reading; now he could draw on the twenty-two folio volumes of the Jansenist antiquarian Le Nain de Tillemont – the *Mémoires ecclésiastiques* and the *Histoire des Empéreurs* on the first six centuries of the Church. The 'scrupulous accuracy' and diligence of his sure-footed guide are often praised. He also had Jean Le Clerc's critical study on the

* The church of Santa Maria in Aracoeli is in fact on the site of the Temple of Juno.

authenticity of texts, Ludovico Muratori's thirty-four folio volumes on the Annals and Antiquities of Italy, Cardinal Baronius' *Annales ecclesiastici*, and many other learned compilations. Gradually he built up a library, which at his death contained about seven thousand volumes, including such unexpected subjects as a translation of the *Bhagavatgita*, a three-volume history of astronomy, Frederick II on falconry, a history of Sumatra, and the natural history of Norway.*

Gibbon's original idea had been to write of the decay of the city of Rome; then he expanded his plan to cover the collapse of the empire of the West; and after he had written the first volume he decided to continue through the Dark and Middle Ages to the Renaissance. He started writing in October 1772, almost as soon as he settled into his new London home in 7 Bentinck Street, and despite an increasingly full social life at the London clubs, he published his first volume on 17 February 1776. This took the history up to Constantine the Great, and ended with two chapters (XV and XVI) on the early Christians. It brought Gibbon immediate fame and quickly ran through three editions. But his 'candid but rational enquiry' into the origins of the Christian Church raised a storm of criticism from the clergy, which Gibbon had to answer in his *Vindicatio*.

From 1774 Gibbon was a Member of Parliament, first for Liskeard and then for Lymington. He never made a speech, but supported Lord North's government through most of the American war, and held a minor post in the Board of Trade, which increased his rather inadequate income by £750 a year. He spent another few months in Paris at the invitation of the Neckers, enjoying his literary success and meeting celebrities – the encyclopaedists d'Alembert and Diderot, and the 'eloquent and philosophic' Comte de Buffon, whose *Histoire naturelle* satisfied his lively curiosity about such subjects as the giraffe, the camel, burning glasses, and 'the new and savage land' of Guyana. Not surprisingly, the next two volumes were delayed until 1 March 1781. They covered chapters XVII to XXXVIII, ending with the deposing of the last emperor of Rome in 476 and Gibbon's 'General observations on the fall of the Roman Empire in the West'.

(The much-quoted 'scribble, scribble' story exists in more than one version, but it was probably the Duke of Gloucester's remark on being presented with the second volume: 'Another damned thick, square book! Always scribble, scribble, scribble! Eh! Mr Gibbon?')†

* See Geoffrey Keynes, *The Library of Edward Gibbon* (London, 1940).
† See D. M. Low, *Edward Gibbon*, p. 315.

With the fall of the North government in March 1782 Gibbon lost his seat and his position in the Board of Trade. He decided not to seek re-election but to join Georges Deyverdun in Lausanne and share his pleasant house on the edge of the lake. The two bachelors suited each other, and the next few years were some of Gibbon's happiest. He had completed his fourth volume before he reached Lausanne in September 1783; it ended with chapter XLVII, and dealt mainly with Justinian's legal code and attempt to reconquer the West. By then Gibbon had covered about 450 years of his appointed period, and was left with 800 more, to fit into two volumes and end at chapter LXXI and the fall of Constantinople. They were written between 1784 and 27 June 1787, and all three were published in April 1788.

At the start of chapter XLVIII Gibbon set out his plan for dealing with such a vast amount of material. Instead of the earlier chronological record which he feared would 'repeat a tedious and uniform tale of weakness and misery . . . I preferred, as I still prefer, the method of grouping my picture by nations; and the seeming neglect of chronological order is surely compensated by the superior merits of interest and perspicuity.' In a single chapter he runs through the emperors of the East, up to the Crusaders' outrageous occupation of Constantinople in 1204, and then paints the components of his picture: the Franks and Charlemagne, the Arabs and Mahommed, the Slavs, the Normans in Italy, the short-lived Latin empire of the East, the fall of Constantinople to the Turks, the rivalries of the western Popes up to the fifteenth century. He surveys the whole medieval world west of India, and with the widening of his horizons Gibbon often writes with a kind of elation, with zest for the opportunities given him to indulge his interest in remote places and exotic peoples. Yet the philosophic historian is always at work, setting out his evidence in a logical order of cause and effect, giving significance to his facts in the way which marks him off from the antiquarian or travel-writer.

Gibbon returned to London to see his three volumes through the press, and came back to Lausanne to find Georges Deyverdun seriously ill. He lived on alone at La Grotte after his friend's death in 1789, writing the drafts for his *Memoirs*, enjoying his fame and his position in local society, welcoming English visitors and the refugees from France, including the Neckers. It is during this period that it is tempting to picture him as a slightly ridiculous figure – only five feet tall, increasingly fat, dandified in dress, mildly flirtatious with his lady friends, complacent and so set in his ways as to lack strong emotions – but this is caricature. With his perceptive intelligence went a warm feeling for humanity, shown in his consistent opposition to slavery, when Sheffield supported it; Gibbon always saw lack of political liberty as a fatal flaw in any society. He was of course a British eighteenth-century Whig, believing in 'rational freedom' for the enlightened upper classes, with no sympathy for 'a wild and mischievous system of democracy'; and he had always criticised the dogmatic enthusiasms of Voltaire and his followers, 'the Gallic frenzy, the wild theories of equal and boundless freedom', which led straight into the atrocities of the French Revolution. The human suffering involved filled him with horror.

His letters also show his kindly affection for his stepmother Dorothea Gibbon and his aunt Catherine Porten, whose death he felt deeply; and nothing could be better proof of his love and sympathy for his close friend than his immediate reaction to the news of Lady Sheffield's sudden death; which was to make the hazardous journey through Mainz and Brussels to offer comfort and support. He reached England in June 1793, spent the summer with Sheffield and other friends, but by November a long-standing hernia could no longer be neglected. Twice the fluid was successfully drawn off, and Gibbon was optimistic of a complete cure and a life of a further twenty years, but the third time lack of antiseptic precautions took effect, infection set in, and he died on 16 January 1794, calmly and bravely, at the age of fifty-six.* Lord Sheffield had the coffin placed in his family mausoleum in the church of Fletching, Sussex, where a splendid Latin tribute can be read.

The Decline and Fall of the Roman Empire is Gibbon's *monumentum aere perennius*. It is also a monument to the best of eighteenth-century European learning, coming at a time when the Age of Enlightenment was about to yield to Rousseau and the romantics, and before the great German scholars and archaeologists were to dominate the next century. There were earlier German works of scholarship which Gibbon could have made more use of: Winckelmann's *History of Ancient Art* for instance, in French translation, if the arts had been among his interests. But the distinction between primary and secondary sources which Niebuhr was to establish for all time was not yet fully understood. Gibbon sometimes noted that coins and inscriptions provided valuable evidence where the literary tradition failed, and he used the best compila-tions available for his 'guides', but where he felt he could trust the transcription of a document, he tended to take the facts it related, however remote from it in time, as equally authentic.

---

* See Gavin de Beer, *Gibbon and his World* (London, 1966), pp. 118–121.

Gibbon's editors of later editions have pointed out occasional errors of fact: the Temple of Juno on the Capitol wrongly named that of Jupiter, the Euphrates once called the Tigris, the Odeum of Pericles confused with that of Herodes, uncertainty on the origins of the Vandals, Ostrogoths and Visigoths, miscalculations of mileage or of the extent of the slave population. Such details are of little importance in the context of the whole. More serious are certain inequalities and flaws which have been fairly criticised. Gibbon lacked sympathy with the elaborate cer-emonial of the Byzantine court and with the abstract speculations of Eastern theologians; he never appreciated the fact that until the Cru-saders of 1204 seized Constantinople it was the greatest city in the world after Rome had collapsed, a bulwark against barbarian assault and a bastion of ancient learning. He could have made more of the Slavs, and more of the work of Saints Cyril and Methodius, the 'Apostles of the Slavs', in civilising the Slav tribes and giving them a Slavonic version of the Scriptures. His dislike of intolerance and extremism when exhibited in monastic life led him to deny credit to the monasteries for what they preserved throughout the Dark Ages; he was apparently unappreciative of the wisdom and humanity of the Rule of St Benedict, and of the work of Cassiodorus in encouraging secular as well as religious learning at Vivarium, and in establishing the monastic tradition of scholarship at a time when the secular world was crumbling around him.

The criticism which greeted Gibbon's treatment of Christianity in his first volume rumbled on amongst churchmen through the editions of Dean Milman (1846) and William Smith (1862). Perhaps we are better able than the Victorians were to understand what Gibbon was doing, without being shocked where we do not agree with him. He never attacked primitive and uncorrupted Christian teaching nor spoke disparagingly of Jesus (who has a rare mention at the start of chapter XLVII), but he refused to put Christianity in a position of superiority over other forms of religion in which he was just as interested – Roman paganism, the cults of the primitive Germans, Islam, Zoroastrianism. As a deist and a sceptic, he believed religious truth to be unobtainable and, indeed, relatively unimportant. The Christian Church must be judged by its works and the good or harm it had done to mankind. That is, Gibbon treated all religions as social phenomena which ought to express the spirit and aims of a society, showing himself a true disciple of Montesquieu. The notorious chapters XV and XVI are directed against institutionalised Christianity as an alien and divisive element in the Roman Empire, one which largely contributed to its downfall. The

Frontispiece to J. Gruter's Inscriptions, *published in 1707*

'cheerful devotion of the pagans', with its practical emphasis on civic and martial virtues had been a support; the antisocial intolerance of the Church – which exceeded that of any other religion in Gibbon's view – was destructive of the old values: 'the active virtues of society were discouraged; and the last remains of military spirit were buried in the cloister.'

Gibbon was very conscious of the power of religion on the individual, and fascinated by heresies and the minutiae of theological arguments, even when he most deplored the 'deluded enthusiasts' who wasted time and even fought over them. With his humanist belief that society should aim at rational freedom and happiness for its members, inevitably he saw Christianity as neither rational, free nor happy; preaching and allegory led to a withdrawal from rational thinking, celibacy and monastic seclusion were 'painful to the individual and useless to mankind', the Christian emphasis on sin and retribution and on preparation for the life to come robbed men of their human right to enjoy life here and now. Consequently, Gibbon devoted the main part of six of his chapters to an attack on the emperor Constantine for establishing Christianity as the official religion of the empire, and Julian the Apostate was one of his heroes for his attempt to restore the old pagan worship.

Travelling in Switzerland with M. Pavilliard at the age of eighteen, Gibbon had been shocked by the Benedictine Abbey of Einsiedeln, 'by the profuse ostentation of riches in the poorest corner of Europe . . . and it was created by the potent magic of religion'. As *The Decline and Fall* advanced into the Middle Ages he showed himself fiercely anticlerical in the manner of the French *philosophes*. It was his withering comments on the ambitions and corruption of the clergy, the ecclesiastical hierarchy, the papacy, and especially on the monks of both East and West which did most to damn him as an enemy of Christianity and give his work the reputation of a shocking book. In chapter LXIII, for example, we are told that 'the heads of the Greek church were ambitious and fanatic monks; and their vices or virtues, their learning or ignorance, were equally mischievous or contemptible', while the asceticism of Mount Athos led to a mystic vision which was 'the production of a distempered fancy, the creature of an empty stomach and an empty brain'. His treatment of miracles also gave great offence, as he attacked them from the standpoint of someone educated by the Enlightenment who accepted the Newtonian laws governing the universe. So in chapter XV: 'Accustomed long since to observe and to respect the invariable order of Nature, our reason, or at least, our imagination, is not sufficiently prepared to sustain the visible action of the Deity.'

Gibbon's ironic comments on clerical lapses, deceived husbands and on colourful figures such as the empress Theodora provoked his contemporary, the scholar Richard Porson, to remark on 'the rage for indecency which pervades the whole work'; and later the critic SainteBeuve was to refer to his *obscenité érudite et froide*. Gibbon defended himself by pointing out that anything which could be found offensive was relegated to the notes, and often left in 'the obscurity of a learned language'. Certainly he can appear to enjoy writing notes with a sexual innuendo, but we can surely be amused by his urbane mockery without finding it excessive or obscene. It is very much of his period, but quite free from anything gross or scatalogical, and far removed from the bitter satire of Pope or Swift. Here again Gibbon is very French, and his model was Pascal. He writes that he reread the *Provincial Letters* every year, and 'learned to manage the weapon of grave and temperate irony'. From Pascal he learned that the most effective way to discomfort an opponent is not denunciation but ridicule (Erasmus had used the same method). For instance, in the paragraph in chapter VI (p. 134 of this volume) on James Macpherson's fabricated poems of Ossian, so hotly debated at the time, 'If we could, with safety, indulge the pleasing supposition that Fingal lived and Ossian sang' makes it quite clear that Gibbon does *not* so indulge himself, while in 'the untutored Caledonians, glowing with the warm virtues of nature' he is teasing the Scots. His technique is often to make his point by no more than a neatly placed epithet, undercutting what is formal and pompous by the juxtaposition of an incongruous or deflating word or phrase. Cyril of Alexandria, in chapter XLVII, 'meditated the works of allegory and metaphysics, whose remains, in seven verbose folios, now peaceably slumber by the side of their rivals'. In the same chapter, in a note on 'the vision of a pretended angel' seen by 'an ambitious monk' we are told that his name of Timothy the Cat came from 'his nocturnal expeditions. In darkness and disguise he crept round the cells of the monastery, and whispered the revelation to his slumbering brethren.' A note in chapter XXVIII (on the worship of saints and relics) says that 'At Minorca, the relics of St Stephen converted in eight days 540 Jews; with the help, indeed, of some wholesome severities, such as burning the synagogue, driving the obstinate infidels to starve among the rocks, etc.' Elsewhere the most frightful imprecations on heretics are 'the charitable wishes of a Christian synod' and 'the deserts of Thebais swarmed with hermits'. Gibbon's disingenuous assumption is that his readers will share his own rational scepticism and find it agreeable to do so. Naturally his mock⁄serious tone could infuriate Christian apologists holding cherished beliefs.

Gibbon elaborated a prose style in *The Decline and Fall* which was in marked contrast with that of his unrevised memoirs and the lighter, more adaptable manner of his letters. As he says himself in the *Autobiography*:

'The style of an author should be the image of his mind, but the choice and command of language is the fruit of exercise. Many experiments were made before I could hit the middle tone between a dull chronicle and a rhetorical declamation: three times did I compose the first chapter, and twice the second and third, before I was tolerably satisfied with their effect.'

Once he found the tone he wanted he moved forward confidently, planning his paragraphs with equal care and testing them by ear. The orotund baroque periods owe a great deal to Cicero and to the great orators of his day, Burke and Sheridan, but the effective thrust of a pointed epigram is more reminiscent of Tacitus. In chapter XI, for example, 'Such, indeed, is the policy of civil war: severely to remember injuries, and to forget the most important services. Revenge is profitable, gratitude is expensive.'

Gibbon's antithetic or tripartite sentences, so much a feature of his style, and his richly Latinized vocabulary have had their critics. Gilbert Highet, in *The Classical Tradition*, finds Gibbon monotonous, while admitting that he is not 'unremittingly solemn – on the contrary, his text is sometimes elegantly witty, and his footnotes . . . scandalously gay'.* Dickens seizes the opportunity to poke fun at the 'gorging Lord⁄Mayor's⁄Show of wollumes', in red and gold with purple ribbon book⁄marks, of Mr Boffin's Decline⁄and⁄Fall⁄Off⁄The⁄Rooshan⁄ Empire; after three chapters read by Mr Silas Wegg 'in a dry, unflinch⁄ ing way', Mr Boffin who 'sat intently staring with his eyes and mind at the confounding enormities of the Romans, was so severely punished that he could hardly wish his literary friend goodnight'.† Dickens reasonably makes the point that the sheer eloquence of Gibbon's style risks carrying his readers on too smoothly to be alert to what he is saying. Coleridge too complains that 'When I read a chapter in Gibbon I seem to be looking through a luminous haze or fog; figures come and go, I know not why, all larger than life. . . .'* But Mme Necker (Suzanne

* Chapter 18, 'Baroque Prose', p. 344.   † *Our Mutual Friend*, chapter 5.

Curchod) speaks for all Gibbon's admirers when she wrote perceptively on receiving his first volume: 'I see that he [Tacitus] was the model and perhaps the source of your work, but the source has been enlarged by the torrents of thought of all the ages; you show what a fertile and sensitive imagination can add to the depth and breadth of intellect.'

Without the working of that fertile imagination *The Decline and Fall* would not be the noble masterpiece it is. There are great imaginative descriptions – of the temple of Apollo at Antioch (Daphne) in chapter XXIII, of a fifth-century Christian church in chapter XXVIII, of the final collapse of Constantinople in chapter LXVIII and desecration of St Sophia where 'a vast and gloomy silence prevailed in that venerable dome, which had so often smoked with a cloud of incense, blazed with innumerable lights, and resounded with the voice of prayer and thanks-giving'. There are the masterly accounts of the primitive Germans and the nomadic tribes of the steppes in chapters IX and XXVI; and there are haunting phrases, Belisarius in chapter XLI having to 'contend at the same time with the wind, the waves, and the barbarians', and one which echoes Montesquieu, at the start of chapter XLVIII, where 'the Roman name . . . is reduced to a narrow corner of Europe, to the lonely suburbs of Constantinople; and the fate of the Greek Empire has been compared to that of the Rhine, which loses itself in the sands before its waters can mingle with the ocean.'

Gibbon has been criticised for speaking of 'the triumph of barbarism and religion', or for giving a confused multiplicity of reasons for the fall of Rome. The epigram is over-simplified; and if the gates were left open to the invading barbarians because Christians were too preoccupied to defend them, that is only one amongst the many contributary causes, economic and socially divisive, which are still debated. But though *The Decline and Fall* covers 'the greatest, perhaps, and most awful scene in the history of mankind' it is not a depressing book, thanks to Gibbon's humanist optimism about man's future in the world he knew. This can appear in unexpected places. When in chapter LXI he judged the two hundred years spent on the wasteful wars of the Crusades as 'having checked rather than forwarded the maturity of Europe', he could also see them as a social and economic turning point, 'undermining the Gothic edifice' of oppressive feudalism and indirectly bringing benefit 'to the most numerous and useful part of the community. The conflagration which destroyed the tall and barren trees of the forest gave air and scope to the vegetation of the smaller and nutritive plants of the soil.'

* Quoted by E. Blunden, *Edward Gibbon and his Age*, p. 11

Gibbon probably saw himself as one of a series of historians who work to rationalise the past, to bring order to the confusion of events whose development was 'insensible', as he called it, to those who lived through them. But for us:

'Edward Gibbon is the greatest of the historians of the Enlightenment, the only one of them who is still read not only as a stylist but also as a historian. Two centuries of massive scholarship and constant intellectual evolution have inevitably left many marks on Roman, Byzantine and even more on medieval European history; but it remains a remarkable fact that any one who wishes to study the later Roman or Byzantine Empire will still find Gibbon's *Decline and Fall of the Roman Empire* the best, as well as the most readable narrative of it. . . . Gibbon is the first great historian of a remote past whom the work of later centuries has not driven from the field.'*

* H. R. Trevor-Roper, Introduction to the abridged Gibbon in the Great Histories series, p. vii.

INTRODUCTION TO VOLUME I

THE FOLIO SOCIETY'S EDITION OF GIBBON'S *The Decline and Fall of the Roman Empire* is planned in eight volumes, which will contain the whole of the original text, based on Dent's Everyman edition of 1910. The notes included are all by Gibbon, but are only a selection from the great number he wrote. They are chosen to illustrate as many aspects as possible of the author, and to refer to points suggested in the present editor's Introduction.

This first volume, entitled *The Turn of the Tide*, comprises chapters I to XII and covers the period from the accession of the Emperor Nerva to that of Diocletian (AD 96–284). (Gibbon's own first of four volumes continued to end at chapter xiv.) Gibbon started with the period which he believed showed the Roman Empire at its peak of prosperity and security: the second century, up to the death of Marcus Aurelius in 196. He gave his first three chapters to this 'happy period', and the next four to the internal disorder under weak or violent rulers, and to the breakdown of army discipline and consequent exposure of the frontiers to 'the rapaciousness or ambition of the barbarians, who soon discovered the decline of the Roman Empire'. Chapter VIII describes the rise of the Persian Empire, which soon 'threatened, as an impending cloud, the eastern provinces of the declining empire of Rome'. Chapter IX deals in masterly fashion with the greater menace to the West: 'the warlike Germans, who first resisted, then invaded, and at length overturned, the western monarchy of Rome', and pays proper tribute to Tacitus, 'the first of historians, who applied the science of philosophy to the study of facts'. The final three chapters cover 'twenty years of shame and misfortune' under a series of military tyrants, and then thirty years of restoration under the 'great princes' Claudius Gothicus, Aurelian, Probus and Diocletian.

The second volume, *Constantine and the Christian Empire*, will contain chapters XIII to XX and concentrate on the struggle for power and victory over his rivals won by Constantine the Great, his Christian conversion and establishment of Christianity as the official religion, and his foundation of Constantinople as capital of the empire. In the celebrated chapters xv and xvi Gibbon traces the origin and influence of the early Christians, and returns to the attack in chapter xx, by analysing the subversive effect on Roman society of the early Christian Church.

THE ROMAN EMPERORS FROM NERVA TO DIOCLETIAN

96–98	Nerva
98–117	Trajan
117–138	Hadrian
138–161	Antoninus Pius
161–180	Marcus Aurelius
161–169	Lucius Verus
180–192	Commodus
193	Pertinax
193	Didius Julianus
193–211	Septimius Severus
211–217	Caracalla
211–212	Geta
217–218	Macrinus
218–222	Elagabalus
222–235	Alexander Severus
235–238	Maximin
238	Gordian I
238	Gordian II
238	Balbinus
238	Pupienus
238–244	Gordian III
244–249	Philip
249–251	Decius
251–253	Trebonianus (Hostilianus)
253	Aemilianus
253–260	Valerian
253–268	Gallienus
268–270	Claudius Gothicus
270–275	Aurelian
275–276	Tacitus
276	Florianus
276–282	Probus
282–283	Carus
283–285	Carinus
283–284	Numerian
284–305	Diocletian

THE TURN OF
THE TIDE

I

THE EXTENT AND MILITARY FORCE OF THE
EMPIRE IN THE AGE OF THE ANTONINES

In THE SECOND CENTURY OF THE CHRISTIAN era, the empire of Rome comprehended the fairest part of the earth, and the most civilised portion of mankind. The frontiers of that extensive monarchy were guarded by ancient renown and disciplined valour. The gentle but powerful influence of laws and manners had gradually cemented the union of the provinces. Their peaceful inhabitants enjoyed and abused the advantages of wealth and luxury. The image of a free constitution was preserved with decent reverence: the Roman senate appeared to possess the sovereign authority, and devolved on the emperors all the executive powers of government. During a happy period (AD 98–180) of more than fourscore years, the public adminis‐tration was conducted by the virtue and abilities of Nerva, Trajan, Hadrian, and the two Antonines. It is the design of this, and of the two succeeding chapters, to describe the prosperous condition of their empire; and afterwards, from the death of Marcus Antoninus, to deduce the most important circumstances of its decline and fall; a revolution which will ever be remembered, and is still felt by the nations of the earth.

The principal conquests of the Romans were achieved under the republic; and the emperors, for the most part, were satisfied with preserving those dominions which had been acquired by the policy of the senate, the active emulation of the consuls, and the martial enthu‐siasm of the people. The seven first centuries were filled with a rapid succession of triumphs; but it was reserved for Augustus to relinquish the ambitious design of subduing the whole earth, and to introduce a spirit of moderation into the public councils. Inclined to peace by his temper and situation, it was easy for him to discover that Rome, in her present exalted situation, had much less to hope than to fear from the chance of arms; and that, in the prosecution of remote wars, the undertaking became every day more difficult, the event more doubtful, and the possesion more precarious, and less beneficial. The experience of Augustus added weight to these salutary reflections, and effectually convinced him that, by the prudent vigour of his counsels, it would be easy to secure every concession which the safety or the dignity of Rome might require from the most formidable Barbarians. Instead of exposing his person and his legions to the arrows of the Parthians, he obtained, by an honourable treaty, the restitution of the standards and prisoners which had been taken in the defeat of Crassus.

His generals, in the early part of his reign, attempted the reduction of Ethiopia and Arabia Felix. They marched near a thousand miles to the south of the tropic; but the heat of the climate soon repelled the invaders, and protected the unwarlike natives of those sequestered regions. The northern countries of Europe scarcely deserved the expense and labour of conquest. The forests and morasses of Germany were filled with a hardy race of barbarians, who despised life when it was separated from freedom; and though, on the first attack, they seemed to yield to the weight of the Roman power, they soon, by a signal act of despair, regained their independence, and reminded Augustus of the vicissitude of fortune. On the death of that emperor, his testament was publicly read in the senate. He bequeathed, as a valuable legacy to his successors, the advice of confining the empire within those limits, which Nature seemed to have placed as its permanent bulwarks and boundaries: on the west the Atlantic ocean; the Rhine and Danube on the north; the Euphrates on the east; and towards the south, the sandy deserts of Arabia and Africa.

Happily for the repose of mankind, the moderate system recommended by the wisdom of Augustus, was adopted by the fears and vices of his immediate successors. Engaged in the pursuit of pleasure, or in the exercise of tyranny, the first Caesars seldom showed themselves to the armies, or to the provinces; nor were they disposed to suffer, that those triumphs which *their* indolence neglected should be usurped by the conduct and valour of their lieutenants. The military fame of a subject was considered as an insolent invasion of the Imperial prerogative; and it became the duty, as well as interest, of every Roman general, to guard the frontiers entrusted to his care, without aspiring to conquests which might have proved no less fatal to himself than to the vanquished barbarians.

The only accession which the Roman Empire received, during the first century of the Christian era, was the province of Britain. In this single instance the successors of Caesar and Augustus were persuaded to follow the example of the former, rather than the precept of the latter. The proximity of its situation to the coast of Gaul seemed to invite their arms; the pleasing, though doubtful intelligence, of a pearl fishery, attracted their avarice; and as Britain was viewed in the light of a distinct and insulated world, the conquest scarcely formed any exception to the general system of continental measures. After a war of about forty years, undertaken by the most stupid, maintained by the most dissolute, and terminated by the most timid of all the emperors, the far greater part of the island submitted to the Roman yoke. The various tribes of Britons possessed valour without conduct, and the love of freedom without the spirit of union. They took up arms with savage fierceness; they laid them down, or turned them against each other, with wild inconstancy; and while they fought singly, they were successively subdued. Neither the fortitude of Caractacus, nor the despair of Boadicea, nor the fanaticism of the Druids, could avert the slavery of their country, or resist the steady progress of the Imperial generals, who maintained the national glory, when the throne was disgraced by the weakest, or the most vicious of mankind. At the very time when Domitian, confined to his palace, felt the terrors which he inspired, his legions, under the command of the virtuous Agricola, defeated the collected force of the Caledonians at the foot of the Grampian hills; and his fleets, venturing to explore an unknown and dangerous navigation, displayed the Roman arms round every part of the island. The conquest of Britain was considered as already achieved; and it was the design of Agricola to complete and ensure his success by the easy reduction of Ireland, for which in his opinion, one legion and a few auxiliaries were sufficient.* The western isle might be improved into a valuable possession, and the Britons would wear their chains with the less reluctance, if the prospect and example of freedom were on every side removed from before their eyes.

But the superior merit of Agricola soon occasioned his removal from the government of Britain; and for ever disappointed this rational, though extensive scheme of conquest. Before his departure, the prudent general had provided for security as well as for dominion. He had observed that the island is almost divided into two unequal parts by the opposite gulfs, or, as they are now called, the Friths of Scotland. Across the narrow interval of about forty miles, he had drawn a line of military stations, which was afterwards fortified in the reign of Antoninus Pius, by a turf rampart erected on foundations of stone. This wall of Antoninus, at a small distance beyond the modern cities of Edinburgh and Glasgow, was fixed as the limit of the Roman province. The native Caledonians preserved in the northern extremity of the island their wild

* The Irish writers, jealous of their national honour, are extremely provoked on this occasion, both with Tacitus and with Agricola.

independence, for which they were not less indebted to their poverty than to their valour. Their incursions were frequently repelled and chastised; but their country was never subdued.* The masters of the fairest and most wealthy climates of the globe turned with contempt from gloomy hills assailed by the winter tempest, from lakes concealed in a blue mist, and from cold and lonely heaths, over which the deer of the forest were chased by a troop of naked barbarians.

Such was the state of the Roman frontiers, and such the maxims of Imperial policy, from the death of Augustus to the accession of Trajan. That virtuous and active prince had received the education of a soldier, and possessed the talents of a general. The peaceful system of his predecessors was interrupted by scenes of war and conquest; and the legions, after a long interval, beheld a military emperor at their head. The first exploits of Trajan were against the Dacians, the most warlike of men, who dwelt beyond the Danube, and who, during the reign of Domitian, had insulted with impunity the majesty of Rome. To the strength and fierceness of barbarians, they added a contempt for life, which was derived from a warm persuasion of the immortality and transmigration of the soul. Decebalus, the Dacian king, approved himself a rival not unworthy of Trajan; nor did he despair of his own and the public fortune, till, by the confession of his enemies, he had exhausted every resource both of valour and policy. This memorable war, with a very short suspension of hostilities, lasted five years; and as the emperor could exert, without control, the whole force of the state, it was terminated by an absolute submission of the barbarians. The new province of Dacia, which formed a second exception to the precept of Augustus, was about 1300 miles in circumference. Its natural boundaries were the Dniester, the Teyss, or Tibiscus, the Lower Danube, and the Euxine Sea. The vestiges of a military road may still be traced from the banks of the Danube to the neighbourhood of Bender, a place famous in modern history, and the actual frontier of the Turkish and Russian empires.

Trajan was ambitious of fame; and as long as mankind shall continue to bestow more liberal applause on their destroyers than on their benefactors, the thirst of military glory will ever be the vice of the most exalted characters. The praises of Alexander, transmitted by a succession of

* The poet Buchanan celebrates, with elegence and spirit (see his *Sylvae* v.), the unviolated independence of his native country. But, if the single testimony of Richard of Cirencester was sufficient to create a Roman province of Vespasiana to the north of the wall, that independence would be reduced within very narrow limits.

poets and historians, had kindled a dangerous emulation in the mind of Trajan. Like him the Roman emperor undertook an expedition against the nations of the east, but he lamented with a sigh, that his advanced age scarcely left him any hopes of equalling the renown of the son of Philip. Yet the success of Trajan, however transient, was rapid and specious. The degenerate Parthians, broken by intestine discord, fled before his arms. He descended the river Tigris in triumph, from the mountains of Armenia to the Persian gulf. He enjoyed the honour of being the first, as he was the last, of the Roman generals, who ever navigated that remote sea. His fleets ravaged the coasts of Arabia; and Trajan vainly flattered himself that he was approaching towards the confines of India. Every day the astonished senate received the intelligence of new names and new nations, that acknowledged his sway. They were informed that the kings of Bosphorus, Colchos, Iberia, Albania, Osrhoene, and even the Parthian monarch himself, had accepted their diadems from the hands of the emperor; that the independent tribes of the Median and Cardu-chian hills had implored his protection; and that the rich countries of Armenia, Mesopotamia, and Assyria, were reduced into the state of provinces. But the death of Trajan soon clouded the splendid prospect; and it was justly to be dreaded, that so many distant nations would throw off the unaccustomed yoke, when they were no longer restrained by the powerful hand which had imposed it.

It was an ancient tradition, that when the Capitol was founded by one of the Roman kings, the god Terminus (who presided over boundaries, and was represented according to the fashion of that age by a large stone) alone, among all the inferior deities, refused to yield his place to Jupiter himself. A favourable inference was drawn from his obstinacy, which was interpreted by the augurs as a sure presage that the boundaries of the Roman power would never recede. During many ages, the prediction, as it is usual, contributed to its own accomplish-ment. But though Terminus had resisted the majesty of Jupiter, he submitted to the authority of the emperor Hadrian.* The resignation of all the eastern conquests of Trajan was the first measure of his reign. He restored to the Parthians the election of an independent sovereign, withdrew the Roman garrisons from the provinces of Armenia, Meso-potamia, and Assyria, and, in compliance with the precept of Augustus, once more established the Euphrates as the frontier of the

* St Augustine is highly delighted with the proof of the weakness of Terminus, and the vanity of the Augurs.

empire. Censure, which arraigns the public actions and the private motive of princes, has ascribed to envy, a conduct which might be attributed to the prudence and moderation of Hadrian. The various character of that emperor, capable, by turns, of the meanest and the most generous sentiments, may afford some colour to the suspicion. It was, however, scarcely in his power to place the superiority of his predecessor in a more conspicuous light, than by thus confessing himself unequal to the task of defending the conquests of Trajan.

The martial and ambitious spirit of Trajan formed a very singular contrast with the moderation of his successor. The restless activity of Hadrian was not less remarkable, when compared with the gentle repose of Antoninus Pius. The life of the former was almost a perpetual journey; and as he possessed the various talents of the soldier, the statesman, and the scholar, he gratified his curiosity in the discharge of his duty. Careless of the difference of seasons and of climates, he marched on foot, and bare-headed, over the snows of Caledonia, and the sultry plains of the Upper Egypt; nor was there a province of the empire which, in the course of his reign, was not honoured with the presence of the monarch.* But the tranquil life of Antoninus Pius was spent in the bosom of Italy; and, during the twenty-three years that he directed the public administration, the longest journeys of that amiable prince extended no farther than from his palace in Rome to the retirement of his Lanuvian villa.

Notwithstanding this difference in their personal conduct, the general system of Augustus was equally adopted and uniformly pursued by Hadrian and by the two Antonines. They persisted in the design of maintaining the dignity of the empire, without attempting to enlarge its limits. By every honourable expedient they invited the friendship of the barbarians; and endeavoured to convince mankind that the Roman power, raised above the temptation of conquest, was actuated only by the love of order and justice. During a long period of forty-three years their virtuous labours were crowned with success; and if we except a few slight hostilities that served to exercise the legions of the frontier, the reigns of Hadrian and Antoninus Pius offer the fair prospect of universal peace. The Roman name was revered among the most remote nations of the earth. The fiercest barbarians frequently submitted their differences to the arbitration of the emperor; and we are informed by a contemporary historian, that he had seen ambassadors who were refused the honour

* If all our historians were lost, medals, inscriptions, and other monuments, would be sufficient to record the travels of Hadrian.

Trajan's Column

which they came to solicit, of being admitted into the rank of subjects.

The terror of the Roman arms added weight and dignity to the moderation of the emperors. They preserved peace by a constant prep-aration for war; and while justice regulated their conduct, they announced to the nations on their confines that they were as little disposed to endure as to offer an injury. The military strength, which it had been sufficient for Hadrian and the elder Antoninus to display, was exerted against the Parthians and the Germans by the emperor Marcus. The hostilities of the barbarians provoked the resentment of that philo-sophic monarch, and, in the prosecution of a just defence, Marcus and his generals obtained many signal victories, both on the Euphrates and on the Danube. The military establishment of the Roman Empire, which thus assured either its tranquillity or success, will now become the proper and important object of our attention.

In the purer ages of the commonwealth, the use of arms was reserved for those ranks of citizens who had a country to love, a property to defend, and some share in enacting those laws, which it was their interest, as well as duty, to maintain. But in proportion as the public freedom was lost in extent of conquest, war was gradually improved into an art, and degraded into a trade. The legions themselves, even at the time when they were recruited in the most distant provinces, were supposed to consist of Roman citizens. That distinction was generally considered either as a legal qualification or as a proper recompense for the soldier; but a more serious regard was paid to the essential merit of age, strength, and military stature. In all levies, a just preference was given to the climates of the north over those of the south: the race of men born to the exercise of arms was sought for in the country rather than in cities; and it was very reasonably presumed, that the hardy occupations of smiths, carpenters, and huntsmen, would supply more vigour and resolution than the sedentary trades which are employed in the service of luxury. After every qualification of property had been laid aside, the armies of the Roman emperors were still commanded, for the most part, by officers of a liberal birth and education; but the common soldiers, like the mercenary troops of modern Europe, were drawn from the meanest, and very frequently from the most profligate, of mankind.

That public virtue which among the ancients was denominated patriotism, is derived from a strong sense of our own interest in the preservation and prosperity of the free government of which we are members. Such a sentiment, which had rendered the legions of the republic almost invincible, could make but a very feeble impression on the mercenary servants of a despotic prince; and it became necessary to supply that defect by other motives, of a different, but not less forcible nature; honour and religion. The peasant, or mechanic, imbibed the useful prejudice that he was advanced to the more dignified profession of arms, in which his rank and reputation would depend on his own valour; and that, although the prowess of a private soldier must often escape the notice of fame, his own behaviour might sometimes confer glory or disgrace on the company, the legion, or even the army, to whose honours he was associated. On his first entrance into the service, an oath was administered to him, with every circumstance of solemnity. He promised never to desert his standard, to submit his own will to the commands of his leaders, and to sacrifice his life for the safety of the emperor and the empire. The attachment of the Roman troops to their standards was inspired by the united influence of religion and of honour. The golden eagle, which glittered in the front of the legion, was the object of their fondest devotion; nor was it esteemed less impious than it was ignominious, to abandon that sacred ensign in the hour of danger. These motives, which derived their strength from the imagination, were enforced by fears and hopes of a more substantial kind. Regular pay, occasional donatives, and a stated recompense, after the appointed time of service, alleviated the hardships of the military life, whilst, on the other hand, it was impossible for cowardice or disobedience to escape the severest punishment. The centurions were authorised to chastise with blows, the generals had a right to punish with death; and it was an inflexible maxim of Roman discipline, that a good soldier should dread his officers far more than the enemy. From such laudable arts did the valour of the Imperial troops receive a degree of firmness and docility, unattainable by the impetuous and irregular passions of barbarians.

And yet so sensible were the Romans of the imperfection of valour without skill and practice, that, in their language, the name of an army was borrowed from the word which signified exercise.* Military exer-cises were the important and unremitted object of their discipline. The recruits and young soldiers were constantly trained both in the morning and in the evening, nor was age or knowledge allowed to excuse the veterans from the daily repetition of what they had completely learnt. Large sheds were erected in the winter-quarters of the troops, that their useful labours might not receive any interruption from the most tempes-

* *Exercitus ab exercitando.* There is room for a very interesting work, which should lay open the connection between the languages and manners of nations.

tuous weather; and it was carefully observed, that the arms destined to this imitation of war, should be of double the weight which was required in real action. It is not the purpose of this work to enter into any minute description of the Roman exercises. We shall only remark, that they comprehended whatever could add strength to the body, activity to the limbs, or grace to the motions. The soldiers were diligently instructed to march, to run, to leap, to swim, to carry heavy burdens, to handle every species of arms that was used either for offence or for defence, either in distant engagement or in a closer onset; to form a variety of evolutions; and to move to the sound of flutes, in the Pyrrhic or martial dance. In the midst of peace, the Roman troops familiarised themselves with the practice of war; and it is prettily remarked by an ancient historian who had fought against them, that the effusion of blood was the only circumstance which distinguished a field of battle from a field of exercise.* It was the policy of the ablest generals, and even of the emperors themselves, to encourage these military studies by their presence and example; and we are informed that Hadrian, as well as Trajan, frequently condescended to instruct the unexperienced soldiers, to re-ward the diligent, and sometimes to dispute with them the prize of superior strength or dexterity. Under the reigns of those princes, the science of tactics was cultivated with success; and as long as the empire retained any vigour, their military instructions were respected as the most perfect model of Roman discipline.

Nine centuries of war had gradually introduced into the service many alterations and improvements. The legions, as they are described by Polybius, in the time of the Punic wars, differed very materially from those which achieved the victories of Caesar, or defended the monarchy of Hadrian and the Antonines. The constitution of the Imperial legion may be described in a few words. The heavy-armed infantry, which composed its principal strength, was divided into ten cohorts, and fifty-five companies, under the orders of a correspondent number of tribunes and centurions. The first cohort, which always claimed the post of honour and the custody of the eagle, was formed of eleven hundred and five soldiers, the most approved for valour and fidelity. The remaining nine cohorts consisted each of five hundred and fifty-five; and the whole body of legionary infantry amounted to six thousand one hundred men. Their arms were uniform, and admirably adapted to the nature of their service: an open helmet, with a lofty crest; a breast-plate, or

* Josephus. We are indebted to this Jew for some very curious details of Roman discipline.

coat of mail; greaves on their legs, and an ample buckler on their left arm. The buckler was of an oblong and concave figure, four feet in length, and two and an half in breadth, framed of a light wood, covered with a bull's hide, and strongly guarded with plates of brass. Besides a lighter spear, the legionary soldier grasped in his right hand the formidable *pilum*, a ponderous javelin, whose utmost length was about six feet, and which was terminated by a massy triangular point of steel of eighteen inches. This instrument was indeed much inferior to our modern fire-arms; since it was exhausted by a single discharge, at the distance of only ten or twelve paces. Yet when it was launched by a firm and skilful hand, there was not any cavalry that durst venture within its reach, nor any shield or corslet that could sustain the impetuosity of its weight. As soon as the Roman had darted his *pilum*, he drew his sword, and rushed forwards to close with the enemy. His sword was a short well-tempered Spanish blade, that carried a double edge, and was alike suited to the purpose of striking or of pushing; but the soldier was always instructed to prefer the latter use of his weapon, as his own body remained less exposed, whilst he inflicted a more dangerous wound on his adversary. The legion was usually drawn up eight deep; and the regular distance of three feet was left between the files as well as ranks. A body of troops, habituated to preserve this open order, in a long front and a rapid charge, found themselves prepared to execute every disposition which the circumstances of war, or the skill of their leader, might suggest. The soldier possessed a free space for his arms and motions, and sufficient intervals were allowed, through which seasonable reinforcements might be introduced to the relief of the exhausted combatants. The tactics of the Greeks and Macedonians were formed on very different principles. The strength of the phalanx depended on sixteen ranks of long pikes, wedged together in the closest array.* But it was soon discovered by reflection, as well by the event, that the strength of the phalanx was unable to contend with the activity of the legion.

The cavalry, without which the force of the legion would have remained imperfect, was divided into ten troops or squadrons; the first, as the companion of the first cohort, consisted of an hundred and thirty-two men; whilst each of the other nine amounted only to sixty-six. The entire establishment formed a regiment, if we may use the modern expression, of seven hundred and twenty-six horse, naturally connected with its respective legion, but occasionally separated to act in the line, and to

* Arrian's *Tactics*. With the true partiality of a Greek, Arrian rather chose to describe the phalanx, of which he had read, than the legions which he had commanded.

compose a part of the wings of the army. The cavalry of the emperors was no longer composed, like that of the ancient republic, of the noblest youths of Rome and Italy, who, by performing their military service on horseback, prepared themselves for the offices of senator and consul; and solicited, by deeds of valour, the future suffrages of their countrymen. Since the alteration of manners and government, the most wealthy of the equestrian order were engaged in the administration of justice, and of the revenue; and whenever they embraced the profession of arms, they were immediately entrusted with a troop of horse, or a cohort of foot. Trajan and Hadrian formed their cavalry from the same provinces, and the same class of their subjects, which recruited the ranks of the legion. The horses were bred, for the most part, in Spain or Cappadocia. The Roman troopers despised the complete armour with which the cavalry of the East was encumbered. *Their* more useful arms consisted in a helmet, an oblong shield, light boots, and a coat of mail. A javelin, and a long broad-sword, were their principal weapons of offence. The use of lances and of iron maces they seem to have borrowed from the barbarians.

The safety and honour of the empire were principally entrusted to the legions, but the policy of Rome condescended to adopt every useful instrument of war. Considerable levies were regularly made among the provincials, who had not yet deserved the honourable distinction of Romans. Many dependant princes and communities, dispersed round the frontiers, were permitted, for a while, to hold their freedom and security by the tenure of military service. Even select troops of hostile barbarians were frequently compelled or persuaded to consume their dangerous valour in remote climates, and for the benefit of the state. All these were included under the general name of auxiliaries; and howsoever they might vary according to the difference of times and circumstances, their numbers were seldom much inferior to those of the legions themselves. Among the auxiliaries, the bravest and most faithful bands were placed under the command of prefects and centurions, and severely trained in the arts of Roman discipline; but the far greater part retained those arms, to which the nature of their country, or their early habits of life, more peculiarly adapted them. By this institution each legion, to whom a certain proportion of auxiliaries was allotted, contained within itself every species of lighter troops, and of missile weapons; and was capable of encountering every nation, with the advantages of its respective arms and discipline. Nor was the legion destitute of what, in modern language, would be styled a train of artillery. It consisted in ten military engines of the largest, and fifty-five of a smaller size; but all of which, either in an oblique or horizontal manner, discharged stones and darts with irresistible violence.*

The camp of a Roman legion presented the appearance of a fortified city. As soon as the space was marked out, the pioneers carefully levelled the ground, and removed every impediment that might interrupt its perfect regularity. Its form was an exact quadrangle; and we may calculate that a square of about seven hundred yards was sufficient for the encampment of twenty thousand Romans; though a similar number of our own troops would expose to the enemy a front of more than treble that extent. In the midst of the camp, the praetorium, or general's quarters, rose above the others; the cavalry, the infantry, and the auxiliaries occupied their respective stations; the streets were broad and perfectly straight, and a vacant space of two hundred feet was left on all sides, between the tents and the rampart. The rampart itself was usually twelve feet high, armed with a line of strong and intricate palisades, and defended by a ditch of twelve feet in depth as well as in breadth. This important labour was performed by the hands of the legionaries them‑ selves, to whom the use of the spade and the pick‑axe was no less familiar than that of the sword or *pilum*. Active valour may often be the present of nature; but such patient diligence can be the fruit only of habit and discipline.

Whenever the trumpet gave the signal of departure, the camp was almost instantly broke up, and the troops fell into their ranks without delay or confusion. Besides their arms, which the legionaries scarcely considered as an encumbrance, they were laden with their kitchen furniture, the instruments of fortification, and the provision of many days. Under this weight, which would oppress the delicacy of a modern soldier, they were trained by a regular step to advance, in about six hours, near twenty miles. On the appearance of an enemy, they threw aside their baggage, and by easy and rapid evolutions converted the column of march into an order of battle. The slingers and archers skirmished in the front; the auxiliaries formed the first line, and were seconded or sustained by the strength of the legions: the cavalry covered the flanks, and the military engines were placed in the rear.

Such were the arts of war by which the Roman emperors defended

* The subject of the ancient machines is treated with great knowledge and ingenuity by the Chevalier Folard. He prefers them in many respects to our modern cannon and mortars. We may observe, that the use of them in the field gradually became more prevalent, in proportion as personal valour and military skill declined with the Roman Empire. When men were no longer found, their place was supplied by machines.

their extensive conquests, and preserved a military spirit, at a time when every other virtue was oppressed by luxury and despotism. If, in the consideration of their armies, we pass from their discipline to their numbers, we shall not find it easy to define them with any tolerable accuracy. We may compute, however, that the legion, which was itself a body of six thousand eight hundred and thirty-one Romans, might, with its attendant auxiliaries, amount to about twelve thousand five hundred men. The peace establishment of Hadrian and his successors was composed of no less than thirty of these formidable brigades; and most probably formed a standing force of three hundred and seventy-five thousand men. Instead of being confined within the walls of fortified cities, which the Romans considered as the refuge of weakness or pusillanimity, the legions were encamped on the banks of the great rivers, and along the frontiers of the barbarians. As their stations, for the most part, remained fixed and permanent, we may venture to describe the distribution of the troops. Three legions were sufficient for Britain. The principal strength lay upon the Rhine and Danube, and consisted of sixteen legions, in the following proportions: two in the Lower and three in the Upper Germany; one in Rhaetia, one in Noricum, four in Pannonia, three in Maesia, and two in Dacia. The defence of the Euphrates was entrusted to eight legions, six of whom were planted in Syria, and the other two in Cappadocia. With regard to Egypt, Africa, and Spain, as they were far removed from any important scene of war, a single legion maintained the domestic tranquillity of each of those great provinces. Even Italy was not left destitute of military force. Above twenty thousand chosen soldiers, distinguished by the titles of City Cohorts and Praetorian Guards, watched over the safety of the monarchs and the capital. As the authors of almost every revolution that distracted the empire, the Praetorians will, very soon, and very loudly, demand our attention; but in their arms and institutions, we cannot find any circumstance which discriminated them from the legions, unless it were a more splendid appearance, and a less rigid discipline.

The navy maintained by the emperors might seem inadequate to their greatness; but it was fully sufficient for every useful purpose of government. The ambition of the Romans was confined to the land; nor was that warlike people ever actuated by the enterprising spirit which had prompted the navigators of Tyre, of Carthage, and even of Marseilles, to enlarge the bounds of the world, and to explore the most remote coasts of the ocean. To the Romans the ocean remained an object of terror rather than of curiosity;* the whole extent of the Mediterranean, after the destruction of Carthage, and the extirpation of the pirates, was included within their provinces. The policy of the emperors was directed only to preserve the peaceful dominion of that sea, and to protect the commerce of their subjects. With these moderate views, Augustus stationed two permanent fleets in the most convenient ports of Italy, the one at Ravenna, on the Adriatic, the other at Misenum, in the bay of Naples. Experience seems at length to have convinced the ancients, that as soon as their galleys exceeded two, or at the most three ranks of oars, they were suited rather for vain pomp than for real service. Augustus himself, in the victory of Actium, had seen the superiority of his own light frigates (they were called Liburnians) over the lofty but unwieldy castles of his rival. Of these Liburnians he composed the two fleets of Ravenna and Misenum, destined to command, the one the eastern, the other the western division of the Mediterranean; and to each of the squadrons he attached a body of several thousand marines. Besides these two ports, which may be considered as the principal seats of the Roman navy, a very considerable force was stationed at Fréjus, on the coast of Provence, and the Euxine was guarded by forty ships, and three thousand soldiers. To all these we add the fleet which preserved the communication between Gaul and Britain, and a great number of vessels constantly maintained on the Rhine and Danube, to harass the country, or to intercept the passage of the barbarians. If we review this general state of the Imperial forces; of the cavalry as well as infantry; of the legions, the auxiliaries, the guards, and the navy; the most liberal computation will not allow us to fix the entire establishment by sea and by land at more than four hundred and fifty thousand men; a military power, which, however formidable it may seem, was equalled by a monarch of the last century, whose kingdom was confined within a single province of the Roman Empire.†

We have attempted to explain the spirit which moderated, and the strength which supported, the power of Hadrian and the Antonines. We shall now endeavour, with clearness and precision, to describe the provinces once united under their sway, but, at present, divided into so many independent and hostile states.

Spain, the western extremity of the empire, of Europe, and of the

---

* The Romans tried to disguise, by the pretence of religious awe, their ignorance and terror.

† Voltaire, *Siècle de Louis XIV*, c. 29. It must, however, be remembered, that France still feels that extraordinary effort.

ancient world, has, in every age, invariably preserved the same natural limits; the Pyrenaean mountains, the Mediterranean, and the Atlantic Ocean. That great peninsula, at present so unequally divided between two sovereigns, was distributed by Augustus into three provinces, Lusitania, Baetica, and Tarraconensis. The kingdom of Portugal now fills the place of the warlike country of the Lusitanians; and the loss sustained by the former, on the side of the East, is compensated by an accession of territory towards the North. The confines of Grenada and Andalusia correspond with those of ancient Baetica. The remainder of Spain, Gallicia and the Asturias, Biscay and Navarre, Leon and the two Castilles, Murcia, Valencia, Catalonia, and Arragon, all contri-buted to form the third and most considerable of the Roman govern-ments, which, from the name of its capital, was styled the province of Tarragona.* Of the native barbarians, the Celtiberians were the most powerful, as the Cantabrians and Asturians proved the most obstinate. Confident in the strength of their mountains, they were the last who submitted to the arms of Rome, and the first who threw off the yoke of the Arabs.

Ancient Gaul, as it contained the whole country between the Pyrenees, the Alps, the Rhine, and the Ocean, was of greater extent than modern France. To the dominions of that powerful monarchy, with its recent acquisitions of Alsace and Lorraine, we must add the duchy of Savoy, the cantons of Switzerland, the four electorates of the Rhine, and the territories of Liège, Luxemburg, Hainault, Flanders, and Brabant. When Augustus gave laws to the conquests of his father, he introduced a division of Gaul equally adapted to the progress of the legions, to the course of the rivers, and to the principal national distinctions, which had comprehended above an hundred independent states. The sea-coast of the Mediterranean, Languedoc, Provence, and Dauphiné, received their provincial appellation from the colony of Narbonne. The government of Aquitaine was extended from the Pyrenees to the Loire. The country between the Loire and the Seine was styled the Celtic Gaul, and soon borrowed a new denomination from the celebrated colony of Lug-dunum, or Lyons. The Belgic lay beyond the Seine, and in more ancient times had been bounded only by the Rhine; but a little before the age of

---

* It is natural enough to suppose, that Arragon is derived from Tarraconensis, and several moderns who have written in Latin, use those words as synonymous. It is however certain, that the Arragon, a little stream which falls from the Pyrenees into the Ebro, first gave its name to a country, and gradually to a kingdom. D'Anville, *Géographie du Moyen Age.*

Caesar the Germans, abusing their superiority of valour, had occupied a considerable portion of the Belgic territory. The Roman conquerors very eagerly embraced so flattering a circumstance, and the Gallic frontier of the Rhine, from Basel to Leyden, received the pompous names of the Upper and the Lower Germany. Such, under the reign of the Antonines, were the six provinces of Gaul: the Narbonnese, Aquitaine, the Celtic, or Lyonnese, the Belgic, and the two Germanies.

We have already had occasion to mention the conquest of Britain, and to fix the boundary of the Roman province in this island. It comprehended all England, Wales, and the Lowlands of Scotland, as far as Dumbarton and Edinburgh. Before Britain lost her freedom, the country was irregularly divided between thirty tribes of barbarians, of whom the most considerable were the Belgae in the West, the Brigantes in the North, the Silures in South Wales, and the Iceni in Norfolk and Suffolk. As far as we can either trace or credit the resemblance of manners and language, Spain, Gaul, and Britain were peopled by the same hardy race of savages. Before they yielded to the Roman arms, they often disputed the field, and often renewed the contest. After their submission they constituted the western division of the European provinces, which extended from the columns of Hercules to the wall of Antoninus and from the mouth of the Tagus to the sources of the Rhine and Danube.

Before the Roman conquest, the country which is now called Lombardy was not considered as a part of Italy. It had been occupied by a powerful colony of Gauls, who settling themselves along the banks of the Po, from Piedmont to Romagna, carried their arms and diffused their name from the Alps to the Apennine. The Ligurians dwelt on the rocky coast, which now forms the republic of Genoa. Venice was yet unborn; but the territories of that state, which lie to the east of the Adige, were inhabited by the Venetians. The middle part of the peninsula that now composes the duchy of Tuscany and the ecclesiastical state, was the ancient seat of the Etruscans and Umbrians; to the former of whom Italy was indebted for the first rudiments of civilised life. The Tiber rolled at the foot of the seven hills of Rome, and the country of the Sabines, the Latins, and the Volsci, from that river to the frontiers of Naples, was the theatre of her infant victories. On that celebrated ground the first consuls deserved triumphs; their successors adorned villas, and *their* posterity have erected convents.* Capua and Campania possessed the immediate

* The first contrast was observed by the ancients. The second must strike every modern traveller.

territory of Naples; the rest of the kingdom was inhabited by many warlike nations, the Marsi, the Samnites, the Apulians, and the Lu-canians; and the sea-coasts had been covered by the flourishing colonies of the Greeks. We may remark, that when Augustus divided Italy into eleven regions, the little province of Istria was annexed to that seat of Roman sovereignty.

The European provinces of Rome were protected by the course of the Rhine and the Danube. The latter of those mighty streams, which rises at the distance of only thirty miles from the former, flows above thirteen hundred miles, for the most part, to the south-east, collects the tribute of sixty navigable rivers, and is, at length, through six mouths, received into the Euxine, which appears scarcely equal to such an accession of waters. The provinces of the Danube soon acquired the general appella-tion of Illyricum, or the Illyrian frontier, and were esteemed the most warlike of the empire; but they deserve to be more particularly considered under the names of Rhaetia, Noricum, Pannonia, Dalmatia, Dacia, Maesia, Thrace, Macedonia, and Greece.

The province of Rhaetia, which soon extinguished the name of the Vindelicians, extended from the summit of the Alps to the banks of the Danube; from its source, as far as its conflux with the Inn. The greatest part of the flat country is subject to the elector of Bavaria; the city of Augsburg is protected by the constitution of the German empire; the Grisons are safe in their mountains, and the country of Tyrol is ranked among the numerous provinces of the house of Austria.

The wide extent of territory, which is included between the Inn, the Danube, and the Save; Austria, Styria, Carinthia, Carniola, the Lower Hungary, and Sclavonia, was known to the ancients under the names of Noricum and Pannonia. In their original state of independence, their fierce inhabitants were intimately connected. Under the Roman govern-ment they were frequently united, and they still remain the patrimony of a single family. They now contain the residence of a German prince, who styles himself Emperor of the Romans, and form the centre, as well as strength, of the Austrian power. It may not be improper to observe, that if we except Bohemia, Moravia, the northern skirts of Austria, and a part of Hungary, between the Theiss and the Danube, all the other dominions of the House of Austria were comprised within the limits of the Roman Empire.

Dalmatia, to which the name of Illyricum more properly belonged, was a long but narrow tract between the Save and the Adriatic. The best part of the sea-coast, which still retains its ancient appellation, is a province of the Venetian state, and the seat of the little republic of Ragusa. The inland parts have assumed the Sclavonian names of Croatia and Bosnia; the former obeys an Austrian governor, the latter a Turkish pasha; but the whole country is still infested by tribes of barbarians, whose savage independence irregularly marks the doubtful limit of the Christian and Mahometan power.

After the Danube had received the waters of the Theiss and the Save, it acquired, at least among the Greeks, the name of Ister. It formerly divided Maesia and Dacia, the latter of which, as we have already seen, was a conquest of Trajan, and the only province beyond the river. If we inquire into the present state of those countries, we shall find that, on the left hand of the Danube, Temeswar and Transylvania have been annexed, after many revolutions, to the crown of Hungary; whilst the principalities of Moldavia and Wallachia acknowledge the supremacy of the Ottoman Porte. On the right hand of the Danube, Maesia, which, during the Middle Ages, was broken into the barbarian king′doms of Servia and Bulgaria, is again united in Turkish slavery.

The appellation of Roumelia, which is still bestowed by the Turks on the extensive countries of Thrace, Macedonia, and Greece, preserves the memory of their ancient state under the Roman Empire. In the time of the Antonines, the martial regions of Thrace, from the mountains of Haemus and Rhodope, to the Bosphorus and the Hellespont, had assumed the form of a province. Notwithstanding the change of masters and of religion, the new city of Rome, founded by Constantine on the banks of the Bosphorus, has ever since remained the capital of a great monarchy. The kingdom of Macedonia, which, under the reign of Alexander, gave laws to Asia, derived more solid advantages from the policy of the two Philips; and with its dependencies of Epirus and Thessaly, extended from the Aegean to the Ionian Sea. When we reflect on the fame of Thebes and Argos, of Sparta and Athens, we can scarcely persuade ourselves that so many immortal republics of ancient Greece were lost in a single province of the Roman Empire, which, from the superior influence of the Achaean league, was usually denominated the province of Achaia.

Such was the state of Europe under the Roman emperors. The provinces of Asia, without excepting the transient conquests of Trajan, are all comprehended within the limits of the Turkish power. But, instead of following the arbitrary divisions of despotism and ignorance, it will be safer for us, as well as more agreeable, to observe the indelible characters of nature. The name of Asia Minor is attributed with some propriety to the peninsula, which, confined betwixt the Euxine and the Mediterranean, advances from the Euphrates towards Europe. The most extensive and flourishing district, westward of Mount Taurus and the river Halys, was dignified by the Romans with the exclusive title of Asia. The jurisdiction of that province extended over the ancient monarchies of Troy, Lydia, and Phrygia, the maritime countries of the Pamphylians, Lycians, and Carians, and the Grecian colonies of Ionia, which equalled in arts, though not in arms, the glory of their parent. The kingdoms of Bithynia and Pontus possessed the northern side of the peninsula from Constantinople to Trebizond. On the opposite side, the province of Cilicia was terminated by the mountains of Syria: the inland country, separated from the Roman Asia by the river Halys, and from Armenia by the Euphrates, had once formed the independent kingdom of Cappadocia. In this place we may observe that the northern shores of the Euxine, beyond Trebizond in Asia, and beyond the Danube in Europe, acknowledged the sovereignty of the emperors, and received at their hands either tributary princes or Roman garrisons. Budzak, Crim Tartary, Circassia, and Mingrelia, are the modern appellations of those savage countries.

Under the successors of Alexander, Syria was the seat of the Seleuci- dae, who reigned over Upper Asia, till the successful revolt of the Parthians confined their dominions between the Euphrates and the Mediterranean. When Syria became subject to the Romans, it formed the eastern frontier of their empire; nor did that province, in its utmost latitude, know any other bounds than the mountains of Cappadocia to the north, and towards the south the confines of Egypt, and the Red Sea. Phoenicia and Palestine were sometimes annexed to, and sometimes separated from, the jurisdiction of Syria. The former of these was a narrow and rocky coast; the latter was a territory scarcely superior to Wales, either in fertility or extent. Yet Phoenicia and Palestine will for ever live in the memory of mankind; since America, as well as Europe, has received letters from the one, and religion from the other.* A sandy desert alike destitute of wood and water skirts along the doubtful confine of Syria, from the Euphrates to the Red Sea. The wandering life of the Arabs was inseparably connected with their independence; and

* The progress of religion is well known. The use of letters was introduced among the savages of Europe about fifteen hundred years before Christ; and the Europeans carried them to America, about fifteen centuries after the Christian era. But in a period of three thousand years, the Phoenician alphabet received considerable alterations, as it passed through the hands of the Greeks and Romans.

wherever, on some spots less barren than the rest, they ventured to form any settled habitation, they soon became subjects to the Roman Empire.

The geographers of antiquity have frequently hesitated to what portion of the globe they should ascribe Egypt. By its situation that celebrated kingdom is included within the immense peninsula of Africa; but it is accessible only on the side of Asia, whose revolutions, in almost every period of history, Egypt has humbly obeyed. A Roman prefect was seated on the splendid throne of the Ptolemies; and the iron sceptre of the Mamalukes is now in the hands of a Turkish pasha. The Nile flows down the country, above five hundred miles from the tropic of Cancer to the Mediterranean, and marks, on either side, the extent of fertility by the measure of its inundations. Cyrene, situate towards the west, and along the sea-coast, was first a Greek colony, afterwards a province of Egypt, and is now lost in the desert of Barca.

From Cyrene to the ocean, the coast of Africa extends above fifteen hundred miles; yet so closely is it pressed between the Mediterranean and the Sahara, or sandy desert, that its breadth seldom exceeds fourscore or an hundred miles. The eastern division was considered by the Romans as the more peculiar and proper province of Africa. Till the arrival of the Phoenician colonies, that fertile country was inhabited by the Libyans, the most savage of mankind. Under the immediate jurisdiction of Carthage, it became the centre of commerce and empire; but the republic of Carthage is now degenerated into the feeble and disorderly states of Tripoli and Tunis. The military government of Algiers oppresses the wide extent of Numidia, as it was once united under Massinissa and Jugurtha: but in the time of Augustus, the limits of Numidia were contracted; and, at least, two-thirds of the country acquiesced in the name of Mauritania, with the epithet of Caesariensis. The genuine Mauritania, or country of the Moors, which, from the ancient city of Tingi, or Tangier, was distinguished by the appellation of Tingitana, is represented by the modern kingdom of Fez. Sallé, on the Ocean, long infamous for its piratical depredations, was noticed by the Romans, as the extreme object of their power, and almost of their geography. A city of their foundation may still be discovered near Mequinez, the residence of the barbarian whom we condescend to style the emperor of Morocco; but it does not appear that his more southern dominions, Morocco itself, and Segelmessa, were ever comprehended within the Roman province. The western parts of Africa are intersected by the branches of Mount Atlas, a name so idly celebrated by the fancy of poets;* but which is now diffused over the immense ocean that rolls between the ancient and the new continent.†

Having now finished the circuit of the Roman Empire, we may observe that Africa is divided from Spain by a narrow strait of about twelve miles, through which the Atlantic flows into the Mediterranean. The columns of Hercules, so famous among the ancients, were two mountains which seemed to have been torn asunder by some convulsion of the elements; and at the foot of the European mountain the fortress of Gibraltar is now seated. The whole extent of the Mediterranean Sea, its coasts, and its islands, were comprised within the Roman dominion. Of the larger islands, the two Baleares, which derive their name of Majorca and Minorca from their respective size, are subject at present, the former to Spain, the latter to Great Britain. It is easier to deplore the fate, than to describe the actual condition, of Corsica. Two Italian sovereigns assume a regal title from Sardinia and Sicily. Crete, or Candia, with Cyprus, and most of the smaller islands of Greece and Asia, have been subdued by the Turkish arms; while the little rock of Malta defies their power, and has emerged, under the government of its military Order, into fame and opulence.

This long enumeration of provinces, whose broken fragments have formed so many powerful kingdoms, might almost induce us to forgive the vanity or ignorance of the ancients. Dazzled with the extensive sway, the irresistible strength, and the real or affected moderation of the emperors, they permitted themselves to despise, and sometimes to forget, the outlying countries which had been left in the enjoyment of a barbarous independence; and they gradually usurped the licence of confounding the Roman monarchy with the globe of the earth. But the temper, as well as knowledge, of a modern historian require a more sober and accurate language. He may impress a juster image of the greatness of Rome, by observing that the empire was above two thousand miles in breadth, from the wall of Antoninus and the northern limits of Dacia, to mount Atlas and the tropic of Cancer; that it extended, in length, more than three thousand miles from the Western Ocean to the Euphrates;

* The long range, moderate height, and gentle declivity of mount Atlas are very unlike a solitary mountain which rears its head into the clouds, and seems to support the heavens. The peak of Teneriffe, on the contrary, rises a league and a half above the surface of the sea, and as it was frequently visited by the Phoenicians, might engage the notice of the Greek poets. Buffon, *Histoire des Voyages*.

† M. de Voltaire, unsupported by either fact or probability, has generously bestowed the Canary Islands on the Roman Empire.

that it was situated in the finest part of the Temperate Zone, between the twenty-fourth and fifty-sixth degrees of northern latitude; and that it was supposed to contain above sixteen hundred thousand square miles, for the most part of fertile and well-cultivated land.*

* Templeman's *Survey of the Globe*; but I distrust both the doctor's learning and his maps.

2

OF THE UNION AND INTERNAL PROSPERITY OF THE ROMAN EMPIRE, IN THE AGE OF THE ANTONINES

It is not alone by the rapidity, or ex-
tent of conquest, that we should estimate the greatness of Rome. The
sovereign of the Russian deserts commands a larger portion of the globe.
In the seventh summer after his passage of the Hellespont, Alexander
erected the Macedonian trophies on the banks of the Hyphasis.* Within
less than a century, the irresistible Zingis, and the Mogul princes of his
race, spread their cruel devastations and transient empire from the sea of
China to the confines of Egypt and Germany. But the firm edifice of
Roman power was raised and preserved by the wisdom of ages. The
obedient provinces of Trajan and the Antonines were united by laws
and adorned by arts. They might occasionally suffer from the partial
abuse of delegated authority; but the general principle of government
was wise, simple, and beneficent. They enjoyed the religion of their
ancestors, whilst in civil honours and advantages they were exalted, by
just degrees, to an equality with their conquerors.

I. The policy of the emperors and the senate, as far as it concerned
religion, was happily seconded by the reflections of the enlightened, and
by the habits of the superstitious, part of their subjects. The various
modes of worship, which prevailed in the Roman world, were all considered by the people, as equally true; by the philosopher, as equally false;
and by the magistrate, as equally useful. And thus toleration produced
not only mutual indulgence, but even religious concord.

The superstition of the people was not embittered by any mixture of
theological rancour; nor was it confined by the chains of any speculative
system. The devout polytheist, though fondly attached to his national
rites, admitted with implicit faith the different religions of the earth.†

* They were erected about midway between Lahor and Delhi. The conquests of
Alexander in Hindostan were confined to the Punjab, a country watered by the five
great streams of the Indus.
† There is not any writer who describes in so lively a manner as Herodotus, the true
genius of Polytheism. The best commentary may be found in Mr Hume's *Natural
History of Religion*; and the best contrast in Bossuet's *Universal History*. Some obscure

Fear, gratitude, and curiosity, a dream or an omen, a singular disorder, or a distant journey, perpetually disposed him to multiply the articles of his belief, and to enlarge the list of his protectors. The thin texture of the Pagan mythology was interwoven with various but not discordant materials. As soon as it was allowed that sages and heroes, who had lived, or who had died for the benefit of their country, were exalted to a state of power and immortality, it was universally confessed that they deserved, if not the adoration, at least the reverence of all mankind. The deities of a thousand groves and a thousand streams possessed, in peace, their local and respective influence; nor could the Roman who depre- cated the wrath of the Tiber, deride the Egyptian who presented his offering to the beneficent genius of the Nile. The visible powers of Nature, the planets, and the elements, were the same throughout the universe. The invisible governors of the moral world were inevitably cast in a similar mould of fiction and allegory. Every virtue, and even vice, acquired its divine representative; every art and profession its patron, whose attributes, in the most distant ages and countries, were uniformly derived from the character of their peculiar votaries. A republic of gods of such opposite tempers and interest required, in every system, the moderating hand of a supreme magistrate, who, by the progress of knowledge and flattery, was gradually invested with the sublime perfec- tions of an Eternal Parent, and an Omnipotent Monarch.* Such was the mild spirit of antiquity, that the nations were less attentive to the difference than to the resemblance of their religious worship. The Greek, the Roman, and the Barbarian, as they met before their respective altars, easily persuaded themselves, that under various names, and with various ceremonies, they adored the same deities. The elegant mythology of Homer gave a beautiful, and almost a regular form, to the polytheism of the ancient world.

The philosophers of Greece deduced their morals from the nature of man, rather than from that of God. They meditated, however, on the Divine Nature, as a very curious and important speculation; and in their profound inquiry, they displayed the strength and weakness of the

* The rights, powers, and pretensions of the sovereign of Olympus, are very clearly described in the xvth book of the *Iliad*: In the Greek original, I mean; for Mr Pope, without perceiving it, has improved the theology of Homer.

traces of an intolerant spirit appear in the conduct of the Egyptians (Juvenal, *Sat.* xv.); and the Christians as well as Jews, who lived under the Roman Empire, formed a very important exception: so important, indeed, that the discussion will require a distinct chapter of this work.

human understanding.* Of the four most celebrated schools, the Stoics and the Platonists endeavoured to reconcile the jarring interests of reason and piety. They have left us the most sublime proofs of the existence and perfections of the first cause; but, as it was impossible for them to conceive the creation of matter, the workman in the Stoic philosophy was not sufficiently distinguished from the work; whilst, on the contrary, the spiritual God of Plato and his disciples resembled an idea rather than a substance. The opinions of the Academics and Epicureans were of a less religious cast; but whilst the modest science of the former induced them to doubt, the positive ignorance of the latter urged them to deny, the providence of a Supreme Ruler. The spirit of inquiry, prompted by emulation, and supported by freedom, had divided the public teachers of philosophy into a variety of contending sects; but the ingenuous youth who, from every part, resorted to Athens, and the other seats of learning in the Roman Empire, were alike instructed in every school to reject and to despise the religion of the multitude. How, indeed, was it possible, that a philosopher should accept, as divine truths, the idle tales of the poets, and the incoherent traditions of antiquity; or, that he should adore, as gods, those imperfect beings whom he must have despised, as men! Against such unworthy adversaries, Cicero condescended to employ the arms of reason and eloquence; but the satire of Lucian was a much more adequate, as well as more efficacious weapon. We may be well assured, that a writer conversant with the world would never have ventured to expose the gods of his country to public ridicule, had they not already been the objects of secret contempt among the polished and enlightened orders of society.†

Notwithstanding the fashionable irreligion which prevailed in the age of the Antonines, both the interests of the priests and the credulity of the people were sufficiently respected. In their writings and conversation, the philosophers of antiquity asserted the independent dignity of reason; but they resigned their actions to the commands of law and of custom. Viewing, with a smile of pity and indulgence, the various errors of the vulgar, they diligently practised the ceremonies of their fathers, devoutly frequented the temples of the gods; and sometimes condescending to act a part on the theatre of superstition, they concealed the sentiments of an atheist under the sacerdotal robes. Reasoners of such a temper were

* The admirable work of Cicero, de Naturâ Deorum, is the best clue we have to guide us through the dark and profound abyss. He represents with candour, and confutes with subtlety, the opinions of the philosophers.
† I do not pretend to assert, that, in this irreligious age, the natural terrors of superstition, dreams, omens, apparitions, etc., had lost their efficacy.

scarcely inclined to wrangle about their respective modes of faith, or of worship. It was indifferent to them what shape the folly of the multitude might choose to assume; and they approached, with the same inward contempt, and the same external reverence, the altars of the Libyan, the Olympian, or the Capitoline Jupiter.

It is not easy to conceive from what motives a spirit of persecution could introduce itself into the Roman councils. The magistrates could not be actuated by a blind, though honest bigotry, since the magistrates were themselves philosophers; and the schools of Athens had given laws to the senate. They could not be impelled by ambition or avarice, as the temporal and ecclesiastical powers were united in the same hands. The pontiffs were chosen among the most illustrious of the senators; and the office of Supreme Pontiff was constantly exercised by the emperors themselves. They knew and valued the advantages of religion, as it is connected with civil government. They encouraged the public festivals which humanise the manners of the people. They managed the arts of divination, as a convenient instrument of policy; and they respected as the firmest bond of society, the useful persuasion that, either in this or in a future life, the crime of perjury is most assuredly punished by the avenging gods. But whilst they acknowledged the general advantages of religion, they were convinced that the various modes of worship contri- buted alike to the same salutary purposes; and that, in every country, the form of superstition, which had received the sanction of time and experience, was the best adapted to the climate and to its inhabitants. Avarice and taste very frequently despoiled the vanquished nations of the elegant statues of their gods, and the rich ornaments of their temples; but, in the exercise of the religion which they derived from their ancestors, they uniformly experienced the indulgence, and even protection, of the Roman conquerors. The province of Gaul seems, and indeed only seems, an exception to this universal toleration. Under the specious pretext of abolishing human sacrifices, the emperors Tiberius and Claudius suppressed the dangerous power of the Druids, but the priests themselves, their gods and their altars, subsisted in peaceful obscurity till the final destruction of paganism.

Rome, the capital of a great monarchy, was incessantly filled with subjects and strangers from every part of the world, who all introduced and enjoyed the favourite superstitions of their native country. Every city in the empire was justified in maintaining the purity of its ancient ceremonies; and the Roman senate, using the common privilege, some- times interposed, to check this inundation of foreign rites. The Egyptian superstition, of all the most contemptible and abject, was frequently prohibited; the temples of Serapis and Isis demolished and their wor- shippers banished from Rome and Italy. But the zeal of fanaticism prevailed over the cold and feeble efforts of policy. The exiles returned, the proselytes multiplied, the temples were restored with increasing splendour, and Isis and Serapis at length assumed their place among the Roman deities. Nor was this indulgence a departure from the old maxims of government. In the purest ages of the commonwealth, Cybele and Aesculapius had been invited by solemn embassies; and it was customary to tempt the protectors of besieged cities, by the promise of more distinguished honours than they possessed in their native country. Rome gradually became the common temple of her subjects; and the freedom of the city was bestowed on all the gods of mankind.

II. The narrow policy of preserving, without any foreign mixture, the pure blood of the ancient citizens, had checked the fortune, and hastened the ruin, of Athens and Sparta. The aspiring genius of Rome sacrificed vanity to ambition, and deemed it more prudent, as well as honourable, to adopt virtue and merit for her own wheresoever they were found, among slaves or strangers, enemies or barbarians. During the most flourishing era of the Athenian commonwealth, the number of citizens gradually decreased from about thirty to twenty-one thousand. If, on the contrary, we study the growth of the Roman republic, we may discover, that, notwithstanding the incessant demands of wars and colonies, the citizens, who, in the first census of Servius Tullius, amounted to no more than eighty-three thousand, were multiplied, before the commencement of the Social War, to the number of four hundred and sixty-three thousand men, able to bear arms in the service of their country. When the allies of Rome claimed an equal share of honours and privileges, the senate indeed preferred the chance of arms to an ignominious concession. The Samnites and the Lucanians paid the severe penalty of their rashness; but the rest of the Italian states, as they successively returned to their duty, were admitted into the bosom of the republic, and soon contributed to the ruin of public freedom. Under a democratical government, the citizens exercise the powers of sovereignty; and those powers will be first abused, and afterwards lost, if they are committed to an unwieldy multitude. But when the popular assemblies had been suppressed by the administration of the emperors, the conquerors were distinguished from the vanquished nations, only as the first and most honourable order of subjects; and their increase, however rapid, was no longer exposed to the same dangers. Yet the wisest princes, who adopted the maxims of

Augustus, guarded with the strictest care the dignity of the Roman name, and diffused the freedom of the city with a prudent liberality.

Till the privileges of Romans had been progressively extended to all the inhabitants of the empire, an important distinction was preserved between Italy and the provinces. The former was esteemed the centre of public unity, and the firm basis of the constitution. Italy claimed the birth, or at least the residence, of the emperors and the senate. The estates of the Italians were exempt from taxes, their persons from the arbitrary jurisdiction of governors. Their municipal corporations, formed after the perfect model of the capital, were entrusted, under the immediate eye of the supreme power, with the execution of the laws. From the foot of the Alps to the extremity of Calabria, all the natives of Italy were born citizens of Rome. Their partial distinctions were obliterated, and they insensibly coalesced into one great nation, united by language, manners, and civil institutions, and equal to the weight of a powerful empire. The republic gloried in her generous policy, and was frequently rewarded by the merit and services of her adopted sons. Had she always confined the distinction of Romans to the ancient families within the walls of the city, that immortal name would have been deprived of some of its noblest ornaments. Virgil was a native of Mantua; Horace was inclined to doubt whether he should call himself an Apulian or a Lucanian: it was in Padua that an historian was found worthy to record the majestic series of Roman victories. The patriot family of the Catos emerged from Tusculum; and the little town of Arpinum claimed the double honour of producing Marius and Cicero, the former of whom deserved, after Romulus and Camillus, to be styled the Third Founder of Rome; and the latter, after saving his country from the designs of Catiline, enabled her to contend with Athens for the palm of eloquence.

The provinces of the empire (as they have been described in the preceding chapter) were destitute of any public force, or constitutional freedom. In Etruria, in Greece, and in Gaul, it was the first care of the senate to dissolve those dangerous confederacies, which taught mankind, that as the Roman arts prevailed by division, they might be resisted by union. Those princes, whom the ostentation of gratitude or generosity permitted for a while to hold a precarious sceptre, were dismissed from their thrones as soon as they had performed their appointed task of fashioning to the yoke the vanquished nations. The free states and cities which had embraced the cause of Rome, were rewarded with a nominal alliance, and insensibly sunk into real servitude. The public authority was everywhere exercised by the ministers of the senate and of the emperors, and that authority was absolute, and without control. But the same salutary maxims of government, which had secured the peace and obedience of Italy, were extended to the most distant conquests. A nation of Romans was gradually formed in the provinces, by the double expedient of introducing colonies, and of admitting the most faithful and deserving of the provincials to the freedom of Rome.

'Wheresoever the Roman conquers, he inhabits,' is a very just observation of Seneca, confirmed by history and experience. The natives of Italy, allured by pleasure or by interest, hastened to enjoy the advantages of victory; and we may remark, that about forty years after the reduction of Asia, eighty thousand Romans were massacred in one day, by the cruel orders of Mithridates. These voluntary exiles were engaged, for the most part, in the occupations of commerce, agriculture, and the farm of the revenue. But after the legions were rendered permanent by the emperors, the provinces were peopled by a race of soldiers; and the veterans, whether they received the reward of their service in land or in money, usually settled with their families in the country where they had honourably spent their youth. Throughout the empire, but more par' ticularly in the western parts, the most fertile districts, and the most convenient situations, were reserved for the establishment of colonies; some of which were of a civil, and others of a military nature. In their manners and internal policy, the colonies formed a perfect representation of their great parent; and they were soon endeared to the natives by the ties of friendship and alliance, they effectually diffused a reverence for the Roman name, and a desire, which was seldom disappointed, of sharing, in due time, its honours and advantages. The municipal cities insensibly equalled the rank and splendour of the colonies; and in the reign of Hadrian, it was disputed which was the preferable condition, of those societies which had issued from, or those which had been received into the bosom of Rome. The right of Latium, as it was called, conferred on the cities to which it had been granted a more partial favour. The magistrates only, at the expiration of their office, assumed the quality of Roman citizens; but as those offices were annual, in a few years they circulated round the principal families. Those of the provincials who were permitted to bear arms in the legions; those who exercised any civil employment; all, in a word, who performed any public service, or displayed any personal talents, were rewarded with a present, whose value was continually diminished by the increasing liberality of the emperors. Yet even, in the age of the Antonines, when the freedom of the city had been bestowed on the greater number of their subjects, it was still accompanied with very solid advantages. The bulk of the people acquired, with that title, the benefit of the Roman laws, particularly in the interesting articles of marriage, testaments, and inheritances; and the road of fortune was open to those whose pretensions were seconded by favour or merit. The grandsons of the Gauls, who had besieged Julius Caesar in Alesia, commanded legions, governed provinces, and were admitted into the senate of Rome. Their ambition, instead of disturbing the tranquillity of the state, was intimately connected with its safety and greatness.

So sensible were the Romans of the influence of language over national manners, that it was their most serious care to extend, with the progress of their arms, the use of the Latin tongue. The ancient dialects of Italy, the Sabine, the Etruscan, and the Venetian, sunk into oblivion; but in the provinces, the east was less docile than the west, to the voice of its victorious preceptors. This obvious difference marked the two por-tions of the empire with a distinction of colours, which, though it was in some degree concealed during the meridian splendour of prosperity, became gradually more visible as the shades of night descended upon the Roman world. The western countries were civilised by the same hands which subdued them. As soon as the barbarians were reconciled to obedience, their minds were opened to any new impressions of know-ledge and politeness. The language of Virgil and Cicero, though with some inevitable mixture of corruption, was so universally adopted in Africa, Spain, Gaul, Britain, and Pannonia,* that the faint traces of the Punic or Celtic idioms were preserved only in the mountains, or among the peasants.† Education and study insensibly inspired the natives of those countries with the sentiments of Romans; and Italy gave fashions as well as laws to her Latin provincials. They solicited with more ardour, and obtained with more facility, the freedom and honours of the state; supported the national dignity in letters and in arms; and, at length, in the person of Trajan, produced an emperor whom the Scipios would not have disowned for their countryman. The situation of the Greeks was very different from that of the Barbarians. The former had been long

* Apuleius and Augustine will answer for Africa; Strabo for Spain and Gaul; Tacitus, in the *Life of Agricola*, for Britain; and Velleius Paterculus, for Pannonia. To them we may add the language of the Inscriptions.

† The Celtic was preserved in the mountains of Wales, Cornwall, and Armorica. We may observe that Apuleius reproaches an African youth, who lived among the populace, with the use of the Punic; whilst he had almost forgot Greek, and neither could nor would speak Latin. The greater part of St Augustine's congregations were strangers to the Punic.

since civilised and corrupted. They had too much taste to relinquish their language, and too much vanity to adopt any foreign institutions. Still preserving the prejudices after they had lost the virtues of their ancestors, they affected to despise the unpolished manners of the Roman conquerors, whilst they were compelled to respect their superior wisdom and power.* Nor was the influence of the Grecian language and sentiments confined to the narrow limits of that once celebrated country. Their empire, by the progress of colonies and conquest, had been diffused from the Hadriatic to the Euphrates and the Nile. Asia was covered with Greek cities, and the long reign of the Macedonian kings had introduced a silent revolution into Syria and Egypt. In their pompous courts those princes united the elegance of Athens with the luxury of the East, and the example of the court was imitated, at an humble distance, by the higher ranks of their subjects. Such was the general division of the Roman Empire into the Latin and Greek languages. To these we may add a third distinction for the body of the natives in Syria, and especially in Egypt. The use of their ancient dialects, by secluding them from the commerce of mankind, checked the improvements of those barbarians. The slothful effeminacy of the former, exposed them to the contempt; the sullen ferociousness of the latter, excited the aversion of the conquerors. Those nations had submitted to the Roman power, but they seldom desired or deserved the freedom of the city; and it was remarked that more than two hundred and thirty years elapsed after the ruin of the Ptolemies before an Egyptian was admitted in the senate of Rome.

It is a just though trite observation, that victorious Rome was herself subdued by the arts of Greece. Those immortal writers who still command the admiration of modern Europe, soon became the favourite object of study and imitation in Italy and the western provinces. But the elegant amusements of the Romans were not suffered to interfere with their sound maxims of policy. Whilst they acknowledged the charms of the Greek, they asserted the dignity of the Latin tongue, and the exclusive use of the latter was inflexibly maintained in the adminis- tration of civil as well as military government. The two languages exercised at the same time their separate jurisdiction throughout the empire: the former as the natural idiom of science; the latter as the legal dialect of public transactions. Those who united letters with business were equally conversant with both; and it was almost impossible, in any

* There is not, I believe, from Dionysius to Libanius, a single Greek critic who mentions Virgil or Horace. They seem ignorant that the Romans had any good writers.

province, to find a Roman subject of a liberal education, who was at once a stranger to the Greek and to the Latin language.

It was by such institutions that the nations of the empire insensibly melted away into the Roman name and people. But there still remained, in the centre of every province and of every family, an unhappy condition of men who endured the weight, without sharing the benefits, of society. In the free states of antiquity the domestic slaves were exposed to the wanton rigour of despotism. The perfect settlement of the Roman Empire was preceded by ages of violence and rapine. The slaves consisted, for the most part, of barbarian captives, taken in thousands by the chance of war, purchased at a vile price, accustomed to a life of independence, and impatient to break and to revenge their fetters. Against such internal enemies, whose desperate insurrections had more than once reduced the republic to the brink of destruction, the most severe regulations, and the most cruel treatment, seemed almost justified by the great law of self-preservation. But when the principal nations of Europe, Asia, and Africa, were united under the laws of one sovereign, the source of foreign supplies flowed with much less abundance, and the Romans were reduced to the milder but more tedious method of propagation. In their numerous families, and particularly in their country estates, they encouraged the marriage of their slaves. The sentiments of nature, the habits of education, and the possession of a dependent species of property, contributed to alleviate the hardships of servitude.* The existence of a slave became an object of greater value, and though his happiness still depended on the temper and circum-stances of the master, the humanity of the latter, instead of being restrained by fear, was encouraged by the sense of his own interest. The progress of manners was accelerated by the virtue or policy of the emperors; and by the edicts of Hadrian and the Antonines the protection of the laws was extended to the most abject part of mankind. The jurisdiction of life and death over the slaves, a power long exercised and often abused, was taken out of private hands, and reserved to the magistrates alone. The subterraneous prisons were abolished; and, upon a just complaint of intolerable treatment, the injured slave obtained either his deliverance, or a less cruel master.

Hope, the best comfort of our imperfect condition, was not denied to the Roman slave; and if he had any opportunity of rendering himself

* See in Gruter, and the other collectors, a great number of inscriptions addressed by slaves to their wives, children, fellow-servants, masters, etc. They are all most probably of the Imperial age.

either useful or agreeable, he might very naturally expect that the diligence and fidelity of a few years would be rewarded with the inestimable gift of freedom. The benevolence of the master was so frequently prompted by the meaner suggestions of vanity and avarice, that the laws found it more necessary to restrain than to encourage a profuse and undistinguishing liberality, which might degenerate into a very dangerous abuse. It was a maxim of ancient jurisprudence, that a slave had not any country of his own, he acquired with his liberty an admission into the political society of which his patron was a member. The consequences of this maxim would have prostituted the privileges of the Roman city to a mean and promiscuous multitude. Some seasonable exceptions were therefore provided; and the honourable distinction was confined to such slaves only, as for just causes, and with the approbation of the magistrate, should receive a solemn and legal manumission. Even these chosen freedmen obtained no more than the private rights of citizens, and were rigorously excluded from civil or military honours. Whatever might be the merit or fortune of their sons, *they* likewise were esteemed unworthy of a seat in the senate; nor were the traces of a servile origin allowed to be completely obliterated till the third or fourth generation. Without destroying the distinction of ranks, a distant prospect of freedom and honours was presented, even to those whom pride and prejudice almost disdained to number among the human species.

It was once proposed to discriminate the slaves by a peculiar habit; but it was justly apprehended that there might be some danger in acquainting them with their own numbers. Without interpreting, in their utmost strictness, the liberal appellations of legions and myriads; we may venture to pronounce, that the proportion of slaves, who were valued as property, was more considerable than that of servants, who can be computed only as an expense.* The youths of a promising genius were instructed in the arts and sciences, and their price was ascertained by the degree of their skill and talents. Almost every profession, either liberal or mechanical, might be found in the household of an opulent senator. The ministers of pomp and sensuality were multiplied beyond the conception of modern luxury. It was more for the interest of the merchant or manufacturer to purchase than to hire his workmen; and in the country, slaves were employed as the cheapest and most laborious instruments of agriculture. To confirm the general observation, and to

* In Paris there are not more than 43,700 domestics of every sort, and not a twelfth part of the inhabitants.

display the multitude of slaves, we might allege a variety of particular instances. It was discovered, on a very melancholy occasion, that four hundred slaves were maintained in a single palace of Rome. The same number of four hundred belonged to an estate which an African widow, of a very private condition, resigned to her son, whilst she reserved for herself a much larger share of her property. A freedman, under the reign of Augustus, though his fortune had suffered great losses in the civil wars, left behind him three thousand six hundred yoke of oxen, two hundred and fifty thousand head of smaller cattle, and, what was almost included in the description of cattle, four thousand one hundred and sixteen slaves.

The number of subjects who acknowledged the laws of Rome, of citizens, of provincials, and of slaves, cannot now be fixed with such a degree of accuracy, as the importance of the object would deserve. We are informed that when the emperor Claudius exercised the office of censor, he took an account of six millions nine hundred and forty-five thousand Roman citizens, who, with the proportion of women and children, must have amounted to about twenty millions of souls. The multitude of subjects of an inferior rank was uncertain and fluctuating. But, after weighing with attention every circumstance which could influence the balance, it seems probable that there existed, in the time of Claudius, about twice as many provincials as there were citizens, of either sex, and of every age; and that the slaves were at least equal in number to the free inhabitants of the Roman world. The total amount of this imperfect calculation would rise to about one hundred and twenty millions of persons; a degree of population which possibly exceeds that of modern Europe,* and forms the most numerous society that has ever been united under the same system of government.

Domestic peace and union were the natural consequences of the moderate and comprehensive policy embraced by the Romans. If we turn our eyes towards the monarchies of Asia, we shall behold despotism in the centre, and weakness in the extremities; the collection of the revenue, or the administration of justice, enforced by the presence of an army; hostile barbarians established in the heart of the country,

---

* Compute twenty millions in France, twenty-two in Germany, four in Hungary, ten in Italy with its islands, eight in Great Britain and Ireland, eight in Spain and Portugal, ten or twelve in the European Russia, six in Poland, six in Greece and Turkey, four in Sweden, three in Denmark and Norway, four in the Low Countries. The whole would amount to one hundred and five or one hundred and seven millions. Voltaire, *Histoire générale.*

hereditary satraps usurping the dominion of the provinces, and subjects inclined to rebellion, though incapable of freedom. But the obedience of the Roman world was uniform, voluntary, and permanent. The vanquished nations, blended into one great people, resigned the hope, nay even the wish, of resuming their independence, and scarcely considered their own existence as distinct from the existence of Rome. The established authority of the emperors pervaded without an effort the wide extent of their dominions, and was exercised with the same facility on the banks of the Thames, or of the Nile, as on those of the Tiber. The legions were destined to serve against the public enemy, and the civil magistrate seldom required the aid of a military force. In this state of general security, the leisure as well as opulence both of the prince and people were devoted to improve and to adorn the Roman Empire.

Among the innumerable monuments of architecture constructed by the Romans, how many have escaped the notice of history, how few have resisted the ravages of time and barbarism! And yet even the majestic ruins that are still scattered over Italy and the provinces, would be sufficient to prove that those countries were once the seat of a polite and powerful empire. Their greatness alone, or their beauty, might deserve our attention; but they are rendered more interesting by two important circumstances, which connect the agreeable history of the arts with the more useful history of human manners. Many of those works were erected at private expense, and almost all were intended for public benefit.

It is natural to suppose that the greatest number, as well as the most considerable of the Roman edifices, were raised by the emperors, who possessed so unbounded a command both of men and money. Augustus was accustomed to boast that he had found his capital of brick, and that he had left it of marble. The strict economy of Vespasian was the source of his magnificence. The works of Trajan bear the stamp of his genius. The public monuments with which Hadrian adorned every province of the empire, were executed not only by his orders, but under his immediate inspection. He was himself an artist; and he loved the arts, as they conduced to the glory of the monarch. They were encouraged by the Antonines, as they contributed to the happiness of the people. But if the emperors were the first, they were not the only architects of their dominions. Their example was universally imitated by their principal subjects, who were not afraid of declaring to the world that they had spirit to conceive, and wealth to accomplish, the noblest undertakings. Scarcely had the proud structure of the Coliseum been dedicated at

Rome, before the edifices of a smaller scale indeed, but of the same design and materials, were erected for the use, and at the expense, of the cities of Capua and Verona. The inscription of the stupendous bridge of Alcantara attests that it was thrown over the Tagus by the contribution of a few Lusitanian communities. When Pliny was entrusted with the government of Bithynia and Pontus, provinces by no means the richest or most considerable of the empire, he found the cities within his jurisdiction striving with each other in every useful and ornamental work, that might deserve the curiosity of strangers, or the gratitude of their citizens. It was the duty of the Proconsul to supply their deficiencies, to direct their taste, and sometimes to moderate their emulation. The opulent senators of Rome and the provinces esteemed it an honour, and almost an obligation, to adorn the splendour of their age and country; and the influence of fashion very frequently supplied the want of taste or generosity. Among a crowd of these private benefactors, we may select Herodes Atticus, an Athenian citizen, who lived in the age of the Antonines. Whatever might be the motive of his conduct, his magnificence would have been worthy of the greatest kings.

The family of Herod, at least after it had been favoured by fortune, was lineally descended from Cimon and Miltiades, Theseus and Cecrops, Aeacus and Jupiter. But the posterity of so many gods and heroes was fallen into the most abject state. His grandfather had suffered by the hands of justice, and Julius Atticus, his father, must have ended his life in poverty and contempt, had he not discovered an immense treasure buried under an old house, the last remains of his patrimony. According to the rigour of law, the emperor might have asserted his claim, and the prudent Atticus prevented, by a frank confession, the officiousness of informers. But the equitable Nerva, who then filled the throne, refused to accept any part of it, and commanded him to use, without scruple, the present of fortune. The cautious Athenian still insisted that the treasure was too considerable for a subject, and that he knew not how to *use it.* '*Abuse it, then,*' replied the monarch, with a good-natured peevishness; 'for it is your own.' Many will be of opinion that Atticus literally obeyed the emperor's last instructions; since he expended the greatest part of his fortune, which was much increased by an advantageous marriage, in the service of the public. He had obtained for his son Herod the prefecture of the free cities of Asia; and the young magistrate, observing that the town of Troas was indifferently supplied with water, obtained from the munificence of Hadrian three hundred myriads of drachms (about a hundred thousand pounds) for the construction of a new aqueduct. But

The Coliseum

The Capitol and the Steps of Santa Maria in Aracoeli

in the execution of the work the charge amounted to more than double the estimate, and the officers of the revenue began to murmur, till the generous Atticus silenced their complaints, by requesting that he might be permitted to take upon himself the whole additional expense.

The ablest preceptors of Greece and Asia had been invited by liberal rewards to direct the education of young Herod. Their pupil soon became a celebrated orator according to the useless rhetoric of that age, which, confining itself to the schools, disdained to visit either the Forum or the Senate. He was honoured with the consulship at Rome; but the greatest part of his life was spent in a philosophic retirement at Athens, and his adjacent villas; perpetually surrounded by sophists, who acknowledged, without reluctance, the superiority of a rich and generous rival. The monuments of his genius have perished; some considerable ruins still preserve the fame of his taste and munificence: modern travellers have measured the remains of the stadium which he constructed at Athens. It was six hundred feet in length, built entirely of white marble, capable of admitting the whole body of the people, and finished in four years, whilst Herod was president of the Athenian games. To the memory of his wife Regilla he dedicated a theatre, scarcely to be paralleled in the empire; no wood except cedar, very curiously carved, was employed in any part of the building. The Odeum, designed by Pericles for musical performances, and the rehearsal of new tragedies, had been a trophy of the victory of the arts over Barbaric greatness; as the timbers employed in the construction consisted chiefly of of the masts of the Persian vessels. Notwithstanding the repairs bestowed on that ancient edifice by a king of Cappadocia, it was again fallen to decay. Herod restored its ancient beauty and magnificence. Nor was the liberality of that illustrious citizen confined to the walls of Athens. The most splendid ornaments bestowed on the temple of Neptune in the Isthmus, a theatre at Corinth, a stadium at Delphi, a bath at Thermopylae; and an aqueduct at Canusium in Italy, were insufficient to exhaust his treasures. The people of Epirus, Thessaly, Euboea, Boeotia, and Peloponnesus, experienced his favours; and many inscriptions of the cities of Greece and Asia gratefully style Herodes Atticus their patron and benefactor.

In the commonwealths of Athens and Rome, the modest simplicity of private houses announced the equal condition of freedom; whilst the sovereignty of the people was represented in the majestic edifices destined to the public use; nor was this republican spirit totally extinguished by the introduction of wealth and monarchy. It was in works of national honour and benefit, that the most virtuous of the emperors affected to display their magnificence. The golden palace of Nero excited a just indignation, but the vast extent of ground which had been usurped by his selfish luxury, was more nobly filled under the succeeding reigns by the Coliseum, the baths of Titus, the Claudian portico, and the temples dedicated to the goddess of Peace, and to the genius of Rome. These monuments of architecture, the property of the Roman people, were adorned with the most beautiful productions of Grecian painting and sculpture; and in the temple of Peace a very curious library was open to the curiosity of the learned. At a small distance from thence was situated the forum of Trajan. It was surrounded with a lofty portico, in the form of a quadrangle, into which four triumphal arches opened a noble and spacious entrance: in the centre arose a column of marble, whose height, of one hundred and ten feet, denoted the elevation of the hill that had been cut away. This column, which still subsists in its ancient beauty, exhibited an exact representation of the Dacian victories of its founder. The veteran soldier contemplated the story of his own campaigns, and by an easy illusion of national vanity, the peaceful citizen associated himself to the honours of the triumph. All the other quarters of the capital, and all the provinces of the empire, were embellished by the same liberal spirit of public magnificence, and were filled with amphi-theatres, theatres, temples, porticos, triumphal arches, baths, and aque-ducts, all variously conducive to the health, the devotion, and the pleasures of the meanest citizen. The last mentioned of those edifices deserve our peculiar attention. The boldness of the enterprise, the solidity of the execution, and the uses to which they were subservient, rank the aqueducts among the noblest monuments of Roman genius and power. The aqueducts of the capital claim a just pre-eminence; but the curious traveller, who, without the light of history, should examine those of Spoleto, of Metz, or of Segovia, would very naturally conclude that those provincial towns had formerly been the residence of some potent monarch. The solitudes of Asia and Africa were once covered with flourishing cities, whose populousness, and even whose existence, was derived from such artificial supplies of a perennial stream of fresh water.

We have computed the inhabitants and contemplated the public works of the Roman Empire. The observation of the number and greatness of its cities will serve to confirm the former, and to multiply the latter. It may not be unpleasing to collect a few scattered instances relative to that subject, without forgetting, however, that from the vanity of nations and the poverty of language, the vague appellation of city has

been indifferently bestowed on Rome and upon Laurentum. *Ancient*
Italy is said to have contained eleven hundred and ninety-seven cities;
and for whatsoever era of antiquity the expression might be intended,
there is not any reason to believe the country less populous in the age of
the Antonines than in that of Romulus. I. The petty states of Latium
were contained within the metropolis of the empire, by whose superior
influence they had been attracted. Those parts of Italy which have so
long languished under the lazy tyranny of priests and viceroys, had been
afflicted only by the more tolerable calamities of war; and the first
symptoms of decay which *they* experienced were amply compensated by
the rapid improvements of the Cisalpine Gaul. The splendour of
Verona may be traced in its remains: yet Verona was less celebrated than
Aquileia or Padua, Milan or Ravenna. II. The spirit of improvement
had passed the Alps, and been felt even in the woods of Britain, which
were gradually cleared away to open a free space for convenient and
elegant habitations. York was the seat of government; London was
already enriched by commerce; and Bath was celebrated for the salutary
effects of its medicinal waters. Gaul could boast of her twelve hundred
cities; and though, in the northern parts, many of them, without
excepting Paris itself, were little more than the rude and imperfect
townships of a rising people, the southern provinces imitated the wealth
and elegance of Italy. Many were the cities of Gaul, Marseilles, Arles,
Nismes, Narbonne, Thoulouse, Bourdeaux, Autun, Vienna, Lyons,
Langres, and Trèves, whose ancient condition might sustain an equal,
and perhaps advantageous comparison with their present state. With
regard to Spain, that country flourished as a province, and has declined
as a kingdom. Exhausted by the abuse of her strength, by America, and
by superstition, her pride might possibly be confounded, if we required
such a list of three hundred and sixty cities, as Pliny has exhibited under
the reign of Vespasian. III. Three hundred African cities had once
acknowledged the authority of Carthage, nor is it likely that their
numbers diminished under the administration of the emperors: Carthage itself rose with new splendour from its ashes; and that capital, as well
as Capua and Corinth, soon recovered all the advantages which can be
separated from independent sovereignty. IV. The provinces of the East
present the contrast of Roman magnificence with Turkish barbarism.
The ruins of antiquity scattered over uncultivated fields, and ascribed, by
ignorance, to the power of magic, scarcely afford a shelter to the
oppressed peasant or wandering Arab. Under the reign of the Caesars,
the proper Asia alone contained five hundred populous cities, enriched

with all the gifts of nature, and adorned with all the refinements of art. Eleven cities of Asia had once disputed the honour of dedicating a temple to Tiberius, and their respective merits were examined by the senate.* Four of them were immediately rejected as unequal to the burden; and among these was Laodicea, whose splendour is still displayed in its ruins.† Laodicea collected a very considerable revenue from its flocks of sheep, celebrated for the fineness of their wool, and had received, a little before the contest, a legacy of above four hundred thousand pounds by the testament of a generous citizen. If such was the poverty of Laodicea, what must have been the wealth of those cities, whose claim appeared preferable, and particularly of Pergamus, of Smyrna, and of Ephesus, who so long disputed with each other the titular primacy of Asia. The capitals of Syria and Egypt held a still superior rank in the empire: Antioch and Alexandria looked down with disdain on a crowd of dependent cities, and yielded, with reluc⁄ tance, to the majesty of Rome itself.

All these cities were connected with each other, and with the capital, by the public highways, which issuing from the forum of Rome, traversed Italy, pervaded the provinces, and were terminated only by the frontiers of the empire. If we carefully trace the distance from the wall of Antoninus to Rome, and from thence to Jerusalem, it will be found that the great chain of communication, from the north⁄west to the south⁄east point of the empire, was drawn out to the length of four thousand and eighty Roman miles. The public roads were accurately divided by mile⁄stones, and ran in a direct line from one city to another, with very little respect for the obstacles either of nature or private property. Mountains were perforated, and bold arches thrown over the broadest and most rapid streams. The middle part of the road was raised into a terrace which commanded the adjacent country, consisted of several strata of sand, gravel, and cement, and was paved with large stones, or in some places, near the capital, with granite. Such was the solid construc⁄ tion of the Roman highways, whose firmness has not entirely yielded to

---

* I have taken some pains in consulting and comparing modern travellers, with regard to the fate of those eleven cities of Asia: seven or eight are totally destroyed, Hypaepe, Tralles, Laodicea, Ilium, Halicarnassus, Miletus, Ephesus, and we may add Sardis. Of the remaining three, Pergamus is a straggling village of two or three thousand inhabitants; Magnesia, under the name of Guzel⁄hissar, a town of some consequence, and Smyrna, a great city, peopled by an hundred thousand souls. But even at Smyrna, while the Franks have maintained commerce, the Turks have ruined the arts.

† See a very exact and pleasing description of the ruins of Laodicea in Chandler's *Travels through Asia Minor*.

the effort of fifteen centuries. They united the subjects of the most distant provinces by an easy and familiar intercourse; but their primary object had been to facilitate the marches of the legions; nor was any country considered as completely subdued, till it had been rendered, in all its parts, pervious to the arms and the authority of the conqueror. The advantage of receiving the earliest intelligence, and of conveying their orders with celerity, induced the emperors to establish throughout their extensive dominions, the regular institution of posts. Houses were everywhere erected at the distance only of five or six miles; each of them was constantly provided with forty horses, and by the help of these relays it was easy to travel an hundred miles in a day along the Roman roads.* The use of the posts was allowed to those who claimed it by an Imperial mandate; but though originally intended for the public service, it was sometimes indulged to the business or conveniency of private citizens. Nor was the communication of the Roman Empire less free and open by sea than it was by land. The provinces surrounded and inclosed the Mediterranean; and Italy, in the shape of an immense promontory, advanced into the midst of that great lake. The coasts of Italy are, in general, destitute of safe harbours; but human industry had corrected the deficiencies of nature; and the artificial port of Ostia, in particular, situate at the mouth of the Tiber, and formed by the emperor Claudius, was a useful monument of Roman greatness. From this port, which was only sixteen miles from the capital, a favourable breeze frequently carried vessels in seven days to the columns of Hercules, and in nine or ten, to Alexandria in Egypt.

Whatever evils either reason or declamation have imputed to exten⁄ sive empire, the power of Rome was attended with some beneficial consequences to mankind; and the same freedom of intercourse which extended the vices, diffused likewise the improvements of social life. In the more remote ages of antiquity the world was unequally divided. The east was in the immemorial possession of arts and luxury; whilst the west was inhabited by rude and warlike barbarians, who either disdained agriculture, or to whom it was totally unknown. Under the protection of an established government, the productions of happier climates, and the industry of more civilised nations, were gradually introduced into the western countries of Europe; and the natives were encouraged, by an

* In the time of Theodosius, Caesarius, a magistrate of high rank, went post from Antioch to Constantinople. He began his journey at night, was in Cappadocia (165 miles from Antioch) the ensuing evening, and arrived at Constantinople the sixth day about noon. The whole distance was 725 Roman, or 665 English miles.

open and profitable commerce, to multiply the former, as well as to improve the latter. It would be almost impossible to enumerate all the articles, either of the animal or the vegetable reign, which were successively imported into Europe, from Asia and Egypt; but it will not be unworthy of the dignity, and much less of the utility, of an historical work, slightly to touch on a few of the principal heads. I. Almost all the flowers, the herbs, and the fruits, that grow in our European gardens, are of foreign extraction, which, in many cases, is betrayed even by their names: the apple was a native of Italy, and when the Romans had tasted the richer flavour of the apricot, the peach, the pomegranate, the citron, and the orange, they contented themselves with applying to all these new fruits the common denomination of apple, discriminating them from each other by the additional epithet of their country. II. In the time of Homer, the vine grew wild in the island of Sicily, and most probably in the adjacent continent; but it was not improved by the skill, nor did it afford a liquor grateful to the taste, of the savage inhabitants. A thousand years afterwards, Italy could boast, that of the fourscore most generous and celebrated wines, more than twothirds were produced from her soil. The blessing was soon communicated to the Narbonnese province of Gaul; but so intense was the cold to the north of the Cevennes, that, in the time of Strabo, it was thought impossible to ripen the grapes in those parts of Gaul. This difficulty, however, was gradually vanquished; and there is some reason to believe, that the vineyards of Burgundy are as old as the age of the Antonines.* The olive, in the western world, followed the progress of peace, of which it was considered as the symbol. Two centuries after the foundation of Rome, both Italy and Africa were strangers to that useful plant; it was naturalised in those countries; and at length carried into the heart of Spain and Gaul. The timid errors of the ancients, that it required a certain degree of heat, and could only flourish in the neighbourhood of the sea, were insensibly exploded by industry and experience. The cultivation of flax was transported from Egypt to Gaul, and enriched the whole country, however it might impoverish the particular lands on which it was sown. III. The use of artificial grasses became familiar to the farmers both of Italy and the provinces, particularly the Lucerne, which derived its name and origin from Media. The assured supply of wholesome and plentiful food for the cattle during

* In the beginning of the fourth century, the orator Eumenius speaks of the vines in the territory of Autun, which were decayed through age, and the first plantation of which was totally unknown. The Pagus Arebrignus is supposed by M. d'Anville to be the district of Beaune, celebrated, even at present, for one of the first growths of Burgundy.

winter, multiplied the number of the flocks and herds, which in their turn contributed to the fertility of the soil. To all these improvements may be added an assiduous attention to mines and fisheries, which, by employing a multitude of laborious hands, serve to increase the pleasures of the rich, and the subsistence of the poor. The elegant treatise of Columella describes the advanced state of the Spanish husbandry, under the reign of Tiberius; and it may be observed, that those famines which so frequently afflicted the infant republic, were seldom or never experienced by the extensive empire of Rome. The accidental scarcity, in any single province, was immediately relieved by the plenty of its more fortunate neighbours.

Agriculture is the foundation of manufactures; since the productions of nature are the materials of art. Under the Roman Empire, the labour of an industrious and ingenious people was variously, but incessantly employed, in the service of the rich. In their dress, their table, their houses, and their furniture, the favourites of fortune united every refine ment of conveniency, of elegance, and of splendour, whatever could soothe their pride or gratify their sensuality. Such refinements, under the odious name of luxury, have been severely arraigned by the moralists of every age; and it might perhaps be more conducive to the virtue, as well as happiness, of mankind, if all possessed the necessaries, and none the superfluities, of life. But in the present imperfect condition of society, luxury, though it may proceed from vice or folly, seems to be the only means that can correct the unequal distribution of property. The diligent mechanic, and the skilful artist, who have obtained no share in the division of the earth, receive a voluntary tax from the possessors of land; and the latter are prompted, by a sense of interest, to improve those estates, with whose produce they may purchase additional pleasures. This operation, the particular effects of which are felt in every society, acted with much more diffusive energy in the Roman world. The provinces would soon have been exhausted of their wealth, if the manufactures and commerce of luxury had not insensibly restored to the industrious subjects the sums which were exacted from them by the arms and authority of Rome. As long as the circulation was confined within the bounds of the empire, it impressed the political machine with a new degree of activity, and its consequences, sometimes beneficial, could never become pernicious.

But it is no easy task to confine luxury within the limits of an empire. The most remote countries of the ancient world were ransacked to supply the pomp and delicacy of Rome. The forests of Scythia afforded some valuable furs. Amber was brought over land from the shores of the Baltic to the Danube; and the barbarians were astonished at the price which they received in exchange for so useless a commodity. There was a considerable demand for Babylonian carpets and other manufactures of the East; but the most important and unpopular branch of foreign trade was carried on with Arabia and India. Every year, about the time of the summer solstice, a fleet of an hundred and twenty vessels sailed from Myos-hormos, a port of Egypt, on the Red Sea. By the periodical assistance of the monsoons, they traversed the ocean in about forty days. The coast of Malabar, or the island of Ceylon, was the usual term of their navigation, and it was in those markets that the merchants from the more remote countries of Asia expected their arrival. The return of the fleet of Egypt was fixed to the months of December or January; and as soon as their rich cargo had been transported on the backs of camels, from the Red Sea to the Nile, and had descended that river as far as Alexandria, it was poured, without delay, into the capital of the empire. The objects of oriental traffic were splendid and trifling: silk, a pound of which was esteemed not inferior in value to a pound of gold; precious stones, among which the pearl claimed the first rank after the diamond;* and a variety of aromatics, that were consumed in religious worship and the pomp of funerals. The labour and risk of the voyage was rewarded with almost incredible profit; but the profit was made upon Roman subjects, and a few individuals were enriched at the expense of the public. As the natives of Arabia and India were contented with the production and manufactures of their own country, silver, on the side of the Romans, was the principal, if not the only instrument of commerce. It was a complaint worthy of the gravity of the senate, that in the purchase of female ornaments, the wealth of the state was irrecoverably given away to foreign and hostile nations. The annual loss is computed, by a writer of an inquisitive but censorious temper, at upwards of eight hundred thousand pounds sterling. Such was the style of discontent, brooding over the dark prospect of approaching poverty. And yet, if we compare the proportion between gold and silver, as it stood in the time of Pliny, and as it was fixed in the reign of Constantine, we shall discover within that period a very considerable increase. There is not the least reason to suppose that gold was become more scarce; it is therefore evident that

* The two great pearl fisheries were the same as at present, Ormuz and Cape Comorin. As well as we can compare ancient with modern geography, Rome was supplied with diamonds from the mine of Jumelpur, in Bengal, which is described in the *Voyages de Tavernier*.

silver was grown more common; that whatever might be the amount of the Indian and Arabian exports, they were far from exhausting the wealth of the Roman world; and that the produce of the mines abundantly supplied the demands of commerce.

Notwithstanding the propensity of mankind to exalt the past, and to depreciate the present, the tranquil and prosperous state of the empire was warmly felt, and honestly confessed, by the provincials as well as Romans. 'They acknowledged that the true principles of social life, laws, agriculture, and science, which had been first invented by the wisdom of Athens, were now firmly established by the power of Rome, under whose auspicious influence the fiercest barbarians were united by an equal government and common language. They affirm, that with the improvement of arts, the human species was visibly multiplied. They celebrate the increasing splendour of the cities, the beautiful face of the country, cultivated and adorned like an immense garden; and the long festival of peace, which was enjoyed by so many nations, forgetful of their ancient animosities, and delivered from the apprehension of future danger.' Whatever suspicions may be suggested by the air of rhetoric and declamation, which seems to prevail in these passages, the substance of them is perfectly agreeable to historic truth.

It was scarcely possible that the eyes of contemporaries should discover in the public felicity the latent causes of decay and corruption. This long peace, and the uniform government of the Romans, intro- duced a slow and secret poison into the vitals of the empire. The minds of men were gradually reduced to the same level, the fire of genius was extinguished, and even the military spirit evaporated. The natives of Europe were brave and robust, Spain, Gaul, Britain, and Illyricum supplied the legions with excellent soldiers, and constituted the real strength of the monarchy. Their personal valour remained, but they no longer possessed that public courage which is nourished by the love of independence, the sense of national honour, the presence of danger, and the habit of command. They received laws and governors from the will of their sovereign, and trusted for their defence to a mercenary army. The posterity of their boldest leaders was contented with the rank of citizens and subjects. The most aspiring spirits resorted to the court or stan- dard of the emperors; and the deserted provinces, deprived of political strength or union, insensibly sunk into the languid indifference of private life.

The love of letters, almost inseparable from peace and refinement, was fashionable among the subjects of Hadrian and the Antonines, who were themselves men of learning and curiosity. It was diffused over the whole extent of their empire; the most northern tribes of Britons had acquired a taste for rhetoric; Homer as well as Virgil were transcribed and studied on the banks of the Rhine and Danube; and the most liberal rewards sought out the faintest glimmerings of literary merit. The sciences of physic and astronomy were successfully cultivated by the Greeks; the observations of Ptolemy and the writings of Galen are studied by those who have improved their discoveries and corrected their errors; but if we except the inimitable Lucian, this age of indolence passed away without having produced a single writer of original genius, or who excelled in the arts of elegant composition. The authority of Plato and Aristotle, of Zeno and Epicurus, still reigned in the schools; and their systems, transmitted with blind deference from one generation of disciples to another, precluded every generous attempt to exercise the powers, or enlarge the limits, of the human mind. The beauties of the poets and orators, instead of kindling a fire like their own, inspired only cold and servile imitations: or if any ventured to deviate from those models, they deviated at the same time from good sense and propriety. On the revival of letters, the youthful vigour of the imagination, after a long repose, national emulation, a new religion, new languages, and a new world, called forth the genius of Europe. But the provincials of Rome, trained by a uniform artificial foreign education, were engaged in a very unequal competition with those bold ancients, who, by express⁄ing their genuine feelings in their native tongue, had already occupied every place of honour. The name of Poet was almost forgotten; that of Orator was usurped by the sophists. A cloud of critics, of compilers, of commentators, darkened the face of learning, and the decline of genius was soon followed by the corruption of taste.

The sublime Longinus, who in a somewhat later period, and in the court of a Syrian queen, preserved the spirit of ancient Athens, observes and laments this degeneracy of his contemporaries, which debased their sentiments, enervated their courage, and depressed their talents. 'In the same manner,' says he 'as some children always remain pygmies, whose infant limbs have been too closely confined; thus our tender minds, fettered by the prejudices and habits of a just servitude, are unable to expand themselves, or to attain that well⁄proportioned greatness which we admire in the ancients; who living under a popular government, wrote with the same freedom as they acted.' This diminutive stature of mankind, if we pursue the metaphor, was daily sinking below the old standard, and the Roman world was indeed peopled by a race of pygmies; when the fierce giants of the north broke in, and mended the puny breed. They restored a manly spirit of freedom; and after the revolution of ten centuries, freedom became the happy parent of taste and science.

OF THE CONSTITUTION OF THE ROMAN EMPIRE, IN THE
AGE OF THE ANTONINES

THE OBVIOUS DEFINITION OF A MONARCHY
seems to be that of a state, in which a single person, by whatsoever name
he may be distinguished, is entrusted with the execution of the laws, the
management of the revenue, and the command of the army. But, unless
public liberty is protected by intrepid and vigilant guardians, the
authority of so formidable a magistrate will soon degenerate into despotism. The influence of the clergy, in an age of superstition, might be
usefully employed to assert the rights of mankind; but so intimate is the
connection between the throne and the altar, that the banner of the
church has very seldom been seen on the side of the people. A martial
nobility and stubborn commons, possessed of arms, tenacious of property,
and collected into constitutional assemblies, form the only balance capable
of preserving a free constitution against enterprises of an aspiring prince.

Every barrier of the Roman constitution had been levelled by the vast
ambition of the dictator; every fence had been extirpated by the cruel
hand of the Triumvir. After the victory of Actium, the fate of the
Roman world depended on the will of Octavianus, surnamed Caesar,
by his uncle's adoption, and afterwards Augustus, by the flattery of the
senate. The conqueror was at the head of forty-four veteran legions,
conscious of their own strength, and of the weakness of the constitution,
habituated, during twenty years of civil war, to every act of blood and
violence, and passionately devoted to the house of Caesar, from whence
alone they had received, and expected, the most lavish rewards. The
provinces, long oppressed by the ministers of the republic, sighed for the
government of a single person, who would be the master, not the
accomplice, of those petty tyrants. The people of Rome, viewing, with a
secret pleasure, the humiliation of the aristocracy, demanded only bread
and public shows; and were supplied with both by the liberal hand of
Augustus. The rich and polite Italians, who had almost universally
embraced the philosophy of Epicurus, enjoyed the present blessings of
ease and tranquillity, and suffered not the pleasing dream to be interrupted
by the memory of their old tumultuous freedom. With its power, the

senate had lost its dignity; many of the most noble families were extinct. The republicans of spirit and ability had perished in the field of battle, or in the proscription. The door of the assembly had been designedly left open, for a mixed multitude of more than a thousand persons, who reflected disgrace upon their rank, instead of deriving honour from it.

The reformation of the senate was one of the first steps in which Augustus laid aside the tyrant, and professed himself the father of his country. He was elected censor; and, in concert with his faithful Agrippa, he examined the list of the senators, expelled a few members, whose vices or whose obstinacy required a public example, persuaded near two hundred to prevent the shame of an expulsion by a voluntary retreat, raised the qualification of a senator to about ten thousand pounds, created a sufficient number of patrician families, and accepted for himself the honourable title of Prince of the Senate, which had always been bestowed, by the censors, on the citizen the most eminent for his honours and services. But whilst he thus restored the dignity, he destroyed the independence of the senate. The principles of a free constitution are irrecoverably lost, when the legislative power is nominated by the executive.

Before an assembly thus modelled and prepared, Augustus pro-nounced a studied oration, which displayed his patriotism, and dis-guised his ambition. 'He lamented, yet excused, his past conduct. Filial piety had required at his hands the revenge of his father's murder; the humanity of his own nature had sometimes given way to the stern laws of necessity, and to a forced connection with two unworthy colleagues: as long as Antony lived, the republic forbade him to abandon her to a degenerate Roman, and a barbarian queen. He was now at liberty to satisfy his duty and his inclination. He solemnly restored the senate and people to all their ancient rights; and wished only to mingle with the crowd of his fellow-citizens, and to share the blessings which he had obtained for his country.'

It would require the pen of Tacitus (if Tacitus had assisted at this assembly) to describe the various emotions of the senate; those that were suppressed, and those that were affected. It was dangerous to trust the sincerity of Augustus; to seem to distrust it was still more dangerous. The respective advantages of monarchy and a republic have often divided speculative inquirers; the present greatness of the Roman state, the corruption of manners, and the licence of the soldiers, supplied new arguments to the advocates of monarchy, and these general views of government were again warped by the hopes and fears of each individual. Amidst this confusion of sentiments, the answer of the senate was unanimous and decisive. They refused to accept the resignation of Augustus; they conjured him not to desert the republic, which he had saved. After a decent resistance, the crafty tyrant submitted to the orders of the senate; and consented to receive the government of the provinces, and the general command of the Roman armies, under the well-known names of Proconsul and Imperator. But he would receive them only for ten years. Even before the expiration of that period, he hoped that the wounds of civil discord would be completely healed, and that the republic, restored to its pristine health and vigour, would no longer require the dangerous interposition of so extraordinary a magistrate. The memory of this comedy, repeated several times during the life of Augustus, was preserved to the last ages of the empire, by the peculiar pomp with which the perpetual monarchs of Rome always solemnised the tenth years of their reign.

Without any violation of the principles of the constitution, the general of the Roman armies might receive and exercise an authority almost despotic over the soldiers, the enemies, and the subjects of the republic. With regard to the soldiers, the jealousy of freedom had, even from the earliest ages of Rome, given way to the hopes of conquest, and a just sense of military discipline. The dictator, or consul, had a right to command the service of the Roman youth; and to punish an obstinate or cowardly disobedience by the most severe and ignominious penalties, by striking the offender out of the list of citizens, by confiscating his property, and by selling his person into slavery. The most sacred rights of freedom, confirmed by the Porcian and Sempronian laws, were suspended by the military engagement. In his camp the general exercised an absolute power of life and death; his jurisdiction was not confined by any forms of trial or rules of proceeding, and the execution of the sentence was immediate and without appeal. The choice of the enemies of Rome was regularly decided by the legislative authority. The most important resolutions of peace and war were seriously debated in the senate, and solemnly ratified by the people. But when the arms of the legions were carried to a great distance from Italy, the generals assumed the liberty of directing them against whatever people, and in whatever manner, they judged most advantageous for the public service. It was from the success, not from the justice, of their enterprises, that they expected the honours of a triumph. In the use of victory, especially after they were no longer controlled by the commissioners of the senate, they exercised the most unbounded despotism. When Pompey commanded in the East, he

Augustus 27 BC – AD 14

Trajan 98–117

Hadrian 117–138

Marcus Aurelius 161–180

Claudius Gothicus 268–270

Aurelian 270–275

Probus 276–282

rewarded his soldiers and allies, dethroned princes, divided kingdoms, founded colonies, and distributed the treasures of Mithridates. On his return to Rome, he obtained by a single act of the senate and people, the universal ratifications of all his proceedings. Such was the power over the soldiers, and over the enemies of Rome, which was either granted to, or assumed by, the generals of the republic. They were, at the same time, the governors, or rather monarchs, of the conquered provinces, united the civil with the military character, administered justice as well as the finances, and exercised both the executive and legislative power of the state.

From what has been already observed in the first chapter of this work, some notion may be formed of the armies and provinces thus intrusted to the ruling hand of Augustus. But as it was impossible that he could personally command the legions of so many distant frontiers, he was indulged by the senate, as Pompey had already been, in the permission of devolving the execution of his great office on a sufficient number of lieutenants. In rank and authority these officers seemed not inferior to the ancient proconsuls; but their station was dependent and precarious. They received and held their commissions at the will of a superior, to whose *auspicious* influence the merit of their action was legally attributed. They were the representatives of the emperor. The emperor alone was the general of the republic, and his jurisdiction, civil as well as military, extended over all the conquests of Rome. It was some satisfaction, however, to the senate, that he always delegated his power to the members of their body. The Imperial lieutenants were of consular or praetorian dignity; the legions were commanded by senators, and the prefecture of Egypt was the only important trust committed to a Roman knight.

Within six days after Augustus had been compelled to accept so very liberal a grant, he resolved to gratify the pride of the senate by an easy sacrifice. He represented to them, that they had enlarged his powers, even beyond that degree which might be required by the melancholy condi-tion of the times. They had not permitted him to refuse the laborious command of the armies and the frontiers; but he must insist on being allowed to restore the more peaceful and secure provinces, to the mild administration of the civil magistrate. In the division of the provinces, Augustus provided for his own power, and for the dignity of the republic. The proconsuls of the senate, particularly those of Asia, Greece, and Africa, enjoyed a more honourable character than the lieutenants of the emperor, who commanded in Gaul or Syria. The former were attended by lictors, the latter by soldiers. A law was passed that wherever the emperor was present, his extraordinary commission should supersede the ordinary jurisdiction of the governor; a custom was introduced, that the new conquest belonged to the Imperial portion; and it was soon discovered that the authority of the *Prince*, the favourite epithet of Augustus, was the same in every part of the empire.

In return for this imaginary concession, Augustus obtained an important privilege, which rendered him master of Rome and Italy. By a dangerous exception to the ancient maxims, he was authorised to preserve his military command, supported by a numerous body of guards, even in time of peace, and in the heart of the capital. His command, indeed, was confined to those citizens who were engaged in the service by the military oath; but such was the propensity of the Romans to servitude, that the oath was voluntarily taken by the magistrates, the senators, and the equestrian order, till the homage of flattery was insensibly converted into an annual and solemn protestation of fidelity.

Although Augustus considered a military force as the firmest founda-tion, he wisely rejected it, as a very odious intrument of government. It was more agreeable to his temper, as well as to his policy, to reign under the venerable names of ancient magistracy, and artfully to collect, in his own person, all the scattered rays of civil jurisdiction. With this view, he permitted the senate to confer upon him, for his life, the powers of the consular and tribunitian offices, which were, in the same manner, continued to all his successors. The consuls had succeeded to the kings of Rome, and represented the dignity of the state. They superintended the ceremonies of religion, levied and commanded the legions, gave audience to foreign ambassadors, and presided in the assemblies both of the senate and people. The general control of the finances was intrusted to their care; and though they seldom had leisure to administer justice in person, they were considered as the supreme guardians of law, equity, and the public peace. Such was their ordinary jurisdiction; but whenever the senate empowered the first magistrate to consult the safety of the commonwealth, he was raised by that degree above the laws, and exercised, in the defence of liberty, a temporary despotism. The character of the tribunes was, in every respect, different from that of the consuls. The appearance of the former was modest and humble; but their persons were sacred and inviolable. Their force was suited rather for opposition than for action. They were instituted to defend the oppressed, to pardon offences, to arraign the enemies of the people, and, when they judged it necessary, to stop, by a single word, the whole machine of government. As long as the republic subsisted, the dangerous influence, which either the consul or the tribune might derive from their respective jurisdiction, was diminished by several important restrictions. Their authority expired with the year in which they were elected; the former office was divided between two, the latter among ten persons; and, as both in their private and public interest they were averse to each other, their mutual conflicts contributed, for the most part, to strengthen rather than to destroy the balance of the constitution. But when the consular and tribunitian powers were united, when they were vested for life in a single person, when the general of the army was, at the same time, the minister of the senate, and the representative of the Roman people, it was impossible to resist the exercise, nor was it easy to define the limits, of his Imperial prerogative.

To these accumulated honours, the policy of Augustus soon added the splendid as well as important dignities of supreme pontiff, and of censor. By the former he acquired the management of the religion, and by the latter a legal inspection over the manners and fortunes, of the Roman people. If so many distinct and independent powers did not exactly unite with each other, the complaisance of the senate was prepared to supply every deficiency by the most ample and extraordinary concessions. The emperors, as the first ministers of the republic, were exempted from the obligation and penalty of many inconvenient laws: they were authorised to convoke the senate, to make several motions in the same day, to recommend candidates for the honours of the state, to enlarge the bounds of the city, to employ the revenue at their discretion, to declare peace and war, to ratify treaties; and by a most comprehensive clause, they were empowered to execute whatsoever they should judge advantageous to the empire, and agreeable to the majesty of things private or public, human or divine.*

When all the various powers of executive government were committed to the *Imperial magistrate*, the ordinary magistrates of the commonwealth languished in obscurity, without vigour, and almost without business. The names and forms of the ancient administration were preserved by Augustus with the most anxious care. The usual number of consuls, praetors, and tribunes, were annually invested with their respective ensigns of office, and continued to discharge some of their least

* See a fragment of a Decree of the Senate, conferring on the emperor Vespasian all the powers granted to his predecessors, Augustus, Tiberius, and Claudius. This curious and important monument is published in Gruter's *Inscriptions*.

important functions. Those honours still attracted the vain ambition of the Romans; and the emperors themselves, though invested for life with the powers of the consulship, frequently aspired to the title of that annual dignity, which they condescended to share with the most illustrious of their fellow-citizens. In the election of these magistrates, the people, during the reign of Augustus, were permitted to expose all the inconveniences of a wild democracy. That artful prince, instead of discovering the least symptom of impatience, humbly solicited their suffrages for himself or his friends, and scrupulously practised all the duties of an ordinary candidate. But we may venture to ascribe to his councils, the first measure of the succeeding reign, by which the elections were transferred to the senate. The assemblies of the people were for ever abolished, and the emperors were delivered from a dangerous multitude, who, without restoring liberty, might have disturbed, and perhaps endangered, the established government.

By declaring themselves the protectors of the people, Marius and Caesar had subverted the constitution of their country. But as soon as the senate had been humbled and disarmed, such an assembly, consisting of five or six hundred persons, was found a much more tractable and useful instrument of dominion. It was on the dignity of the senate, that Augustus and his successors founded their new empire; and they affected, on every occasion, to adopt the language and principles of patricians. In the administration of their own powers they frequently consulted the great national council, and *seemed* to refer to its decision the most important concerns of peace and war. Rome, Italy, and the internal provinces, were subject to the immediate jurisdiction of the senate. With regard to civil objects, it was the supreme court of appeal; with regard to criminal matters, a tribunal constituted for the trial of all offences that were committed by men in any public station, or that affected the peace and majesty of the Roman people. The exercise of the judicial power became the most frequent and serious occupation of the senate; and the important causes that were pleaded before them afforded a last refuge to the spirit of ancient eloquence. As a council of state, and as a court of justice, the senate possessed very considerable prerogatives; but in its legislative capacity, in which it was supposed virtually to represent the people, the rights of sovereignty were acknowledged to reside in that assembly. Every power was derived from their authority, every law was ratified by their sanction. Their regular meetings were held on three stated days in every month, the Calends, the Nones, and the Ides. The debates were conducted with decent freedom; and the emperors themselves, who gloried in the name of senators, sat, voted, and divided with their equals.

To resume, in a few words, the system of the Imperial government, as it was instituted by Augustus, and maintained by those princes who understood their own interest and that of the people, it may be defined an absolute monarchy disguised by the forms of a commonwealth. The masters of the Roman world surrounded their throne with darkness, concealed their irresistible strength, and humbly professed themselves the accountable ministers of the senate, whose supreme decrees they dictated and obeyed.

The face of the court corresponded with the forms of the adminis-tration. The emperors, if we except those tyrants whose capricious folly violated every law of nature and decency, disdained that pomp and ceremony which might offend their countrymen, but could add nothing to their real power. In all the offices of life they affected to confound themselves with their subjects, and maintained with them an equal intercourse of visits and entertainments. Their habit, their palace, their table, were suited only to the rank of an opulent senator. Their family, however numerous or splendid, was composed entirely of their domestic slaves and freedmen.* Augustus or Trajan would have blushed at employing the meanest of the Romans in those menial offices, which, in the household and bed-chamber of a limited monarch, are so eagerly solicited by the proudest nobles of Britain.

The deification of the emperors is the only instance in which they departed from their accustomed prudence and modesty. The Asiatic Greeks were the first inventors, the successors of Alexander the first objects, of this servile and impious mode of adulation. It was easily transferred from the kings to the governors of Asia; and the Roman magistrates very frequently were adored as provincial deities, with the pomp of altars and temples, of festivals and sacrifices. It was natural that the emperors should not refuse what the proconsuls had accepted; and the divine honours which both the one and the other received from the provinces, attested rather the despotism than the servitude of Rome. But the conquerors soon imitated the vanquished nations in the arts of flattery; and the imperious spirit of the first Caesar too easily consented to assume, during his lifetime, a place among the tutelar deities of Rome. The milder temper of his successor declined so dangerous an ambition,

---

* A weak prince will always be governed by his domestics. The power of slaves aggravated the shame of the Romans; and the senate paid court to a Pallas or a Narcissus. There is a chance that a modern favourite may be a gentleman.

which was never afterwards revived, except by the madness of Caligula and Domitian. Augustus permitted indeed some of the provincial cities to erect temples to his honour, on condition that they should associate the worship of Rome with that of the sovereign; he tolerated private superstition, of which he might be the object; but he contented himself with being revered by the senate and people in his human character, and wisely left to his successor the care of his public deification. A regular custom was introduced, that on the decease of every emperor who had neither lived nor died like a tyrant, the senate by a solemn decree should place him in the number of the gods: and the ceremonies of his Apotheosis were blended with those of his funeral. This legal, and, as it should seem, injudicious profanation, so abhorrent to our stricter princi, ples, was received with a faint murmur, by the easy nature of polytheism; but it was received as an institution, not of religion, but of policy. We should disgrace the virtues of the Antonines, by comparing them with the vices of Hercules or Jupiter. Even the characters of Caesar or Augustus were far superior to those of the popular deities. But it was the misfortune of the former to live in an enlightened age, and their actions were too faithfully recorded to admit of such a mixture of fable and mystery, as the devotion of the vulgar requires. As soon as their divinity was established by law, it sunk into oblivion, without contributing either to their own fame, or to the dignity of succeeding princes.

In the consideration of the Imperial government, we have frequently mentioned the artful founder, under his well-known title of Augustus, which was not however conferred upon him till the edifice was almost completed. The obscure name of Octavianus he derived from a mean family in the little town of Aricia. It was stained with the blood of the proscription; and he was desirous, had it been possible, to erase all memory of his former life. The illustrious surname of Caesar he had assumed as the adopted son of the dictator; but he had too much good sense, either to hope to be confounded, or to wish to be compared, with that extraordinary man. It was proposed in the senate, to dignify their minister with a new appellation: and after a very serious discussion, that of Augustus was chosen, among several others, as being the most expressive of the character of peace and sanctity, which he uniformly affected. *Augustus* was therefore a personal, *Caesar* a family distinction. The former should naturally have expired with the prince on whom it was bestowed; and however the latter was diffused by adoption and female alliance, Nero was the last prince who could allege any hereditary claim to the honours of the Julian line. But, at the time of his death, the practice of a century had inseparably connected those appellations with the Imperial dignity, and they have been preserved by a long succession of emperors, Romans, Greeks, Franks, and Germans, from the fall of the republic to the present time. A distinction was, however, soon introduced. The sacred title of Augustus was always reserved for the monarch, whilst the name of Caesar was more freely communicated to his relations; and, from the reign of Hadrian, at least, was appropriated to the second person in the state, who was considered as the presumptive heir of the empire.

The tender respect of Augustus for a free constitution which he had destroyed, can only be explained by an attentive consideration of the character of that subtle tyrant. A cool head, an unfeeling heart, and a cowardly disposition, prompted him, at the age of nineteen, to assume the mask of hypocrisy, which he never afterwards laid aside. With the same hand, and probably with the same temper, he signed the proscription of Cicero, and the pardon of Cinna. His virtues, and even his vices, were artificial; and according to the various dictates of his interest, he was at first the enemy, and at last the father, of the Roman world.* When he framed the artful system of the Imperial authority, his moderation was inspired by his fears. He wished to deceive the people by an image of civil liberty, and the armies by an image of civil government.

I. The death of Caesar was ever before his eyes. He had lavished wealth and honours on his adherents; but the most favoured friends of his uncle were in the number of the conspirators. The fidelity of the legions might defend his authority against open rebellion; but their vigilance could not secure his person from the dagger of a determined republican; and the Romans, who revered the memory of Brutus, would applaud the imitation of his virtue. Caesar had provoked his fate, as much by the ostentation of his power as by his power itself. The consul or the tribune might have reigned in peace. The title of king had armed the Romans against his life. Augustus was sensible that mankind is governed by names; nor was he deceived in his expectation, that the senate and people would submit to slavery, provided they were respectfully assured that they still enjoyed their ancient freedom. A feeble senate

---

* 'As Octavianus advanced to the banquet of the Caesars, his colour changed like that of the Camelion; pale at first, then red, afterwards black, he at last assumed the mild livery of Venus and the graces.' This image employed by Julian in his ingenious fiction, is just and elegant; but when he considers this change of character as real, and ascribes it to the power of philosophy, he does too much honour to philosophy, and to Octavianus.

and enervated people cheerfully acquiesced in the pleasing illusion, as long as it was supported by the virtue, or even by the prudence, of the succession of Augustus. It was a motive of self-preservation, not a principle of liberty, that animated the conspirators against Caligula, Nero, and Domitian. They attacked the person of the tyrant, without aiming their blow at the authority of the emperor.

There appears, indeed, *one* memorable occasion, in which the senate, after seventy years of patience, made an ineffectual attempt to reassume its long-forgotten rights. When the throne was vacant by the murder of Caligula, the consuls convoked that assembly in the Capitol, condemned the memory of the Caesars, gave the watchword *liberty* to the few cohorts who faintly adhered to their standard, and during eight and forty hours acted as the independent chiefs of a free commonwealth. But while they deliberated, the Praetorian Guards had resolved. The stupid Claudius, brother of Germanicus, was already in their camp, invested with the Imperial purple, and prepared to support his election by arms. The dream of liberty was at an end; and the senate awoke to all the horrors of inevitable servitude. Deserted by the people, and threatened by a military force, that feeble assembly was compelled to ratify the choice of the Praetorians, and to embrace the benefit of an amnesty, which Claudius had the prudence to offer, and the generosity to observe.*

II. The insolence of the armies inspired Augustus with fears of a still more alarming nature. The despair of the citizens could only attempt what the power of the soldiers was, at any time, able to execute. How precarious was his own authority over men whom he had taught to violate every social duty! He had heard their seditious clamours; he dreaded their calmer moments of reflection. One revolution had been purchased by immense rewards; but a second revolution might double those rewards. The troops professed the fondest attachment to the house of Caesar; but the attachment of the multitude are capricious and inconstant. Augustus summoned to his aid whatever remained in those fierce minds of Roman prejudices; enforced the rigour of discipline by the sanction of law; and interposing the majesty of the senate between the emperor and the army, boldly claimed their allegiance, as the first magistrate of the republic.

During a long period of two hundred and twenty years, from the establishment of this artful system to the death of Commodus, the

* It is much to be regretted that we have lost the part of Tacitus which treated of that transaction. We are forced to content ourselves with the popular rumours of Josephus, and the imperfect hints of Dion and Suetonius.

dangers inherent to a military government were, in a great measure, suspended. The soldiers were seldom roused to that fatal sense of their own strength, and of the weakness of the civil authority, which was, before and afterwards, productive of such dreadful calamities. Caligula and Domitian were assassinated in their palace by their own domestics; the convulsions which agitated Rome on the death of the former, were confined to the walls of the city. But Nero involved the whole empire in his ruin. In the space of eighteen months, four princes perished by the sword; and the Roman world was shaken by the fury of the contending armies. Excepting only this short, though violent, eruption of military licence, the two centuries from Augustus to Commodus passed away unstained with civil blood, and undisturbed by revolutions. The emperor was elected by *the authority of the senate*, and *the consent of the soldiers*. The legions respected their oath of fidelity; and it requires a minute inspection of the Roman annals to discover three inconsiderable rebellions, which were all suppressed in a few months, and without even the hazard of a battle.

In elective monarchies, the vacancy of the throne is a moment big with danger and mischief. The Roman emperors, desirous to spare the legions that interval of suspense, and the temptation of an irregular choice, invested their designed successor with so large a share of present power, as should enable him, after their decease, to assume the remainder, without suffering the empire to perceive the change of masters. Thus Augustus, after all his fairer prospects had been snatched from him by untimely deaths, rested his last hopes on Tiberius, obtained for his adopted son the censorial and tribunitian powers, and dictated a law by which the future prince was invested with an authority equal to his own, over the provinces and the armies. Thus Vespasian subdued the generous mind of his eldest son. Titus was adored by the eastern legions, which, under his command, had recently achieved the conquest of Judea. His power was dreaded and as his virtues were clouded by the intemperance of youth, his designs were suspected. Instead of listening to such unworthy suspicions, the prudent monarch associated Titus to the full powers of the Imperial dignity; and the grateful son ever approved himself the humble and faithful minister of so indulgent a father.

The good sense of Vespasian engaged him indeed to embrace every measure that might confirm his recent and precarious elevation. The military oath, and the fidelity of the troops, had been consecrated by the habits of an hundred years, to the name and family of the Caesars; and although that family had been continued only by the fictitious rite of adoption, the Romans still revered, in the person of Nero, the grandson of Germanicus, and the lineal successor of Augustus. It was not without reluctance and remorse that the Praetorian Guards had been persuaded to abandon the cause of the tyrant. The rapid downfall of Galba, Otho, and Vitellius, taught the armies to consider the emperors as the creatures of *their* will, and the instruments of *their* licence. The birth of Vespasian was mean; his grandfather had been a private soldier, his father a petty officer of the revenue; his own merit had raised him, in an advanced age, to the empire; but his merit was rather useful, than shining, and his virtues were disgraced by a strict and even sordid parsimony. Such a prince consulted his true interest by the association of a son, whose more splendid and amiable character might turn the public attention from the obscure origin to the future glories of the Flavian house. Under the mild administration of Titus, the Roman world enjoyed a transient felicity, and his beloved memory served to protect, above fifteen years, the vices of his brother Domitian.

Nerva had scarcely accepted the purple from the assassins of Domitian before he discovered that his feeble age was unable to stem the torrent of public disorders, which had multiplied under the long tyranny of his predecessor. His mild disposition was respected by the good; but the degenerate Romans required a more vigorous character, whose justice should strike terror into the guilty. Though he had several relations, he fixed his choice on a stranger. He adopted Trajan, then about forty years of age, and who commanded a powerful army in the Lower Germany; and immediately, by a decree of the senate, declared him his colleague and successor in the empire. It is sincerely to be lamented, that whilst we are fatigued with the disgustful relation of Nero's crimes and follies, we are reduced to collect the actions of Trajan from the glimmerings of an abridgment, or the doubtful light of a panegyric. There remains, however, one panegyric far removed beyond the suspicion of flattery. Above two hundred and fifty years after the death of Trajan, the senate, in pouring out the customary acclamations on the accession of a new emperor, wished that he might surpass the felicity of Augustus, and the virtue of Trajan.

We may readily believe, that the father of his country hesitated whether he ought to entrust the various and doubtful character of his kinsman Hadrian with sovereign power. In his last moments, the arts of the empress Plotina either fixed the irresolution of Trajan, or boldly supposed a fictitious adoption; the truth of which could not be safely disputed, and Hadrian was peaceably acknowledged as his lawful successor. Under his reign, as has been already mentioned, the empire flourished in peace and prosperity. He encouraged the arts, reformed the laws, asserted military discipline, and visited all his provinces in person. His vast and active genius was equally suited to the most enlarged views, and the minute details of civil policy. But the ruling passions of his soul were curiosity and vanity. As they prevailed, and as they were attracted by different objects, Hadrian was, by turns, an excellent prince, a ridiculous sophist, and a jealous tyrant. The general tenor of his conduct deserved praise for its equity and moderation. Yet in the first days of his reign, he put to death four consular senators, his personal enemies, and men who had been judged worthy of empire; and the tediousness of a painful illness rendered him, at last, peevish and cruel. The senate doubted whether they should pronounce him a god or a tyrant; and the honours decreed to his memory were granted to the prayers of the pious Antoninus.

The caprice of Hadrian influenced his choice of a successor. After revolving in his mind several men of distinguished merit, whom he esteemed and hated, he adopted Aelius Verus, a gay and voluptuous nobleman, recommended by uncommon beauty to the lover of Antinous.* But while Hadrian was delighting himself with his own applause, and the acclamations of the soldiers, whose consent had been secured by an immense donative, the new Caesar was ravished from his embraces by an untimely death. He left only one son. Hadrian commended the boy to the gratitude of the Antonines. He was adopted by Pius; and, on the accession of Marcus, was invested with an equal share of sovereign power. Among the many vices of this younger Verus he possessed one virtue; a dutiful reverence for his wiser colleague, to whom he willingly abandoned the ruder cares of empire. The philosophic emperor dissembled his follies, lamented his early death, and cast a decent veil over his memory.

As soon as Hadrian's passion was either gratified or disappointed, he resolved to deserve the thanks of posterity, by placing the most exalted merit on the Roman throne. His discerning eye easily discovered a senator about fifty years of age, blameless in all the offices of life, and a youth of about seventeen, whose riper years opened the fair prospect of every virtue: the elder of these was declared the son and successor of

---

* The deification of Antinous, his medals, statues, temples, city, oracles, and constellation, are well known, and still dishonour the memory of Hadrian. Yet we may remark, that of the first fifteen emperors, Claudius was the only one whose taste in love was entirely correct.

Hadrian, on condition, however, that he himself should immediately adopt the younger. The two Antonines (for it is of them that we are now speaking) governed the Roman world forty-two years, with the same invariable spirit of wisdom and virtue. Although Pius had two sons,* he preferred the welfare of Rome to the interest of his family, gave his daughter Faustina in marriage to young Marcus, obtained from the senate the tribunitian and preconsular powers, and with a noble disdain, or rather ignorance of jealousy, associated him to all the labours of government. Marcus, on the other hand, revered the character of his benefactor, loved him as a parent, obeyed him as his sovereign, and, after he was no more, regulated his own administration by the example and maxims of his predecessor. Their united reigns are possibly the only period of history in which the happiness of a great people was the sole object of government.

Titus Antoninus Pius has been justly denominated a second Numa. The same love of religion, justice, and peace, was the distinguishing characteristic of both princes. But the situation of the latter opened a much larger field for the exercise of those virtues. Numa could only prevent a few neighbouring villages from plundering each other's harvests. Antoninus diffused order and tranquillity over the greatest part of the earth. His reign is marked by the rare advantage of furnishing very few materials for history; which is, indeed, little more than the register of the crimes, follies, and misfortunes of mankind. In private life, he was an amiable as well as a good man. The native simplicity of his virtue was a stranger to vanity or affectation. He enjoyed with moderation the conveniencies of his fortune, and the innocent pleasures of society: and the benevolence of his soul displayed itself in a cheerful serenity of temper.

The virtue of Marcus Aurelius Antoninus was of a severer and more laborious kind.† It was the well-earned harvest of many a learned conference, of many a patient lecture, and many a midnight lucubration. At the age of twelve years he embraced the rigid system of the Stoics,

* Without the help of medals and inscriptions we should be ignorant of this fact, so honourable to the memory of Pius.

† The enemies of Marcus charged him with hypocrisy, and with a want of that simplicity which distinguished Pius and even Verus. This suspicion, unjust as it was, may serve to account for the superior applause bestowed upon personal qualifications, in preference to the social virtues. Even Marcus Antoninus has been called a hypocrite; but the wildest scepticism never insinuated that Caesar might possibly be a coward, or Tully a fool. Wit and valour are qualifications more easily ascertained, than humanity or the love of justice.

which taught him to submit his body to his mind, his passions to his reason; to consider virtue as the only good, vice as the only evil, all things external as things indifferent. His meditations, composed in the tumult of a camp, are still extant; and he even condescended to give lessons of philosophy in a more public manner than was perhaps consistent with the modesty of a sage, or the dignity of an emperor. But his life was the noblest commentary on the precepts of Zeno. He was severe to himself, indulgent to the imperfections of others, just and beneficent to all mankind. He regretted that Avidius Cassius, who excited a rebellion in Syria, had disappointed him, by a voluntary death, of the pleasure of converting an enemy into a friend; and he justified the sincerity of that sentiment, by moderating the zeal of the senate against the adherents of the traitor. War he detested, as the disgrace and calamity of human nature; but when the necessity of a just defence called upon him to take up arms, he readily exposed his person to eight winter campaigns on the frozen banks of the Danube, the severity of which was at last fatal to the weakness of his constitution. His memory was revered by a grateful posterity, and above a century after his death, many persons preserved the image of Marcus Antoninus, among those of their household gods.

If a man were called to fix the period in the history of the world, during which the condition of the human race was most happy and prosperous, he would, without hesitation, name that which elapsed from the death of Domitian to the accession of Commodus. The vast extent of the Roman Empire was governed by absolute power, under the guid-ance of virtue and wisdom. The armies were restrained by the firm but gentle hand of four successive emperors, whose characters and authority commanded involuntary respect. The forms of the civil administration were carefully preserved by Nerva, Trajan, Hadrian, and the Antonines, who delighted in the image of liberty, and were pleased with considering themselves as the accountable ministers of the laws. Such princes deserved the honour of restoring the republic had the Romans of their days been capable of enjoying a rational freedom.

The labours of these monarchs were overpaid by the immense reward that inseparably waited on their success; by the honest pride of virtue, and by the exquisite delight of beholding the general happiness of which they were the authors. A just, but melancholy reflection embittered, however, the noblest of human enjoyments. They must often have recollected the instability of a happiness which depended on the charac-ter of a single man. The fatal moment was perhaps approaching, when some licentious youth, or some jealous tyrant, would abuse, to the destruction, that absolute power which they had exerted for the benefit of their people. The ideal restraints of the senate and the laws might serve to display the virtues, but could never correct the vices, of the emperor. The military force was a blind and irresistible instrument of oppression; and the corruption of Roman manners would always supply flatterers eager to applaud, and ministers prepared to serve the fear or the avarice, the lust or the cruelty, of their masters.

These gloomy apprehensions had been already justified by the experience of the Romans. The annals of the emperors exhibit a strong and various picture of human nature, which we should vainly seek among the mixed and doubtful characters of modern history. In the conduct of those monarchs we may trace the utmost lines of vice and virtue; the most exalted perfection, and the meanest degeneracy of our own species. The golden age of Trajan and the Antonines had been preceded by an age of iron. It is almost superfluous to enumerate the unworthy successors of Augustus. Their unparalleled vices, and the splendid theatre on which they were acted, have saved them from oblivion. The dark unrelenting Tiberius, the furious Caligula, the feeble Claudius, the profligate and cruel Nero, the beastly Vitellius,* and the timid inhuman Domitian, are condemned to everlasting infamy. During fourscore years (excepting only the short and doubtful respite of Vespasian's reign) Rome groaned beneath an unremitting tyranny, which exterminated the ancient families of the republic, and was fatal to almost every virtue, and every talent, that arose in that unhappy period.

Under the reign of these monsters the slavery of the Romans was accompanied with two peculiar circumstances, the one occasioned by their former liberty, the other by their extensive conquests, which rendered their condition more completely wretched than that of the victims of tyranny in any other age or country. From these causes were derived, 1: The exquisite sensibility of the sufferers; and, 2: the impossibility of escaping from the hand of the oppressor.

I. When Persia was governed by the descendants of Sefi, a race of princes whose wanton cruelty often stained their divan, their table, and their bed, with the blood of their favourites, there is a saying recorded of a young nobleman, that he never departed from the sultan's presence without satisfying himself whether his head was still on his shoulders. The experience of every day might almost justify the scepticism of Rustan. Yet the fatal sword, suspended above him by a single thread,

* Vitellius consumed in mere eating, at least six millions of our money in about seven months. It is not easy to express his vices with dignity, or even decency.

seems not to have disturbed the slumbers, or interrupted the tranquillity, of the Persian. The monarch's frown, he well knew, could level him with the dust; but the stroke of lightning or apoplexy might be equally fatal; and it was the part of a wise man to forget the inevitable calamities of human life in the enjoyment of the fleeting hour. He was dignified with the appellation of the king's slave; had, perhaps, been purchased from obscure parents in a country which he had never known; and was trained up from his infancy in the severe discipline of the seraglio.* His name, his wealth, his honours, were the gift of a master, who might, without injustice, resume what he had bestowed. Rustan's knowledge, if he possessed any, could only serve to confirm his habits by prejudices. His language afforded no words for any form of government, except absolute monarchy. The history of the East informed him, that such had ever been the condition of mankind. The Koran, and the interpreters of that divine book, inculcated to him, that the sultan was the descendant of the prophet, and the vice-regent of heaven; that patience was the first virtue of a Mussulman, and unlimited obedience the great duty of a subject.

The minds of the Romans were very differently prepared for slavery. Oppressed beneath the weight of their own corruption and of military violence, they for a long while preserved the sentiments, or at least the ideas, of their free-born ancestors. The education of Helvidius and Thrasea, of Tacitus and Pliny, was the same as that of Cato and Cicero. From Grecian philosophy they had imbibed the justest and most liberal notions of the dignity of human nature, and the origin of civil society. The history of their own country had taught them to revere a free, a virtuous, and a victorious commonwealth; to abhor the successful crimes of Caesar and Augustus; and inwardly to despise those tyrants whom they adored with the most abject flattery. As magistrates and senators, they were admitted into the great council which had once dictated laws to the earth, whose name still gave a sanction to the acts of the monarch, and whose authority was so often prostituted to the vilest purposes of tyranny. Tiberius, and those emperors who adopted his maxims, attempted to disguise their murders by the formalities of justice, and perhaps enjoyed a secret pleasure in rendering the senate their accomplice as well as their victim. By this assembly the last of the Romans were condemned for imaginary crimes and real virtues. Their infamous

* The practice of raising slaves to the great offices of state is still more common among the Turks than among the Persians. The miserable countries of Georgia and Circassia supply rulers to the greatest part of the East.

accusers assumed the language of independent patriots, who arraigned a dangerous citizen before the tribunal of his country; and the public service was rewarded by riches and honours. The servile judges professed to assert the majesty of the commonwealth, violated in the person of its first magistrate; whose clemency they most applauded when they trem╱bled the most at his inexorable and impending cruelty. The tyrant beheld their baseness with just contempt, and encountered their secret sentiments of detestation with sincere and avowed hatred for the whole body of the senate.

II. The division of Europe into a number of independent states, connected, however, with each other, by the general resemblance of religion, language, and manners, is productive of the most beneficial consequences to the liberty of mankind. A modern tyrant, who should find no resistance either in his own breast, or in his people, would soon experience a gentle restraint from the example of his equals, the dread of present censure, the advice of his allies, and the apprehension of his enemies. The object of his displeasure, escaping from the narrow limits of his dominions, would easily obtain, in a happier climate, a secure refuge, a new fortune adequate to his merit, the freedom of complaint, and perhaps the means of revenge. But the empire of the Romans filled the world, and when the empire fell into the hands of a single person, the world became a safe and dreary prison for his enemies. The slave of Imperial despotism, whether he was condemned to drag his gilded chain in Rome and the senate, or to wear out a life of exile on the barren rock of Seriphus, or the frozen banks of the Danube, expected his fate in silent despair.* To resist was fatal, and it was impossible to fly. On every side he was encompassed with a vast extent of sea and land, which he could never hope to traverse without being discovered, seized and restored to his irritated master. Beyond the frontiers, his anxious view could discover nothing, except the ocean, inhospitable deserts, hostile tribes of barbarians, of fierce manners and unknown language, or dependent kings, who would gladly purchase the emperor's protection by the sacrifice of an obnoxious fugitive. 'Wherever you are,' said Cicero to the exiled Marcellus, 'remember that you are equally within the power of the conqueror.'

* Seriphus was a small rocky island in the Aegean Sea, the inhabitants of which were despised for their ignorance and obscurity. The place of Ovid's exile is well known, by his just, but unmanly lamentations. It should seem, that he only received an order to leave Rome in so many days, and to transport himself to Tomi. Guards and gaolers were unnecessary.

THE CRUELTY, FOLLIES, AND MURDER OF COMMO-
DUS — ELECTION OF PERTINAX — HIS ATTEMPTS TO
REFORM THE STATE — HIS ASSASSINATION BY THE
PRAETORIAN GUARDS

THE MILDNESS OF MARCUS, WHICH THE
rigid discipline of the Stoics was unable to eradicate, formed, at the same
time, the most amiable, and the only defective, part of his character. His
excellent understanding was often deceived by the unsuspecting goodness of his heart. Artful men, who study the passions of princes, and
conceal their own, approached his person in the disguise of philosophic
sanctity, and acquired riches and honours by affecting to despise them.
His excessive indulgence to his brother, his wife, and his son, exceeded
the bounds of private virtue, and became a public injury, by the example
and consequences of their vices.

Faustina, the daughter of Pius and the wife of Marcus, has been as
much celebrated for her gallantries as for her beauty. The grave simplicity of the philosopher was ill calculated to engage her wanton levity, or
to fix that unbounded passion for variety, which often discovered
personal merit in the meanest of mankind. The Cupid of the ancients
was, in general, a very sensual deity; and the amours of an empress, as
they exact on her side the plainest advances, are seldom susceptible of
much sentimental delicacy. Marcus was the only man in the empire who
seemed ignorant or insensible of the irregularities of Faustina; which,
according to the prejudices of every age, reflected some disgrace on the
injured husband. He promoted several of her lovers to posts of honour
and profit, and during a connection of thirty years, invariably gave her
proofs of the most tender confidence, and of a respect which ended not
with her life. In his *Meditations*, he thanks the gods, who had bestowed
on him a wife, so faithful, so gentle, and of such a wonderful simplicity
of manners. The obsequious senate, at his earnest request, declared her a
goddess. She was represented in her temples, with the attributes of Juno,
Venus, and Ceres; and it was decreed, that on the day of their nuptials,
the youth of either sex should pay their vows before the altar of their
chaste patroness.

The monstrous vices of the son have cast a shade on the purity of the father's virtues. It has been objected to Marcus, that he sacrificed the happiness of millions to a fond partiality for a worthless boy; and that he chose a successor in his own family, rather than in the republic. Nothing, however, was neglected by the anxious father, and by the men of virtue and learning whom he summoned to his assistance, to expand the narrow mind of young Commodus, to correct his growing vices, and to render him worthy of the throne, for which he was designed. But the power of instruction is seldom of much efficacy, except in those happy dispositions where it is almost superfluous. The distasteful lesson of a grave philosopher was in a moment obliterated by the whisper of a profligate favourite; and Marcus himself blasted the fruits of this laboured education, by admitting his son, at the age of fourteen or fifteen, to a full participation of the Imperial power. He lived but four years afterwards; but he lived long enough to repent a rash measure, which raised the impetuous youth above the restraint of reason and authority.

Most of the crimes which disturb the internal peace of society are produced by the restraints which the necessary, but unequal, laws of property have imposed on the appetites of mankind, by confining to a few the possession of those objects that are coveted by many. Of all our passions and appetites, the love of power is of the most imperious and unsociable nature, since the pride of one man requires the submission of the multitude. In the tumult of civil discord, the laws of society lose their force, and their place is seldom supplied by those of humanity. The ardour of contention, the pride of victory, the despair of success, the memory of past injuries, and the fear of future dangers, all contribute to inflame the mind, and to silence the voice of pity. From such motives almost every page of history has been stained with civil blood; but these motives will not account for the unprovoked cruelties of Commodus, who had nothing to wish for and everything to enjoy. The beloved son of Marcus succeeded (AD 180) to his father, amidst the acclamations of the senate and armies, and when he ascended the throne the happy youth saw round him neither competitor to remove nor enemies to punish. In this calm elevated station it was surely natural that he should prefer the love of mankind to their detestation, the mild glories of his five predecessors, to the ignominious fate of Nero and Domitian.

Yet Commodus was not, as he has been represented, a tiger born with an insatiate thirst of human blood, and capable, from his infancy, of the most inhuman actions. Nature had formed him of a weak, rather than a wicked, disposition. His simplicity and timidity rendered him the slave of his attendants, who gradually corrupted his mind. His cruelty, which at first obeyed the dictates of others, degenerated into habit, and at length became the ruling passion of his soul.

Upon the death of his father, Commodus found himself embarrassed with the command of a great army, and the conduct of a difficult war against the Quadi and Marcomanni. The servile and profligate youths whom Marcus had banished, soon regained their station and influence about the new emperor. They exaggerated the hardships and dangers of a campaign in the wild countries beyond the Danube; and they assured the indolent prince, that the terror of his name and the arms of his lieutenants would be sufficient to complete the conquest of the dismayed barbarians; or to impose such conditions as were more advantageous than any conquest. By a dexterous application to his sensual appetites, they compared the tranquillity, the splendour, the refined pleasures of Rome, with the tumult of a Pannonian camp, which afforded neither leisure nor materials for luxury. Commodus listened to the pleasing advice; but whilst he hesitated between his own inclination and the awe which he still retained for his father's counsellors, the summer insensibly elapsed, and his triumphal entry into the capital was deferred till the autumn. His graceful person, popular address, and imagined virtues, attracted the public favour; the honourable peace which he had recently granted to the barbarians diffused an universal joy; his impatience to revisit Rome was fondly ascribed to the love of his country; and his dissolute course of amusements was faintly condemned in a prince of nineteen years of age.

During the three first years of his reign, the forms, and even the spirit, of the old administration were maintained by those faithful counsellors, to whom Marcus had recommended his son, and for whose wisdom and integrity Commodus still entertained a reluctant esteem. The young prince and his profligate favourites revelled in all the licence of sovereign power; but his hands were yet unstained with blood; and he had even displayed a generosity of sentiment, which might perhaps have ripened into solid virtue. A fatal incident decided his fluctuating character.

One evening (AD 183), as the emperor was returning to the palace through a dark and narrow portico in the amphitheatre, an assassin, who waited in his passage, rushed upon him with a drawn sword, loudly exclaiming, '*The senate sends you this.*' The menace prevented the deed; the assassin was seized by the guards, and immediately revealed the authors of the conspiracy. It had been formed, not in the senate, but within the walls of the palace. Lucilla, the emperor's sister, and widow of Lucius Verus, impatient of the second rank, and jealous of the reigning empress, had armed the murderer against her brother's life. She had not ventured to communicate the black design to her second husband Claudius Pompeianus, a senator of distinguished merit and unshaken loyalty; but among the crowd of her lovers (for she imitated the manners of Faustina), she found men of desperate fortunes and wild ambition, who were prepared to serve her more violent as well as her tender passions. The conspirators experienced the rigour of justice, and the abandoned princess was punished, first with exile, and afterwards with death.

But the words of the assassin sunk deep into the mind of Commodus, and left an indelible impression of fear and hatred against the whole body of the senate. Those whom he had dreaded as importunate ministers, he now suspected as secret enemies. The Delators, a race of men discouraged, and almost extinguished, under the former reigns, again became formidable, as soon as they discovered that the emperor was desirous of finding disaffection and treason in the senate. That assembly, whom Marcus had ever considered as the great council of the nation, was composed of the most distinguished of the Romans; and distinction of every kind soon became criminal. The possession of wealth stimulated the diligence of the informers; rigid virtue implied a tacit censure of the irregularities of Commodus; important services implied a dangerous superiority of merit; and the friendship of the father always insured the aversion of the son. Suspicion was equivalent to proof; trial to condemnation. The execution of a considerable senator was attended with the death of all who might lament or revenge his fate; and when Commodus had once tasted human blood, he became incapable of pity or remorse.

Of these innocent victims of tyranny, none died more lamented than the two brothers of the Quintilian family, Maximus and Condianus; whose fraternal love has saved their names from oblivion, and endeared their memory to posterity. Their studies and their occupations, their pursuits and their pleasures, were still the same. In the enjoyment of a great estate, they never admitted the idea of a separate interest; some fragments are now extant of a treatise which they composed in common; and in every action of life it was observed that their two bodies were animated by one soul. The Antonines, who valued their virtues, and delighted in their union, raised them, in the same year, to the consulship: and Marcus afterwards entrusted to their joint care the civil administration of Greece, and a great military command, in which they obtained a signal victory over the Germans. The kind cruelty of Commodus united them in death.

The tyrant's rage, after having shed the noblest blood of the senate, at length recoiled on the principal instrument of his cruelty. Whilst Commodus was immersed in blood and luxury, he devolved the detail of the public business on Perennis; a servile and ambitious minister, who had obtained his post by the murder of his predecessor, but who possessed a considerable share of vigour and ability. By acts of extortion, and the forfeited estates of the nobles sacrificed to his avarice, he had accumulated an immense treasure. The Praetorian Guards were under his immediate command; and his son, who already discovered a military genius, was at the head of the Illyrian legions. Perennis aspired to the empire; or what, in the eyes of Commodus, amounted to the same crime, he was capable of aspiring to it, had he not been prevented, surprised, and (AD 186) put to death. The fall of a minister is a very trifling incident in the general history of the empire; but it was hastened by an extraordinary circumstance, which proved how much the nerves of discipline were already relaxed. The legions of Britain, discontented with the administration of Perennis, formed a deputation of fifteen hundred select men, with instructions to march to Rome, and lay their complaints before the emperor. These military petitioners, by their own determined behaviour, by inflaming the divisions of the guards, by exaggerating the strength of the British army, and by alarming the fears of Commodus, exacted and obtained the minister's death, as the only redress of their grievances. This presumption of a distant army, and their discovery of the weakness of government, was a sure presage of the most dreadful convulsions.

The negligence of the public administration was betrayed soon afterwards by a new disorder which arose from the smallest beginnings. A spirit of desertion began to prevail among the troops; and the deserters, instead of seeking their flight in safety or concealment, infested the highways. Maternus, a private soldier, of a daring boldness above his station, collected these bands of robbers into a little army, set open the prisons, invited the slaves to assert their freedom, and plundered with impunity the rich and defenceless cities of Gaul and Spain. The governors of the provinces, who had long been the spectators, and perhaps the partners, of his depredations, were, at length, roused from their supine indolence by the threatening commands of the emperor. Maternus found that he was encompassed, and foresaw that he must be overpowered. A great effort of despair was his last resource. He ordered his followers to disperse, to pass the Alps in small parties and various disguises, and to assemble at Rome, during the licentious tumult of the festival of Cybele.* To murder Commodus, and to ascend the vacant throne, was the ambition of no vulgar robber. His measures were so ably concerted, that his concealed troops already filled the streets of Rome. The envy of an accomplice discovered and ruined this singular enter- prise, in the moment when it was ripe for execution.

Suspicious princes often promote the last of mankind from a vain persuasion, that those who have no dependence, except on their favour, will have no attachment, except to the person of their benefactor. Cleander, the successor of Perennis, was a Phrygian by birth; of a nation, over whose stubborn, but servile temper, blows only could prevail. He had been sent from his native country to Rome, in the capacity of a slave. As a slave he entered the Imperial palace, rendered himself useful to his master's passions, and rapidly ascended to the most exalted station which a subject could enjoy. His influence over the mind of Commodus was much greater than that of his predecessor; for Cleander was devoid of any ability or virtue which could inspire the emperor with envy or distrust. Avarice was the reigning passion of his soul, and the great principle of his administration. The rank of Consul, of Patrician, of Senator, was exposed to public sale; and it would have been considered as disaffection if any one had refused to purchase these empty and disgraceful honours with the greatest part of his fortune. In the lucrative provincial employments, the minister shared with the governor the spoils of the people. The execution of the laws was venal and arbitrary. A wealthy criminal might obtain, not only the reversal of the sentence by which he was justly condemned; but might likewise inflict whatever punishment he pleased on the accuser, the witnesses, and the judge.

By these means, Cleander, in the space of three years, had accumu- lated more wealth than had ever yet been possessed by any freedman. Commodus was perfectly satisfied with the magnificent presents which the artful courtier laid at his feet in the most seasonable moments. To divert the public envy, Cleander, under the emperor's name, erected baths, porticos, and places of exercise, for the use of the people. He flattered himself that the Romans, dazzled and amused by this apparent liberality, would be less affected by the bloody scenes which were daily

* During the second Punic war, the Romans imported from Asia the worship of the mother of the gods. Her festival, the *Megalesia*, began on the fourth of April, and lasted six days. The streets were crowded with mad processions, the theatres with spectators, and the public tables with unbidden guests. Order and police were suspended, and pleasure was the only serious business of the city. See Ovid, *de Fastis*, iv, 189.

The Arch of Titus

The Forum of Nerva (interior of enclosure walls with the two half-buried Corinthian Columns)

exhibited; that they would forget the death of Byrrhus, a senator to whose superior merit the late emperor had granted one of his daughters; and that they would forgive the execution of Arrius Antoninus, the last representative of the name and virtues of the Antonines. The former, with more integrity than prudence, had attempted to disclose, to his brother-in-law, the true character of Cleander. An equitable sentence pronounced by the latter, when proconsul of Asia, against a worthless creature of the favourite, proved fatal to him. After the fall of Perennis, the terrors of Commodus had, for a short time, assumed the appearance of a return to virtue. He repealed the most odious of his acts, loaded his memory with the public execration, and ascribed to the pernicious counsels of that wicked minister, all the errors of his inexperienced youth. But his repentance lasted only thirty days; and, under Cleander's tyranny, the administration of Perennis was often regretted.

Pestilence and famine contributed to fill up the measure of the calamities of Rome. The first could be only imputed to the just indignation of the gods; but (AD 189) a monopoly of corn, supported by the riches and power of the minister, was considered as the immediate cause of the second. The popular discontent, after it had long circulated in whispers, broke out in the assembled circus. The people quitted their favourite amusements for the more delicious pleasure of revenge, rushed in crowds towards a palace in the suburbs, one of the emperor's retirements, and demanded, with angry clamours, the head of the public enemy. Cleander, who commanded the Praetorian Guards, ordered a body of cavalry to sally forth, and disperse the seditious multitude. The multitude fled with precipitation towards the city; several were slain, and many more were trampled to death: but when the cavalry entered the streets, their pursuit was checked by a shower of stones and darts from the roofs and windows of the houses. The foot guards, who had been long jealous of the prerogatives and insolence of the Praetorian cavalry, embraced the party of the people. The tumult became a regular engage-ment, and threatened a general massacre. The Praetorians, at length, gave way, oppressed with numbers; and the tide of popular fury returned with redoubled violence against the gates of the palace, where Com-modus lay, dissolved in luxury, and alone unconscious of the civil war. It was death to approach his person with the unwelcome news. He would have perished in this supine security, had not two women, his elder sister Fadilla, and Marcia, the most favoured of his concubines, ventured to break into his presence. Bathed in tears, and with dishevelled hair, they threw themselves at his feet; and with all the pressing eloquence of fear, discovered to the affrighted emperor, the crimes of the minister, the rage of the people, and the impending ruin, which, in a few minutes, would burst over his palace and person. Commodus started from his dream of pleasure, and commanded that the head of Cleander should be thrown out to the people. The desired spectacle instantly appeased the tumult; and the son of Marcus might even yet have regained the affection and confidence of his outraged subjects.

But every sentiment of virtue and humanity was extinct in the mind of Commodus. Whilst he thus abandoned the reins of empire to these unworthy favourites, he valued nothing in sovereign power, except the unbounded licence of indulging his sensual appetites. His hours were spent in a seraglio of three hundred beautiful women, and as many boys, of every rank, and of every province; and, wherever the arts of seduction proved ineffectual, the brutal lover had recourse to violence. The ancient historians have expatiated on these abandoned scenes of prostitution, which scorned every restraint of nature or modesty; but it would not be easy to translate their too faithful descriptions into the decency of modern language. The intervals of lust were filled up with the basest amusements. The influence of a polite age, and the labour of an attentive education, had never been able to infuse into his rude and brutish mind the least tincture of learning; and he was the first of the Roman emperors totally devoid of taste for the pleasures of the understanding. Nero himself excelled, or affected to excel, in the elegant arts of music and poetry; nor should we despise his pursuits had he not converted the pleasing relaxation of a leisure hour into the serious business and ambition of his life. But Commodus, from his earliest infancy, discovered an aversion to whatever was rational or liberal, and a fond attachment to the amusements of the populace; the sports of the circus and amphitheatre, the combats of gladiators, and the hunting of wild beasts. The masters in every branch of learning, whom Marcus provided for his son, were heard with inattention and disgust; whilst the Moors and Parthians, who taught him to dart the javelin and to shoot with the bow, found a disciple who delighted in his application, and soon equalled the most skilful of his instructors, in the steadiness of the eye, and the dexterity of the hand.

The servile crowd, whose fortune depended on their master's vices, applauded these ignoble pursuits. The perfidious voice of flattery reminded him that by exploits of the same nature, by the defeat of the Nemaean lion, and the slaughter of the wild boar of Erymanthus, the Grecian Hercules had acquired a place among the gods, and an immortal memory among men. They only forgot to observe, that, in the first ages of society, when the fiercer animals often dispute with man the possession of an unsettled country, a successful war against those savages is one of the most innocent and beneficial labours of heroism. In the civilised state of the Roman Empire, the wild beasts had long since retired from the face of man, and the neighbourhood of populous cities. To surprise them in their solitary haunts, and to transport them to Rome, that they might be slain in pomp by the hand of an emperor, was an enterprise equally ridiculous for the prince, and oppressive for the people.* Ignorant of these distinctions, Commodus eagerly embraced the glorious resemblance, and styled himself (as we still read on his medals) the *Roman Hercules*. The club and the lion's hide were placed by the side of the throne, amongst the ensigns of sovereignty; and statues were erected, in which Commodus was represented in the character, and with the attributes, of the god, whose valour and dexterity he endeavoured to emulate in the daily course of his ferocious amusements.

Elated with these praises, which gradually extinguished the innate sense of shame, Commodus resolved to exhibit, before the eyes of the Roman people, those exercises, which till then he had decently confined within the walls of his palace, and to the presence of a few favourites. On the appointed day, the various motives of flattery, fear, and curiosity, attracted to the amphitheatre an innumerable multitude of spectators: and some degree of applause was deservedly bestowed on the uncommon skill of the Imperial performer. Whether he aimed at the head or heart of the animal, the wound was alike certain and mortal. With arrows, whose point was shaped into the form of a crescent, Commodus often intercepted the rapid career, and cut asunder the long bony neck of the ostrich.† A panther was let loose; and the archer waited till he had leaped upon a trembling malefactor. In the same instant the shaft flew, the beast dropped dead, and the man remained unhurt. The dens of the amphitheatre disgorged at once a hundred lions; a hundred darts from the unerring hand of Commodus laid them dead as they ran raging round the *Arena*. Neither the huge bulk of the elephant, nor the scaly hide of the rhinoceros, could defend them from his stroke. Ethiopia and

* The African lions, when pressed by hunger, infested the open villages and cultivated country, and they infested them with impunity. The royal beast was reserved for the pleasures of the emperor and the capital; and the unfortunate peasant, who killed one of them, though in his own defence, incurred a very heavy penalty. This extraordinary gamelaw was mitigated by Honorius, and finally repealed by Justinian.

† The ostrich's neck is three feet long, and composed of seventeen vertebrae. Buffon, *Histoire naturelle*.

India yielded their most extraordinary productions; and several animals were slain in the amphitheatre, which had been seen only in the representations of art, or perhaps of fancy.* In all these exhibitions, the securest precautions were used to protect the person of the Roman Hercules from the desperate spring of any savage; who might possibly disregard the dignity of the emperor, and the sanctity of the god.

But the meanest of the populace were affected with shame and indignation when they beheld their sovereign enter the lists as a gladiator, and glory in a profession which the laws and manners of the Romans had branded with the justest note of infamy. He chose the habit and arms of the *Secutor*, whose combat with the *Retiarius* formed one of the most lively scenes in the bloody sports of the amphitheatre. The *Secutor* was armed with an helmet, sword, and buckler; his naked antagonist had only a large net and a trident; with the one he endeavoured to entangle, with the other to dispatch, his enemy. If he missed the first throw, he was obliged to fly from the pursuit of the *Secutor*, till he had prepared his net for a second cast. The emperor fought in this character seven hundred and thirty-five several times. These glorious achievements were carefully recorded in the public acts of the empire; and that he might omit no circumstance of infamy, he received from the common fund of gladia, tors, a stipend so exorbitant, that it became a new and most ignominious tax upon the Roman people. It may be easily supposed that in these engagements the master of the world was always successful: in the amphitheatre his victories were not often sanguinary; but when he exercised his skill in the school of gladiators, or his own palace, his wretched antagonists were frequently honoured with a mortal wound from the hand of Commodus, and obliged to seal their flattery with their blood. He now disdained the appellation of Hercules. The name of Paulus, a celebrated *Secutor*, was the only one which delighted his ear. It was inscribed on his colossal statues, and repeated in the redoubled acclamations of the mournful and applauding senate. Claudius Pom, peianus, the virtuous husband of Lucilla, was the only senator who asserted the honour of his rank. As a father, he permitted his sons to consult their safety by attending the amphitheatre. As a Roman, he declared, that his own life was in the emperor's hands, but that he would

---

* Commodus killed a camelopardalis or giraffe, the tallest, the most gentle, and the most useless of the large quadrupeds. This singular animal, a native only of the interior parts of Africa, has not been seen in Europe since the revival of letters, and though M. de Buffon (*Histoire naturelle*) has endeavoured to describe, he has not ventured to delineate, the giraffe.

never behold the son of Marcus prostituting his person and dignity. Notwithstanding his manly resolution, Pompeianus escaped the resent⁄ment of the tyrant, and with his honour had the good fortune to preserve his life.

Commodus had now attained the summit of vice and infamy. Amidst the acclamations of a flattering court, he was unable to disguise, from himself, that he had deserved the contempt and hatred of every man of sense and virtue in his empire. His ferocious spirit was irritated by the consciousness of that hatred, by the envy of every kind of merit, by the just apprehension of danger, and by the habit of slaughter, which he contracted in his daily amusements. History has preserved a long list of consular senators sacrificed to his wanton suspicion, which sought out, with peculiar anxiety, those unfortunate persons connected, however remotely, with the family of the Antonines, without sparing even the ministers of his crimes or pleasures. His cruelty proved at last fatal to himself. He had shed with impunity the noblest blood of Rome: he perished as soon as he was dreaded by his own domestics. Marcia his favourite concubine, Eclectus his chamberlain, and Laetus his Praetor⁄ian prefect, alarmed by the fate of their companions and predecessors, resolved to prevent the destruction which every hour hung over their heads, either from the mad caprice of the tyrant, or the sudden indigna⁄tion of the people. Marcia seized the occasion of presenting a draught of wine to her lover, after he had fatigued himself with hunting some wild beasts. Commodus retired to sleep; but whilst he was labouring with the effects of poison and drunkenness, a robust youth, by profession a wrestler, entered his chamber, and strangled him without resistance. The body was secretly conveyed out of the palace, before the least suspicion was entertained in the city, or even in the court, of the emperor's death. Such was the fate of the son of Marcus, and so easy was it to destroy a hated tyrant, who, by the artificial powers of government, had oppressed, during thirteen years, so many millions of subjects, each of whom was equal to their master in personal strength and personal abilities.

The measures of the conspirators were conducted with the deliberate coolness and celerity which the greatness of the occasion required. They resolved instantly to fill the vacant throne with an emperor whose character would justify and maintain the action that had been commit⁄ted. They fixed on Pertinax, prefect of the city, an ancient senator of consular rank, whose conspicuous merit had broke through the obscur⁄ity of his birth, and raised him to the first honours of the state. He had successively governed most of the provinces of the empire; and in all his

great employments, military as well as civil, he had uniformly distinguished himself by the firmness, the prudence, and the integrity of his
conduct. He now remained almost alone of the friends and ministers of
Marcus; and when, at a late hour of the night, he was awakened with the
news, that the chamberlain and the prefect were at his door, he received
them with intrepid resignation, and desired they would execute their
master's orders. Instead of death, they offered him the throne of the
Roman world. During some moments he distrusted their intentions and
assurances. Convinced at length of the death of Commodus, he
accepted the purple with a sincere reluctance, the natural effect of his
knowledge both of the duties and of the dangers of the supreme rank.

Laetus conducted without delay his new emperor to the camp of the
Praetorians, diffusing at the same time through the city a seasonable
report that Commodus died suddenly of an apoplexy; and that the
virtuous Pertinax had *already* succeeded to the throne. The guards were
rather surprised than pleased with the suspicious death of a prince whose
indulgence and liberality they alone had experienced; but the emergency
of the occasion, the authority of their prefect, the reputation of Pertinax,
and the clamours of the people, obliged them to stifle their secret
discontents, to accept the donative promised of the new emperor, to
swear allegiance to him, and with joyful acclamations and laurels in
their hands to conduct him to the senate-house, that the military consent
might be ratified by the civil authority.

This important night was now far spent; with the dawn of day, and
(AD 193, 1 January) the commencement of the new year, the senators
expected a summons to attend an ignominious ceremony. In spite of all
remonstrances, even of those of his creatures, who yet preserved any
regard for prudence or decency, Commodus had resolved to pass the
night in the gladiators' school, and from thence to take possession of the
consulship, in the habit and with the attendance of that infamous crew.
On a sudden, before the break of day, the senate was called together in
the temple of Concord, to meet the guards, and to ratify the election of a
new emperor. For a few minutes they sat in silent suspense, doubtful of
their unexpected deliverance, and suspicious of the cruel artifices of
Commodus; but when at length they were assured that the tyrant was no
more, they resigned themselves to all the transports of joy and indignation. Pertinax, who modestly represented the meanness of his extraction,
and pointed out several noble senators more deserving than himself of the
empire, was constrained by their dutiful violence to ascend the throne,
and received all the titles of Imperial power, confirmed by the most

sincere vows of fidelity. The memory of Commodus was branded with eternal infamy. The names of tyrant, of gladiator, of public enemy, resounded in every corner of the house. They decreed in tumultuous votes, that his honours should be reversed, his titles erased from the public monuments, his statues thrown down, his body dragged with a hook into the stripping-room of the gladiators, to satiate the public fury; and they expressed some indignation against those officious servants who had already presumed to screen his remains from the justice of the senate. But Pertinax could not refuse those last rites to the memory of Marcus, and the tears of his first protector Claudius Pompeianus, who lamented the cruel fate of his brother-in-law, and lamented still more that he had deserved it.

These effusions of impotent rage against a dead emperor, whom the senate had flattered when alive with the most abject servility, betrayed a just but ungenerous spirit of revenge. The legality of these decrees was however supported by the principles of the Imperial constitution. To censure, to depose, or to punish with death, the first magistrate of the republic, who had abused his delegated trust, was the ancient and undoubted prerogative of the Roman senate; but that feeble assembly was obliged to content itself with inflicting on a fallen tyrant that public justice, from which, during his life and reign, he had been shielded by the strong arm of military despotism.

Pertinax found a nobler way of condemning his predecessor's memory; by the contrast of his own virtues with the vices of Commodus. On the day of his accession, he resigned over to his wife and son his whole private fortune; that they might have no pretence to solicit favours at the expense of the state. He refused to flatter the vanity of the former with the title of Augusta; or to corrupt the inexperienced youth of the latter by the rank of Caesar. Accurately distinguishing between the duties of a parent and those of a sovereign, he educated his son with a severe simplicity, which, while it gave him no assured prospect of the throne, might in time have rendered him worthy of it. In public, the behaviour of Pertinax was grave and affable. He lived with the virtuous part of the senate (and in a private station, he had been acquainted with the true character of each individual), without either pride or jealousy; considered them as friends and companions, with whom he had shared the dangers of the tyranny, and with whom he wished to enjoy the security of the present time. He very frequently invited them to familiar entertainments, the frugality of which was ridiculed by those who remembered and regretted the luxurious prodigality of Commodus.

To heal, as far as it was possible, the wounds inflicted by the hand of tyranny, was the pleasing, but melancholy, task of Pertinax. The innocent victims, who yet survived, were recalled from exile, released from prison, and restored to the full possession of their honours and fortunes. The unburied bodies of murdered senators (for the cruelty of Commodus endeavoured to extend itself beyond death) were deposited in the sepulchres of their ancestors; their memory was justified; and every consolation was bestowed on their ruined and afflicted families. Among these consolations, one of the most grateful was the punishment of the Delators: the common enemies of their master, of virtue, and of their country. Yet even in the inquisition of these legal assassins, Pertinax proceeded with a steady temper, which gave everything to justice, and nothing to popular prejudice and resentment.

The finances of the state demanded the most vigilant care of the emperor. Though every measure of injustice and extortion had been adopted, which could collect the property of the subject into the coffers of the prince; the rapaciousness of Commodus had been so very inadequate to his extravagance, that, upon his death, no more than eight thousand pounds were found in the exhausted treasury, to defray the current expenses of government, and to discharge the pressing demand of a liberal donative, which the new emperor had been obliged to promise to the Praetorian Guards. Yet under these distressed circumstances, Pertinax had the generous firmness to remit all the oppressive taxes invented by Commodus, and to cancel all the unjust claims of the treasury; declaring, in a decree of the senate, 'that he was better satisfied to administer a poor republic with innocence than to acquire riches by the ways of tyranny and dishonour.' Economy and industry he considered as the pure and genuine sources of wealth; and from them he soon derived a copious supply for the public necessities. The expense of the household was immediately reduced to one half. All the instruments of luxury, Pertinax exposed to public auction, gold and silver plate, chariots of a singular construction, a superfluous wardrobe of silk and embroidery, and a great number of beautiful slaves of both sexes; excepting only, with attentive humanity, those who were born in a state of freedom, and had been ravished from the arms of their weeping parents. At the same time that he obliged the worthless favourites of the tyrant to resign a part of their ill-gotten wealth, he satisfied the just creditors of the state, and unexpectedly discharged the long arrears of honest services. He removed the oppressive restrictions which had been laid upon commerce, and granted all the uncultivated lands in Italy and the provinces to those who would improve them, with an exemption from tribute, during the term of ten years.

Such an uniform conduct had already secured to Pertinax the noblest reward of a sovereign, the love and esteem of his people. Those who remembered the virtues of Marcus were happy to contemplate in their new emperor the features of that bright original; and flattered themselves that they should long enjoy the benign influence of his administration. A hasty zeal to reform the corrupted state, accompanied with less prudence than might have been expected from the years and experience of Pertinax, proved fatal to himself and to his country. His honest indiscretion united against him the servile crowd, who found their private benefit in the public disorders, and who preferred the favour of a tyrant to the inexorable equality of the laws.

Amidst the general joy, the sullen and angry countenance of the Praetorian Guards betrayed their inward dissatisfaction. They had reluctantly submitted to Pertinax; they dreaded the strictness of the ancient discipline which he was preparing to restore; and they regretted the licence of the former reign. Their discontents were secretly fomented by Laetus their prefect, who found, when it was too late, that his new emperor would reward a servant, but would not be ruled by a favourite. On the third day of his reign the soldiers seized on a noble senator, with a design to carry him to the camp, and to invest him with the Imperial purple. Instead of being dazzled by the dangerous honour, the affrighted victim escaped from their violence, and took refuge at the feet of Pertinax. A short time afterwards Sosius Falco, one of the consuls of the year, a rash youth, but of an ancient and opulent family, listened to the voice of ambition; and a conspiracy was formed during a short absence of Pertinax, which was crushed by his sudden return to Rome, and his resolute behaviour. Falco was on the point of being justly condemned to death as a public enemy, had he not been saved by the earnest and sincere entreaties of the injured emperor; who conjured the senate, that the purity of his reign might not be stained by the blood even of a guilty senator.

These disappointments served only to irritate the rage of the Praetorian Guards. On the twenty-eighth of March, eighty-six days only after the death of Commodus, a general sedition broke out in the camp, which the officers wanted either power or inclination to suppress. Two or three hundred of the most desperate soldiers marched at noon-day, with arms in their hands and fury in their looks, towards the Imperial palace. The gates were thrown open by their companions upon guard; and by the domestics of the old court, who had already formed a secret conspiracy against the life of the too virtuous emperor. On the news of their approach, Pertinax, disdaining either flight or concealment, advanced to meet his assassins; and recalled to their minds his own innocence, and the sanctity of their recent oath. For a few moments they stood in silent suspense, ashamed of their atrocious design, and awed by the venerable aspect and majestic firmness of their sovereign, till at length the despair of pardon reviving their fury, a barbarian of the country of Tongres* levelled the first blow against Pertinax, who was instantly dispatched with a multitude of wounds. His head separated from his body, and placed on a lance, was carried in triumph to the Praetorian camp, in the sight of a mournful and indignant people, who lamented the unworthy fate of that excellent prince, and the transient blessings of a reign, the memory of which could serve only to aggravate their approaching misfortunes.

* The modern bishopric of Liège. This soldier probably belonged to the Batavian horseguards, who were mostly raised in the duchy of Gueldres and the neighbourhood, and were distinguished by their valour, and by the boldness with which they swam their horses across the broadest and most rapid rivers.

5

PUBLIC SALE OF THE EMPIRE TO DIDIUS JULIANUS BY
THE PRAETORIAN GUARDS — CLODIUS ALBINUS IN BRI-
TAIN, PESCENNIUS NIGER IN SYRIA, AND SEPTIMIUS
SEVERUS IN PANNONIA, DECLARE AGAINST THE MUR-
DERERS OF PERTINAX — CIVIL WARS AND VICTORY OF
SEVERUS OVER HIS THREE RIVALS — RELAXATION OF
DISCIPLINE — NEW MAXIMS OF GOVERNMENT

THE POWER OF THE SWORD IS MORE
sensibly felt in an extensive monarchy than in a small community. It has
been calculated by the ablest politicians, that no state, without being
soon exhausted, can maintain above the hundredth part of its members
in arms and idleness. But although this relative proportion may be
uniform, the influence of the army over the rest of the society will vary
according to the degree of its positive strength. The advantages of
military science and discipline cannot be exerted, unless a proper
number of soldiers are united into one body, and actuated by one soul.
With a handful of men, such an union would be ineffectual; with an
unwieldy host, it would be impracticable; and the powers of the
machine would be alike destroyed by the extreme minuteness, or the
excessive weight, of its springs. To illustrate this observation we need
only reflect, that there is no superiority of natural strength, artificial
weapons, or acquired skill, which could enable one man to keep in
constant subjection one hundred of his fellow-creatures: the tyrant of a
single town, or a small district, would soon discover that an hundred
armed followers were a weak defence against ten thousand peasants or
citizens; but an hundred thousand well-disciplined soldiers will command, with despotic sway, ten millions of subjects; and a body of ten or
fifteen thousand guards will strike terror into the most numerous
populace that ever crowded the streets of an immense capital.

The Praetorian bands, whose licentious fury was the first symptom
and cause of the decline of the Roman Empire, scarcely amounted to the
last-mentioned number. They derived their institution from Augustus.
That crafty tyrant, sensible that laws might colour, but that arms alone
could maintain, his usurped dominion, had gradually formed this

powerful body of guards in constant readiness to protect his person, to awe the senate, and either to prevent or to crush the first motions of rebellion. He distinguished these favoured troops by a double pay, and superior privileges; but, as their formidable aspect would at once have alarmed and irritated the Roman people, three cohorts only were stationed in the capital; whilst the remainder was dispersed in the adjacent towns of Italy. But after fifty years of peace and servitude, Tiberius ventured on a decisive measure, which for ever riveted the fetters of his country. Under the fair pretences of relieving Italy from the heavy burthen of military quarters, and of introducing a stricter discipline among the guards, he assembled them at Rome, in a permanent camp, which was fortified with skilful care, and placed on a commanding situation.

Such formidable servants are always necessary, but often fatal to the throne of despotism. By thus introducing the Praetorian Guards, as it were into the palace and the senate, the emperors taught them to perceive their own strength, and the weakness of the civil government; to view the vices of their masters with familiar contempt, and to lay aside that reverential awe, which distance only, and mystery, can preserve towards an imaginary power. In the luxurious idleness of an opulent city, their pride was nourished by the sense of their irresistible weight; nor was it possible to conceal from them, that the person of the sovereign, the authority of the senate, the public treasure, and the seat of empire, were all in their hands. To divert the Praetorian bands from these dangerous reflections, the firmest and best established princes were obliged to mix blandishments with commands, rewards with punishments, to flatter their pride, indulge their pleasures, connive at their irregularities, and to purchase their precarious faith by a liberal donative; which, since the elevation of Claudius, was exacted as a legal claim, on the accession of every new emperor.

The advocates of the guards endeavoured to justify by arguments, the power which they asserted by arms; and to maintain that, according to the purest principles of the constitution, *their* consent was essentially necessary in the appointment of an emperor. The election of consuls, of generals, and of magistrates, however it had been recently usurped by the senate, was the ancient and undoubted right of the Roman people. But where was the Roman people to be found? Not surely amongst the mixed multitude of slaves and strangers that filled the streets of Rome; a servile populace, as devoid of spirit as destitute of property. The defenders of the state, selected from the flower of the Italian youth, and trained in the exercise of arms and virtue, were the genuine representatives of the people, and the best entitled to elect the military chief of the republic. These assertions, however defective in reason, became unanswerable, when the fierce Praetorians increased their weight, by throwing, like the barbarian conqueror of Rome, their swords into the scale.

The Praetorians had violated the sanctity of the throne, by the atrocious murder of Pertinax; they dishonoured the majesty of it, by their subsequent conduct. The camp was without a leader, for even the prefect Laetus, who had excited the tempest, prudently declined the public indignation. Amidst the wild disorder Sulpicianus, the emperor's father-in-law, and governor of the city, who had been sent to the camp on the first alarm of mutiny, was endeavouring to calm the fury of the multitude, when he was silenced by the clamorous return of the murderers, bearing on a lance the head of Pertinax. Though history has accustomed us to observe every principle and every passion yielding to the imperious dictates of ambition, it is scarcely credible that, in these moments of horror, Sulpicianus should have aspired to ascend a throne polluted with the recent blood of so near a relation, and so excellent a prince. He had already begun to use the only effectual argument, and to treat for the Imperial dignity; but the more prudent of the Praetorians, apprehensive that, in this private contract, they should not obtain a just price for so valuable a commodity, ran out upon the ramparts; and, with a loud voice, proclaimed that the Roman world was to be disposed of to the best bidder by public auction.

This infamous offer, the most insolent excess of military licence, diffused an universal grief, shame, and indignation throughout the city. It reached at length the ears of Didius Julianus, a wealthy senator, who, regardless of the public calamities, was indulging himself in the luxury of the table. His wife and his daughter, his freedmen and his parasites, easily convinced him that he deserved the throne, and earnestly conjured him to embrace so fortunate an opportunity. The vain old man (AD 193, 28 March) hastened to the Praetorian camp, where Sulpicianus was still in treaty with the guards; and began to bid against him from the foot of the rampart. The unworthy negotiation was transacted by faithful emissaries, who passed alternately from one candidate to the other, and acquainted each of them with the offers of his rival. Sulpicianus had already promised a donative of five thousand drachms (above one hundred and sixty pounds) to each soldier; when Julian, eager for the prize, rose at once to the sum of six thousand two hundred and fifty drachms, or upwards of two hundred pounds sterling. The gates of the camp were instantly thrown open to the purchaser; he was declared emperor, and received an oath of allegiance from the soldiers, who retained humanity enough to stipulate that he should pardon and forget the competition of Sulpicianus.

It was now incumbent on the Praetorians to fulfil the conditions of the sale. They placed their new sovereign, whom they served and despised, in the centre of their ranks, surrounded him on every side with their shields, and conducted him in close order of battle through the deserted streets of the city. The senate was commanded to assemble; and those who had been the distinguished friends of Pertinax, or the personal enemies of Julian, found it necessary to affect a more than common share of satisfaction at this happy revolution. After Julian had filled the senate-house with armed soldiers, he expatiated on the freedom of his election, his own eminent virtues, and his full assurance of the affections of the senate. The obsequious assembly congratulated their own and the public felicity; engaged their allegiance, and conferred on him all the several branches of the Imperial power. From the senate Julian was conducted, by the same military procession, to take possession of the palace. The first objects that struck his eyes were the abandoned trunk of Pertinax and the frugal entertainment prepared for his supper. The one he viewed with indifference; the other with contempt. A magnificent feast was prepared by his order, and he amused himself till a very late hour with dice, and the performances of Pylades, a celebrated dancer. Yet it was observed, that after the crowd of flatterers dispersed, and left him to darkness, solitude, and terrible reflection, he passed a sleepless night; revolving most probably in his mind his own rash folly, the fate of his virtuous predecessor, and the doubtful and dangerous tenure of an empire, which had not been acquired by merit, but purchased by money.

He had reason to tremble. On the throne of the world he found himself without a friend, and even without an adherent. The guards themselves were ashamed of the prince whom their avarice had per-suaded them to accept; nor was there a citizen who did not consider his elevation with horror, as the last insult on the Roman name. The nobility, whose conspicuous station and ample possessions exacted the strictest caution, dissembled their sentiments, and met the affected civility of the emperor with smiles of complacency and professions of duty. But the people, secure in their numbers and obscurity, gave a free vent to their passions. The streets and public places of Rome resounded with clamours and imprecations. The enraged multitude affronted the person of Julian, rejected his liberality, and conscious of the impotence of their own resentment, they called aloud on the legions of the frontiers to assert the violated majesty of the Roman Empire.

The public discontent was soon diffused from the centre to the frontiers of the empire. The armies of Britain, of Syria, and of Illyricum, lamented the death of Pertinax, in whose company, or under whose command, they had so often fought and conquered. They received with surprise, with indignation, and perhaps with envy, the extraordinary intelligence that the Praetorians had disposed of the empire by public auction; and they sternly refused to ratify the ignominious bargain. Their immediate and unanimous revolt was fatal to Julian, but it was fatal at the same time to the public peace; as the generals of the respective armies, Clodius Albinus, Pescennius Niger, and Septimius Severus, were still more anxious to succeed than to revenge the murdered Pertinax. Their forces were exactly balanced. Each of them was at the head of three legions, with a numerous train of auxiliaries; and however different in their characters, they were all soldiers of experience and capacity.

Clodius Albinus, governor of Britain, surpassed both his competitors in the nobility of his extraction, which he derived from some of the most illustrious names of the old republic. But the branch from whence he claimed his descent was sunk into mean circumstances, and transplanted into a remote province. It is difficult to form a just idea of his true character. Under the philosophic cloak of austerity, he stands accused of concealing most of the vices which degrade human nature.* But his accusers are those venal writers who adored the fortune of Severus, and trampled on the ashes of an unsuccessful rival. Virtue, or the appearances of virtue, recommended Albinus to the confidence and good opinion of Marcus; and his preserving with the son the same interest which he had acquired with the father, is a proof at least that he was possessed of a very flexible disposition. The favour of a tyrant does not always suppose a want of merit in the object of it; he may, without intending it, reward a man of worth and ability, or he may find such a man useful to his own service. It does not appear that Albinus served the son of Marcus, either as the minister of his cruelties, or even as the associate of his pleasures. He was employed in a distant honourable command, when he received a confidential letter from the emperor, acquainting him of the treasonable designs of some discontented generals, and authorising him to declare himself the guardian and

---

* Spartianus, in his undigested collections, mixes up all the virtues and all the vices that enter into the human composition, and bestows them on the same object. Such, indeed, are many of the characters in the Augustan History.

successor of the throne, by assuming the title and ensigns of Caesar. The governor of Britain wisely declined the dangerous honour, which would have marked him for the jealousy, or involved him in the approaching ruin, of Commodus. He courted power by nobler, or, at least, by more specious arts. On a premature report of the death of the emperor, he assembled his troops; and, in an eloquent discourse, deplored the inevitable mischiefs of despotism, described the happiness and glory which their ancestors had enjoyed under the consular government, and declared his firm resolution to reinstate the senate and people in their legal authority. The popular harangue was answered by the loud acclamations of the British legions, and received at Rome with a secret murmur of applause. Safe in the possession of this little world, and in the command of an army less distinguished indeed for discipline than for numbers and valour, Albinus braved the menaces of Commodus, maintained towards Pertinax a stately ambiguous reserve, and instantly declared against the usurpation of Julian. The convulsions of the capital added new weight to his sentiments, or rather to his professions of patriotism. A regard to decency induced him to decline the lofty titles of Augustus and Emperor; and he imitated perhaps the example of Galba, who, on a similar occasion, had styled himself the Lieutenant of the senate and people.

Personal merit alone had raised Pescennius Niger from an obscure birth and station to the government of Syria; a lucrative and important command, which in times of civil confusion gave him a near prospect of the throne. Yet his parts seem to have been better suited to the second than to the first rank; he was an unequal rival, though he might have approved himself an excellent lieutenant to Severus, who afterwards displayed the greatness of his mind by adopting several useful institutions from a vanquished enemy. In his government, Niger acquired the esteem of the soldiers, and the love of the provincials. His rigid discipline fortified the valour and confirmed the obedience of the former, whilst the voluptuous Syrians were less delighted with the mild firmness of his administration, than with the affability of his manners, and the apparent pleasure with which he attended their frequent and pompous festivals.* As soon as the intelligence of the atrocious murder of Pertinax had reached Antioch, the wishes of Asia invited Niger to assume the Imperial purple and revenge his death. The legions of the eastern frontier

* The chronicle of John Malala, of Antioch, shows the zealous attachment of his countrymen to these festivals, which at once gratified their superstition and their love of pleasure.

embraced his cause; the opulent but unarmed provinces from the frontiers of Ethiopia to the Hadriatic cheerfully submitted to his power; and the kings beyond the Tigris and the Euphrates congratulated his election, and offered him their homage and services. The mind of Niger was not capable of receiving this sudden tide of fortune; he flattered himself that his accession would be undisturbed by competition, and unstained by civil blood; and whilst he enjoyed the vain pomp of triumph, he neglected to secure the means of victory. Instead of entering into an effectual negotiation with the powerful armies of the west, whose resolution might decide, or at least must balance, the mighty contest; instead of advancing without delay towards Rome and Italy, where his presence was impatiently expected, Niger trifled away in the luxury of Antioch those irretrievable moments which were diligently improved by the decisive activity of Severus.

The country of Pannonia and Dalmatia, which occupied the space between the Danube and the Hadriatic, was one of the last and most difficult conquests of the Romans. In the defence of national freedom, two hundred thousand of these barbarians had once appeared in the field, alarmed the declining age of Augustus, and exercised the vigilant prudence of Tiberius at the head of the collected force of the empire. The Pannonians yielded at length to the arms and institution of Rome. Their recent subjection, however, the neighbourhood, and even the mixture, of the unconquered tribes, and perhaps the climate, adapted, as it has been observed, to the production of great bodies and slow minds,* all contributed to preserve some remains of their original ferocity, and under the tame and uniform countenance of Roman provincials, the hardy features of the natives were still to be discerned. Their warlike youth afforded an inexhaustible supply of recruits to the legions stationed on the banks of the Danube, and which, from a perpetual warfare against the Germans and Sarmatians, were deservedly esteemed the best troops in the service.

The Pannonian army was at this time commanded by Septimius Severus, a native of Africa, who in the gradual ascent of private honours, had concealed his daring ambition, which was never diverted from its steady course by the allurements of pleasure, the apprehension of danger, or the feelings of humanity. On the first news of the murder of Pertinax, he assembled his troops, painted in the most lively colours the crime, the insolence, and the weakness of the Praetorian Guards, and animated the legions to arms and to revenge. He concluded (and the

* Such is the reflection of Herodian. Will the modern Austrians allow the influence?

peroration was thought extremely eloquent) with promising every sol-dier about four hundred pounds; an honourable donative, double in value to the infamous bribe with which Julian had purchased the empire. The acclamations of the army immediately saluted Severus with the names of Augustus, Pertinax, and Emperor; and he (AD 193, 13 April) thus attained the lofty station to which he was invited, by conscious merit and a long train of dreams and omens, the fruitful offspring either of his superstition or policy.*

The new candidate for empire saw and improved the peculiar advantage of his situation. His province extended to the Julian Alps, which gave an easy access into Italy; and he remembered the saying of Augustus, that a Pannonian army might in ten days appear in sight of Rome. By a celerity proportioned to the greatness of the occasion, he might reasonably hope to revenge Pertinax, punish Julian, and receive the homage of the senate and people, as their lawful emperor, before his competitors, separated from Italy by an immense tract of sea and land, were apprised of his success, or even of his election. During the whole expedition he scarcely allowed himself any moments for sleep or food; marching on foot, and in complete armour, at the head of his columns, he insinuated himself into the confidence and affection of his troops, pressed their diligence, revived their spirits, animated their hopes, and was well satisfied to share the hardships of the meanest soldier, whilst he kept in view the infinite superiority of this reward.

The wretched Julian had expected, and thought himself prepared, to dispute the empire with the governor of Syria; but in the invincible and rapid approach of the Pannonian legions, he saw his inevitable ruin. The hasty arrival of every messenger increased his just apprehensions. He was successively informed that Severus had passed the Alps; that the Italian cities, unwilling or unable to oppose his progress, had received him with the warmest professions of joy and duty; that the important place of Ravenna had surrendered without resistance, and that the Hadriatic fleet was in the hands of the conqueror. The enemy was now within two hundred and fifty miles of Rome; and every moment diminished the narrow span of life and empire allotted to Julian.

He attempted, however, to prevent, or at least to protract, his ruin. He

---

* Severus was declared emperor on the banks of the Danube, either at Carnuntum, according to Spartianus, or else at Sabaria, according to Victor. Mr Hume, in supposing that the birth and dignity of Severus were too much inferior to the Imperial crown, and that he marched into Italy as general only, has not considered this transaction with his usual accuracy.

implored the venal faith of the Praetorians, filled the city with unavailing preparations for war, drew lines round the suburbs, and even strength-ened the fortification of the palace; as if those last intrenchments could be defended without hope of relief against a victorious invader. Fear and shame prevented the guards from deserting his standard; but they trembled at the name of the Pannonian legions, commanded by an experienced general, and accustomed to vanquish the barbarians on the frozen Danube. They quitted, with a sigh, the pleasures of the baths and theatres, to put on arms, whose use they had almost forgotten, and beneath the weight of which they were oppressed. The unpractised elephants, whose uncouth appearance, it was hoped, would strike terror into the army of the north, threw their unskilful riders; and the awkward evolutions of the marines, drawn from the fleet of Misenum, were an object of ridicule to the populace; whilst the senate enjoyed, with secret pleasure, the distress and weakness of the usurper.*

Every motion of Julian betrayed his trembling perplexity. He insisted that Severus should be declared a public enemy by the senate. He intreated that the Pannonian general might be associated to the empire. He sent public ambassadors of consular rank to negotiate with his rival; he dispatched private assassins to take away his life. He designed that the vestal virgins, and all the colleges of priests, in their sacerdotal habits, and bearing before them the sacred pledges of the Roman religion, should advance, in solemn procession, to meet the Pannonian legions; and, at the same time, he vainly tried to interrogate, or to appease, the fates, by magic ceremonies, and unlawful sacrifices.

Severus, who dreaded neither his arms nor his enchantments, guarded himself from the only danger of secret conspiracy, by the faithful attendance of six hundred chosen men, who never quitted his person or their cuirasses, either by night or by day, during the whole march. Advancing with a steady and rapid course, he passed, without diffi-culty, the defiles of the Apennine, received into his party the troops and ambassadors sent to retard his progress, and made a short halt at Interamnia, about seventy miles from Rome. His victory was already secure; but the despair of the Praetorians might have rendered it bloody; and Severus had the laudable ambition of ascending the throne without drawing the sword. His emissaries, dispersed in the capital, assured the guards that provided they would abandon their worthless prince, and

* There is no surer proof of the military skill of the Romans, than their first surmounting the idle terror, and afterwards disdaining the dangerous use, of elephants in war.

the perpetrators of the murder of Pertinax, to the justice of the conqueror, he would no longer consider that melancholy event as the act of the whole body. The faithless Praetorians, whose resistance was supported only by sullen obstinacy, gladly complied with the easy conditions, seized the greatest part of the assassins, and signified to the senate that they no longer defended the cause of Julian. That assembly, convoked by the consul, unanimously acknowledged Severus as lawful emperor, decreed divine honours to Pertinax, and pronounced a sentence of depositon and death against his unfortunate successor. Julian was conducted into a private apartment of the baths of the palace, and (AD 193, 2 June) beheaded as a common criminal, after having purchased, with an immense treasure, an anxious and precarious reign of only sixty-six days. The almost incredible expedition of Severus, who, in so short a space of time, conducted a numerous army from the banks of the Danube to those of the Tiber, proves at once the plenty of provisions produced by agriculture and commerce, the goodness of the roads, the discipline of the legions, and the indolent subdued temper of the provinces.

The first cares of Severus were bestowed on two measures, the one dictated by policy, the other by decency; the revenge, and the honours, due to the memory of Pertinax. Before the new emperor entered Rome, he issued his commands to the Praetorian Guards, directing them to wait his arrival on a large plain near the city, without arms, but in the habits of ceremony, in which they were accustomed to attend their sovereign. He was obeyed by those haughty troops, whose contrition was the effect of their just terrors. A chosen part of the Illyrian army encompassed them with levelled spears. Incapable of flight or resistance, they expected their fate in silent consternation. Severus mounted the tribunal, sternly reproached them with perfidy and cowardice, dismissed them with ignominy from the trust which they had betrayed, despoiled them of their splendid ornaments, and banished them, on pain of death, to the distance of an hundred miles from the capital. During the transaction, another detachment had been sent to seize their arms, occupy their camp, and prevent the hasty consequences of their despair.

The funeral and consecration of Pertinax was next solemnised with every circumstance of sad magnificence. The senate, with a melancholy pleasure, performed the last rites to that excellent prince, whom they had loved, and still regretted. The concern of his successor was probably less sincere. He esteemed the virtues of Pertinax, but those virtues would for ever have confined his ambition to a private station. Severus pronounced his funeral oration with studied eloquence, inward satisfaction, and

The Column of Marcus Aurelius

well-acted sorrow; and by this pious regard to his memory, convinced the credulous multitude that *he alone* was worthy to supply his place. Sensible, however, that arms, not ceremonies, must assert his claim to the empire, he left Rome at the end of thirty days, and, without suffering himself to be elated by this easy victory, prepared to encounter his more formidable rivals.

The uncommon abilities and fortune of Severus have induced an elegant historian to compare him with the first and greatest of the Caesars. The parallel is, at least, imperfect. Where shall we find, in the character of Severus, the commanding superiority of soul, the generous clemency, and the various genius, which could reconcile and unite the love of pleasure, the thirst of knowledge, and the fire of ambition?* In one instance only they may be compared with some degree of propriety, in the celerity of their motions and their civil victories. In less than four years (AD 193–197), Severus subdued the riches of the east, and the valour of the west. He vanquished two competitors of reputation and ability, and defeated numerous armies, provided with weapons and discipline equal to his own. In that age, the art of fortification, and the principles of tactics, were well understood by all the Roman generals; and the constant superiority of Severus was that of an artist who uses the same instruments with more skill and industry than his rivals. I shall not, however, enter into a minute narrative of these military operations; but as the two civil wars against Niger and against Albinus were almost the same in their conduct, event, and consequences, I shall collect into one point of view the most striking circumstances, tending to develop the character of the conqueror, and the state of the empire.

Falsehood and insincerity, unsuitable as they seem to the dignity of public transactions, offend us with a less degrading idea of meanness than when they are found in the intercourse of private life. In the latter, they discover a want of courage; in the other, only a defect of power: and, as it is impossible for the most able statesman to subdue millions of followers and enemies by their own personal strength, the world, under the name of policy, seems to have granted them a very liberal indulgence of craft and dissimulation. Yet the arts of Severus cannot be justified by the most ample privileges of state reason. He promised only to betray, he

* Though it is not, most assuredly, the intention of Lucan to exalt the character of Caesar, yet the idea he gives of that hero, in the tenth book of the *Pharsalia*, where he describes him, at the same time, making love to Cleopatra, sustaining a siege against the power of Egypt, and conversing with the sages of the country, is, in reality, the noblest panegyric.

flattered only to ruin; and however he might occasionally bind himself by oaths and treaties, his conscience, obsequious to his interest, always released him from the inconvenient obligation.

If his two competitors, reconciled by their common danger, had advanced upon him without delay, perhaps Severus would have sunk under their united effort. Had they even attacked him, at the same time, with separate views and separate armies, the contest might have been long and doubtful. But they fell, singly and successively, an easy prey to the arts as well as arms of their subtle enemy, lulled into security by the moderation of his professions, and overwhelmed by the rapidity of his action. He first marched against Niger, whose reputation and power he the most dreaded: but he declined any hostile declarations, suppressed the name of his antagonist, and only signified to the senate and people, his intention of regulating the eastern provinces. In private he spoke of Niger, his old friend and intended successor, with the most affectionate regard, and highly applauded his generous design of revenging the murder of Pertinax. To punish the vile usurper of the throne, was the duty of every Roman general. To persevere in arms, and to resist a lawful emperor, acknowledged by the senate, would alone render him criminal. The sons of Niger had fallen into his hands among the children of the provincial governors, detailed at Rome as pledges for the loyalty of their parents. As long as the power of Niger inspired terror, or even respect, they were educated with the most tender care, with the children of Severus himself; but they were soon involved in their father's ruin, and removed, first by exile, and afterwards by death, from the eye of public compassion.

Whilst Severus was engaged in his eastern war, he had reason to apprehend that the governor of Britain might pass the sea and the Alps, occupy the vacant seat of empire, and oppose his return with the authority of the senate and the forces of the west. The ambiguous conduct of Albinus, in not assuming the Imperial title, left room for negotiation. Forgetting, at once, his professions of patriotism, and the jealousy of sovereign power, he accepted the precarious rank of Caesar, as a reward for his fatal neutrality. Till the first contest was decided, Severus treated the man, whom he had doomed to destruction, with every mark of esteem and regard. Even in the letter, in which he announced his victory over Niger, he styles Albinus the brother of his soul and empire, sends him the affectionate salutations of his wife, Julia, and his young family, and intreats him to preserve the armies and the republic faithful to their common interest. The messengers charged with this letter were instructed to accost the Caesar with respect, to desire a private audience, and to plunge their daggers into his heart. The conspiracy was discovered, and the too credulous Albinus, at length, passed over to the continent, and prepared for an unequal contest with his rival, who rushed upon him at the head of a veteran and victorious army.

The military labours of Severus seem inadequate to the importance of his conquests. Two engagements, the one near the Hellespont, the other in the narrow defiles of Cilicia, decided the fate of his Syrian competitor; and the troops of Europe asserted their usual ascendant over the effe/minate natives of Asia. The battle of Lyons, where one hundred and fifty thousand Romans were engaged, was equally fatal to Albinus. The valour of the British army maintained, indeed, a sharp and doubtful contest with the hardy discipline of the Illyrian legions. The fame and person of Severus appeared, during a few moments, irrecoverably lost, till that warlike prince rallied his fainting troops, and led them on to a decisive victory. The war was finished by that memorable day.

The civil wars of modern Europe have been distinguished, not only by the fierce animosity, but likewise by the obstinate perseverance, of the contending factions. They have generally been justified by some princi/ple, or, at least, coloured by some pretext, of religion, freedom, or loyalty. The leaders were nobles of independent property and hereditary in/fluence. The troops fought like men interested in a decision of the quarrel; and as military spirit and party zeal were strongly diffused throughout the whole community, a vanquished chief was immediately supplied with new adherents, eager to shed their blood in the same cause. But the Romans, after the fall of the republic, combated only for the choice of masters. Under the standard of a popular candidate for empire, a few enlisted from affection, some from fear, many from interest, none from principle. The legions, uninflamed by party zeal, were allured into civil war by liberal donatives, and still more liberal promises. A defeat, by disabling the chief from the performance of his engagements, dis/solved the mercenary allegiance of his followers; and left them to consult their own safety, by a timely desertion of an unsuccessful cause. It was of little moment to the provinces, under whose name they were oppressed or governed; they were driven by the impulsion of the present power, and as soon as that power yielded to a superior force, they hastened to implore the clemency of the conqueror, who, as he had an immense debt to discharge, was obliged to sacrifice the most guilty countries to the avarice of his soldiers. In the vast extent of the Roman Empire, there were few fortified cities capable of protecting a routed army; nor was there any person, or family, or order of men, whose natural interest, unsupported by the powers of government, was capable of restoring the cause of a sinking party.*

Yet, in the contest between Niger and Severus, a single city deserves an honourable exception. As Byzantium was one of the greatest passages from Europe into Asia, it had been provided with a strong garrison, and a fleet of five hundred vessels was anchored in the harbour. The impetuosity of Severus disappointed this prudent scheme of defence; he left to his generals the siege of Byzantium, forced the less guarded passage of the Hellespont, and, impatient of a meaner enemy, pressed forward to encounter his rival. Byzantium, attacked by a numerous and increasing army, and afterwards by the whole naval power of the empire, sustained a siege of three years, and remained faithful to the name and memory of Niger. The citizens and soldiers (we know not from what cause) were animated with equal fury; several of the principal officers of Niger, who despaired of, or who disdained, a pardon, had thrown themselves into this last refuge: the fortifications were esteemed impregnable, and, in the defence of the place, a celebrated engineer displayed all the mechanical powers known to the ancients. Byzantium, at length, surrendered to famine. The magistrates and soldiers were put to the sword, the walls demolished, the privileges suppressed, and the destined capital of the east subsisted only as an open village, subject to the insulting jurisdiction of Perinthus. The historian Dion, who had admired the flourishing, and lamented the desolate, state of Byzantium, accused the revenge of Severus, for depriving the Roman people of the strongest bulwark against the barbarians of Pontus and Asia. The truth of this observation was but too well justified in the succeeding age, when the Gothic fleets covered the Euxine, and passed through the undefended Bosphorus into the centre of the Mediterranean.

Both Niger and Albinus were discovered and put to death in their flight from the field of battle. Their fate excited neither surprise nor compassion. They had staked their lives against the chance of empire, and suffered what they would have inflicted; nor did Severus claim the arrogant superiority of suffering his rivals to live in a private station. But his unforgiving temper, stimulated by avarice, indulged a spirit of revenge where there was no room for apprehension. The most consider-able of the provincials, who, without any dislike to the fortunate candidate, had obeyed the governor under whose authority they were

* Montesquieu, *Considérations sur la grandeur et la décadence des Romains*, c. xii.

accidentally placed, were punished by death, exile, and especially by the confiscation of their estates. Many cities of the east were stript of their ancient honours, and obliged to pay, into the treasury of Severus, four times the amount of the sums contributed by them for the service of Niger.

Till the final decision of the war, the cruelty of Severus was, in some measure, restrained by the uncertainty of the event, and his pretended reverence for the senate. The head of Albinus, accompanied with a menacing letter, announced to the Romans, that he was resolved to spare none of the adherents of his unfortunate competitors. He was irritated by the just suspicion, that he had never possessed the affections of the senate, and he concealed his old malevolence under the recent discovery of some treasonable correspondences. Thirty-five senators, however, accused of having favoured the party of Albinus, he freely pardoned; and, by his subsequent behaviour, endeavoured to convince them that he had forgotten, as well as forgiven, their supposed offences. But, at the same time, he condemned forty-one other senators, whose names history has recorded; their wives, children, and clients attended them in death, and the noblest provincials of Spain and Gaul were involved in the same ruin. Such rigid justice, for so he termed it, was, in the opinion of Severus, the only conduct capable of ensuring peace to the people, or stability to the prince; and he condescended slightly to lament, that, to be mild, it was necessary that he should first be cruel.

The true interest of an absolute monarch generally coincides with that of his people. Their numbers, their wealth, their order, and their security, are the best and only foundations of his real greatness; and were he totally devoid of virtue, prudence might supply its place, and would dictate the same rule of conduct. Severus considered the Roman Empire as his property, and had no sooner secured the possession, than he bestowed his care on the cultivation and improvement of so valuable an acquisition. Salutary laws, executed with inflexible firmness, soon corrected most of the abuses with which, since the death of Marcus, every part of the government had been infected. In the administration of justice, the judgments of the emperor were characterised by attention, discernment, and impartiality; and whenever he deviated from the strict line of equity, it was generally in favour of the poor and oppressed; not so much indeed from any sense of humanity, as from the natural propensity of a despot, to humble the pride of greatness, and to sink all his subjects to the same common level of absolute dependence. His expensive taste for building, magnificent shows, and above all a constant and liberal distribution of corn and provisions, were the surest means of captivating the affection of the Roman people. The misfortunes of civil discord were obliterated. The calm of peace and prosperity was once more experienced in the provinces; and many cities, restored by the munificence of Severus, assumed the title of his colonies, and attested by public monuments their gratitude and felicity.* The fame of the Roman arms was revived by that warlike and successful emperor, and he boasted with a just pride, that, having received the empire oppressed with foreign and domestic wars, he left it established in profound, universal, and honourable peace.

Although the wounds of civil war appeared completely healed, its mortal poison still lurked in the vitals of the constitution. Severus possessed a considerable share of vigour and ability; but the daring soul of the first Caesar, or the deep policy of Augustus, were scarcely equal to the task of curbing the insolence of the victorious legions. By gratitude, by misguided policy, by seeming necessity, Severus was induced to relax the nerves of discipline. The vanity of his soldiers was flattered with the honour of wearing gold rings; their ease was indulged in the permission of living with their wives in the idleness of quarters. He increased their pay beyond the example of former times, and taught them to expect, and soon to claim, extraordinary donatives on every public occasion of danger or festivity. Elated by success, enervated by luxury, and raised above the level of subjects by their dangerous privileges, they soon became incapable of military fatigue, oppressive to the country, and impatient of a just subordination. Their officers asserted the superiority of rank by a more profuse and elegant luxury. There is still extant a letter of Severus, lamenting the licentious state of the army, and exhorting one of his generals, to begin the necessary reformation from the tribunes themselves; since, as he justly observes, the officer who has forfeited the esteem, will never command the obedience, of his soldiers. Had the emperor pursued the train of reflection, he would have discovered that the primary cause of this general corruption might be ascribed, not indeed to the example, but to the pernicious indulgence, however, of the commander in chief.

The Praetorians, who murdered their emperor and sold the empire, had received the just punishment of their treason; but the necessary, though dangerous, institution of guards, was soon restored on a new

* See Spanheim's treatise of ancient medals, the inscriptions, and our learned travellers, Spon and Wheeler, Shaw, Pocock, etc., who, in Africa, Greece, and Asia, have found more monuments of Severus than of any other Roman emperor whatsoever.

model by Severus, and increased to four times the ancient number. Formerly these troops had been recruited in Italy; and as the adjacent provinces gradually imbibed the softer manners of Rome, the levies were extended to Macedonia, Noricum, and Spain. In the room of these elegant troops, better adapted to the pomp of courts than to the uses of war, it was established by Severus, that from all the legions of the frontiers, the soldiers most distinguished for strength, valour, and fide-lity, should be occasionally draughted; and promoted, as an honour and reward, into the more eligible service of the guards. By this new institution, the Italian youth were diverted from the exercise of arms, and the capital was terrified by the strange aspect and manners of a multitude of barbarians. But Severus flattered himself that the legions would consider these chosen Praetorians as the representatives of the whole military order; and that the present aid of fifty thousand men, superior in arms and appointments to any force that could be brought into the field against them, would for ever crush the hopes of rebellion, and secure the empire to himself and his posterity.

The command of these favoured and formidable troops soon became the first office of the empire. As the government degenerated into military despotism, the Praetorian prefect, who in his origin had been a simple captain of the guards, was placed, not only at the head of the army, but of the finances, and even of the law. In every department of administration he represented the person and exercised the authority of the emperor. The first prefect who enjoyed and abused this immense power was Plau-tianus, the favourite minister of Severus. His reign lasted above ten years, till the marriage of his daughter with the eldest son of the emperor, which seemed to assure his fortune, proved the occasion of his ruin.* The animosities of the palace, by irritating the ambition and alarming the fears of Plautianus, threatened to produce a revolution, and obliged the emperor, who still loved him, to consent with reluctance to his death. After the fall of Plautianus an eminent lawyer, the cele-brated Papinian, was appointed to execute the motley office of Prae-torian prefect.

Till the reign of Severus, the virtue and even the good sense of the emperors had been distinguished by their zeal or affected reverence for the senate, and by a tender regard to the nice frame of civil policy

* One of his most daring and wanton acts of power, was the castration of an hundred free Romans, some of them married men, and even fathers of families; merely that his daughter, on her marriage with the young emperor, might be attended by a train of eunuchs worthy of an eastern queen.

instituted by Augustus. But the youth of Severus had been trained in the implicit obedience of camps, and his riper years spent in the despotism of military command. His haughty and inflexible spirit could not discover, or would not acknowledge, the advantage of preserving an intermediate power, however imaginary, between the emperor and the army. He disdained to profess himself the servant of an assembly that detested his person and trembled at his frown; he issued his commands, where his request would have proved as effectual; assumed the conduct and style of a sovereign and a conqueror, and exercised, without disguise, the whole legislative as well as the executive power.

The victory over the senate was easy and inglorious. Every eye and every passion was directed to the supreme magistrate, who possessed the arms and treasure of the state; whilst the senate, neither elected by the people, nor guarded by military force, nor animated by public spirit, rested its declining authority on the frail and crumbling basis of ancient opinion. The fine theory of a republic insensibly vanished, and made way for the more natural and substantial feelings of monarchy. As the freedom and honours of Rome were successively communicated to the provinces, in which the old government had been either unknown, or was remembered with abhorrence, the tradition of republican maxims was gradually obliterated. The Greek historians of the age of the Antonines observe with a malicious pleasure, that although the sovereign of Rome, in compliance with an obsolete prejudice, abstained from the name of king, he possessed the full measure of regal power. In the reign of Severus, the senate was filled with polished and eloquent slaves from the eastern provinces, who justified personal flattery by speculative principles of servitude. These new advocates of prerogative were heard with pleasure by the court, and with patience by the people, when they inculcated the duty of passive obedience, and descanted on the inevitable mischiefs of freedom. The lawyers and the historians concurred in teaching that the Imperial authority was held, not by the delegated commission, but by the irrevocable resignation of the senate; that the emperor was freed from the restraint of civil laws, could command by his arbitrary will the lives and fortunes of his subjects, and might dispose of the empire as of his private patrimony. The most eminent of the civil lawyers, and particularly Papinian, Paulus, and Ulpian, flourished under the house of Severus; and the Roman jurisprudence having closely united itself with the system of monarchy, was supposed to have attained its full maturity and perfection.

The contemporaries of Severus, in the enjoyment of the peace and glory of his reign, forgave the cruelties by which it had been introduced. Posterity, who experienced the fatal effects of his maxims and example, justly considered him as the principal author of the decline of the Roman Empire.

6

THE DEATH OF SEVERUS — TYRANNY OF CARACALLA —
USURPATION OF MACRINUS — FOLLIES OF ELAGABALUS —
VIRTUES OF ALEXANDER SEVERUS — LICENTIOUSNESS OF
THE ARMY — GENERAL STATE OF THE ROMAN FINANCES

THE ASCENT TO GREATNESS, HOWEVER
steep and dangerous, may entertain an active spirit with the consciousness and exercise of its own powers; but the possession of a throne could
never yet afford a lasting satisfaction to an ambitious mind. This
melancholy truth was felt and acknowledged by Severus. Fortune and
merit had, from an humble station, elevated him to the first place among
mankind. 'He had been all things,' as he said himself, 'and all was of
little value.' Distracted with the care, not of acquiring, but of preserving
an empire, oppressed with age and infirmities, careless of fame, and
satiated with power, all his prospects of life were closed. The desire of
perpetuating the greatness of his family was the only remaining wish of
his ambition and paternal tenderness.

Like most of the Africans, Severus was passionately addicted to the
vain studies of magic and divination, deeply versed in the interpretation
of dreams and omens, and perfectly acquainted with the science of
judicial astrology; which, in almost every age, except the present, has
maintained its dominion over the mind of man. He had lost his first wife
whilst he was governor of the Lyonnese Gaul.* In the choice of a
second, he sought only to connect himself with some favourite of fortune;
and as soon as he had discovered that a young lady of Emesa in Syria had
a royal nativity, he solicited, and obtained her hand. Julia Domna (for
that was her name) deserved all that the stars could promise her. She
possessed, even in an advanced age, the attractions of beauty, and united
to a lively imagination, a firmness of mind, and strength of judgment,

* About the year 186; M. de Tillemont is miserably embarrassed with a passage of
Dion, in which the empress Faustina, who died in the year 175, is introduced as having
contributed to the marriage of Severus and Julia. The learned compiler forgot, that
Dion is relating, not a real fact, but a dream of Severus; and dreams are circumscribed
to no limits of time or space.

seldom bestowed on her sex. Her amiable qualities never made any deep impression on the dark and jealous temper of her husband; but in her son's reign she administered the principal affairs of the empire, with a prudence that supported his authority; and with a moderation that sometimes corrected his wild extravagancies. Julia applied herself to letters and philosophy, with some success, and with the most splendid reputation. She was the patroness of every art, and the friend of every man of genius. The grateful flattery of the learned has celebrated her virtue; but, if we may credit the scandal of ancient history, chastity was very far from being the most conspicuous virtue of the empress Julia.

Two sons, Caracalla and Geta, were the fruit of this marriage, and the destined heirs of the empire. The fond hopes of the father, and of the Roman world, were soon disappointed by these vain youths, who displayed the indolent security of hereditary princes; and a presumption that fortune would supply the place of merit and application. Without any emulation of virtue or talents, they discovered, almost from their infancy, a fixed and implacable antipathy for each other. Their aversion, confirmed by years, and fomented by the arts of their interested favourites, broke out in childish, and gradually in more serious, competitions; and, at length, divided the theatre, the circus, and the court, into two factions; actuated by the hopes and fears of their respective leaders. The prudent emperor endeavoured, by every expedient of advice and authority, to allay this growing animosity. The unhappy discord of his sons clouded all his prospects, and threatened to overturn a throne raised with so much labour, cemented with so much blood, and guarded with every defence of arms and treasure. With an impartial hand he maintained between them an exact balance of favour, conferred on both the rank of Augustus, with the revered name of Antoninus; and for the first time the Roman world beheld three emperors. Yet even this equal conduct served only to inflame the contest, whilst the fierce Caracalla asserted the right of primogeniture, and the milder Geta courted the affections of the people and the soldiers. In the anguish of a disappointed father, Severus foretold that the weaker of his sons would fall a sacrifice to the stronger; who, in his turn, would be ruined by his own vices.

In these circumstances the intelligence of a war in Britain and of an invasion (AD 208) of the province by the barbarians of the North, was received with pleasure by Severus. Though the vigilance of his lieu-tenants might have been sufficient to repel the distant enemy, he resolved to embrace the honourable pretext of withdrawing his sons from the luxury of Rome, which enervated their minds and irritated their passions; and of inuring their youth to the toils of war and government. Notwithstanding his advanced age (for he was above three score), and his gout, which obliged him to be carried in a litter, he transported himself in person into that remote island, attended by his two sons, his whole court, and a formidable army. He immediately passed the walls of Hadrian and Antoninus, and entered the enemy's country, with a design of completing the long-attempted conquest of Britain. He penetrated to the northern extremity of the island without meeting an enemy. But the concealed ambuscades of the Caledonians, who hung unseen on the rear and flanks of his army, the coldness of the climate, and the severity of a winter march across the hills and morasses of Scotland, are reported to have cost the Romans above fifty thousand men. The Caledonians at length yielded to the powerful and obstinate attack, sued for peace, and surrendered a part of their arms, and a large tract of territory. But their apparent submission lasted no longer than the present terror. As soon as the Roman legions had retired, they resumed their hostile independence. Their restless spirit provoked Severus to send a new army into Caledonia, with the most bloody orders, not to subdue but to extirpate the natives. They were saved by the death of their haughty enemy.

This Caledonian war, neither marked by decisive events, nor attended with any important consequences, would ill deserve our attention; but it is supposed, not without a considerable degree of probability, that the invasion of Severus is connected with the most shining period of the British history or fable. Fingal, whose fame, with that of his heroes and bards, has been revived in our language by a recent publication, is said to have commanded the Caledonians in that memorable juncture, to have eluded the power of Severus, and to have obtained a signal victory on the banks of the Carun, in which the son of *the King of the World*, Caracalla, fled from his arms along the fields of his pride. Something of a doubtful mist still hangs over these Highland traditions; nor can it be entirely dispelled by the most ingenious researches of modern criticism; but if we could, with safety, indulge the pleasing supposition, that Fingal lived, and that Ossian sung, the striking contrast of the situation and manners of the contending nations might amuse a philosophic mind. The parallel would be little to the advantage of the more civilised people, if we compared the unrelenting revenge of Severus with the generous clemency of Fingal; the timid and brutal cruelty of Caracalla, with the bravery, the tenderness, the elegant genius of Ossian; the mercenary chiefs who, from motives of fear or interest, served under the Imperial standard, with the freeborn warriors who started to arms at the voice of the king of Morven; if, in a word, we contemplated the untutored Caledonians, glowing with the warm virtues of nature, and the degenerate Romans, polluted with the mean vices of wealth and slavery.

The declining health and last illness of Severus inflamed the wild ambition and black passions of Caracalla's soul. Impatient of any delay or division of empire, he attempted, more than once, to shorten the small remainder of his father's days, and endeavoured, but without success, to excite a mutiny among the troops. The old emperor had often censured the misguided lenity of Marcus, who, by a single act of justice, might have saved the Romans from the tyranny of his worthless son. Placed in the same situation, he experienced how easily the rigour of a judge dissolves away in the tenderness of a parent. He deliberated, he threat/ ened, but he could not punish; and this last and only instance of mercy was more fatal to the empire than a long series of cruelty. The disorder of his mind irritated the pains of his body; he wished impatiently for death, and hastened the instant of it by his impatience. He expired (AD 211, 4 February) at York in the sixty/fifth year of his life, and in the eighteenth of a glorious and successful reign. In his last moments he recommended concord to his sons, and his sons to the army. The salutary advice never reached the heart, or even the understanding, of the impetuous youths; but the more obedient troops, mindful of their oath of allegiance, and of the authority of their deceased master, resisted the solicitations of Cara/ calla, and proclaimed both brothers emperors of Rome. The new princes soon left the Caledonians in peace, returned to the capital, celebrated their father's funeral with divine honours, and were cheerfully acknowledged as lawful sovereigns, by the senate, the people, and the provinces. Some pre/eminence of rank seems to have been allowed to the elder brother; but they both administered the empire with equal and independent power.

Such a divided form of government would have proved a source of discord between the most affectionate brothers. It was impossible that it could long subsist between two implacable enemies, who neither desired nor could trust a reconciliation. It was visible that one only could reign, and that the other must fall; and each of them judging of his rival's designs by his own, guarded his life with the most jealous vigilance from the repeated attacks of poison or the sword. Their rapid journey through Gaul and Italy, during which they never ate at the same table, or slept in the same house, displayed to the provinces the odious spectacle of fraternal discord. On their arrival at Rome, they immediately divided the vast extent of the Imperial palace.* No communication was allowed between their apartments: the doors and passages were diligently forti' fied, and guards posted and relieved with the same strictness as in a besieged place. The emperors met only in public, in the presence of their afflicted mother; and each surrounded by a numerous train of armed followers. Even on these occasions of ceremony, the dissimulation of courts could ill disguise the rancour of their hearts.

This latent civil war already distracted the whole government, when a scheme was suggested that seemed of mutual benefit to the hostile brothers. It was proposed, that since it was impossible to reconcile their minds, they should separate their interest, and divide the empire between them. The conditions of the treaty were already drawn with some accuracy. It was agreed that Caracalla, as the elder brother, should remain in possession of Europe and the western Africa; and that he should relinquish the sovereignty of Asia and Egypt to Geta, who might fix his residence at Alexandria or Antioch, cities little inferior to Rome itself in wealth and greatness; that numerous armies should be constantly encamped on either side of the Thracian Bosphorus, to guard the frontiers of the rival monarchies; and that the senators of European extraction should acknowledge the sovereign of Rome, whilst the natives of Asia followed the emperor of the East. The tears of the empress Julia interrupted the negotiation, the first idea of which had filled every Roman breast with surprise and indignation. The mighty mass of conquest was so intimately united by the hand of time and policy, that it required the most forcible violence to rend it asunder. The Romans had reason to dread that the disjointed members would soon be reduced by a civil war under the dominion of one master; but if the separation was permanent, the division of the provinces must terminate

* Mr Hume is justly surprised at a passage in Herodian who, on this occasion, represents the Imperial palace as equal in extent to the rest of Rome. The whole region of the Palatine Mount on which it was built, occupied, at most, a circumference of eleven or twelve thousand feet. But we should recollect that the opulent senators had almost surrounded the city with their extensive gardens and suburban palaces, the greatest part of which had been gradually confiscated by the emperors. If Geta resided in the gardens that bore his name in the Janiculum; and if Caracalla inhabited the gardens of Maecenas on the Esquiline, the rival brothers were separated from each other by the distance of several miles; and yet the intermediate space was filled by the imperial gardens of Sallust, of Lucullus, of Agrippa, of Domitian, of Caius, etc., all skirting round the city, and all connected with each other, and with the palace, by bridges thrown over the Tiber and the streets. But this explanation of Herodian would require, though it ill deserves, a particular dissertation, illustrated by a map of ancient Rome.

in the dissolution of an empire whose unity had hitherto remained inviolate.

Had the treaty been carried into execution, the sovereign of Europe might soon have been the conqueror of Asia; but Caracalla obtained an easier though a more guilty victory. He artfully listened to his mother's entreaties, and consented (AD 212, 27 February) to meet his brother in her apartment, on terms of peace and reconciliation. In the midst of their conversation, some centurions, who had contrived to conceal them-selves, rushed with drawn swords upon the unfortunate Geta. His distracted mother strove to protect him in her arms; but, in the unavail-ing struggle, she was wounded in the hand, and covered with the blood of her younger son, while she saw the elder animating and assisting the fury of the assassins. As soon as the deed was perpetrated, Caracalla, with hasty steps, and horror in his countenance, ran towards the Praetorian camp as his only refuge, and threw himself on the ground before the statues of the tutelar deities.* The soldiers attempted to raise and comfort him. In broken and disordered words he informed them of his imminent danger and fortunate escape; insinuating that he had prevented the designs of his enemy, and declared his resolution to live and die with his faithful troops. Geta had been the favourite of the soldiers; but complaint was useless, revenge was dangerous, and they still reverenced the son of Severus. The discontent died away in idle murmurs, and Caracalla soon convinced them of the justice of his cause, by distributing in one lavish donative the accumulated treasures of his father's reign. The real *sentiments* of the soldiers alone were of importance to his power or safety. Their declaration in his favour, commanded the dutiful *professions* of the senate. The obsequious assembly was always prepared to ratify the decision of fortune; but as Caracalla wished to assuage the first emotions of public indignation, the name of Geta was men-tioned with decency, and he received the funeral honours of a Roman emperor.† Posterity, in pity to his misfortune, has cast a veil over his vices. We consider that young prince as the innocent victim of his brother's ambition, without recollecting that he himself wanted power, rather than inclination, to consummate the same attempts of revenge and murder.

* In every Roman camp there was a small chapel near the headquarters, in which the statues of the tutelar deities were preserved and adored; and we may remark, that the eagles, and other military ensigns, were in the first rank of these deities: an excellent institution, which confirmed discipline by the sanction of religion.
† Geta was placed among the gods. *Sit divus dum non sit vivus*, said his brother. [Let him be a god as he's not alive.] Some marks of Geta's consecration are still found upon medals.

The crime went not unpunished. Neither business, nor pleasure, nor flattery, could defend Caracalla from the stings of a guilty conscience; and he confessed, in the anguish of a tortured mind, that his disordered fancy often beheld the angry forms of his father and his brother rising into life, to threaten and upbraid him. The consciousness of his crime, should have induced him to convince mankind, by the virtues of his reign, that the bloody deed had been the involuntary effect of fatal necessity. But the repentance of Caracalla only prompted him to remove from the world whatever could remind him of his guilt, or recall the memory of his murdered brother. On his return from the senate to the palace, he found his mother in the company of several noble matrons, weeping over the untimely fate of her son. The jealous emperor threatened them with instant death; the sentence was executed against Fadilla, the last remain-ing daughter of the emperor Marcus; and even the afflicted Julia was obliged to silence her lamentations, to suppress her sighs, and to receive the assassin with smiles of joy and approbation. It was computed that, under the vague appellation of the friends of Geta, above twenty thousand persons of both sexes suffered death. His guards and freedmen, the ministers of his serious business, and the companions of his looser hours, those who by his interest had been promoted to any commands in the army or provinces, with the long-connected chain of their depen-dents, were included in the proscription; which endeavoured to reach every one who had maintained the smallest correspondence with Geta, who lamented his death, or who even mentioned his name. Helvius Pertinax, son to the prince of that name, lost his life by an unseasonable witticism. It was a sufficient crime of Thrasea Priscus, to be descended from a family in which the love of liberty seemed an hereditary quality.* The particular causes of calumny and suspicion were at length exhausted; and when a senator was accused of being a secret enemy to the government, the emperor was satisfied with the general proof that he was a man of property and virtue. From this well-grounded principle he frequently drew the most bloody inferences.

The execution of so many innocent citizens was bewailed by the secret tears of their friends and families. The death of Papinian, the Praetorian prefect, was lamented as a public calamity. During the last seven years of Severus, he had exercised the most important offices of the state, and, by his salutary influence, guided the emperor's steps in the

* He was probably descended from Helvidius Priscus and Thrasea Paetus, those patriots whose firm, but useless and unseasonable, virtue has been immortalised by Tacitus.

paths of justice and moderation. In full assurance of his virtues and abilities, Severus, on his death-bed, had conjured him to watch over the prosperity and union of the Imperial family. The honest labours of Papinian served only to inflame the hatred which Caracalla had already conceived against his father's minister. After the murder of Geta, the prefect was commanded to exert the powers of his skill and eloquence in a studied apology for that atrocious deed. The philosophic Seneca had condescended to compose a similar epistle to the senate, in the name of the son and assassin of Agrippina. That it was easier to commit than to justify a 'parricide', was the glorious reply of Papinian, who did not hesitate between the loss of life and that of honour. Such intrepid virtue, which had escaped pure and unsullied from the intrigues of courts, the habits of business and the arts of his profession, reflects more lustre on the memory of Papinian, than all his great employments, his numerous writings, and the superior reputation as a lawyer, which he has preserved through every age of the Roman jurisprudence.

It had hitherto been the peculiar felicity of the Romans, and in the worst of times their consolation, that the virtue of the emperors was active, and their vice indolent. Augustus, Trajan, Hadrian, and Marcus, visited their extensive dominions in person, and their progress was marked by acts of wisdom and beneficence. The tyranny of Tiberius, Nero, and Domitian, who resided almost constantly at Rome, or in the adjacent villas, was confined to the senatorial and equestrian orders. But Caracalla was the common enemy of mankind. He left (AD 213) the capital (and he never returned to it) about a year after the murder of Geta. The rest of his reign was spent in the several provinces of the empire, particularly those of the East, and every province was by turns the scene of his rapine and cruelty. The senators, compelled by fear to attend his capricious motions, were obliged to provide daily entertain-ments at an immense expense, which he abandoned with contempt to his guards; and to erect, in every city, magnificent palaces and theatres, which he either disdained to visit, or ordered to be immediately thrown down. The most wealthy families were ruined by partial fines and confiscations, and the great body of his subjects oppressed by ingenious and aggravated taxes. In the midst of peace, and upon the slightest provocation, he issued his commands, at Alexandria in Egypt, for a general massacre. From a secure post in the temple of Serapis, he viewed and directed the slaughter of many thousand citizens, as well as strangers, without distinguishing either the number or the crime of the sufferers; since, as he coolly informed the senate, *all* the Alexandrians, those who had perished and those who had escaped, were alike guilty.

The wise instructions of Severus never made any lasting impression on the mind of his son, who, although not destitute of imagination and eloquence, was equally devoid of judgment and humanity. One dan-gerous maxim, worthy of a tyrant, was remembered and abused by Caracalla, 'To secure the affections of the army, and to esteem the rest of his subjects as of little moment.' But the liberality of the father had been restrained by prudence, and his indulgence to the troops was tempered by firmness and authority. The careless profusion of the son was the policy of one reign, and the inevitable ruin both of the army and of the empire. The vigour of the soldiers, instead of being confirmed by the severe discipline of camps, melted away in the luxury of cities. The excessive increase of their pay and donatives exhausted the state to enrich the military order, whose modesty in peace, and service in war, is best secured by an honourable poverty. The demeanour of Caracalla was haughty and full of pride; but with the troops he forgot even the proper dignity of his rank, encouraged their insolent familiarity, and neglecting the essential duties of a general, affected to imitate the dress and manners of a common soldier.

It was impossible that such a character, and such a conduct as that of Caracalla, could inspire either love or esteem; but as long as his vices were beneficial to the armies, he was secure from the danger of rebellion. A secret conspiracy, provoked by his own jealousy, was fatal to the tyrant. The Praetorian prefecture was divided between two ministers. The military department was entrusted to Adventus, an experienced rather than an able soldier; and the civil affairs were transacted by Opilius Macrinus, who, by his dexterity in business, had raised himself, with a fair character, to that high office. But his favour varied with the caprice of the emperor, and his life might depend on the slightest suspicion, or the most casual circumstance. Malice or fanaticism had suggested to an African, deeply skilled in the knowledge of futurity, a very dangerous prediction, that Macrinus and his son were destined to reign over the empire. The report was soon diffused through the province; and when the man was sent in chains to Rome, he still asserted, in the presence of the prefect of the city, the faith of his prophecy. That magistrate, who had received the most pressing instructions to inform himself of the *successors* of Caracalla, immediately communicated the examination of the African to the Imperial court, which at that time resided in Syria. But, notwithstanding the diligence of the public messengers, a friend of Macrinus found means to apprise him of the approaching danger. The emperor received the letters from Rome; and as he was then engaged in the conduct of a chariot-race, he delivered them unopened to the Praetorian prefect, directing him to dispatch the ordinary affairs, and to report the more important business that might be contained in them. Macrinus read his fate, and resolved to prevent it. He inflamed the discontents of some inferior officers, and employed the hand of Martialis, a desperate soldier, who had been refused the rank of centurion. The devotion of Caracalla prompted him to make a pilgrimage from Edessa to the celebrated temple of the Moon at Carrhae. He (AD 217, 8 March) was attended by a body of cavalry; but having stopped on the road for some necessary occasion, his guards preserved a respectful distance, and Martialis approaching his person under a pretence of duty, stabbed him with a dagger. The bold assassin was instantly killed by a Scythian archer of the Imperial guard. Such was the end of a monster whose life disgraced human nature, and whose reign accused the patience of the Romans. The grateful soldiers forgot his vices, remembered only his partial liberality, and obliged the senate to prostitute their own dignity and that of religion by granting him a place among the gods. Whilst he was upon earth, Alexander the Great was the only hero whom this god deemed worthy of his admiration. He assumed the name and ensigns of Alexander, formed a Macedonian phalanx of guards, persecuted the disciples of Aristotle, and displayed with a puerile enthusiasm the only sentiment by which he discovered any regard for virtue or glory. We can easily conceive, that after the battle of Narva, and the conquest of Poland, Charles the Twelfth (though he still wanted the more elegant accomplishments of the son of Philip) might boast of having rivalled his valour and magnanimity; but in no one action of his life did Caracalla express the faintest resemblance of the Macedonian hero, except in the murder of a great number of his own and of his father's friends.

After the extinction of the house of Severus, the Roman world remained three days without a master. The choice of the army (for the authority of a distant and feeble senate was little regarded) hung in an anxious suspense; as no candidate presented himself whose distinguished birth and merit could engage their attachment and unite their suffrages. The decisive weight of the Praetorian guards elevated the hopes of their prefects, and these powerful ministers began to assert their *legal* claim to fill the vacancy of the Imperial throne. Adventus, however, the senior prefect, conscious of his age and infirmities, of his small reputation, and his smaller abilities, resigned the dangerous honour to the crafty ambition of his colleague Macrinus, whose well-dissembled grief removed all suspicion of his being accessory to his master's death. The troops neither loved nor esteemed his character. They cast their eyes around in search of a competitor, and at last yielded with reluctance to his promises of unbounded liberality and indulgence. A short time after his accession (AD 217, 11 March) he conferred on his son Diadu- menianus, at the age of only ten years, the Imperial title and the popular name of Antoninus. The beautiful figure of the youth, assisted by an additional donative, for which the ceremony furnished a pretext, might attract, it was hoped, the favour of the army, and secure the doubtful throne of Macrinus.

The authority of the new sovereign had been ratified by the cheerful submission of the senate and provinces. They exulted in their unex- pected deliverance from a hated tyrant, and it seemed of little conse- quence to examine into the virtues of the successor of Caracalla. But as soon as the first transports of joy and surprise had subsided, they began to scrutinise the merits of Macrinus with a critical severity, and to arraign the hasty choice of the army. It had hitherto been considered as a fundamental maxim of the constitution, that the emperor must be chosen in the senate, and the sovereign power, no longer exercised by the whole body, was always delegated to one of its members. But Macrinus was not a senator. The sudden elevation of the Praetorian prefects betrayed the meanness of their origin; and the equestrian order was still in possession of that great office, which commanded with arbitrary sway the lives and fortunes of the senate. A murmur of indignation was heard, that a man whose obscure extraction had never been illustrated by any signal service, should dare to invest himself with the purple, instead of bestowing it on some distinguished senator, equal in birth and dignity to the splendour of the Imperial station.

As soon as the character of Macrinus was surveyed by the sharp eye of discontent, some vices, and many defects, were easily discovered. The choice of his ministers was in many instances justly censured, and the dissatisfied people, with their usual candour, accused at once his indolent tameness and his excessive severity.

His rash ambition had climbed a height where it was difficult to stand with firmness, and impossible to fall without instant destruction. Trained in the arts of courts, and the forms of civil business, he trembled in the presence of the fierce and undisciplined multitude, over whom he had assumed the command; his military talents were despised, and his

The Forum Romanum, or Campo Vaccino, with the Temple of Antoninus and Faustina in the foreground, left; and the Temple of Castor and Pollux, right; and the Coliseum in the distance

The Piazza della Rotunda with the Pantheon and the Obelisk

personal courage suspected; a whisper that circulated in the camp, disclosed the fatal secret of the conspiracy against the late emperor, aggravated the guilt of murder by the baseness of hypocrisy, and heightened contempt by detestation. To alienate the soldiers, and to provoke inevitable ruin, the character of a reformer was only wanting: and such was the peculiar hardship of his fate, that Macrinus was compelled to exercise that invidious office. The prodigality of Caracalla had left behind it a long train of ruin and disorder; and if that worthless tyrant had been capable of reflecting on the sure consequences of his own conduct, he would perhaps have enjoyed the dark prospect of the distress and calamities which he bequeathed to his successors.

In the management of this necessary reformation, Macrinus proceeded with a cautious prudence, which would have restored health and vigour to the Roman army, in an easy and almost imperceptible manner. To the soldiers already engaged in the service, he was constrained to leave the dangerous privileges and extravagant pay given by Caracalla; but the new recruits were received on the more moderate though liberal establishment of Severus, and gradually formed to modesty and obedience. One fatal error destroyed the salutary effects of this judicious plan. The numerous army, assembled in the East by the late emperor, instead of being immediately dispersed by Macrinus through the several provinces, was suffered to remain united in Syria, during the winter that followed his elevation. In the luxurious idleness of their quarters, the troops viewed their strength and numbers, communicated their complaints, and revolved in their minds the advantages of another revolution. The veterans, instead of being flattered by the advantageous distinction, were alarmed by the first steps of the emperor, which they considered as the presage of his future intentions. The recruits, with sullen reluctance, entered on a service, whose labours were increased while its rewards were diminished by a covetous and unwarlike sovereign. The murmurs of the army swelled with impunity into seditious clamours; and the partial mutinies betrayed a spirit of discontent and disaffection, that waited only for the slightest occasion to break out on every side into a general rebellion. To minds thus disposed, the occasion soon presented itself.

The empress Julia had experienced all the vicissitudes of fortune. From an humble station she had been raised to greatness, only to taste the superior bitterness of an exalted rank. She was doomed to weep over the death of one of her sons, and over the life of the other. The cruel fate of Caracalla, though her good sense must have long taught her to expect it, awakened the feelings of a mother and of an empress. Notwithstanding the respectful civility expressed by the usurper towards the widow of Severus, she descended with a painful struggle into the condition of a subject, and soon withdrew herself by a voluntary death from the anxious and humiliating dependence. Julia Maesa, her sister, was ordered to leave the court and Antioch. She retired to Emesa with an immense fortune, the fruit of twenty years' favour, accompanied by her two daughters, Soaemias and Mamaea, each of whom was a widow, and each had an only son. Bassianus, for that was the name of the son of Soaemias, was consecrated to the honourable ministry of high priest of the Sun; and this holy vocation, embraced either from prudence or superstititon, contributed to raise the Syrian youth to the empire of Rome. A numerous body of troops was stationed at Emesa; and, as the severe discipline of Macrinus had constrained them to pass the winter encamped, they were eager to revenge the cruelty of such unaccustomed hardships. The soldiers, who resorted in crowds to the temple of the Sun, beheld with veneration and delight the elegant dress and figure of a young Pontiff: they recognised, or they thought that they recognised, the features of Caracalla, whose memory they now adored. The artful Maesa saw and cherished their rising partiality, and readily sacrificing her daughter's reputation to the fortune of her grandson, she insinuated that Bassianus was the natural son of their murdered sovereign. The sums distributed by her emissaries with a lavish hand silenced every objection, and the profusion sufficiently proved the affinity, or at least the resem⁄ blance, of Bassianus with the great original. The young Antoninus (for he had assumed and polluted that respectable name) was (AD 218, 16 May) declared emperor by the troops of Emesa, asserted his hereditary right, and called aloud on the armies to follow the standard of a young and liberal prince, who had taken up arms to revenge his father's death and the oppression of the military order.

Whilst a conspiracy of women and eunuchs was concerted with prudence, and conducted with rapid vigour, Macrinus, who, by a decisive motion, might have crushed his infant enemy, floated between the opposite extremes of terror and security, which alike fixed him inactive at Antioch. A spirit of rebellion diffused itself through all the camps and garrisons of Syria, successive detachments murdered their officers, and joined the party of the rebels; and the tardy restitution of military pay and privileges was imputed to the acknowledged weakness of Macrinus. At length he marched out of Antioch, to meet the increasing and zealous army of the young pretender. His own troops seemed to take the field with faintness and reluctance; but (AD 218, 7 June), in the heat of the battle, the Praetorian Guards, almost by an involuntary impulse, asserted the superiority of their valour and disci-pline. The rebel ranks were broken; when the mother and grandmother of the Syrian prince, who, according to their eastern custom, had attended the army, threw themselves from their covered chariots, and, by exciting the compassion of the soldiers, endeavoured to animate their drooping courage. Antoninus himself, who, in the rest of his life, never acted like a man, in this important crisis of his fate approved himself a hero, mounted his horse, and, at the head of his rallied troops, charged sword in hand among the thickest of the enemy; whilst the eunuch Gannys, whose occupations had been confined to female cares and the soft luxury of Asia, displayed the talents of an able and experienced general. The battle still raged with doubtful violence, and Macrinus might have obtained the victory, had he not betrayed his own cause by a shameful and precipitate flight. His cowardice served only to protract his life a few days, and to stamp deserved ignominy on his misfortunes. It is scarcely necessary to add, that his son Diadumenianus was involved in the same fate. As soon as the stubborn Praetorians could be convinced that they fought for a prince who had basely deserted them, they surrendered to the conqueror; the contending parties of the Roman army, mingling tears of joy and tenderness, united under the banners of the imagined son of Caracalla, and the East acknowledged with pleasure the first emperor of Asiatic extraction.

The letters of Macrinus had condescended to inform the senate of the slight disturbance occasioned by an impostor in Syria, and a decree immediately passed, declaring the rebel and his family public enemies; with a promise of pardon, however, to such of his deluded adherents as should merit it by an immediate return to their duty. During the twenty days that elapsed from the declaration to the victory of Antoninus (for in so short an interval was the fate of the Roman world decided), the capital and the provinces, more especially those of the East, were distracted with hopes and fears, agitated with tumult, and stained with a useless effusion of civil blood, since whosoever of the rivals prevailed in Syria, must reign over the empire. The specious letters in which the young conqueror announced his victory to the obedient senate, were filled with professions of virtue and moderation; the shining examples of Marcus and Augustus he should ever consider as the great rule of his administration; and he affected to dwell with pride on the striking resemblance of his own age and fortunes with those of Augustus, who in the earliest youth had revenged by a successful war the murder of his father. By adopting the style of Marcus Aurelius Antoninus, son of Antoninus and grand-son of Severus, he tacitly asserted his hereditary claim to the empire; but, by assuming the tribunitian and proconsular powers before they had been conferred on him by a decree of the senate, he offended the delicacy of Roman prejudice. This new and injudicious violation of the constitu-tion was probably dictated either by the ignorance of his Syrian courtiers, or the fierce disdain of his military followers.

As the attention of the new emperor was diverted by the most trifling amusements, he (AD 219) wasted many months in his luxurious progress from Syria to Italy, passed at Nicomedia his first winter after his victory, and deferred till the ensuing summer his triumphal entry into the capital. A faithful picture, however, which preceded his arrival, and was placed by his immediate order over the altar of Victory in the senate-house, conveyed to the Romans the just but unworthy resemblance of his person and manners. He was drawn in his sacerdotal robes of silk and gold, after the loose flowing fashion of the Medes and Phoenicians; his head was covered with a lofty tiara, his numerous collars and bracelets were adorned with gems of an inestimable value. His eyebrows were tinged with black, and his cheeks painted with an artificial red and white. The grave senators confessed with a sigh, that, after having long experienced the stern tyranny of their own countrymen, Rome was at length humbled beneath the effeminate luxury of Oriental despotism.

The Sun was worshipped at Emesa, under the name of Elagabalus,* and under the form of a black conical stone, which, as it was universally believed, had fallen from heaven on that sacred place. To this protecting deity, Antoninus, not without some reason, ascribed his elevation to the throne. The display of superstitious gratitude was the only serious business of his reign. The triumph of the God of Emesa over all the religions of the earth, was the great object of his zeal and vanity: and the appellation of Elagabalus (for he presumed as Pontiff and favourite to adopt that sacred name) was dearer to him than all the titles of Imperial greatness. In a solemn procession through the streets of Rome, the way was strewed with gold dust; the black stone, set in precious gems, was placed on a chariot drawn by six milk-white horses richly caparisoned. The pious emperor held the reins, and, supported by his ministers, moved slowly backwards, that he might perpetually enjoy the felicity of the divine presence. In a magnificent temple raised on the Palatine

* This name is derived by the learned from two Syriac words, *Ela* a God, and *Gabal*, to form, the forming or plastic God, a proper, and even happy epithet for the Sun.

Mount, the sacrifices of the god of Elagabalus were celebrated with every circumstance of cost and solemnity. The richest wines, the most extra- ordinary victims, and the rarest aromatics, were profusely consumed on his altar. Around the altar a chorus of Syrian damsels performed their lascivious dances to the sound of barbarian music, whilst the gravest personages of the state and army, clothed in long Phoenician tunics, officiated in the meanest functions, with affected zeal and secret indigna- tion.

To this temple, as to the common centre of religious worship, the Imperial fanatic attempted to remove the Ancilia, the Palladium,* and all the sacred pledges of the faith of Numa. A crowd of inferior deities attended in various stations the majesty of the god of Emesa; but his court was still imperfect, till a female of distinguished rank was admitted to his bed. Pallas had been first chosen for his comfort; but as it was dreaded lest her warlike terrors might affright the soft delicacy of a Syrian deity, the Moon, adored by the Africans under the name of Astarte, was deemed a more suitable companion for the Sun. Her image, with the rich offerings of her temple as a marriage portion, was transported with solemn pomp from Carthage to Rome, and the day of these mystic nuptials was a general festival in the capital and throughout the empire.

A rational voluptuary adheres with invariable respect to the temperate dictates of nature, and improves the gratifications of sense by social intercourse, endearing connections, and the soft colouring of taste and the imagination. But Elagabalus (I speak of the emperor of that name), corrupted by his youth, his country, and his fortune, abandoned himself to the grossest pleasures with ungoverned fury, and soon found disgust and satiety in the midst of his enjoyments. The inflammatory powers of art were summoned to his aid: the confused multitude of women, of wines, and of dishes, and the studied variety of attitudes and sauces, served to revive his languid appetites. New terms and new inventions in these sciences, the only ones cultivated and patronised by the monarch,† signalised his reign, and transmitted his infamy to succeeding times. A capricious prodigality supplied the want of taste and elegance; and whilst Elagabalus lavished away the treasures of his people in the wildest

* He broke into the sanctuary of Vesta, and carried away a statue, which he supposed to be the Palladium; but the vestals boasted, that, by a pious fraud, they had imposed a counterfeit image on the profane intruder.
† The invention of a new sauce was liberally rewarded; but if it was not relished, the inventor was confined to eat of nothing else, till he had discovered another more agreeable to the Imperial palate.

extravagance, his own voice and that of his flatterers applauded a spirit and magnificence unknown to the tameness of his predecessors. To confound the order of seasons and climates, to sport with the passions and prejudices of his subjects, and to subvert every law of nature and decency, were in the number of his most delicious amusements. A long train of concubines, and a rapid succession of wives, among whom was a vestal virgin, ravished by force from her sacred asylum, were insufficient to satisfy the impotence of his passions. The master of the Roman world affected to copy the dress and manners of the female sex, preferred the distaff to the sceptre, and dishonoured the principal dignities of the empire by distributing them among his numerous lovers; one of whom was publicly invested with the title and authority of the emperor's, or, as he more properly styled himself, of the empress's husband.

It may seem probable, the vices and follies of Elagabalus have been adorned by fancy, and blackened by prejudice. Yet confining ourselves to the public scenes displayed before the Roman people, and attested by grave and contemporary historians, their inexpressible infamy surpasses that of any other age or country. The licence of an eastern monarch is secluded from the eye of curiosity by the inaccessible walls of his seraglio. The sentiments of honour and gallantry have introduced a refinement of pleasure, a regard for decency, and a respect for the public opinion, into the modern courts of Europe; but the corrupt and opulent nobles of Rome gratified every vice that could be collected from the mighty conflux of nations and manners. Secure of impunity, careless of censure, they lived without restraint in the patient and humble society of their slaves and parasites. The emperor, in his turn, viewing every rank of his subjects with the same contemptuous indifference, asserted without control his sovereign privilege of lust and luxury.

The most worthless of mankind are not afraid to condemn in others the same disorders which they allow in themselves; and can readily discover some nice difference of age, character, or station, to justify the partial distinction. The licentious soldiers, who had raised to the throne the dissolute son of Caracalla, blushed at their ignominious choice, and turned with disgust from that monster, to contemplate with pleasure the opening virtues of his cousin Alexander the son of Mamaea. The crafty Maesa, sensible that her grandson Elagabalus must inevitably destroy himself by his own vices, had provided another and surer support of her family. Embracing a favourable moment of fondness and devotion, she had persuaded the young emperor to adopt Alexander, and to invest him (AD 221) with the title of Caesar, that his own divine occupations might be no longer interrupted by the care of the earth. In the second rank that amiable prince soon acquired the affections of the public, and excited the tyrant's jealousy, who resolved to terminate the dangerous competition, either by corrupting the manners, or by taking away the life, of his rival. His arts proved unsuccessful; his vain designs were constantly discovered by his own loquacious folly, and disappointed by those virtuous and faithful servants whom the prudence of Mamaea had placed about the person of her son. In a hasty sally of passion, Elagabalus resolved to execute by force what he had been unable to compass by fraud, and by a despotic sentence degraded his cousin from the rank and honours of Caesar. The message was received in the senate with silence, and in the camp with fury. The Praetorian Guards swore to protect Alexander, and to revenge the dishonoured majesty of the throne. The tears and promises of the trembling Elagabalus, who only begged them to spare his life, and to leave him in the possession of his beloved Hierocles, diverted their just indignation; and they contented themselves with empowering their prefects to watch over the safety of Alexander, and the conduct of the emperor.

It was impossible that such a reconciliation should last, or that even the mean soul of Elagabalus could hold an empire on such humiliating terms of dependence. He soon attempted, by a dangerous experiment, to try the temper of the soldiers. The report of the death of Alexander, and the natural suspicion that he had been murdered, inflamed their passions into fury, and the tempest of the camp could only be appeased by the presence and authority of the popular youth. Provoked at this new instance of their affection for his cousin, and their contempt for his person, the emperor ventured to punish some of the leaders of the mutiny. His unseasonable severity proved instantly fatal to his minions, his mother, and himself. Elagabalus was (AD 222, 10 March) massacred by the indignant Praetorians, his mutilated corpse dragged through the streets of the city, and thrown into the Tiber. His memory was branded with eternal infamy by the senate; the justice of whose decree has been ratified by posterity.

In the room of Elagabalus, his cousin Alexander was raised to the throne by the Praetorian Guards. His relation to the family of Severus, whose name he assumed, was the same as that of his predecessor; his virtue and his danger had already endeared him to the Romans, and the eager liberality of the senate conferred upon him, in one day, the various titles and powers of the Imperial dignity. But as Alexander was a modest and dutiful youth, of only seventeen years of age, the reins of government were in the hands of two women, of his mother Mamaea, and of Maesa, his grandmother. After the death of the latter, who survived but a short time the elevation of Alexander, Mamaea remained the sole regent of her son and of the empire.

In every age and country, the wiser, or at least the stronger, of the two sexes, has usurped the powers of the state, and confined the other to the cares and pleasures of domestic life. In hereditary monarchies, however, and especially in those of modern Europe, the gallant spirit of chivalry, and the law of succession, have accustomed us to allow a singular exception; and a woman is often acknowledged the absolute sovereign of a great kingdom, in which she would be deemed incapable of exercising the smallest employment, civil or military. But as the Roman emperors were still considered as the generals and magistrates of the republic, their wives and mothers, although distinguished by the name of Augusta, were never associated to their personal honours; and a female reign would have appeared an inexpiable prodigy in the eyes of those primitive Romans, who married without love, or loved without delicacy and respect.* The haughty Agrippina aspired, indeed, to share the honours of the empire, which she had conferred on her son; but her mad ambition, detested by every citizen who felt for the dignity of Rome, was disappointed by the artful firmness of Seneca and Burrus. The good sense, or the indifference, of succeeding princes, restrained them from offending the prejudices of their subjects; and it was reserved for the profligate Elagabalus, to discharge the acts of the senate, with the name of his mother Soaemias, who was placed by the side of the consuls, and subscribed, as a regular member, the decrees of the legislative assembly. Her more prudent sister, Mamaea, declined the useless and odious prerogative, and a solemn law was enacted, excluding women for ever from the senate, and devoting to the infernal gods, the head of the wretch by whom this sanction should be violated. The substance, not the pageantry, of power was the object of Mamaea's manly ambition. She maintained an absolute and lasting empire over the mind of her son, and in his affection the mother could not brook a rival. Alexander, with her consent, married the daughter of a patrician; but his respect for his father-in-law, and love for the empress, were inconsistent with the tenderness or interest of Mamaea. The patrician was executed on the

---

* Metellus Numidicus, the censor, acknowledged to the Roman people in a public oration that had kind Nature allowed us to exist without the help of women, we should be delivered from a very troublesome companion; and he could recommend matri-mony, only as the sacrifice of private pleasure to public duty.

ready accusation of treason, and the wife of Alexander driven with ignominy from the palace, and banished into Africa.

Notwithstanding this act of jealous cruelty, as well as some instances of avarice, with which Mamaea is charged; the general tenor of her administration was equally for the benefit of her son and of the empire. With the approbation of the senate, she chose sixteen of the wisest and most virtuous senators, as a perpetual council of state, before whom every public business of moment was debated and determined. The celebrated Ulpian, equally distinguished by his knowledge of, and his respect for, the laws of Rome, was at their head; and the prudent firmness of this aristocracy restored order and authority to the government. As soon as they had purged the city from foreign superstition and luxury, the remains of the capricious tyranny of Elagabalus, they applied themselves to remove his worthless creatures from every department of public administration, and to supply their places with men of virtue and ability. Learning, and the love of justice, became the only recommendations for civil offices. Valour, and the love of discipline, the only qualifications for military employments.

But the most important care of Mamaea and her wise counsellors, was to form the character of the young emperor, on whose personal qualities the happiness or misery of the Roman world must ultimately depend. The fortunate soil assisted, and even prevented, the hand of cultivation. An excellent understanding soon convinced Alexander of the advantages of virtue, the pleasure of knowledge, and the necessity of labour. A natural mildness and moderation of temper preserved him from the assaults of passion, and the allurements of vice. His unalterable regard for his mother, and his esteem for the wise Ulpian, guarded his inexperienced youth from the poison of flattery.

The simple journal of his ordinary occupations exhibits a pleasing picture of an accomplished emperor, and with some allowance for the difference of manners, might well deserve the imitation of modern princes. Alexander rose early; the first moments of the day were consecrated to private devotion, and his domestic chapel was filled with the images of those heroes, who, by improving or reforming human life, had deserved the grateful reverence of posterity. But, as he deemed the service of mankind the most acceptable worship of the gods, the greatest part of his morning hours was employed in his council, where he discussed public affairs, and determined private causes, with a patience and discretion above his years. The dryness of business was relieved by the charms of literature: and a portion of time was always set apart for his favourite studies of poetry, history, and philosophy. The works of Virgil and Horace, the *Republics* of Plato and Cicero, formed his taste, enlarged his understanding, and gave him the noblest ideas of man and government. The exercises of the body succeeded to those of the mind; and Alexander, who was tall, active, and robust, surpassed most of his equals in the gymnastic arts. Refreshed by the use of the bath and a slight dinner, he resumed, with new vigour, the business of the day; and, till the hour of supper, the principal meal of the Romans, he was attended by his secretaries, with whom he read and answered the multitude of letters, memorials, and petitions, that must have been addressed to the master of the greatest part of the world. His table was served with the most frugal simplicity; and whenever he was at liberty to consult his own inclination, the company consisted of a few select friends, men of learning and virtue, amongst whom Ulpian was constantly invited. Their conversation was familiar and instructive; and the pauses were occasionally enlivened by the recital of some pleasing composition, which supplied the place of the dancers, comedians, and even gladiators, so frequently summoned to the tables of the rich and luxurious Romans. The dress of Alexander was plain and modest, his demeanour courteous and affable: at the proper hours his palace was open to all his subjects, but the voice of a crier was heard, as in the Eleusinian mysteries, pronouncing the same salutary admonition; 'Let none enter those holy walls, unless he is conscious of a pure and innocent mind.'

Such an uniform tenor of life, which left not a moment for vice or folly, is a better proof of the wisdom and justice of Alexander's government, than all the trifling details preserved in the compilation of Lampridius. Since the accession of Commodus, the Roman world had experienced, during a term of forty years, the successive and various vices of four tyrants. From the death of Elagabalus it enjoyed (AD 222–235) an auspicious calm of thirteen years. The provinces, relieved from the oppressive taxes invented by Caracalla and his pretended son, flourished in peace and prosperity, under the administration of magistrates, who were convinced by experience, that to deserve the love of the subjects was their best and only method of obtaining the favour of their sovereign. While some gentle restraints were imposed on the innocent luxury of the Roman people, the price of provisions, and the interest of money, were reduced, by the paternal care of Alexander, whose prudent liberality, without distressing the industrious, supplied the wants and amusements of the populace. The dignity, the freedom, the authority of the senate were restored; and every virtuous senator might approach the person of the emperor, without fear, and without a blush.

The name of Antoninus, ennobled by the virtues of Pius and Marcus, had been communicated by adoption to the dissolute Verus, and by descent to the cruel Commodus. It became the honourable appellation of the sons of Severus, was bestowed on young Diadu-menianus, and at length prostituted to the infamy of the high priest of Emesa. Alexander, though pressed by the studied, and perhaps sincere, importunity of the senate, nobly refused the borrowed lustre of a name; whilst in his whole conduct he laboured to restore the glories and felicity of the age of the genuine Antonines.

In the civil administration of Alexander, wisdom was enforced by power, and the people, sensible of the public felicity, repaid their benefactor with their love and gratitude. There still remained a greater, a more necessary, but a more difficult enterprise; the reformation of the military order, whose interest and temper, confirmed by long impunity, rendered them impatient of the restraints of discipline, and careless of the blessings of public tranquillity. In the execution of his design the emperor affected to display his love, and to conceal his fear, of the army. The most rigid economy in every other branch of the administration, supplied a fund of gold and silver for the ordinary pay and the extraordinary rewards of the troops. In their marches he relaxed the severe obligation of carrying seventeen days' provision on their shoulders. Ample magazines were formed along the public roads, and as soon as they entered the enemy's country, a numerous train of mules and camels waited on their haughty laziness. As Alexander despaired of correcting the luxury of his soldiers, he attempted, at least, to direct it to objects of martial pomp and ornament, fine horses, splendid armour, and shields enriched with silver and gold. He shared whatever fatigues he was obliged to impose, visited, in person, the sick and wounded, preserved an exact register of their services and his own gratitude, and expressed, on every occasion, the warmest regard for a body of men, whose welfare, as he affected to declare, was so closely connected with that of the state. By the most gentle arts he laboured to inspire the fierce multitude with a sense of duty, and to restore at least a faint image of that discipline to which the Romans owed their empire over so many other nations, as warlike and more powerful than themselves. But his pru-dence was vain, his courage fatal, and the attempt towards a reformation served only to inflame the ills it was meant to cure.

The Praetorian Guards were attached to the youth of Alexander.

They loved him as a tender pupil, whom they had saved from a tyrant's fury, and placed on the Imperial throne. That amiable prince was sensible of the obligation; but as his gratitude was restrained within the limits of reason and justice, they soon were more dissatisfied with the virtues of Alexander, than they had ever been with the vices of Elagabalus. Their prefect, the wise Ulpian, was the friend of the laws and of the people; he was considered as the enemy of the soldiers, and to his pernicious counsels every scheme of reformation was imputed. Some trifling accident blew up their discontent into a furious mutiny; and a civil war raged, during three days, in Rome, whilst the life of that excellent minister was defended by the grateful people. Terrified, at length, by the sight of some houses in flames, and by the threats of a general conflagration, the people yielded with a sigh, and left the virtuous, but unfortunate, Ulpian to his fate. He was pursued into the Imperial palace, and massacred at the feet of his master, who vainly strove to cover him with the purple, and to obtain his pardon from the inexorable soldiers. Such was the deplorable weakness of government, that the emperor was unable to revenge his murdered friend and his insulted dignity, without stooping to the arts of patience and dissimulation. Epagathus, the principal leader of the mutiny, was removed from Rome, by the honourable employment of prefect of Egypt; from that high rank he was gently degraded to the government of Crete; and when, at length, his popularity among the guards was effaced by time and absence, Alexander ventured to inflict the tardy, but deserved punishment of his crimes. Under the reign of a just and virtuous prince, the tyranny of the army threatened with instant death his most faithful ministers, who were suspected of an intention to correct their intolerable disorders. The historian Dion Cassius had commended the Pannonian legions with the spirit of ancient discipline. Their brethren of Rome, embracing the common cause of military licence, demanded the head of the reformer. Alexander, however, instead of yielding to their seditious clamours, showed a just sense of his merit and services, by appointing him his colleague in the consulship, and defraying from his own treasury the expense of that vain dignity: but as it was justly apprehended, that if the soldiers beheld him with the ensigns of his office, they would revenge the insult in his blood, the nominal first magistrate of the state retired, by the emperor's advice, from the city, and spent the greatest part of his consulship at his villas in Campania.

The lenity of the emperor confirmed the insolence of the troops; the legions imitated the example of the guards, and defended their prerogative of licentiousness with the same furious obstinacy. The administration of Alexander was an unavailing struggle against the corruption of his age. In Illyricum, in Mauritania, in Armenia, in Mesopotamia, in Germany, fresh mutinies perpetually broke out; his officers were murdered, his authority was insulted, and his life at last sacrificed to the fierce discontents of the army. One particular fact well deserves to be recorded, as it illustrates the manners of the troops, and exhibits a singular instance of their return to a sense of duty and obedience. While the emperor lay at Antioch, in his Persian expedition, the particulars of which we shall hereafter relate, the punishment of some soldiers, who had been discovered in the baths of women, excited a sedition in the legion to which they belonged. Alexander ascended his tribunal, and with a modest firmness represented to the armed multitude, the absolute necessity as well as his inflexible resolution of correcting the vices introduced by his impure predecessor, and of maintaining the discipline, which could not be relaxed without the ruin of the Roman name and empire. Their clamours interrupted his mild expostulation. 'Reserve your shouts,' said the undaunted emperor, 'till you take the field against the Persians, the Germans, and the Sarmatians. Be silent in the presence of your sovereign and benefactor, who bestows upon you the corn, the clothing, and the money of the provinces. Be silent, or I shall no longer style you soldiers, but *citizens*, if those indeed who disclaim the laws of Rome deserve to be ranked among the meanest of the people.' His menaces inflamed the fury of the legion, and their brandished arms already threatened his person. 'Your courage,' resumed the intrepid Alexander, 'would be more nobly displayed in the field of battle; *me* you may destroy, you cannot intimidate; and the severe justice of the republic would punish your crime, and revenge my death.' The legion still persisted in clamorous sedition, when the emperor pronounced, with a loud voice, the decisive sentence, '*Citizens!* lay down your arms, and depart in peace to your respective habitations.' The tempest was instantly appeased; the soldiers, filled with grief and shame, silently confessed the justice of their punishment and the power of discipline, yielded up their arms and military ensigns, and retired in confusion, not to their camp, but to the several inns of the city. Alexander enjoyed, during thirty days, the edifying spectacle of their repentance; nor did he restore them to their former rank in the army, till he had punished with death those tribunes whose connivance had occasioned the mutiny. The grateful legion served the emperor, whilst living, and revenged him when dead.

The resolutions of the multitude generally depend on a moment; and the caprice of passion might equally determine the seditious legion to lay down their arms at the emperor's feet, or to plunge them into his breast. Perhaps, if the singular transaction had been investigated by the pene- tration of a philosopher, we should discover the secret causes which on that occasion authorised the boldness of the prince, and commanded the obedience of the troops; and perhaps, if it had been related by a judicious historian, we should find this action, worthy of Caesar himself, reduced nearer to the level of probability and the common standard of the character of Alexander Severus. The abilities of that amiable prince seem to have been inadequate to the difficulties of his situation, the firmness of his conduct inferior to the purity of his intentions. His virtues, as well as the vices of Elagabalus, contracted a tincture of weakness and effeminacy from the soft climate of Syria, of which he was a native; though he blushed at his foreign origin, and listened with a vain complacency to the flattering genealogists, who derived his race from the ancient stock of Roman nobility. The pride and avarice of his mother cast a shade on the glories of his reign; and by exacting from his riper years the same dutiful obedience which she had justly claimed from his inexperienced youth, Mamaea exposed to public ridicule, both her son's character and her own. The fatigues of the Persian war irritated the military discontent; the unsuccessful event degraded the reputation of the emperor as a general, and even as a soldier. Every cause prepared, and every circumstance hastened, a revolution, which distracted the Roman Empire with a long series of intestine calamities.

The dissolute tyranny of Commodus, the civil wars occasioned by his death, and the new maxims of policy introduced by the house of Severus, had all contributed to increase the dangerous power of the army, and to obliterate the faint image of laws and liberty that was still impressed on the minds of the Romans. This internal change, which undermined the foundations of the empire, we have endeavoured to explain with some degree of order and perspicuity. The personal characters of the emperors, their victories, laws, follies, and fortunes, can interest us no farther than as they are connected with the general history of the decline and fall of the monarchy. Our constant attention to that great object will not suffer us to overlook a most important edict of Antoninus Caracalla, which communicated to all the free inhabitants of the empire the name and privileges of Roman citizens. His unbounded liberality flowed not, however, from the sentiments of a generous mind; it was the sordid result of avarice, and will naturally be illustrated by some observations on the finances of that state, from the victorious ages of the commonwealth to the reign of Alexander Severus.

The siege of Veii in Tuscany, the first considerable enterprise of the Romans, was protracted to the tenth year, much less by the strength of the place than by the unskilfulness of the besiegers. The unaccustomed hardships of so many winter campaigns, at the distance of near twenty miles from home, required more than common encouragements; and the senate wisely prevented the clamours of the people, by the institution of a regular pay for the soldiers, which was levied by a general tribute, assessed according to an equitable proportion on the property of the citizens. During more than two hundred years after the conquest of Veii, the victories of the republic added less to the wealth than to the power of Rome. The states of Italy paid their tribute in military service only, and the vast force both by sea and land, which was exerted in the Punic wars, was maintained at the expense of the Romans themselves. That high-spirited people (such is often the generous enthusiasm of freedom) cheerfully submitted to the most excessive but voluntary burdens, in the just confidence that they should speedily enjoy the rich harvest of their labours. Their expectations were not disappointed. In the course of a few years, the riches of Syracuse, of Carthage, of Macedonia, and of Asia, were brought in triumph to Rome. The treasures of Perseus alone amounted to near two millions sterling, and the Roman people, the sovereign of so many nations, was for ever delivered from the weight of taxes. The increasing revenue of the provinces was found sufficient to defray the ordinary establishment of war and government, and the superfluous mass of gold and silver was deposited in the temple of Saturn, and reserved for any unforeseen emergency of the state.

History has never perhaps suffered a greater or more irreparable injury, than in the loss of the curious register bequeathed by Augustus to the senate, in which that experienced prince so accurately balanced the revenues and expenses of the Roman Empire. Deprived of this clear and comprehensive estimate, we are reduced to collect a few imperfect hints from such of the ancients as have accidentally turned aside from the splendid to the more useful parts of history. We are informed that, by the conquest of Pompey, the tributes of Asia were raised from fifty to one hundred and thirty-five millions of drachms; or about four millions and a half sterling. Under the last and most indolent of the Ptolemies, the revenue of Egypt is said to have amounted to twelve thousand five hundred talents; a sum equivalent to more than two millions and a half of our money, but which was afterwards considerably improved by the more exact economy of the Romans, and the increase of the trade of Ethiopia and India. Gaul was enriched by rapine, as Egypt was by commerce, and the tributes of those two great provinces have been compared as nearly equal to each other in value. The ten thousand Euboic or Phoenician talents, about four millions sterling, which vanquished Carthage was condemned to pay within the term of fifty years, were a slight acknowledgment of the superiority of Rome, and cannot bear the least proportion with the taxes afterwards raised both on the lands and on the persons of the inhabitants, when the fertile coast of Africa was reduced into a province.

Spain, by a very singular fatality, was the Peru and Mexico of the old world. The discovery of the rich western continent by the Phoenicians, and the oppression of the simple natives, who were compelled to labour in their own mines for the benefit of strangers, form an exact type of the more recent history of Spanish America. The Phoenicians were acquainted only with the sea-coast of Spain; avarice, as well as ambition, carried the arms of Rome and Carthage into the heart of the country, and almost every part of the soil was found pregnant with copper, silver, and gold. Mention is made of a mine near Carthagena which yielded every day twenty-five thousand drachms of silver, or about three hundred thousand pounds a year. Twenty thousand pound weight of gold was annually received from the provinces of Asturia, Gallicia, and Lusitania.

We want both leisure and materials to pursue this curious inquiry through the many potent states that were annihilated in the Roman Empire. Some notion, however, may be formed of the revenue of the provinces where considerable wealth had been deposited by nature, or collected by man, if we observe the severe attention that was directed to the abodes of solitude and sterility. Augustus once received a petition from the inhabitants of Gyarus, humbly praying that they might be relieved from one-third of their excessive impositions. Their whole tax amounted indeed to no more than one hundred and fifty drachms, or about five pounds; but Gyarus was a little island, or rather a rock, of the Aegean Sea, destitute of fresh water and every necessary of life, and inhabited only by a few wretched fishermen.

From the faint glimmerings of such doubtful and scattered lights we should be inclined to believe, first, that (with every fair allowance for the difference of times and circumstances) the general income of the Roman provinces could seldom amount to less than fifteen or twenty millions of our money; and secondly, that so ample a revenue must have been fully adequate to all the expenses of the moderate government instituted by Augustus, whose court was the modest family of a private senator, and

whose military establishment was calculated for the defence of the
frontiers, without any aspiring views of conquest, or any serious apprehension of a foreign invasion.

Notwithstanding the seeming probability of both these conclusions,
the latter of them at least is positively disowned by the language and
conduct of Augustus. It is not easy to determine whether, on this
occasion, he acted as the common father of the Roman world, or as the
oppressor of liberty; whether he wished to relieve the provinces, or to
impoverish the senate and the equestrian order. But no sooner had he
assumed the reins of government than he frequently intimated the
insufficiency of the tributes, and the necessity of throwing an equitable
proportion of the public burden upon Rome and Italy. In the prosecution of this unpopular design, he advanced, however, by cautious and
well-weighed steps. The introduction of customs was followed by the
establishment of an excise, and the scheme of taxation was completed by
an artful assessment on the real and personal property of the Roman
citizens, who had been exempted from any kind of contribution above a
century and a half.

I. In a great empire like that of Rome, a natural balance of money
must have gradually established itself. It has been already observed, that
as the wealth of the provinces was attracted to the capital by the strong
hand of conquest and power, so a considerable part of it was restored to
the industrious provinces by the gentle influence of commerce and arts.
In the reign of Augustus and his successors, duties were imposed on
every kind of merchandise, which through a thousand channels flowed
to the great centre of opulence and luxury; and in whatsoever manner the
law was expressed, it was the Roman purchaser, and not the provincial
merchant, who paid the tax. The rate of the customs varied from the
eighth to the fortieth part of the value of the commodity; and we have a
right to suppose that the variation was directed by the unalterable
maxims of policy: that a higher duty was fixed on the articles of luxury
than on those of necessity, and that the productions raised or manufac-
tured by the labour of the subjects of the empire, were treated with more
indulgence than was shown to the pernicious, or at least the unpopular,
commerce of Arabia and India. There is still extant a long but imperfect
catalogue of eastern commodities, which about the time of Alexander
Severus were subject to the payment of duties; cinnamon, myrrh,
pepper, ginger, and the whole tribe of aromatics, a great variety of
precious stones, among which the diamond was the most remarkable for
its price, and the emerald for its beauty. Parthian and Babylonian

leather, cottons, silks, both raw and manufactured, ebony, ivory, and eunuchs. We may observe that the use and value of those effeminate slaves gradually rose with the decline of the empire.

II. The excise, introduced by Augustus after the civil wars, was extremely moderate, but it was general. It seldom exceeded one per cent; but it comprehended whatever was sold in the markets or by public auction, from the most considerable purchases of lands and houses to those minute objects which can only derive a value from their infinite multitude and daily consumption. Such a tax, as it affects the body of the people, has ever been the occasion of clamour and discontent. An emperor well acquainted with the wants and resources of the state, was obliged to declare by a public edict that the support of the army depended in a great measure on the produce of the excise.

III. When Augustus resolved to establish a permanent military force for the defence of his government against foreign and domestic enemies, he instituted a peculiar treasury for the pay of the soldiers, the rewards of the veterans, and the extraordinary expenses of war. The ample revenue of the excise, though peculiarly appropriated to those uses, was found inadequate. To supply the deficiency, the emperor suggested a new tax of five per cent on all legacies and inheritances. But the nobles of Rome were more tenacious of property than of freedom. Their indignant murmurs were received by Augustus with his usual temper. He candidly referred the whole business to the senate, and exhorted them to provide for the public service by some other expedient of a less odious nature. They were divided and perplexed. He insinuated to them that their obstinacy would oblige him to *propose* a general land-tax and capitation. They acquiesced in silence. The new imposition on legacies and inheritances was however mitigated by some restrictions. It did not take place unless the object was of a certain value, most probably of fifty or an hundred pieces of gold, nor could it be exacted from the nearest of kin on the father's side. When the rights of nature and poverty were thus secured, it seemed reasonable that a stranger, or a distant relation, who acquired an unexpected accession of fortune, should cheerfully resign a twentieth part of it for the benefit of the state.

Such a tax, plentiful as it must prove in every wealthy community, was most happily suited to the situation of the Romans, who could frame their arbitrary wills, according to the dictates of reason or caprice, without any restraint from the modern fetters of entails and settlements. From various causes the partiality of paternal affection often lost its influence over the stern patriots of the commonwealth and the dissolute nobles of the empire; and if the father bequeathed to his son the fourth part of his estate, he removed all ground of legal complaint. But a rich childless old man was a domestic tyrant, and his power increased with his years and infirmities. A servile crowd, in which he frequently reckoned praetors and consuls, courted his smiles, pampered his avarice, applauded his follies, served his passions, and waited with impatience for his death. The arts of attendance and flattery were formed into a most lucrative science; those who professed it acquired a peculiar appellation; and the whole city, according to the lively descriptions of satire, was divided between two parties, the hunters and their game. Yet, while so many unjust and extravagant wills were every day dictated by cunning, and subscribed by folly, a few were the result of rational esteem and virtuous gratitude. Cicero, who had so often defended the lives and fortunes of his fellow-citizens, was rewarded with legacies to the amount of an hundred and seventy thousand pounds; nor do the friends of the younger Pliny seem to have been less generous to that amiable orator. Whatever was the motive of the testator, the treasury claimed, without distinction, the twentieth part of his estate; and in the course of two or three generations, the whole property of the subject must have gradually passed through the coffers of the state.

In the first and golden years of the reign of Nero, that prince, from a desire of popularity, and perhaps from a blind impulse of benevolence, conceived a wish of abolishing the oppression of the customs and excise. The wisest senators applauded his magnanimity; but they diverted him from the execution of a design, which would have dissolved the strength and resources of the republic. Had it indeed been possible to realise this dream of fancy, such princes as Trajan and the Antonines would surely have embraced with ardour the glorious opportunity of conferring so signal an obligation on mankind. Satisfied, however, with alleviating the public burden, they attempted not to remove it. The mildness and precision of their laws ascertained the rule and measure of taxation, and protected the subject of every rank against arbitrary interpretations, antiquated claims, and the insolent vexation of the farmers of the revenue. For it is somewhat singular that, in every age, the best and wisest of the Roman governors persevered in this pernicious method of collect-ing the principal branches at least of the excise and customs.

The sentiments, and, indeed, the situation of Caracalla, were very different from those of the Antonines. Inattentive, or rather averse, to the welfare of his people, he found himself under the necessity of gratifying the insatiate avarice, which he had excited in the army. Of the several impositions introduced by Augustus, the twentieth on inheritances and legacies was the most fruitful, as well as the most comprehensive. As its influence was not confined to Rome or Italy, the produce continually increased with the gradual extension of the Roman City. The new citizens, though charged, on equal terms, with the payment of new taxes, which had not affected them as subjects, derived an ample compensation from the rank they obtained, the privileges they acquired, and the fair prospect of honours and fortune that was thrown open to their ambition. But the favour which implied a distinction, was lost in the prodigality of Caracalla, and the reluctant provincials were compelled to assume the vain title, and the real obligations, of Roman citizens. Nor was the rapacious son of Severus contented with such a measure of taxation, as had appeared sufficient to his moderate predecessors. Instead of a twentieth, he exacted a tenth of all legacies and inheritances; and during his reign (for the ancient proportion was restored after his death) he crushed alike every part of the empire under the weight of his iron sceptre.

When all the provincials became liable to the peculiar impositions of Roman citizens, they seemed to acquire a legal exemption from the tributes which they paid in their former condition of subjects. Such were not the maxims of government adopted by Caracalla and his pretended son. The old as well as the new taxes were, at the same time, levied in the provinces. It was reserved for the virtue of Alexander to relieve them in a great measure from this intolerable grievance, by reducing the tributes to a thirtieth part of the sum exacted at the time of his accession. It is impossible to conjecture the motive that engaged him to spare so trifling a remnant of the public evil; but the noxious weed, which had not been totally eradicated, again sprang up with the most luxuriant growth, and in the succeeding age darkened the Roman world with its deadly shade. In the course of this history, we shall be too often summoned to explain the land-tax, the capitation, and the heavy contributions of corn, wine, oil, and meat, which were exacted from the provinces for the use of the court, the army, and the capital.

As long as Rome and Italy were respected as the centre of govern-ment, a national spirit was preserved by the ancient, and insensibly imbibed by the adopted, citizens. The principal commands of the army were filled by men who had received a liberal education, were well instructed in the advantages of laws and letters, and who had risen, by equal steps, through the regular succession of civil and military honours. To their influence and example we may partly ascribe the modest obedience of the legions during the two first centuries of the Imperial history.

But when the last enclosure of the Roman constitution was trampled down by Caracalla, the separation of professions gradually succeeded to the distinction of ranks. The more polished citizens of the internal provinces were alone qualified to act as lawyers and magistrates. The rougher trade of arms was abandoned to the peasants and barbarians of the frontiers, who knew no country but their camp, no science but that of war, no civil laws, and scarcely those of military discipline. With bloody hands, savage manners, and desperate resolutions, they sometimes guarded, but much oftener subverted, the throne of the emperors.

THE ELEVATION AND TYRANNY OF MAXIMIN — REBEL⁄
LION IN AFRICA AND ITALY, UNDER THE AUTHORITY OF
THE SENATE — CIVIL WARS AND SEDITIONS — VIOLENT
DEATHS OF MAXIMIN AND HIS SON, OF MAXIMUS AND
BALBINUS, AND OF THE THREE GORDIANS — USURPA⁄
TION AND SECULAR GAMES OF PHILIP

OF THE VARIOUS FORMS OF GOVERNMENT
which have prevailed in the world, an hereditary monarchy seems to
present the fairest scope for ridicule. Is it possible to relate, without an
indignant smile, that, on the father's decease, the property of a nation,
like that of a drove of oxen, descends to his infant son, as yet unknown to
mankind and to himself; and that the bravest warriors and the wisest
statesmen, relinquishing their natural right to empire, approach the royal
cradle with bended knees and protestations of inviolable fidelity? Satire
and declamation may paint these obvious topics in the most dazzling
colours, but our more serious thoughts will respect a useful prejudice,
that establishes a rule of succession, independent of the passions of
mankind; and we shall cheerfully acquiesce in any expedient which
deprives the multitude of the dangerous, and indeed the ideal, power of
giving themselves a master.

In the cool shade of retirement, we may easily devise imaginary forms
of government, in which the sceptre shall be constantly bestowed on the
most worthy, by the free and incorrupt suffrage of the whole community.
Experience overturns these airy fabrics, and teaches us that, in a large
society, the election of a monarch can never devolve to the wisest, or to
the most numerous, part of the people. The army is the only order of men
sufficiently united to concur in the same sentiments, and powerful
enough to impose them on the rest of their fellow⁄citizens: but the temper
of soldiers, habituated at once to violence and to slavery, renders them
very unfit guardians of a legal, or even a civil, constitution. Justice,
humanity, or political wisdom, are qualities they are too little acquainted
with in themselves, to appreciate them in others. Valour will acquire
their esteem, and liberality will purchase their suffrage; but the first of

these merits is often lodged in the most savage breasts; the latter can only exert itself at the expense of the public; and both may be turned against the possessor of the throne, by the ambition of a daring rival.

The superior prerogative of birth, when it has obtained the sanction of time and popular opinion, is the plainest and least invidious of all distinctions among mankind. The acknowledged right extinguishes the hopes of faction, and the conscious security disarms the cruelty of the monarch. To the firm establishment of this idea, we owe the peaceful succession, and mild administration, of European monarchies. To the defect of it, we must attribute the frequent civil wars, through which an Asiatic despot is obliged to cut his way to the throne of his fathers. Yet, even in the East, the sphere of contention is usually limited to the princes of the reigning house, and as soon as the more fortunate competitor has removed his brethren, by the sword and the bow-string, he no longer entertains any jealousy of his meaner subjects. But the Roman Empire, after the authority of the senate had sunk into contempt, was a vast scene of confusion. The royal, and even noble, families of the provinces, had long since been led in triumph before the car of the haughty republicans. The ancient families of Rome had successively fallen beneath the tyranny of the Caesars; and whilst those princes were shackled by the forms of a commonwealth, and disappointed by the repeated failure of their pos- terity, it was impossible that any idea of hereditary succession should have taken root in the minds of their subjects. The right to the throne, which none could claim from birth, every one assumed from merit. The daring hopes of ambition were set loose from the salutary restraints of law and prejudice; and the meanest of mankind might, without folly, entertain a hope of being raised by valour and fortune to a rank in the army, in which a single crime would enable him to wrest the sceptre of the world from his feeble and unpopular master. After the murder of Alexander Severus, and the elevation of Maximin, no emperor could think himself safe upon the throne, and every barbarian peasant of the frontier might aspire to that august, but dangerous station.

About thirty-two years before the event, the Emperor Severus, returning from an eastern expedition, halted in Thrace, to celebrate, with military games, the birthday of his younger son, Geta. The country flocked in crowds to behold their sovereign, and a young barbarian of gigantic stature earnestly solicited, in his rude dialect, that he might be allowed to contend for the prize of wrestling. As the pride of discipline would have been disgraced in the overthrow of a Roman soldier by a Thracian peasant, he was matched with the stoutest followers of the camp, sixteen of whom he successively laid on the ground. His victory was rewarded by some trifling gifts, and a permission to inlist in the troops. The next day, the happy barbarian was distinguished above a crowd of recruits, dancing and exulting after the fashion of his country. As soon as he perceived that he had attracted the emperor's notice, he instantly ran up to his horse, and followed him on foot, without the least appearance of fatigue, in a long and rapid career. 'Thracian,' said Severus, with astonishment, 'art thou disposed to wrestle after thy race?' 'Most willingly, Sir,' replied the unwearied youth, and, almost in a breath, overthrew seven of the strongest soldiers in the army. A gold collar was the prize of his matchless vigour and activity, and he was immediately appointed to serve in the horse-guards who always attended on the person of the sovereign.

Maximin, for that was his name, though born on the territories of the empire, descended from a mixed race of barbarians. His father was a Goth, and his mother of the nation of the Alani. He displayed, on every occasion, a valour equal to his strength; and his native fierceness was soon tempered or disguised by the knowledge of the world. Under the reign of Severus and his son, he obtained the rank of centurion, with the favour and esteem of both those princes, the former of whom was an excellent judge of merit. Gratitude forbade Maximin to serve under the assassin of Caracalla. Honour taught him to decline the effeminate insults of Elagabalus. On the accession of Alexander he returned to court, and was placed by that prince in a station useful to the service and honourable to himself. The fourth legion, to which he was appointed tribune, soon became, under his care, the best disciplined of the whole army. With the general applause of the soldiers, who bestowed on their favourite hero the names of Ajax and Hercules, he was successively promoted to the first military command; and had not he still retained too much of his savage origin, the emperor might perhaps have given his own sister in marriage to the son of Maximin.

Instead of securing his fidelity, these favours served only to inflame the ambition of the Thracian peasant, who deemed his fortune inadequate to his merit, as long as he was constrained to acknowledge a superior. Though a stranger to real wisdom, he was not devoid of a selfish cunning, which showed him that the emperor had lost the affection of the army, and taught him to improve their discontent to his own advantage. It is easy for faction and calumny to shed their poison on the administration of the best of princes, and to accuse even their virtues, by artfully confounding them with those vices to which they bear the nearest affinity. The troops listened with pleasure to the emissaries of Maximin. They blushed at their own ignominious patience, which, during thir-teen years, had supported the vexatious discipline imposed by an effeminate Syrian, the timid slave of his mother and of the senate. It was time, they cried, to cast away that useless phantom of the civil power, and to elect for their prince and general a real soldier, educated in camps, exercised in war, who would assert the glory, and distribute among his companions the treasures, of the empire. A great army was at that time assembled on the banks of the Rhine, under the command of the emperor himself, who, almost immediately after his return from the Persian war, had been obliged to march against the barbarians of Germany. The important care of training and reviewing the new levies was entrusted to Maximin. One day (AD 235, 19 March), as he entered the field of exercise, the troops, either from a sudden impulse or a formed conspiracy, saluted him emperor, silenced by their loud acclamations his obstinate refusal, and hastened to consummate their rebellion by the murder of Alexander Severus.

The circumstances of his death are variously related. The writers, who suppose that he died in ignorance of the ingratitude and ambition of Maximin, affirm that, after taking a frugal repast in the sight of the army, he retired to sleep, and that, about the seventh hour of the day, a part of his own guards broke into the imperial tent, and with many wounds assassinated their virtuous and unsuspecting prince. If we credit another, and indeed a more probable account, Maximin was invested with the purple by a numerous detachment, at the distance of several miles from the headquarters; and he trusted for success rather to the secret wishes than to the public declarations of the great army. Alexander had sufficient time to awaken a faint sense of loyalty among his troops; but their reluctant professions of fidelity quickly vanished on the appearance of Maximin, who declared himself the friend and advocate of the military order, and was unanimously acknowledged emperor of the Romans by the applauding legions. The son of Mamaea, betrayed and deserted, withdrew into his tent, desirous at least to conceal his approaching fate from the insults of the multitude. He was soon followed by a tribune and some centurions, the ministers of death; but, instead of receiving with manly resolution the inevitable stroke, his unavailing cries and entreaties disgraced the last moments of his life, and converted into contempt some portion of the just pity which his innocence and misfortunes must inspire. His mother Mamaea, whose pride and avarice he loudly accused as the cause of his ruin, perished with her son. The most faithful of his friends were sacrificed to the first fury of the soldiers. Others were reserved for the more deliberate cruelty of the usurper; and those who experienced the mildest treatment, were stripped of their employments, and ignominiously driven from the court and army.

The former tyrants, Caligula and Nero, Commodus and Caracalla, were all dissolute and inexperienced youths, educated in the purple, and corrupted by the pride of empire, the luxury of Rome, and the perfidious voice of flattery. The cruelty of Maximin was derived from a different source, the fear of contempt. Though he depended on the attachment of the soldiers, who loved him for virtues like their own, he was conscious that his mean and barbarian origin, his savage appearance, and his total ignorance of the arts and institutions of civil life,* formed a very unfavourable contrast with the amiable manners of the unhappy Alexander. He remembered that, in his humbler fortune, he had often waited before the door of the haughty nobles of Rome, and had been denied admittance by the insolence of their slaves. He recollected too the friendship of a few who had relieved his poverty, and assisted his rising hopes. But those who had spurned, and those who had protected the Thracian, were guilty of the same crime, the knowledge of his original obscurity. For this crime many were put to death; and by the execution of several of his benefactors, Maximin published, in characters of blood, the indelible history of his baseness and ingratitude.

The dark and sanguinary soul of the tyrant was open to every suspicion against those among his subjects who were the most distinguished by their birth or merit. Whenever he was alarmed with the sound of treason, his cruelty was unbounded and unrelenting. A conspiracy against his life was either discovered or imagined, and Magnus, a consular senator, was named as the principal author of it. Without a witness, without a trial, and without an opportunity of defence, Magnus, with four thousand of his supposed accomplices, were put to death. Italy and the whole empire were infested with innumerable spies and informers. On the slightest accusation, the first of the Roman nobles, who had governed provinces, commanded armies, and been adorned with the consular and triumphal ornaments, were chained on the public carriages, and hurried away to the emperor's presence. Confiscation, exile, or simple death, were esteemed uncommon instances of his lenity. Some of the unfortunate sufferers he ordered to be sewed up in the hides of slaughtered animals, others to be exposed to

* It appears that he was totally ignorant of the Greek language: which, from its universal use in conversation and letters, was an essential part of every liberal education.

wild beasts, others again to be beaten to death with clubs. During the three years of his reign, he disdained to visit either Rome or Italy. His camp, occasionally removed from the banks of the Rhine to those of the Danube, was the seat of his stern despotism, which trampled on every principle of law and justice, and was supported by the avowed power of the sword. No man of noble birth, elegant accomplishments, or know-ledge of civil business, was suffered near his person; and the court of a Roman emperor revived the idea of those ancient chiefs of slaves and gladiators, whose savage power had left a deep impression of terror and detestation.

As long as the cruelty of Maximin was confined to the illustrious senators, or even to the bold adventurers, who in the court or army expose themselves to the caprice of fortune, the body of the people viewed their sufferings with indifference, or perhaps with pleasure. But the tyrant's avarice, stimulated by the insatiate desires of the soldiers, at length attacked the public property. Every city of the empire was possessed of an independent revenue, destined to purchase corn for the multitude, and to supply the expenses of the games and entertainments. By a single act of authority, the whole mass of wealth was at once confiscated for the use of the Imperial treasury. The temples were stripped of their most valuable offerings of gold and silver, and the statues of gods, heroes, and emperors, were melted down and coined into money. These impious orders could not be executed without tumults and massacres, as in many places the people chose rather to die in the defence of their altars, than to behold in the midst of peace their cities exposed to the rapine and cruelty of war. The soldiers themselves, among whom this sacrilegious plunder was distributed, received it with a blush; and, hardened as they were in acts of violence, they dreaded the just reproaches of their friends and relations. Throughout the Roman world a general cry of indignation was heard, imploring vengeance on the common enemy of human kind; and at length, by an act of private oppression, a peaceful and unarmed province was driven into rebellion against him.

The procurator of Africa was a servant worthy of such a master, who considered the fines and confiscations of the rich as one of the most fruitful branches of the Imperial revenue. An iniquitous sentence had been (AD 237, April) pronounced against some opulent youths of that country, the execution of which would have stripped them of far the greater part of their patrimony. In this extremity, a resolution that must either complete or prevent their ruin, was dictated by despair. A respite of three days, obtained with difficulty from the rapacious treasurer, was employed in collecting from their estates a great number of slaves and peasants, blindly devoted to the commands of their lords, and armed with the rustic weapons of clubs and axes. The leaders of the conspiracy, as they were admitted to the audience of the procurator, stabbed him with the daggers concealed under their garments, and, by the assistance of their tumultuary train, seized on the little town of Thysdrus, and erected the standard of rebellion against the sovereign of the Roman Empire. They rested their hopes on the hatred of mankind against Maximin, and they judiciously resolved to oppose to that detested tyrant, an emperor whose mild virtues had already acquired the love and esteem of the Romans, and whose authority over the province would give weight and stability to the enterprise. Gordianus, their proconsul, and the object of their choice, refused, with unfeigned reluctance, the dangerous honour, and begged with tears that they would suffer him to terminate in peace a long and innocent life, without staining his feeble age with civil blood. Their menaces compelled him to accept the Imperial purple, his only refuge indeed against the jealous cruelty of Maximin; since, according to the reasoning of tyrants, those who have been esteemed worthy of the throne deserve death, and those who deliberate have already rebelled.

The family of Gordianus was one of the most illustrious of the Roman senate. On the father's side, he was descended from the Gracchi; on his mother's, from the emperor Trajan. A great estate enabled him to support the dignity of this birth, and, in the enjoyment of it, he displayed an elegant taste and beneficent disposition. The palace in Rome, formerly inhabited by the great Pompey, had been, during several generations, in the possession of Gordian's family. It was distinguished by ancient trophies of naval victories, and decorated with the works of modern painting. His villa on the road to Praeneste was celebrated for baths of singular beauty and extent, for three stately rooms of an hundred feet in length, and for a magnificent portico, supported by two hundred columns of the four most curious and costly sorts of marble.* The public shows exhibited at his expense, and in which the people were entertained with many hundreds of wild beasts and gladiators, seem to surpass the fortune of a subject; and whilst the liberality of other

* The Claudian, the Numidian, the Carystian, and the Synnadian. The colours of Roman marbles have been faintly described and imperfectly distinguished. It appears, however, that the Carystian was a sea-green, and that the marble of Synnada was white mixed with oval spots of purple.

A bird's-eye view of the Baths of Caracalla

The interior of the Pantheon

magistrates was confined to a few solemn festivals in Rome, the magnificence of Gordian was repeated, when he was aedile, every month in the
year, and extended, during his consulship, to the principal cities of Italy.
He was twice elevated to the last-mentioned dignity, by Caracalla and
by Alexander; for he possessed the uncommon talent of acquiring the
esteem of virtuous princes, without alarming the jealousy of tyrants. His
long life was innocently spent in the study of letters and the peaceful
honours of Rome; and, till he was named proconsul of Africa by the
voice of the senate and the approbation of Alexander, he appears
prudently to have declined the command of armies and the government
of provinces. As long as that emperor lived, Africa was happy under the
administration of his worthy representative; after the barbarous Maximin
had usurped the throne, Gordianus alleviated the miseries which he was
unable to prevent. When he reluctantly accepted the purple, he was
above fourscore years old; a last and valuable remains of the happy age of
the Antonines, whose virtues he revived in his own conduct and
celebrated in an elegant poem of thirty books. With the venerable
proconsul, his son, who had accompanied him into Africa as his
lieutenant, was likewise declared emperor. His manners were less pure,
but his character was equally amiable with that of his father. Twenty-
two acknowledged concubines, and a library of sixty-two thousand
volumes, attested the variety of his inclinations, and from the productions which he left behind him, it appears that the former as well as the
latter were designed for use rather than ostentation.* The Roman people
acknowledged in the features of the younger Gordian the resemblance of
Scipio Africanus, recollected with pleasure that his mother was the
grand-daughter of Antoninus Pius, and rested the public hope on those
latent virtues which had hitherto, as they fondly imagined, lain concealed in the luxurious indolence of a private life.

As soon as the Gordians had appeased the first tumult of a popular
election, they removed their court to Carthage. They were received with
the acclamations of the Africans, who honoured their virtues, and who,
since the visit of Hadrian, had never beheld the majesty of a Roman
emperor. But these vain acclamations neither strengthened nor confirmed the title of the Gordians. They were induced by principle, as well
as interest, to solicit the approbation of the senate; and a deputation of the
noblest provincials was sent, without delay, to Rome, to relate and justify
the conduct of their countrymen, who, having long suffered with

* By each of his concubines, the younger Gordian left three or four children. His
literary productions were by no means contemptible.

patience, were at length resolved to act with vigour. The letters of the new princes were modest and respectful, excusing the necessity which had obliged them to accept the Imperial title; but submitting their election and their fate to the supreme judgment of the senate.

The inclinations of the senate were neither doubtful nor divided. The birth and noble alliances of the Gordians had intimately connected them with the most illustrious houses of Rome. Their fortune had created many dependents in that assembly, their merit had acquired many friends. Their mild administration opened the flattering prospect of the restoration not only of the civil but even of the republican government. The terror of military violence, which had first obliged the senate to forget the murder of Alexander, and to ratify the election of a barbarian peasant, now produced a contrary effect, and provoked them to assert the injured rights of freedom and humanity. The hatred of Maximin towards the senate was declared and implacable; the tamest submission had not appeased his fury, the most cautious innocence would not remove his suspicions; and even the care of their own safety urged them to share the fortune of an enterprise, of which (if unsuccessful) they were sure to be the first victims. These considerations, and perhaps others of a more private nature, were debated in a previous conference of the consuls and the magistrates. As soon as their resolution was decided, they convoked in the temple of Castor the whole body of the senate, according to an ancient form of secrecy, calculated to awaken their attention, and to conceal their decrees. 'Conscript fathers,' said the consul Syllanus, 'the two Gordians, both of consular dignity, the one your proconsul, the other your lieutenant, have been declared emperors by the general consent of Africa. Let us return thanks,' he boldly continued, 'to the youth of Thysdrus; let us return thanks to the faithful people of Carthage, our generous deliverers from an horrid mon-ster — Why do you hear me thus coolly, thus timidly? Why do you cast those anxious looks on each other? why hesitate? Maximin is a public enemy! may his enmity soon expire with him, and may we long enjoy the prudence and felicity of Gordian the father, the valour and constancy of Gordian the son!' The noble ardour of the consul revived the languid spirit of the senate. By an unanimous decree the election of the Gordians was ratified, Maximin, his son, and his adherents, were pronounced enemies of their country, and liberal rewards were offered to whomsoever had the courage and good fortune to destroy them.

During the emperor's absence, a detachment of the Praetorian Guards remained at Rome, to protect, or rather to command, the capital.

The prefect Vitalianus had signalised his fidelity to Maximin, by the alacrity with which he had obeyed, and even prevented, the cruel mandates of the tyrant. His death alone could rescue the authority of the senate, and the lives of the senators, from a state of danger and suspense. Before their resolves had transpired, a quaestor and some tribunes were commissioned to take his devoted life. They executed the order with equal boldness and success; and, with their bloody daggers in their hands, ran through the streets proclaiming to the people and the soldiers the news of the happy revolution. The enthusiasm of liberty was seconded by the promise of a large donative, in lands and money; the statues of Maximin were thrown down; the capital of the empire acknowledged, with transport, the authority of the two Gordians and the senate, and the example of Rome was followed by the rest of Italy.

A new spirit had arisen in that assembly, whose long patience had been insulted by wanton despotism and military licence. The senate assumed the reins of government, and, with a calm intrepidity, prepared to vindicate by arms the cause of freedom. Among the consular senators recommended by their merit and services to the favour of the emperor Alexander, it was easy to select twenty, not unequal to the command of an army, and the conduct of a war. To these was the defence of Italy intrusted. Each was appointed to act in his respective department, authorised to enrol and discipline the Italian youth; and instructed to fortify the ports and highways against the impending invasion of Maximin. A number of deputies, chosen from the most illustrious of the senatorian and equestrian orders, were dispatched at the same time to the governors of the several provinces, earnestly conjuring them to fly to the assistance of their country, and to remind the nations of their ancient ties of friendship with the Roman senate and people. The general respect with which these deputies were received, and the zeal of Italy and the provinces in favour of the senate, sufficiently prove that the subjects of Maximin were reduced to that uncommon distress, in which the body of the people has more to fear from oppression than from resistance. The consciousness of that melancholy truth inspires a degree of persevering fury seldom to be found in those civil wars which are artificially supported for the benefit of a few factious and designing leaders.

For while the cause of the Gordians was embraced with such diffusive ardour, the Gordians themselves (AD 237, 3 July) were no more. The feeble court of Carthage was alarmed with the rapid approach of Capelianus, governor of Mauritania, who, with a small band of veterans, and a fierce host of barbarians, attacked a faithful but unwarlike province. The younger Gordian sallied out to meet the enemy at the head of a few guards, and a numerous undisciplined multitude, educated in the peaceful luxury of Carthage. His useless valour served only to procure him an honourable death, in the field of battle. His aged father, whose reign had not exceeded thirty-six days, put an end to his life on the first news of the defeat. Carthage, destitute of defence, opened her gates to the conqueror, and Africa was exposed to the rapacious cruelty of a slave, obliged to satisfy his unrelenting master with a large account of blood and treasure.

The fate of the Gordians filled Rome with just, but unexpected terror. The senate convoked in the temple of Concord, affected to transact the common business of the day; and seemed to decline, with trembling anxiety, the consideration of their own and the public danger. A silent consternation prevailed on the assembly, till a senator, of the name and family of Trajan, awakened his brethren from their fatal lethargy. He represented to them, that the choice of cautious dilatory measures had been long since out of their power; that Maximin, implacable by nature, and exasperated by injuries, was advancing towards Italy, at the head of the military force of the empire; and that their only remaining alternative was either to meet him bravely in the field, or tamely to expect the tortures and ignominious death reserved for unsuccessful rebellion. 'We have lost,' continued he, 'two excellent princes; but unless we desert ourselves, the hopes of the republic have not perished with the Gordians. Many are the senators, whose virtues have deserved, and whose abilities would sustain, the Imperial dignity. Let us elect two emperors, one of whom may conduct the war against the public enemy, whilst his colleague remains at Rome to direct the civil administration. I cheerfully expose myself to the danger and envy of the nomination, and give my vote in favour of Maximus and Balbinus. Ratify my choice, conscript fathers or appoint, in their place, others more worthy of the empire.' The general apprehension silenced the whispers of jealousy; the merit of the candi-dates was universally acknowledged; and the house resounded with the sincere acclamations, of 'Long life and victory to the emperors Maximus and Balbinus. You are happy in the judgment of the senate; may the republic be happy under your administration!'

The virtues and the reputation of the new emperors justified the most sanguine hopes of the Romans. The various nature of their talents seemed to appropriate to each his peculiar department of peace and war, without leaving room for jealous emulation. Balbinus was an admired orator, a poet of distinguished fame, and a wise magistrate, who had exercised with innocence and applause the civil jurisdiction in almost all the interior provinces of the empire. His birth was noble,* his fortune affluent, his manners liberal and affable. In him the love of pleasure was corrected by a sense of dignity, nor had the habits of ease deprived him of a capacity for business. The mind of Maximus was formed in a rougher mould. By his valour and abilities he had raised himself from the meanest origin to the first employments of the state and army. His victories over the Sarmatians and the Germans, the austerity of his life, and the rigid impartiality of his justice, whilst he was prefect of the city, commanded the esteem of a people, whose affections were engaged in favour of the more amiable Balbinus. The two colleagues had both been consuls (Balbinus had twice enjoyed that honourable office), both had been named among the twenty lieutenants of the senate; and since the one was sixty and the other seventy-four years old,† they had both attained the full maturity of age and experience.

After the senate had conferred on Maximus and Balbinus an equal portion of the consular and tribunitian powers, the title of Fathers of their country, and the joint office of Supreme Pontiff, they ascended to the Capitol, to return thanks to the gods, protectors of Rome. The solemn rites of sacrifice were disturbed by a sedition of the people. The licentious multitude neither loved the rigid Maximus, nor did they sufficiently fear the mild and humane Balbinus. Their increasing numbers surrounded the temple of Jupiter; with obstinate clamours they asserted their inherent right of consenting to the election of their sovereign; and demanded, with an apparent moderation, that, besides the two emperors chosen by the senate, a third should be added of the family of the Gordians, as a just return of gratitude to those princes who had sacrificed their lives for the republic. At the head of the city-guards, and the youth of the equestrian order, Maximus and Balbinus attempted to cut their way through the

* He was descended from Cornelius Balbus, a noble Spaniard, and the adopted son of Theophanes, the Greek historian. Balbus obtained the freedom of Rome by the favour of Pompey, and preserved it by the eloquence of Cicero. The friendship of Caesar (to whom he rendered the most important secret services in the civil war) raised him to the consulship and the pontificate, honours never yet possessed by a stranger. The nephew of this Balbus triumphed over the Garamantes. See *Dictionnaire de Bayle, au mot* Balbus, where he distinguishes the several persons of that name, and rectifies, with his usual accuracy, the mistakes of former writers concerning them.

† Zonaras. But little dependence is to be had on the authority of a moderate Greek, so grossly ignorant of the history of the third century, that he creates several imaginary emperors, and confounds those who really existed.

seditious multitude. The multitude, armed with sticks and stones, drove them back into the Capitol. It is prudent to yield when the contest, whatever may be the issue of it, must be fatal to both parties. A boy, only thirteen years of age, the grandson of the elder, and nephew of the younger, Gordian, was produced to the people, invested with the ornaments and title of Caesar. The tumult was appeased by this easy condescension; and the two emperors, as soon as they had been peace-ably acknowledged in Rome, prepared to defend Italy against the common enemy.

While in Rome and Africa revolutions succeeded each other with such amazing rapidity, the mind of Maximin was agitated by the most furious passions. He is said to have received the news of the rebellion of the Gordians, and of the decree of the senate against him, not with the temper of a man, but the rage of a wild beast; which, as it could not discharge itself on the distant senate, theatened the life of his son, of his friends, and of all who ventured to approach his person. The grateful intelligence of the death of the Gordians was quickly followed by the assurance that the senate, laying aside all hopes of pardon or accommo-dation, had substituted in their room two emperors, with whose merit he could not be unacquainted. Revenge was the only consolation left to Maximin, and revenge could only be obtained by arms. The strength of the legions had been assembled by Alexander from all parts of the empire. Three successful campaigns against the Germans and the Sarmatians had raised their fame, confirmed their discipline, and even increased their numbers, by filling the ranks with the flower of the barbarian youth. The life of Maximin had been spent in war, and the candid severity of history cannot refuse him the valour of a soldier, or even the abilities of an experienced general. It might naturally be expected, that a prince of such a character, instead of suffering the rebellion to gain stability by delay, should immediately have marched from the banks of the Danube to those of the Tiber, and that his victorious army, instigated by contempt for the senate, and eager to gather the spoils of Italy, should have burned with impatience to finish the easy and lucrative conquest. Yet as far as we can trust to the obscure chronology of that period, it appears that the operations of some foreign war deferred the Italian expedition till the ensuing spring. From the prudent conduct of Maximin, we may learn that the savage features of his character have been exaggerated by the pencil of party, that his passions, however impetuous, submitted to the force of reason, and that the barbarian possessed something of the generous spirit of Sylla, who subdued the enemies of Romes before he suffered himself to revenge his private injuries.*

When the troops of Maximin, advancing in excellent order, arrived at the foot of the Julian Alps, they were terrified by the silence and desolation that reigned on the frontiers of Italy. The villages and open towns had been abandoned on their approach by the inhabitants, the cattle was driven away, the provisions removed, or destroyed, the bridges broke down, nor was anything left which could afford either shelter or give subsistence to an invader. Such had been the wise orders of the generals of the senate, whose design was to protract the war, to ruin the army of Maximin by the slow operation of famine, and to consume his strength in the sieges of the principal cities of Italy, which they had plentifully stored with men and provisions from the deserted country. Aquileia received and withstood the first shock of the invasion. The streams that issue from the head of the Hadriatic gulf, swelled by the melting of the winter snows,† opposed an unexpected obstacle to the arms of Maximin. At length, on a singular bridge, constructed with art and difficulty of large hogsheads, he transported his army to the opposite bank, rooted up the beautiful vineyards in the neighbourhood of Aquileia, demolished the suburbs, and employed the timber of the buildings in the engines and towers, with which on every side he attacked the city. The walls, fallen to decay during the security of a long peace, had been hastily repaired on this sudden emergency; but the firmest defence of Aquileia consisted in the constancy of the citizens; all ranks of whom, instead of being dismayed, were animated by the extreme danger, and their knowledge of the tyrant's unrelenting temper. Their courage was supported and directed by Crispinus and Meno-philus, two of the twenty lieutenants of the senate, who, with a small body of regular troops, had thrown themselves into the besieged place. The army of Maximin was repulsed on repeated attacks, his machines

---

* The president de Montesquieu (in his dialogue between Sylla and Eucrates) expresses the sentiments of the dictator, in a spirited and even a sublime manner.

† Muratori (*Annali d'Italia*) thinks the melting of the snows suits better with the months of June or July, than with that of February. The opinion of a man who passed his life between the Alps and the Apennines, is undoubtedly of great weight; yet I observe, 1. That the long winter, of which Muratori takes advantage, is to be found only in the Latin version, and not in the Greek text of Herodian. 2. That the vicissitude of suns and rains to which the soldiers of Maximin were exposed, denotes the spring rather than the summer. We may observe likewise, that these several streams, as they melted into one, composed the Timavus, so poetically (in every sense of the word) described by Virgil. They are about twelve miles to the east of Aquileia.

destroyed by showers of artificial fire; and the generous enthusiasm of the Aquileians was exalted into a confidence of success, by the opinion, that Belenus, their tutelar deity, combated in person in the defence of his distressed worshippers.*

The Emperor Maximus, who had advanced as far as Ravenna, to secure that important place, and to hasten the military preparations, beheld the event of the war in the more faithful mirror of reason and policy. He was too sensible, that a single town could not resist the persevering efforts of a great army; and he dreaded lest the enemy, tired with the obstinate resistance of Aquileia, should on a sudden relinquish the fruitless siege, and march directly towards Rome. The fate of the empire and the cause of freedom must then be committed to the chance of a battle; and what arms could he oppose to the veteran legions of the Rhine and the Danube? Some troops newly levied among the generous but enervated youth of Italy; and a body of German auxiliaries, on whose firmness, in the hour of trial, it was dangerous to depend. In the midst of these just alarms, the stroke of domestic conspiracy punished the crimes of Maximin, and delivered Rome and the senate from the calamities that would surely have attended the victory of an enraged barbarian.

The people of Aquileia had scarcely experienced any of the common miseries of a siege, their magazines were plentifully supplied, and several fountains within the walls assured them of an inexhaustible resource of fresh water. The soldiers of Maximin were, on the contrary, exposed to the inclemency of the season, the contagion of disease, and the horrors of famine. The open country was ruined, the rivers filled with the slain, and polluted with blood. A spirit of despair and disaffection began to diffuse itself among the troops; and as they were cut off from all intelligence, they easily believed that the whole empire had embraced the cause of the senate, and that they were left as devoted victims to perish under the impregnable walls of Aquileia. The fierce temper of the tyrant was exasperated by disappointments, which he imputed to the cowardice of his army; and his wanton and ill-timed cruelty, instead of striking terror, inspired hatred and a just desire of revenge. A party of Praetorian Guards, who trembled for their wives and children in the camp of Alba, near Rome, executed the sentence of the senate. Maximin, abandoned by his guards, was (AD 238, April) slain in his tent, with his son (whom he

* The Celtic deity was supposed to be Apollo, and received under that name the thanks of the senate. A temple was likewise built to Venus the Bald, in honour of the women of Aquileia, who had given up their hair to make ropes for the military engines.

had associated to the honours of the purple), Anulinus the prefect, and the principal ministers of his tyranny. The sight of their heads, borne on the point of spears, convinced the citizens of Aquileia, that the siege was at an end; the gates of the city were thrown open, a liberal market was provided for the hungry troops of Maximin, and the whole army joined in solemn protestations of fidelity to the senate and the people of Rome, and to their lawful emperors Maximus and Balbinus. Such was the deserved fate of a brutal savage, destitute, as he has generally been represented, of every sentiment that distinguishes a civilised, or even a human being. The body was suited to the soul. The stature of Maximin exceeded the measure of eight feet, and circumstances almost incredible are related of his matchless strength and appetite.* Had he lived in a less enlightened age, tradition and poetry might well have described him as one of those monstrous giants, whose supernatural power was constantly exerted for the destruction of mankind.

It is easier to conceive than to describe the universal joy of the Roman world on the fall of the tyrant, the news of which is said to have been carried in four days from Aquileia to Rome. The return of Maximus was a triumphal procession, his colleague and young Gordian went out to meet him, and the three princes made their entry into the capital, attended by the ambassadors of almost all the cities of Italy, saluted with the splendid offerings of gratitude and superstition, and received with the unfeigned acclamations of the senate and people, who persuaded them-selves that a golden age would succeed to an age of iron. The conduct of the two emperors corresponded with these expectations. They adminis-tered justice in person; and the rigour of the one was tempered by the other's clemency. The oppressive taxes with which Maximin had loaded the rights of inheritance and succession were repealed, or at least moderated. Discipline was revived, and with the advice of the senate many wise laws were enacted by their imperial ministers, who endea-voured to restore a civil constitution on the ruins of military tyranny. 'What reward may we expect for delivering Rome from a monster?' was the question asked by Maximus, in a moment of freedom and confi-dence. Balbinus answered it without hesitation. 'The love of the senate,

---

* Eight Roman feet and one third, which are equal to above eight English feet, as the two measures are to each other in the proportion of 967 to 1000. See Greave's discourse on the Roman foot. We are told that Maximin could drink in a day an amphora (or about seven gallons of wine), and eat thirty or forty pounds of meat. He could move a loaded waggon, break a horse's leg with his fist, crumble stones in his hand, and tear up small trees by the roots. See his life in the Augustan History.

of the people, and of all mankind.' 'Alas!' replied his more penetrating colleague, 'Alas! I dread the hatred of the soldiers, and the fatal effects of their resentment.' His apprehensions were but too well justified by the event.

Whilst Maximus was preparing to defend Italy against the common foe, Balbinus, who remained at Rome, had been engaged in scenes of blood and intestine discord. Distrust and jealousy reigned in the senate; and even in the temples where they assembled, every senator carried either open or concealed arms. In the midst of their deliberations, two veterans of the guards, actuated either by curiosity or a sinister motive, audaciously thrust themselves into the house, and advanced by degrees beyond the altar of Victory. Gallicanus, a consular, and Maecenas, a Praetorian senator, viewed with indignation their insolent intrusion: drawing their daggers, they laid the spies, for such they deemed them, dead at the foot of the altar, and then advancing to the door of the senate, imprudently exhorted the multitude to massacre the Praetorians, as the secret adherents of the tyrant. Those who escaped the first fury of the tumult took refuge in the camp, which they defended with superior advantage against the reiterated attacks of the people, assisted by the numerous bands of gladiators, the property of opulent nobles. The civil war lasted many days, with infinite loss and confusion on both sides. When the pipes were broken that supplied the camp with water, the Praetorians were reduced to intolerable distress; but in their turn they made desperate sallies into the city, set fire to a great number of houses, and filled the street with the blood of the inhabitants. The emperor Balbinus attempted, by ineffectual edicts and precarious truces, to reconcile the factions at Rome. But their animosity, though smothered for a while, burnt with redoubled violence. The soldiers, detesting the senate and the people, despised the weakness of a prince who wanted either the spirit or the power to command the obedience of his subjects.

After the tyrant's death, his formidable army had acknowledged, from necessity rather than from choice, the authority of Maximus, who transported himself without delay to the camp before Aquileia. As soon as he had received their oath of fidelity, he addressed them in terms full of mildness and moderation; lamented, rather than arraigned, the wild disorders of the times, and assured the soldiers, that of all their past conduct, the senate would remember only their generous desertion of the tyrant, and their voluntary return to their duty. Maximus enforced his exhortations by a liberal donative, purified the camp by a solemn sacrifice of expiation, and then dismissed the legions to their several provinces, impressed, as he hoped, with a lively sense of gratitude and obedience. But nothing could reconcile the haughty spirit of the Praetor- ians. They attended the emperors on the memorable day of their public entry into Rome; but amidst the general acclamations, the sullen dejected countenance of the guards sufficiently declared that they consi- dered themselves as the object, rather than the partners, of the triumph. When the whole body was united in their camp, those who had served under Maximin, and those who had remained at Rome, insensibly communicated to each other their complaints and apprehensions. The emperors chosen by the army had perished with ignominy; those elected by the senate were seated on the throne. The long discord between the civil and military powers was decided by a war, in which the former had obtained a complete victory. The soldiers must now learn a new doctrine of submission to the senate; and whatever clemency was affected by that politic assembly, they dreaded a slow revenge, coloured by the name of discipline, and justified by fair pretence of the public good. But their fate was still in their own hands; and if they had courage to despise the vain terrors of an impotent republic, it was easy to convince the world that those who were masters of the arms, were masters of the authority of the state.

When the senate elected two princes, it is probable that, besides the declared reason of providing for the various emergencies of peace and war, they were actuated by the secret desire of weakening by division the despotism of the supreme magistrate. Their policy was effectual, but it proved fatal both to their emperors and to themselves. The jealousy of power was soon exasperated by the difference of character. Maximus despised Balbinus as a luxurious noble, and was in his turn disdained by his colleague as an obscure soldier. Their silent discord was understood rather than seen; but the mutual consciousness prevented them from uniting in any vigorous measures of defence against their common enemies of the Praetorian camp. The whole city was (AD 238, 15 July) employed in the Capitoline games, and the emperors were left almost alone in the palace. On a sudden they were alarmed by the approach of a troop of desperate assassins. Ignorant of each other's situation or designs, for they already occupied very distant apartments, afraid to give or to receive assistance, they wasted the important moments in idle debates and fruitless recriminations. The arrival of the guards put an end to the vain strife. They seized on these emperors of the senate, for such they called them with malicious contempt, stripped them of their garments, and dragged them in insolent triumph through the streets of Rome, with a design of inflicting a slow and cruel death on those unfortunate princes. The fear of a rescue from the faithful Germans of the Imperial guards, shortened their tortures; and their bodies, mangled with a thousand wounds, were left exposed to the insults or to the pity of the populace.

In the space of a few months, six princes had been cut off by the sword. Gordian, who had already received the title of Caesar, was the only person that occurred to the soldiers as proper to fill the vacant throne. They carried him to the camp, and unanimously saluted him Augustus and Emperor. His name was dear to the senate and people; his tender age promised a long impunity of military licence; and the submission of Rome and the provinces to the choice of the Praetorian Guards, saved the republic, at the expense indeed of its freedom and dignity, from the horrors of a new civil war in the heart of the capital.

As the third Gordian was only nineteen years of age at the time of his death, the history of his life, were it known to us with greater accuracy than it really is, would contain little more than the account of his education, and the conduct of the ministers, who by turns abused or guided the simplicity of his inexperienced youth. Immediately after his accession, he fell into the hands of his mother's eunuchs, that pernicious vermin of the East, who, since the days of Elagabalus, had infested the Roman palace. By the artful conspiracy of these wretches, an impenetrable veil was drawn between an innocent prince and his oppressed subjects, the virtuous disposition of Gordian was deceived, and the honours of the empire sold without his knowledge, though in a very public manner, to the most worthless of mankind. We are ignorant by what fortunate accident the emperor escaped from this ignominious slavery, and devolved his confidence on a minister whose wise counsels had no object except the glory of his sovereign and the happiness of the people. It should seem that (AD 240) love and learning introduced Misitheus to the favour of Gordian. The young prince married the daughter of his master of rhetoric, and promoted his father-in-law to the first offices of the empire. Two admirable letters that passed between them are still extant. The minister, with the conscious dignity of virtue, congratulates Gordian that he is delivered from the tyranny of the eunuchs, and still more that he is sensible of his deliverance. The emperor acknowledges, with an amiable confusion, the errors of his past conduct; and laments, with singular propriety, the misfortune of a monarch, from whom a venal tribe of courtiers perpetually labour to conceal the truth.

The life of Misitheus had been spent in the profession of letters, not

of arms; yet such was the versatile genius of that great man, that, when
(AD 242) he was appointed Praetorian prefect, he discharged the military
duties of his place with vigour and ability. The Persians had invaded
Mesopotamia, and threatened Antioch. By the persuasion of his father-
in-law, the young emperor quitted the luxury of Rome, opened, for the
last time recorded in history, the temple of Janus, and marched in person
into the East. On his approach with a great army, the Persians withdrew
their garrisons from the cities which they had already taken, and retired
from the Euphrates to the Tigris. Gordian enjoyed the pleasure of
announcing to the senate the first success of his arms, which he ascribed
with a becoming modesty and gratitude to the wisdom of his father and
prefect. During the whole expedition, Misitheus watched over the safety
and discipline of the army; whilst he prevented their dangerous murmurs
by maintaining a regular plenty in the camp, and by establishing ample
magazines of vinegar, bacon, straw, barley, and wheat, in all the cities of
the frontier. But the prosperity of Gordian expired with Misitheus, who
died of a flux, not without very strong suspicions of poison. Philip, his
successor (AD 243) in the prefecture, was an Arab by birth, and
consequently in the earlier part of his life, a robber by profession. His rise
from so obscure a station to the first dignities of the empire, seems to prove
that he was a bold and able leader. But his boldness prompted him to
aspire to the throne, and his abilities were employed to supplant, not to
serve, his indulgent master. The minds of the soldiers were irritated by an
artificial scarcity, created by his contrivance in the camp; and the distress
of the army was attributed to the youth and incapacity of the prince. It is
not in our power to trace the successive steps of the secret conspiracy and
open sedition, which were at length fatal to Gordian. A sepulchral
monument was erected to his memory of the spot where (AD 244,
March) he was killed, near the conflux of the Euphrates with the little
river Aboras. The fortunate Philip, raised to the empire by the votes of
the soldiers, found a ready obedience from the senate and the provinces.

   We cannot forbear transcribing the ingenious, though somewhat
fanciful description, which a celebrated writer of our own times has
traced of the military government of the Roman Empire. 'What in that
age was called the Roman Empire, was only an irregular republic, not
unlike the Aristocracy* of Algiers,† where the militia, possessed of the

* Can the epithet of *Aristocracy* be applied, with any propriety, to the government of
Algiers? Every military government floats between the extremes of absolute monarchy
and wild democracy.
† The military republic of the Mamalukes in Egypt, would have afforded M. de

sovereignty, creates and deposes a magistrate, who is styled a Dey.
Perhaps, indeed, it may be laid down as a general rule, that a military
government is, in some respects, more republican than monarchical.
Nor can it be said that the soldiers only partook of the government by
their disobedience and rebellions. The speeches made to them by the
emperors, were they not at length of the same nature as those formerly
pronounced to the people by the consuls and the tribunes? And
although the armies had no regular place or forms of assembly; though
their debates were short, their action sudden, and their resolves seldom
the result of cool reflection, did they not dispose, with absolute sway, of
the public fortune? What was the emperor, except the minister of a
violent government elected for the private benefit of the soldiers?

'When the army had elected Philip, who was Praetorian prefect to the
third Gordian; the latter demanded that he might remain sole emperor;
he was unable to obtain it. He requested that the power might be equally
divided between them; the army would not listen to his speech. He
consented to be degraded to the rank of Caesar; the favour was refused
him. He desired, at least, he might be appointed Praetorian prefect; his
prayer was rejected. Finally, he pleaded for his life. The army, in these
several judgments, exercised the supreme magistracy.' According to the
historian, whose doubtful narrative the president de Montesquieu has
adopted, Philip, who, during the whole transaction, had preserved a
sullen silence, was inclined to spare the innocent life of his benefactor;
till, recollecting that his innocence might excite a dangerous compassion
in the Roman world, he commanded, without regard to his suppliant
cries, that he should be seized, stript, and led away to instant death. After
a moment's pause the inhuman sentence was executed.

On his return from the East to Rome, Philip, desirous of obliterating
the memory of his crimes, and of captivating the affections of the people,
solemnised (AD 248, 21 April) the Secular games with infinite pomp
and magnificence. Since their institution or revival by Augustus,* they
had been celebrated by Claudius, by Domitian, and by Severus, and
were now renewed the fifth time, on the accomplishment of the full
period of a thousand years from the foundation of Rome. Every

* The account of the last supposed celebration, though in an enlightened period of
history, was so very doubtful and obscure, that the alternative seems not doubtful.
When the popish jubilees, the copy of the secular games, were invented by Boniface
VIII, the crafty pope pretended that he only revived an ancient institution.

Montesquieu (*Considérations sur la grandeur et la décadence des Romains*, c. 16) a juster and
more noble parallel.

circumstance of the Secular games was skilfully adapted to inspire the superstitious mind with deep and solemn reverence. The long interval between them* exceeded the term of human life; and as none of the spectators had already seen them, none could flatter themselves with the expectation of beholding them a second time. The mystic sacrifices were performed, during three nights, on the banks of the Tiber; and the Campus Martius resounded with music and dances, and was illu-minated with innumerable lamps and torches. Slaves and strangers were excluded from any participation in these national ceremonies. A chorus of twenty-seven youths, and as many virgins, of noble families, and whose parents were both alive, implored the propitious gods in favour of the present, and for the hope of the rising generation; requesting, in religious hymns, that, according to the faith of their ancient oracles, they would still maintain the virtue, the felicity, and the empire of the Roman people. The magnificence of Philip's shows and entertainments dazzled the eyes of the multitude. The devout were employed in the rites of superstition, whilst the reflecting few revolved in their anxious minds the past history and the future fate of the empire.

Since Romulus, with a small band of shepherds and outlaws, fortified himself on the hills near the Tiber, ten centuries had already elapsed. During the first four ages, the Romans, in the laborious school of poverty, had acquired the virtues of war and government; by the vigorous exertion of those virtues, and by the assistance of fortune, they had obtained, in the course of the three succeeding centuries, an absolute empire over many countries of Europe, Asia, and Africa. The last three hundred years had been consumed in apparent prosperity and internal decline. The nation of soldiers, magistrates, and legislators, who com-posed the thirty-five tribes of the Roman people, was dissolved into the common mass of mankind and confounded with the millions of servile provincials, who had received the name without adopting the spirit of Romans. A mercenary army, levied among the subjects and barbarians of the frontier, was the only order of men who preserved and abused their independence. By their tumultuary election, a Syrian, a Goth, or an Arab, was exalted to the throne of Rome, and invested with despotic power over the conquests and over the country of the Scipios.

The limits of the Roman Empire still extended from the Western Ocean to the Tigris, and from Mount Atlas to the Rhine and the

---

* Either of a hundred, or a hundred and ten years. Varro and Livy adopted the former opinion, but the infallible authority of the Sibyl consecrated the latter. The emperors Claudius and Philip, however, did not treat the oracle with implicit respect.

Danube. To the undiscerning eye of the vulgar, Philip appeared a monarch no less powerful than Hadrian or Augustus had formerly been. The form was still the same, but the animating health and vigour were fled. The industry of the people was discouraged and exhausted by a long series of oppression. The discipline of the legions, which alone, after the extinction of every other virtue, had propped the greatness of the state, was corrupted by the ambition, or relaxed by the weakness, of the emperors. The strength of the frontiers, which had always consisted in arms rather than in fortifications, was insensibly undermined; and the fairest provinces were left exposed to the rapaciousness or ambition of the barbarians, who soon discovered the decline of the Roman Empire.

8

OF THE STATE OF PERSIA AFTER THE RESTORATION OF
THE MONARCHY BY ARTAXERXES

W HENEVER TACITUS INDULGES HIMSELF in those beautiful episodes, in which he relates some domestic trans-action of the Germans or of the Parthians, his principal object is to relieve the attention of the reader from a uniform scene of vice and mis-ery. From the reign of Augustus to the time of Alexander Severus, the enemies of Rome were in her bosom; the tyrants, and the soldiers; and her prosperity had a very distant and feeble interest in the revolutions that might happen beyond the Rhine and the Euphrates. But when the military order had levelled, in wild anarchy, the power of the prince, the laws of the senate, and even the discipline of the camp, the barbarians of the north and of the east, who had long hovered on the frontier, boldly attacked the provinces of a declining monarchy. Their vexatious inroads were changed into formidable irruptions, and, after a long vicissitude of mutual calamities, many tribes of the victorious invaders established themselves in the provinces of the Roman Empire. To obtain a clearer knowledge of these great events, we shall endeavour to form a previous idea of the character, forces, and designs of those nations who avenged the cause of Hannibal and Mithridates.

In the more early ages of the world, whilst the forest that covered Europe afforded a retreat to a few wandering savages, the inhabitants of Asia were already collected into populous cities, and reduced under extensive empires, the seat of the arts, of luxury, and of despotism. The Assyrians reigned over the East, till the sceptre of Ninus and Semiramis dropt from the hands of their enervated successors. The Medes and the Babylonians divided their power, and were themselves swallowed up in the monarchy of the Persians, whose arms could not be confined within the narrow limits of Asia. Followed, as it is said, by two millions of *men*, Xerxes, the descendant of Cyrus, invaded Greece. Thirty thousand *soldiers*, under the command of Alexander, the son of Philip, who was entrusted by the Greeks with their glory and revenge, were sufficient to subdue Persia. The princes of the house of Seleucus usurped and lost the Macedonian command over the East. About the same time that, by an

ignominious treaty, they resigned to the Romans the country on this side
Mount Taurus, they were driven by the Parthians, an obscure horde of
Scythian origin, from all the provinces of Upper Asia. The formidable
power of the Parthians, which spread from India to the frontiers of Syria,
was in its turn subverted by Ardshir, or Artaxerxes; the founder of a
new dynasty, which, under the name of Sassanides, governed Persia till
the invasion of the Arabs. This great revolution, whose fatal influence
was soon experienced by the Romans, happened in the fourth year of
Alexander Severus, two hundred and twenty-six years after the Christian era.

Artaxerxes had served with great reputation in the armies of Artaban, the last king of the Parthians, and it appears that he was driven into
exile and rebellion by royal ingratitude, the customary reward for
superior merit. His birth was obscure, and the obscurity equally gave
room to the aspersions of his enemies, and the flattery of his adherents. If
we credit the scandal of the former, Artaxerxes sprang from the
illegitimate commerce of a tanner's wife with a common soldier. The
latter represent him as descended from a branch of the ancient kings of
Persia, though time and misfortune had gradually reduced his ancestors
to the humble station of private citizens. As the lineal heir of the
monarchy, he asserted his right to the throne, and challenged the noble
task of delivering the Persians from the oppression under which they
groaned above five centuries since the death of Darius. The Parthians
were defeated in three great battles. In the last of these their king Artaban
was slain, and the spirit of the nation was for ever broken. The authority
of Artaxerxes was solemnly acknowledged in a great assembly held at
Balch in Khorasan. Two younger branches of the royal house of
Arsaces were confounded among the prostrate satraps. A third, more
mindful of ancient grandeur than of present necessity, attempted to retire,
with a numerous train of vassals, towards their kinsman, the king of
Armenia; but this little army of deserters was intercepted, and cut off, by
the vigilance of the conqueror, who boldly assumed the double diadem,
and the title of King of Kings, which had been enjoyed by his
predecessor. But these pompous titles, instead of gratifying the vanity of
the Persian, served only to admonish him of his duty, and to inflame in
his soul the ambition of restoring, in their full splendour, the religion and
empire of Cyrus.

I. During the long servitude of Persia under the Macedonian and the
Parthian yoke, the nations of Europe and Asia had mutually adopted
and corrupted each other's superstitions. The Arsacides, indeed, prac-

The Aqueduct of Nero leading to the Palatine; a branch of the Aqua Claudia

The Temple of Saturn with the Arch of Septimus Severus in the background

tised the worship of the Magi; but they disgraced and polluted it with a various mixture of foreign idolatry. The memory of Zoroaster, the ancient prophet and philosopher of the Persians, was still revered in the East; but the obsolete and mysterious language in which the Zendavesta was composed, opened a field of dispute to seventy sects, who variously explained the fundamental doctrines of their religion, and were all indifferently derided by a crowd of infidels, who rejected the divine mission and miracles of the Prophet. To suppress the idolaters, reunite the schismatics, and confute the unbelievers, by the infallible decision of a general council, the pious Artaxerxes summoned the Magi from all parts of his dominions. These priests, who had so long sighed in contempt and obscurity, obeyed the welcome summons; and on the appointed day appeared, to the number of about eighty thousand. But as the debates of so tumultuous an assembly could not have been directed by the authority of reason, or influenced by the art of policy, the Persian synod was reduced, by successive operations, to forty thousand, to four thousand, to four hundred, to forty, and at last to seven Magi, the most respected for their learning and piety. One of these, Erdaviraph, a young but holy prelate, received from the hands of his brethren three cups of soporiferous wine. He drank them off, and instantly fell into a long and profound sleep. As soon as he waked, he related to the king and to the believing multitude his journey to Heaven, and his intimate conferences with the Deity. Every doubt was silenced by this supernatural evidence; and the articles of the faith of Zoroaster were fixed with equal authority and precision. A short delineation of that celebrated system will be found useful, not only to display the character of the Persian nation, but to illustrate many of their most important transactions, both in peace and war, with the Roman Empire.*

The great and fundamental article of the system was the celebrated doctrine of the two principles; a bold and injudicious attempt of Eastern philosophy to reconcile the existence of moral and physical evil with the attributes of a beneficent Creator and Governor of the world. The first and original Being, in whom, or by whom, the universe exists, is denominated in the writings of Zoroaster, *Time without bounds;* but it must be confessed that this infinite substance seems rather a metaphysical abstraction

---

* I have principally drawn this account from the Zendavesta of M. d'Anquetil, and the Sadder, subjoined to Dr Hyde's treatise. It must, however, be confessed, that the studied obscurity of a prophet, the figurative style of the East, and the deceitful medium of a French or Latin version, may have betrayed us into error and heresy in this abridgment of Persian theology.

of the mind, than a real object endowed with selfconsciousness, or possessed of moral perfections. From either the blind or the intelligent operation of this infinite Time, which bears but too near an affinity with the chaos of the Greeks, the two secondary but active principles of the universe were from all eternity produced, Ormusd and Ahriman, each of them possessed of the powers of creation, but each disposed, by his invariable nature, to exercise them with different designs. The principle of good is eternally absorbed in light; the principle of evil eternally buried in darkness. The wise benevolence of Ormusd formed man capable of virtue, and abundantly provided his fair habitation with the materials of happiness. By his vigilant providence, the motion of the planets, the order of the seasons, and the temperate mixture of the elements, are preserved. But the malice of Ahriman has long since pierced *Ormusd's egg;* or, in other words, has violated the harmony of his works. Since that fatal irruption, the most minute articles of good and evil are intimately intermingled and agitated together; the rankest poisons spring up amidst the most salutary plants; deluges, earthquakes, and conflagrations, attest the conflict of Nature, and the little world of man is perpetually shaken by vice and misfortune. Whilst the rest of human kind are led away captives in the chains of their infernal enemy, the faithful Persian alone reserves his religious adoration for his friend and protector Ormusd, and fights under his banner of light, in the full confidence that he shall, in the last day, share the glory of his triumph. At that decisive period, the enlightened wisdom of goodness will render the power of Ormusd superior to the furious malice of his rival. Ahriman and his followers, disarmed and subdued, will sink into their native darkness; and virtue will maintain the eternal peace and harmony of the universe.

The theology of Zoroaster was darkly comprehended by foreigners, and even by the far greater number of his disciples; but the most careless observers were struck with the philosophic simplicity of the Persian worship. 'That people,' says Herodotus, 'rejects the use of temples, of altars, and of statues, and smiles at the folly of those nations who imagine that the gods are sprung from, or bear any affinity with, the human nature. The tops of the highest mountains are the places chosen for sacrifices. Hymns and prayers are the principal worship; the Supreme God who fills the wide circle of Heaven is the object to whom they are addressed.' Yet, at the same time, in the true spirit of a polytheist, he accuses them of adoring Earth, Water, Fire, the Winds, and the Sun and Moon. But the Persians of every age have denied the charge, and explained the equivocal conduct, which might appear to give a colour to it. The elements, and more particularly Fire, Light, and the Sun, whom they called Mithra, were the objects of their religious reverence, because they considered them as the purest symbols, the noblest productions, and the most powerful agents of the Divine Power and Nature.

Every mode of religion, to make a deep and lasting impression on the human mind, must exercise our obedience, by enjoining practices of devotion; and must acquire our esteem, by inculcating moral duties analogous to the dictates of our own hearts. The religion of Zoroaster was abundantly provided with the former, and possessed a sufficient portion of the latter. At the age of puberty, the faithful Persian was invested with a mysterious girdle, the badge of the divine protection, and from that moment all the actions of his life, even the most indifferent, or the most necessary, were sanctified by their peculiar prayers, ejaculations, or genuflexions; the omission of which, under any circumstances, was a grievous sin, not inferior in guilt to the violation of the moral duties. The moral duties, however, of justice, mercy, liberality, etc., were in their turn required of the disciple of Zoroaster, who wished to escape the persecution of Ahriman, and to live with Ormusd in a blissful eternity, where the degree of felicity will be exactly proportioned to the degree of virtue and piety.*

But there are some remarkable instances, in which Zoroaster lays aside the prophet, assumes the legislator, and discovers a liberal concern for private and public happiness, seldom to be found among the grovelling or visionary schemes of superstition. Fasting and celibacy, the common means of purchasing the Divine favour, he condemns with abhorrence, as a criminal rejection of the best gifts of Providence. The saint, in the Magian religion, is obliged to beget children, to plant useful trees, to destroy noxious animals, to convey water to the dry lands of Persia, and to work out his salvation by pursuing all the labour of agriculture. We may quote from the Zendavesta a wise and benevolent maxim, which compensates for many an absurdity. 'He who sows the ground with care and diligence, acquires a greater stock of religious merit, than he could gain by the repetition of ten thousand prayers.' In the spring of every year a festival was celebrated, destined to represent the primitive equality, and the present connection, of mankind. The stately kings of Persia, exchanging their vain pomp for more genuine greatness,

---

* See the Sadder, the smallest part of which consists of moral precepts. The ceremonies enjoined are infinite and trifling. Fifteen genuflexions, prayers, etc., were required whenever the devout Persian cut his nails or made water; or as often as he put on the sacred girdle.

freely mingled with the humblest but most useful of their subjects. On that day the husbandmen were admitted, without distinction, to the table of the king, and his satraps. The monarch accepted their petition, inquired into their grievances, and conversed with them on the most equal terms. 'From your labours,' was he accustomed to say (and to say with truth, if not with sincerity), 'from your labours, we receive our subsistence; you derive your tranquillity from our vigilance; since, therefore, we are mutually necessary to each other, let us live together like brothers in concord and love.' Such a festival must indeed have degenerated, in a wealthy and despotic empire, into a theatrical represen‑tation; but it was at least a comedy well worthy of a royal audience, and which might sometimes imprint a salutary lesson on the mind of a young prince.

Had Zoroaster, in all his institutions, invariably supported this exalted character, his name would deserve a place with those of Numa and Confucius, and his system would be justly entitled to all the applause which it has pleased some of our divines, and even some of our philosophers, to bestow on it. But in that motley composition, dictated by reason and passion, by enthusiasm and by selfish motives, some useful and sublime truths were disgraced by a mixture of the most abject and dangerous superstition. The Magi, or sacerdotal order, were extremely numerous, since, as we have already seen, fourscore thousand of them were convened in a general council. Their forces were multiplied by discipline. A regular hierarchy was diffused through all the provinces of Persia; and the Archimagus, who resided at Balch, was respected as the visible head of the church, and the lawful successor of Zoroaster. The property of the Magi was very considerable. Besides the less invidious possession of a large tract of the most fertile lands of Media, they levied a general tax on the fortunes and the industry of the Persians. 'Though your good works,' says the interested prophet, 'exceed in number the leaves of the trees, the drops of rain, the stars in the heaven, or the sands on the sea‑shore, they will all be unprofitable to you, unless they are accepted by the *destour*, or priest. To obtain the acceptation of this guide to salvation, you must faithfully pay him *tithes* of all you possess, of your goods, of your lands, and of your money. If the destour be satisfied, your soul will escape hell tortures; you will secure praise in this world and happiness in the next. For the destours are the teachers of religion; they know all things, and they deliver all men.'

These convenient maxims of reverence and implicit faith were doubtless imprinted with care on the tender minds of youth; since the

Magi were the masters of education in Persia, and to their hands the children even of the royal family were entrusted. The Persian priests, who were of a speculative genius, preserved and investigated the secrets of Oriental philosophy; and acquired, either by superior knowledge or superior art, the reputation of being well versed in some occult sciences, which have derived their appellation from the Magi. Those of more active dispositions mixed with the world in courts and cities; and it is observed, that the administration of Artaxerxes was in a great measure directed by the counsels of the sacerdotal order, whose dignity, either from policy or devotion, that prince restored to its ancient splendour.

The first counsel of the Magi was agreeable to the unsociable genius of their faith,* to the practice of ancient kings, and even to the example of their legislator, who had fallen a victim to a religious war, excited by his own intolerant zeal. By an edict of Artaxerxes, the exercise of every worship, except that of Zoroaster, was severely prohibited. The temples of the Parthians, and the statues of their deified monarchs, were thrown down with ignominy. The sword of Aristotle (such was the name given by the Orientals to the polytheism and philosophy of the Greeks) was easily broken; the flames of persecution soon reached the more stubborn Jews and Christians; nor did they spare the heretics of their own nation and religion. The majesty of Ormusd, who was jealous of a rival, was seconded by the despotism of Artaxerxes, who could not suffer a rebel; and the schismatics within his vast empire were soon reduced to the inconsiderable number of eighty thousand. This spirit of persecution reflects dishonour on the religion of Zoroaster; but as it was not productive of any civil commotion, it served to strengthen the new monarchy, by uniting all the various inhabitants of Persia in the bands of religious zeal.

II. Artaxerxes, by his valour and conduct, had wrested the sceptre of the East from the ancient royal family of Parthia. There still remained the more difficult task of establishing, throughout the vast extent of Persia, a uniform and vigorous administration. The weak indulgence of the Arsacides had resigned to their sons and brothers the principal pro- vinces, and the greatest offices of the kingdom, in the nature of hereditary possessions. The *vitaxae*, or eighteen most powerful satraps, were permit- ted to assume the regal title; and the vain pride of the monarch was delighted with a nominal dominion over so many vassal kings. Even tribes of barbarians in their mountains, and the Greek cities of Upper

* Mr Hume, in the *Natural History of Religion*, remarks that the most refined and philosophic sects are the most intolerant.

Asia, within their walls, scarcely acknowledged, or seldom obeyed, any superior; and the Parthian empire exhibited, under other names, a lively image of the feudal system which has since prevailed in Europe. But the active victor, at the head of a numerous and disciplined army, visited in person every province of Persia. The defeat of the boldest rebels, and the reduction of the strongest fortifications, diffused the terror of his arms, and prepared the way for the peaceful reception of his authority. An obstinate resistance was fatal to the chiefs; but their followers were treated with lenity.* A cheerful submission was rewarded with honours and riches; but the prudent Artaxerxes, suffering no person except himself to assume the title of king, abolished every intermediate power between the throne and the people. His kingdom, nearly equal in extent to modern Persia, was, on every side, bounded by the sea, or by great rivers; by the Euphrates, the Tigris, the Araxes, the Oxus, and the Indus, by the Caspian Sea, and the Gulf of Persia. That country was computed to contain, in the last century, five hundred and fifty-four cities, sixty thousand villages, and about forty millions of souls. If we compare the administration of the house of Sassan with that of the house of Sefi, the political influence of the Magian with that of the Mahometan religion, we shall probably infer, that the kingdom of Artaxerxes contained at least as great a number of cities, villages, and inhabitants. But it must likewise be confessed, that in every age the want of harbours on the sea-coast, and the scarcity of fresh water in the inland provinces, have been very unfavourable to the commerce and agriculture of the Persians; who, in the calculation of their numbers, seem to have indulged one of the meanest, though most common, articles of national vanity.

As soon as the ambitious mind of Artaxerxes had triumphed over the resistance of his vassals, he began to threaten the neighbouring states, who, during the long slumber of his predecessors, had insulted Persia with impunity. He obtained some easy victories over the wild Scythians and the effeminate Indians; but the Romans were an enemy who, by their past injuries and present power, deserved the utmost efforts of his arms. A forty years' tranquillity, the fruit of valour and moderation, had succeeded the victories of Trajan. During the period that elapsed from the accession of Marcus to the reign of Alexander, the Roman and the Parthian empires were twice engaged in war; and although the whole

* The princes of Segestan defended their independence during many years. As romances generally transport to an ancient period the events of their own time, it is not impossible that the fabulous exploits of Rustan prince of Segestan may have been grafted on this real history.

strength of the Arsacides contended with a part only of the forces of Rome, the event was most commonly in favour of the latter. Macrinus, indeed, prompted by his precarious situation and pusillanimous temper, purchased a peace at the expense of near two millions of our money; but the generals of Marcus, the emperor Severus, and his son, erected many trophies in Armenia, Mesopotamia, and Assyria. Among their exploits, the imperfect relation of which would have unseasonably interrupted the more important series of domestic revolutions, we shall only mention the repeated calamities of the two great cities of Seleucia and Ctesiphon.

Seleucia, on the western bank of the Tigris, about forty-five miles to the north of ancient Babylon, was the capital of the Macedonian conquests in Upper Asia. Many ages after the fall of their empire, Seleucia retained the genuine characters of a Grecian colony, arts, military virtue, and the love of freedom. The independent republic was governed by a senate of three hundred nobles; the people consisted of six hundred thousand citizens; the walls were strong, and as long as concord prevailed among the several orders of the state, they viewed with contempt the power of the Parthian: but the madness of faction was sometimes provoked to implore the dangerous aid of the common enemy, who was posted almost at the gates of the colony. The Parthian monarchs, like the Mogul sovereigns of Hindostan, delighted in the pastoral life of their Scythian ancestor; and the Imperial camp was frequently pitched in the plain of Ctesiphon, on the eastern bank of the Tigris, at the distance of only three miles from Seleucia. The innumer-able attendants on luxury and despotism resorted to the court, and the little village of Ctesiphon insensibly swelled into a great city. Under the reign of Marcus, the Roman generals (AD 165) penetrated as far as Ctesiphon and Seleucia. They were received as friends by the Greek colony; they attacked as enemies the seat of the Parthian kings; yet both cities experienced the same treatment. The sack and conflagration of Seleucia, with the massacre of three hundred thousand of the inhabi-tants, tarnished the glory of the Roman triumph. Seleucia, already exhausted by the neighbourhood of a too powerful rival, sunk under the fatal blow; but Ctesiphon (AD 198), in about thirty-three years, had sufficiently recovered its strength to maintain an obstinate siege against the emperor Severus. The city was, however, taken by assault; the king, who defended it in person, escaped with precipitation; an hundred thousand captives, and a rich booty, rewarded the fatigues of the Roman soldiers. Notwithstanding these misfortunes, Ctesiphon succeeded to

Babylon and to Seleucia, as one of the great capitals of the East. In summer, the monarch of Persia enjoyed at Ecbatana the cool breezes of the mountains of Media; but the mildness of the climate engaged him to prefer Ctesiphon for his winter residence.

From these successful inroads, the Romans derived no real or lasting benefit; nor did they attempt to preserve such distant conquests, separated from the provinces of the empire by a large tract of intermediate desert. The reduction of the kingdom of Osrhoene, was an acquisition of less splendour indeed, but of a far more solid advantage. That little state occupied the northern and most fertile part of Mesopotamia, between the Euphrates and the Tigris. Edessa, its capital, was situated about twenty miles beyond the former of those rivers; and the inhabitants, since the time of Alexander, were a mixed race of Greeks, Arabs, Syrians, and Armenians. The feeble sovereigns of Osrhoene, placed on the dangerous verge of two contending empires, were attached from inclination to the Parthian cause; but the superior power of Rome exacted from them a reluctant homage, which is still attested by their medals. After the conclusion of the Parthian war under Marcus, it was judged prudent to secure some substantial pledges of their doubtful fidelity. Forts were constructed in several parts of the country, and a Roman garrison was fixed in the strong town of Nisibis. During the troubles that followed the death of Commodus, the princes of Osrhoene attempted to shake off the yoke; but the stern policy of Severus confirmed their dependence, and the perfidy of Caracalla completed the easy conquest. Abgarus, the last king of Edessa, was (AD 216) sent in chains to Rome, his dominions reduced into a province, and his capital dignified with the rank of colony; and thus the Romans, about ten years before the fall of the Parthian monarchy, obtained a firm and permanent establishment beyond the Euphrates.

Prudence as well as glory might have justified a war on the side of Artaxerxes, had his views been confined to the defence or the acquisition of a useful frontier. But the ambitious Persian openly avowed a far more extensive design of conquest; and (AD 230) he thought himself able to support his lofty pretensions by the arms of reason as well as by those of power. Cyrus, he alleged, had first subdued, and his successors had for a long time possessed, the whole extent of Asia, as far as the Propontis and the Aegean sea; the provinces of Caria and Ionia, under their empire, had been governed by Persian satraps, and all Egypt, to the confines of Ethiopia, had acknowledged their sovereignty. Their right had been suspended, but not destroyed, by a long usurpation; and as soon as he received the Persian diadem, which birth and successful valour had placed upon his head, the first great duty of his station called upon him to restore the ancient limits and splendour of the monarchy. The Great King, therefore (such was the haughty style of his embassies to the emperor Alexander), commanded the Romans instantly to depart from all the provinces of his ancestors, and, yielding to the Persians the empire of Asia, to content themselves with the undisturbed possession of Europe. This haughty mandate was delivered by four hundred of the tallest and most beautiful of the Persians; who, by their fine horses, splendid arms, and rich apparel, displayed the pride and greatness of their master. Such an embassy was much less an offer of negotiation than a declaration of war. Both Alexander Severus and Artaxerxes, collecting the military force of the Roman and Persian monarchies, resolved in this important contest to lead their armies in person.

If we credit what should seem the most authentic of all records, an oration, still extant, and delivered by the emperor himself to the senate, we must allow that the victory of Alexander Severus was not inferior to any of those formerly obtained over the Persians by the son of Philip. The army of the Great King consisted of one hundred and twenty thousand horse, clothed in complete armour of steel; of seven hundred elephants, with towers filled with archers on their backs; and of eighteen hundred chariots, armed with scythes. This formidable host, the like of which is not to be found in eastern history, and has scarcely been imagined in eastern romance,* was (AD 233) discomfited in a great battle, in which the Roman Alexander approved himself an intrepid soldier and a skilful general. The Great King fled before his valour; an

* There were two hundred scythed chariots at the battle of Arbela, in the host of Darius. In the vast army of Tigranes, which was vanquished by Lucullus, seventeen thousand horse only were completely armed. Antiochus brought fiftyfour elephants into the field against the Romans: by his frequent wars and negotiations with the princes of India, he had once collected an hundred and fifty of those great animals; but it may be questioned whether the most powerful monarch of Hindostan ever formed a line of battle of seven hundred elephants. Instead of three or four thousand elephants, which the Great Mogul was supposed to possess, Tavernier (*Voyages*) discovered, by a more accurate inquiry, that he had only five hundred for his baggage, and eighty or ninety for the service of war. The Greeks have varied with regard to the number which Porus brought into the field: but Quintus Curtius, in this instance judicious and moderate, is contented with eightyfive elephants, distinguished by their size and strength. In Siam, where these animals are the most numerous and the most esteemed, eighteen elephants are allowed as a sufficient proportion for each of the nine brigades into which a just army is divided. The whole number, of one hundred and sixtytwo elephants of war, may sometimes be doubled.

immense booty, and the conquest of Mesopotamia, were the immediate fruits of this signal victory. Such are the circumstances of this osten-tatious and improbable relation, dictated, as it too plainly appears, by the vanity of the monarch, adorned by the unblushing servility of his flatterers, and received without contradiction by a distant and obse-quious senate. Far from being inclined to believe that the arms of Alexander obtained any memorable advantage over the Persians, we are induced to suspect that all this blaze of imaginary glory was designed to conceal some real disgrace.

Our suspicions are confirmed by the authority of a contemporary historian, who mentions the virtues of Alexander with respect, and his faults with candour. He describes the judicious plan which had been formed for the conduct of the war. Three Roman armies were destined to invade Persia at the same time, and by different roads. But the operations of the campaign, though wisely concerted, were not executed either with ability or success. The first of these armies, as soon as it had entered the marshy plains of Babylon, towards the artificial conflux of the Euphrates and the Tigris, was encompassed by the superior numbers, and des-troyed by the arrows, of the enemy. The alliance of Chosroes, king of Armenia, and the long tract of mountainous country, in which the Persian cavalry was of little service, opened a secure entrance into the heart of Media to the second of the Roman armies. These brave troops laid waste the adjacent provinces, and by several successful actions against Artaxerxes, gave a faint colour to the emperor's vanity. But the retreat of this victorious army was imprudent, or at least unfortunate. In repassing the mountains great numbers of soldiers perished by the badness of the roads, and the severity of the winter season. It had been resolved, that whilst these two great detachments penetrated into the opposite extremes of the Persian dominions, the main body, under the command of Alexander himself, should support their attack by invad-ing the centre of the kingdom. But the inexperienced youth, influenced by his mother's counsels, and perhaps by his own fears, deserted the bravest troops and the fairest prospect of victory; and after consuming in Mesopotamia an inactive, and inglorious summer, he led back to Antioch an army diminished by sickness, and provoked by disappoint-ment. The behaviour of Artaxerxes had been very different. Flying with rapidity from the hills of Media to the marshes of the Euphrates, he had everywhere opposed the invaders in person; and in either fortune had united with the ablest conduct the most undaunted resolution. But in several obstinate engagements against the veteran legions of Rome, the

Persian monarch had lost the flower of his troops. Even his victories had weakened his power. The favourable opportunities of the absence of Alexander, and of the confusions that followed that emperor's death, presented themselves in vain to his ambition. Instead of expelling the Romans, as he pretended, from the continent of Asia, he found himself unable to wrest from their hands the little province of Mesopotamia.

The reign of Artaxerxes, which from the last defeat of the Parthians (AD 240) lasted only fourteen years, forms a memorable era in the history of the East, and even in that of Rome. His character seems to have been marked by those bold and commanding features that generally dis⁄ tinguished the princes who conquer, from those who inherit, an empire. Till the last period of the Persian monarchy his code of laws was respected as the ground⁄work of their civil and religious policy. Several of his sayings are preserved. One of them in particular discovers a deep insight into the constitution of government. 'The authority of the prince,' said Artaxerxes, 'must be defended by a military force; that force can only be maintained by taxes; all taxes must, at last, fall upon agriculture; and agriculture can never flourish except under the protec⁄ tion of justice and moderation.'* Artaxerxes bequeathed his new empire, and his ambitious designs against the Romans, to Sapor, a son not unworthy of his great father; but those designs were too extensive for the power of Persia, and served only to involve both nations in a long series of destructive wars and reciprocal calamities.

The Persians, long since civilised and corrupted, were very far from possessing the martial independence and the intrepid hardness, both of mind and body, which have rendered the northern barbarians masters of the world. The science of war, that constituted the more rational force of Greece and Rome, as it now does of Europe, never made any considerable progress in the East. Those disciplined evolutions which harmonise and animate a confused multitude were unknown to the Persians. They were equally unskilled in the arts of constructing, besieging, or defending regular fortifications. They trusted more to their courage than to their discipline. The infantry was a half⁄armed spiritless crowd of peasants, levied in haste by the allurements of plunder, and as easily dispersed by a victory as by a defeat. The monarch and his nobles transported into the camp the pride and luxury of the seraglio. Their military operations were impeded by a useless train of women, eunuchs,

* D'Herbelot, *Bibliothèque orientale,* au mot *Ardshir.* We may observe, that after an ancient period of fables, and a long interval of darkness, the modern histories of Persia begin to assume an air of truth with the dynasty of the Sassanides.

horses, and camels, and in the midst of a successful campaign the Persian host was often separated or destroyed by an unexpected famine.

But the nobles of Persia, in the bosom of luxury and despotism, preserved a strong sense of personal gallantry and national honour. From the age of seven years they were taught to speak truth, to shoot with the bow, and to ride; and it was universally confessed, that in the two last of these arts they had made a more than common proficiency.* The most distinguished youth were educated under the monarch's eye, practised their exercises in the gate of his palace, and were severely trained up to the habits of temperance and obedience in their long and laborious parties of hunting. In every province the satrap maintained a like school of military virtue. The Persian nobles (so natural is the idea of feudal tenures) received from the king's bounty lands and houses, on the condition of their service in war. They were ready on the first summons to mount on horseback, with a martial and splendid train of followers, and to join the numerous bodies of guards, who were carefully selected from amongst the most robust slaves, and the bravest adventurers of Asia. These armies, both of light and of heavy cavalry, equally formidable by the impetuosity of their charge, and the rapidity of their motions, threatened, as an impending cloud, the eastern provinces of the declining empire of Rome.

* The Persians are still the most skilful horsemen, and their horses the finest, in the East.

THE STATE OF GERMANY TILL THE INVASION OF THE BARBARIANS, IN THE TIME OF THE EMPEROR DECIUS

THE GOVERNMENT AND RELIGION OF Persia have deserved some notice from their connection with the decline and fall of the Roman Empire. We shall occasionally mention the Scythian or Sarmatian tribes, which, with their arms and horses, their flocks and herds, their wives and families, wandered over the immense plains which spread themselves from the Caspian Sea to the Vistula, from the confines of Persia to those of Germany. But the warlike Germans, who first resisted, then invaded, and at length overturned, the western monarchy of Rome, will occupy a much more important place in this history, and possess a stronger, and, if we may use the expression, a more domestic, claim to our attention and regard. The most civilised nations of modern Europe issued from the woods of Germany, and in the rude institutions of those barbarians we may still distinguish the original principles of our present laws and manners. In their primitive state of simplicity and independence the Germans were surveyed by the discerning eye, and delineated by the masterly pencil, of Tacitus, the first of historians who applied the science of philosophy to the study of facts. The expressive conciseness of his descriptions has deserved to exercise the diligence of innumerable antiquarians, and to excite the genius and penetration of the philosophic historians of our own times. The subject, however various and important, has already been so frequently, so ably, and so successfully discussed, that it is now grown familiar to the reader, and difficult to the writer. We shall therefore content ourselves with observing, and indeed with repeating, some of the most important circumstances of climate, of manners, and of institutions, which ren-dered the wild barbarians of Germany such formidable enemies to the Roman power.

Ancient Germany, excluding from its independent limits the prov-ince westward of the Rhine, which had submitted to the Roman yoke, extended itself over a third part of Europe. Almost the whole of modern Germany, Denmark, Norway, Sweden, Finland, Livonia, Prussia, and the greater part of Poland, were peopled by the various tribes of one great nation, whose complexion, manners, and language denoted a common origin and preserved a striking resemblance. On the west, ancient Germany was divided by the Rhine from the Gallic, and on the south by the Danube from the Illyrian, provinces of the empire. A ridge of hills, rising from the Danube, and called the Carpathian mountains, covered Germany on the side of Dacia or Hungary. The eastern frontier was faintly marked by the mutual fears of the Germans and the Sarmatians, and was often confounded by the mixture of warring and confederating tribes of the two nations. In the remote darkness of the north, the ancients imperfectly descried a frozen ocean that lay beyond the Baltic Sea, and beyond the Peninsula, or islands,* of Scandinavia.

Some ingenious writers have suspected that Europe was much colder formerly than it is at present; the most ancient descriptions of the climate of Germany tend exceedingly to confirm their theory. The general complaints of intense frost, and eternal winter, are perhaps little to be regarded, since we have no method of reducing to the accurate standard of the thermometer the feelings or the expressions of an orator, born in the happier regions of Greece or Asia. But I shall select two remarkable circumstances of a less equivocal nature. 1. The great rivers which covered the Roman provinces, the Rhine and the Danube, were frequently frozen over, and capable of supporting the most enormous weights. The barbarians, who often chose that severe season for their inroads, transported, without apprehension or danger, their numerous armies, their cavalry, and their heavy waggons, over a vast and solid bridge of ice. Modern ages have not presented an instance of a like phenomenon. 2. The reindeer, that useful animal, from whom the savage of the North derives the best comforts of his dreary life, is of a constitution that supports, and even requires, the most intense cold. He is found on the rock of Spitzberg, within ten degrees of the Pole; he seems to delight in the snows of Lapland and Siberia; but at present he cannot subsist, much less multiply, in any country to the south of the Baltic. In the time of Caesar, the reindeer, as well as the elk and the wild bull, was a native of the Hercynian forest, which then overshadowed a great part of

* The modern philosophers of Sweden seem agreed that the waters of the Baltic gradually sink in a regular proportion, which they have ventured to estimate at half an inch every year. Twenty centuries ago, the flat country of Scandinavia must have been covered by the sea; while the high lands rose above the waters, as so many islands of various forms and dimensions. Such indeed is the notion given us by Mela, Pliny, and Tacitus, of the vast countries round the Baltic. See in the *Bibliothèque raisonnée*, tom. xl and xlv, a large abstract of Dalin's *History of Sweden*, composed in the Swedish language.

Germany and Poland.* The modern improvements sufficiently explain the causes of the diminution of the cold. These immense woods have been gradually cleared, which intercepted from the earth the rays of the sun. The morasses have been drained, and, in proportion as the soil has been cultivated, the air has become more temperate. Canada, at this day, is an exact picture of ancient Germany. Although situated in the same parallel with the finest provinces of France and England, that country experiences the most rigorous cold. The reindeer are very numerous, the ground is covered with deep and lasting snow, and the great river of St Lawrence is regularly frozen, in a season when the waters of the Seine and the Thames are usually free from ice.

It is difficult to ascertain, and easy to exaggerate, the influence of the climate of ancient Germany over the minds and bodies of the natives. Many writers have supposed, and most have allowed, though, as it should seem, without any adequate proof, that the rigorous cold of the North was favourable to long life and generative vigour, that the women were more fruitful, and the human species more prolific, than in warmer or more temperate climates.† We may assert, with greater confidence, that the keen air of Germany formed the large and masculine limbs of the natives, who were, in general, of a more lofty stature than the people of the South, gave them a kind of strength better adapted to violent exertions than to patient labour, and inspired them with constitutional bravery, which is the result of nerves and spirits. The severity of a winter campaign, that chilled the courage of the Roman troops, was scarcely felt by these hardy children of the North,‡ who in their turn were unable to resist the summer heats, and dissolved away in languor and sickness under the beams of an Italian sun.§

There is not anywhere upon the globe a large tract of country which we have discovered destitute of inhabitants, or whose first population

* Caesar *de Bell, Gallic,* vi. 23, etc. The most inquisitive of the Germans were ignorant of its utmost limits, although some of them had travelled in it more than sixty days' journey.

† Olaus Rudbeck asserts that the Swedish women often bear ten or twelve children, and not uncommonly twenty or thirty; but the authority of Rudbeck is much to be suspected.

‡ Plutarch, in *Mario.* The Cimbri, by way of amusement, often slid down mountains of snow on their broad shields.

§ The Romans made war in all climates, and by their excellent discipline were in a great measure preserved in health and vigour. It may be remarked, that man is the only animal which can live and multiply in every country from the equator to the poles. The hog seems to approach the nearest to our species in that privilege.

can be fixed with any degree of historical certainty. And yet, as the most philosophic minds can seldom refrain from investigating the infancy of great nations, our curiosity consumes itself in toilsome and disappointed efforts. When Tacitus considered the purity of the German blood, and the forbidding aspect of the country, he was disposed to pronounce those barbarians *Indigenae*, or natives of the soil. We may allow with safety, and perhaps with truth, that ancient Germany was not originally peopled by any foreign colonies already formed into a political society; but that the name and nation received their existence from the gradual union of some wandering savages of the Hercynian woods. To assert those savages to have been the spontaneous production of the earth which they inhabited would be a rash inference, condemned by religion and unwarranted by reason.

Such rational doubt is but ill-suited with the genius of popular vanity. Among the nations who have adopted the Mosaic history of the world, the ark of Noah has been of the same use as was formerly to the Greeks and Romans the siege of Troy. On a narrow basis of acknowledged truth an immense but rude superstructure of fable has been erected, and the 'Wild Irishman', as well as the Wild Tartar, could point out the individual son of Japhet, from whose loins his ancestors were lineally descended. The last century abounded with antiquarians of profound learning and easy faith, who by the dim light of legends and traditions, of conjectures and etymologies, conducted the great-grandchildren of Noah from the tower of Babel to the extremities of the globe. Of these judicious critics, one of the most entertaining was Olaus Rudbeck, professor in the University of Upsal. Whatever is celebrated, either in history or fable, this zealous patriot ascribes to his country. From Sweden (which formed so considerable a part of ancient Germany) the Greeks themselves derived their alphabetical characters, their astronomy, and their religion. Of that delightful region (for such it appeared to the eyes of a native) the Atlantis of Plato, the country of the Hyperboreans, the gardens of the Hesperides, the Fortunate Islands, and even the Elysian Fields, were all but faint and imperfect transcripts. A clime so profusely favoured by Nature could not long remain desert after the flood. The learned Rudbeck allows the family of Noah a few years to multiply from eight to about twenty thousand persons. He then disperses them into small colonies to replenish the earth and to propagate the human species. The German or Swedish detachment (which marched, if I am not mistaken, under the command of Askenaz, the son of Gomer, the son of Japhet) distinguished itself by a more than common diligence in the prosecution of this great work. The northern hive cast its swarms over the greatest part of Europe, Africa, and Asia; and (to use the author's metaphor) the blood circulated from the extremities to the heart.

But all this well-laboured system of German antiquities is annihilated by a single fact, too well attested to admit of any doubt, and of too decisive a nature to leave room for any reply. The Germans, in the age of Tacitus, were unacquainted with the use of letters;* and the use of letters is the principal circumstance that distinguishes a civilised people from a herd of savages incapable of knowledge or reflection. Without that artificial help, the human memory soon dissipates or corrupts the ideas intrusted to her charge; and the nobler faculties of the mind, no longer supplied with models or with materials, gradually forget their powers; the judgment becomes feeble and lethargic, the imagination languid or irregular. Fully to apprehend this important truth, let us attempt, in an improved society, to calculate the immense distance between the man of learning and the *illiterate* peasant. The former, by reading and reflection, multiplies his own experience, and lives in distant ages and remote countries; whilst the latter, rooted to a single spot, and confined to a few years of existence, surpasses, but very little, his fellow-labourer the ox in the exercise of his mental faculties. The same, and even a greater, difference will be found between nations than between individuals; and we may safely pronounce that, without some species of writing, no people has ever preserved the faithful annals of their history, ever made any considerable progress in the abstract sciences, or ever possessed, in any tolerable degree of perfection, the useful and agreeable arts of life.

Of these arts, the ancient Germans were wretchedly destitute. They passed their lives in a state of ignorance and poverty, which it has pleased some declaimers to dignify with the appellation of virtuous simplicity. Modern Germany is said to contain about two thousand three hundred walled towns. In a much wider extent of country, the geographer Ptolemy could discover no more than ninety places, which he decorates with the name of cities; though, according to our ideas, they would but

---

* We may rest contented with this decisive authority, without entering into the obscure disputes concerning the antiquity of the Runic characters. The learned Celsius, a Swede, a scholar, and a philosopher, was of opinion, that they were nothing more than the Roman letters, with the curves changed into straight lines for the ease of engraving. We may add, that the oldest Runic inscriptions are supposed to be of the third century, and the most ancient writer who mentions the Runic characters is Venantius Fortunatus, who lived towards the end of the sixth century.

ill deserve that splendid title. We can only suppose them to have been rude fortifications, constructed in the centre of the woods, and designed to secure the women, children, and cattle, whilst the warriors of the tribe marched out to repel a sudden invasion. But Tacitus asserts, as a well-known fact, that the Germans, in his time, had *no* cities; and that they affected to despise the works of Roman industry as places of confinement rather than of security. Their edifices were not even con-tiguous, or formed into regular villas; each barbarian fixed his indepen-dent dwelling on the spot to which a plain, a wood, or a stream of fresh water had induced him to give the preference. Neither stone, nor brick, nor tiles, were employed in these slight habitations. They were indeed no more than low huts of a circular figure, built of rough timber, thatched with straw, and pierced at the top to leave a free passage for the smoke. In the most inclement winter, the hardy German was satisfied with a scanty garment made of the skin of some animal. The nations who dwelt towards the North clothed themselves in furs; and the women manufac-tured for their own use a coarse kind of linen. The game of various sorts, with which the forests of Germany were plentifully stocked, supplied its inhabitants with food and exercise. Their monstrous herds of cattle, less remarkable indeed for their beauty than for their utility, formed the principal object of their wealth. A small quantity of corn was the only produce exacted from the earth: the use of orchards or artificial meadows was unknown to the Germans; nor can we expect any improvements in agriculture from a people whose property every year experienced a general change by a new division of the arable lands, and who, in that strange operation, avoided disputes by suffering a great part of their territory to lie waste and without tillage.

Gold, silver, and iron were extremely scarce in Germany. Its bar-barous inhabitants wanted both skill and patience to investigate those rich veins of silver, which have so liberally rewarded the attention of the princes of Brunswick and Saxony. Sweden, which now supplies Europe with iron, was equally ignorant of its own riches; and the appearance of the arms of the Germans furnished a sufficient proof how little iron they were able to bestow on what they must have deemed the noblest use of that metal. The various transactions of peace and war had introduced some Roman coins (chiefly silver) among the borderers of the Rhine and Danube; but the more distant tribes were absolutely unac-quainted with the use of money, carried on their confined traffic by the exchange of commodities, and prized their rude earthen vessels as of equal value with the silver vases, the presents of Rome to their princes

The Sepulchral Monument at Mylasa

The Arch of Hadrian

and ambassadors. To a mind capable of reflection, such leading facts convey more instruction than a tedious detail of subordinate circum, stances. The value of money has been settled by general consent to express our wants and our property, as letters were invented to express our ideas; and both these institutions, by giving a more active energy to the powers and passions of human nature, have contributed to multiply the objects they were designed to represent. The use of gold and silver is in a great measure fictitious; but it would be impossible to enumerate the important and various services which agriculture, and all the arts, have received from iron, when tempered and fashioned by the operation of fire and the dexterous hand of man. Money, in a word, is the most universal incitement, iron the most powerful instrument, of human industry; and it is very difficult to conceive by what means a people, neither actuated by the one nor seconded by the other, could emerge from the grossest barbarism.*

If we contemplate a savage nation in any part of the globe, a supine indolence and a carelessness of futurity will be found to constitute their general character. In a civilised state, every faculty of man is expanded and exercised; and the great chain of mutual dependence connects and embraces the several members of society. The most numerous portion of it is employed in constant and useful labour. The select few, placed by fortune above that necessity, can, however, fill up their time by the pursuits of interest or glory, by the improvement of their estate or of their understanding, by the duties, the pleasures, and even the follies of social life. The Germans were not possessed of these varied resources. The care of the house and family, the management of the land and cattle, were delegated to the old and the infirm, to women and slaves. The lazy warrior, destitute of every art that might employ his leisure hours, consumed his days and nights in the animal gratifications of sleep and food. And yet, by a wonderful diversity of Nature (according to the remark of a writer who had pierced into its darkest recesses), the same barbarians are by turns the most indolent and the most restless of mankind. They delight in sloth, they detest tranquillity. The languid soul, oppressed with its own weight, anxiously required some new and powerful sensation; and war and danger were the only amusements adequate to its fierce temper. The sound that summoned the German to arms was grateful to his ear. It roused him from his uncomfortable

* It is said that the Mexicans and Peruvians, without the use of either money or iron, had made a very great progress in the arts. Those arts, and the monuments they produced, have been strangely magnified. *Recherches sur les Américains.*

lethargy, gave him an active pursuit, and, by strong exercise of the body, and violent emotions of the mind, restored him to a more lively sense of his existence. In the dull intervals of peace, these barbarians were immoderately addicted to deep gaming and excessive drinking; both of which, by different means, the one by inflaming their passions, the other by extinguishing their reason, alike relieved them from the pain of thinking. They gloried in passing whole days and nights at table; and the blood of friends and relations often stained their numerous and drunken assemblies. Their debts of honour (for in that light they have transmitted to us those of play) they discharged with the most romantic fidelity. The desperate gamester, who had staked his person and liberty on a last throw of the dice, patiently submitted to the decision of fortune, and suffered himself to be bound, chastised, and sold into remote slavery, by his weaker but more lucky antagonist.*

Strong beer, a liquor extracted with very little art from wheat or barley, and *corrupted* (as it is strongly expressed by Tacitus) into a certain semblance of wine, was sufficient for the gross purposes of German debauchery. But those who had tasted the rich wines of Italy, and afterwards of Gaul, sighed for that more delicious species of intoxication. They attempted not, however (as has since been executed with so much success), to naturalise the vine on the banks of the Rhine and Danube; nor did they endeavour to procure by industry the materials of an advantageous commerce. To solicit by labour what might be ravished by arms was esteemed unworthy of the German spirit. The intemperate thirst of strong liquors often urged the barbarians to invade the provinces on which art or nature had bestowed those much envied presents. The Tuscan who betrayed his country to the Celtic nations attracted them into Italy by the prospect of the rich fruits and delicious wines, the productions of a happier climate. And in the same manner the German auxiliaries, invited into France during the civil wars of the sixteenth century, were allured by the promise of plenteous quarters in the provinces of Champagne and Burgundy. Drunkenness, the most illiberal, but not the most dangerous, of *our* vices, was sometimes capable, in a less civilised state of mankind, of occasioning a battle, a war, or a revolution.

The climate of ancient Germany has been mollified, and the soil fertilised, by the labour of ten centuries from the time of Charlemagne. The same extent of ground which at present maintains, in ease and

* Tacitus, *Germ.* 24. The Germans might borrow the *arts* of play from the Romans, but the *passion* is wonderfully inherent in the human species.

plenty, a million of husbandmen and artificers, was unable to supply an hundred thousand lazy warriors with the simple necessaries of life.* The Germans abandoned their immense forests to the exercise of hunting, employed in pasturage the most considerable part of their lands, be- stowed on the small remainder a rude and careless cultivation, and then accused the scantiness and sterility of a country that refused to maintain the multitude of his inhabitants. When the return of famine severely admonished them of the importance of the arts, the national distress was sometimes alleviated by the emigration of a third, perhaps, or a fourth part of their youth. The possession and the enjoyment of property are the pledges which bind a civilised people to an improved country. But the Germans, who carried with them what they most valued, their arms, their cattle, and their women, cheerfully abandoned the vast silence of their woods for the unbounded hopes of plunder and conquest. The innumerable swarms that issued, or seemed to issue, from the great storehouse of nations, were multiplied by the fears of the vanquished and by the credulity of succeeding ages. And from facts thus exaggerated, an opinion was gradually established, and has been supported by writers of distinguished reputation, that, in the age of Caesar and Tacitus, the inhabitants of the North were far more numerous than they are in our days.† A more serious inquiry into the causes of population seems to have convinced modern philosophers of the falsehood, and indeed the impossibility, of the supposition. To the names of Mariana and of Machiavel, we can oppose the equal names of Robertson and Hume.

A warlike nation like the Germans, without either cities, letters, arts, or money, found some compensation for this savage state in the enjoy- ment of liberty. Their poverty secured their freedom, since our desires and our possessions are the strongest fetters of despotism. 'Among the Suiones (says Tacitus), riches are held in honour. They are *therefore* subject to an absolute monarch, who, instead of intrusting his people with the free use of arms, as is practised in the rest of Germany, commits them to the safe custody not of a citizen, or even of a freedman, but of a slave. The neighbours of the Suiones, the Sitones, are sunk even below

* The Helvetian nation, which issued from the country called Switzerland, contained, of every age and sex, 368,000 persons (Caesar, *de Bell. Gall.* i 29). At present, the number of people in the Pays de Vaud (a small district on the banks of the Leman Lake, much more distinguished for politeness than for industry) amounts to 112,591. See an excellent tract of M. Muret, in the *Mémoires de la Societé de Bern.*

† Sir William Temple and Montesquieu have indulged, on this subject, the usual liveliness of their fancy.

servitude; they obey a woman.'* In the mention of these exceptions, the great historian sufficiently acknowledges the general theory of govern, ment. We are only at a loss to conceive by what means riches and despotism could penetrate into a remote corner of the North, and extinguish the generous flame that blazed with such fierceness on the frontier of the Roman provinces: or how the ancestors of those Danes and Norwegians, so distinguished in latter ages by their unconquered spirit, could thus tamely resign the great character of German liberty.† Some tribes, however, on the coast of the Baltic, acknowledged the authority of kings, though without relinquishing the rights of men; but in the far greater part of Germany, the form of government was a democracy tempered indeed, and controlled, not so much by general and positive laws, as by the occasional ascendant of birth or valour, of eloquence or superstition.

Civil governments, in their first institutions, are voluntary associ, ations for mutual defence. To obtain the desired end, it is absolutely necessary that each individual should conceive himself obliged to submit his private opinion and actions to the judgment of the greater number of his associates. The German tribes were contented with this rude but liberal outline of political society. As soon as a youth, born of free parents, had attained the age of manhood, he was introduced into the general council of his countrymen, solemnly invested with a shield and spear, and adopted as an equal and worthy member of the military commonwealth. The assembly of the warriors of the tribe was convened at stated seasons or on sudden emergencies. The trial of public offences, the election of magistrates, and the great business of peace and war, were determined by its independent voice. Sometimes, indeed, these impor, tant questions were previously considered and prepared in a more select council of the principal chieftains. The magistrates might deliberate and persuade, the people only could resolve and execute; and the resolutions of the Germans were for the most part hasty and violent. Barbarians

* Frenshemius (who dedicated his supplement to Livy to Christina of Sweden) thinks proper to be very angry with the Roman who expressed so very little reverence for Northern queens.

† May we not suspect that superstition was the parent of despotism? The descendants of Odin (whose race was not extinct till the year 1060) are said to have reigned in Sweden above a thousand years. The temple of Upsal was the ancient seat of religion and empire. In the year 1153 I find a singular law, prohibiting the use and profession of arms to any except the king's guards. Is it not probable that it was coloured by the pretence of reviving an old institution? Dalin's *History of Sweden* in the *Bibliothèque raisonnée*.

accustomed to place their freedom in gratifying the present passion, and their courage in overlooking all future consequences, turned away with indignant contempt from the remonstrance of justice and policy, and it was the practice to signify by a hollow murmur their dislike of such timid counsels. But whenever a more popular orator proposed to vindicate the meanest citizen from either foreign or domestic injury, whenever he called upon his fellow-countrymen to assert the national honour, or to pursue some enterprise full of danger and glory, a loud clashing of shields and spears expressed the eager applause of the assembly. For the Germans always met in arms, and it was constantly to be dreaded lest an irregular multitude, inflamed with faction and strong liquors, should use those arms to enforce, as well as to declare, their furious resolves. We may recollect how often the diets of Poland have been polluted with blood, and the more numerous party has been compelled to yield to the more violent and seditious.*

A general of the tribe was elected on occasions of danger; and, if the danger was pressing and extensive, several tribes concurred in the choice of the same general. The bravest warrior was named to lead his countrymen into the field, by his example rather than by his commands. But this power, however limited, was still invidious. It expired with the war, and in time of peace the German tribes acknowledged not any supreme chief. *Princes* were, however, appointed in the general assembly, to administer justice, or rather to compose differences, in their respective districts. In the choice of these magistrates as much regard was shown to birth as to merit. To each was assigned, by the public, a guard and a council of an hundred persons; and the first of the princes appears to have enjoyed a pre-eminence of rank and honour which sometimes tempted the Romans to compliment him with the regal title.

The comparative view of the powers of the magistrates, in two remarkable instances, is alone sufficient to represent the whole system of German manners. The disposal of the landed property within their district was absolutely vested in their hands, and they distributed it every year according to a new division. At the same time they were not authorised to punish with death, to imprison, or even to strike, a private citizen. A people thus jealous of their persons, and careless of their possessions, must have been totally destitute of industry and the arts, but animated with a high sense of honour and independence.

The Germans respected only those duties which they imposed on

* Even in *our* ancient parliament, the barons often carried a question, not so much by the number of votes, as by that of their armed followers.

themselves. The most obscure soldier resisted with disdain the authority of the magistrates. 'The noblest youths blushed not to be numbered among the faithful companions of some renowned chief, to whom they devoted their arms and service. A noble emulation prevailed among the companions to obtain the first place in the esteem of their chief; amongst the chiefs, to acquire the greatest number of valiant companions. To be ever surrounded by a band of select youths was the pride and strength of the chiefs, their ornament in peace, their defence in war. The glory of such distinguished heroes diffused itself beyond the narrow limits of their own tribe. Presents and embassies solicited their friendship, and the fame of their arms often ensured victory to the party which they espoused. In the hour of danger it was shameful for the chief to be surpassed in valour by his companions; shameful for the companions not to equal the valour of their chief. To survive his fall in battle was indelible infamy. To protect his person and to adorn his glory with the trophies of their own exploits were the most sacred of their duties. The chiefs combated for victory, the companions for the chief. The noblest warriors, whenever their native country was sunk in the laziness of peace, maintained their numerous bands in some distant scene of action, to exercise their restless spirit and to acquire renown by voluntary dangers. Gifts worthy of soldiers, the warlike steed, the bloody and ever victorious lance, were the rewards which the companions claimed from the liberality of their chief. The rude plenty of his hospitable board was the only pay that *he* could bestow or *they* would accept. War, rapine, and the free-will offerings of his friends, supplied the materials of this munificence.' This institution, however it might accidentally weaken the several republics, invigorated the general character of the Germans, and even ripened amongst them all the virtues of which barbarians are susceptible; the faith and valour, the hospitality and the courtesy, so conspicuous long afterwards in the ages of chivalry. The honourable gifts, bestowed by the chief on his brave companions, have been supposed, by an ingenious writer, to contain the first rudiments of the fiefs, distributed, after the conquest of the Roman provinces, by the barbarian lords among their vassals, with a similar duty of homage and military service.* These conditions are, however, very repugnant to the maxims of the ancient Germans, who delighted in mutual presents; but without either imposing, or accepting, the weight of obligations.

* *Esprit des Lois*, l. xxx. c. 5. The brilliant imagination of Montesquieu is corrected, however, by the dry cold reason of the Abbé de Mably. *Observations sur l'histoire de France.*

'In the days of chivalry, or more properly of romance, all the men were brave, and all the women were chaste;' and notwithstanding the latter of these virtues is acquired and preserved with much more difficulty than the former, it is ascribed, almost without exception, to the wives of the ancient Germans. Polygamy was not in use, except among the princes, and among them only for the sake of multiplying their alliances. Divorces were prohibited by manners rather than by laws. Adulteries were punished as rare and inexpiable crimes; nor was seduction justified by example and fashion.* We may easily discover that Tacitus indulges an honest pleasure in the contrast of barbarian virtue with the dissolute conduct of the Roman ladies; yet there are some striking circumstances that give an air of truth, or at least of probability, to the conjugal faith and chastity of the Germans.

Although the progress of civilisation has undoubtedly contributed to assuage the fiercer passions of human nature, it seems to have been less favourable to the virtue of chastity, whose most dangerous enemy is the softness of the mind. The refinements of life corrupt while they polish the intercourse of the sexes. The gross appetite of love becomes most dangerous when it is elevated, or rather, indeed, disguised by sentimental passion. The elegance of dress, of motion, and of manners gives a lustre to beauty, and inflames the senses through the imagination. Luxurious entertainments, midnight dances, and licentious spectacles, present at once temptation and opportunity to female frailty.† From such dangers the unpolished wives of the barbarians were secured by poverty, solitude, and the painful cares of domestic life. The German huts, open on every side to the eye of indiscretion or jealousy, were a better safeguard of conjugal fidelity than the walls, the bolts, and the eunuchs of a Persian harem. To this reason, another may be added of a more honourable nature. The Germans treated their women with esteem and confidence, consulted them on every occasion of importance, and fondly believed that in their breasts resided a sanctity and wisdom more than human. Some of these interpreters of fate, such as Velleda, in the Batavian war, governed, in the name of the deity, the fiercest nations of Germany. The rest of the sex, without being adored as goddesses, were respected as the free and equal companions of soldiers; associated even by the marriage ceremony to a life of toil, of danger, and of glory. In their great invasions,

* The adulteress was whipped through the village. Neither wealth nor beauty could inspire compassion, or procure her a second husband.
† Ovid considers the theatre as the best adapted to collect the beauties of Rome, and to melt them into tenderness and sensuality.

the camps of the barbarians were filled with a multitude of women, who remained firm and undaunted amidst the sound of arms, the various forms of destruction, and the honourable wounds of their sons and husbands. Fainting armies of Germans have more than once been driven back upon the enemy by the generous despair of the women who dreaded death much less than servitude. If the day was irrecoverably lost, they well knew how to deliver themselves and their children, with their own hands, from an insulting victor. Heroines of such a cast may claim our admiration; but they were most assuredly neither lovely, nor very susceptible of love. Whilst they affected to emulate the stern virtues of *man*, they must have resigned that attractive softness in which principally consists the charm of *woman*. Conscious pride taught the German females to suppress every tender emotion that stood in competition with honour, and the first honour of the sex has ever been that of chastity. The sentiments and conduct of these high-spirited matrons may, at once, be considered as a cause, as an effect, and as a proof of the general character of the nation. Female courage, however it may be raised by fanaticism, or confirmed by habit, can be only a faint and imperfect imitation of the manly valour that distinguishes the age or country in which it may be found.

The religious system of the Germans (if the wild opinions of savages can deserve that name) was dictated by their wants, their fears, and their ignorance.* They adored the great visible objects and agents of nature, the Sun and the Moon, the Fire and the Earth; together with those imaginary deities, who were supposed to preside over the most important occupations of human life. They were persuaded that, by some ridiculous arts of divination, they could discover the will of the superior beings, and that human sacrifices were the most precious and acceptable offering to their altars. Some applause has been hastily bestowed on the sublime notion, entertained by that people, of the Deity, whom they neither confined within the walls of a temple, nor represented by any human figure; but when we recollect that the Germans were unskilled in architecture, and totally unacquainted with the art of sculpture, we shall readily assign the true reason of a scruple which arose not so much from a superiority of reason as from a want of ingenuity. The only temples in Germany were dark and ancient groves, consecrated by the reverence of

---

* Tacitus has employed a few lines, and Cluverius one hundred and twenty-four pages, on this obscure subject. The former discovers in Germany the gods of Greece and Rome. The latter is positive, that under the emblems of the sun, the moon, and the fire, his pious ancestors worshipped the Trinity in unity.

succeeding generations. Their secret gloom, the imagined residence of an invisible power, by presenting no distinct object of fear or worship, impressed the mind with a still deeper sense of religious horror; and the priests, rude and illiterate as they were, had been taught by experience the use of every artifice that could preserve and fortify impressions so well suited to their own interest.

The same ignorance, which renders barbarians incapable of conceiv- ing or embracing the useful restraints of laws, exposes them naked and unarmed to the blind terrors of superstition. The German priests, improving this favourable temper of their countrymen, had assumed a jurisdiction, even in temporal concerns, which the magistrate could not venture to exercise; and the haughty warrior patiently submitted to the lash of correction, when it was inflicted, not by any human power, but by the immediate order of the god of war. The defects of civil policy were sometimes supplied by the interposition of ecclesiastical authority. The latter was constantly exerted to maintain silence and decency in the popular assemblies; and was sometimes extended to a more enlarged concern for the national welfare. A solemn procession was occasionally celebrated in the present countries of Mecklenburgh and Pomerania. The unknown symbol of the *Earth*, covered with a thick veil, was placed on a carriage drawn by cows; and in this manner the goddess, whose common residence was in the isle of Rugen, visited several adjacent tribes of her worshippers. During her progress the sound of war was hushed, quarrels were suspended, arms laid aside, and the restless Germans had an opportunity of tasting the blessings of peace and harmony. The *truce of God*, so often and so ineffectually proclaimed by the clergy of the eleventh century, was an obvious imitation of this ancient custom.

But the influence of religion was far more powerful to inflame than to moderate the fierce passions of the Germans. Interest and fanaticism often prompted its ministers to sanctify the most daring and the most unjust enterprises, by the approbation of Heaven, and full assurances of success. The consecrated standards, long revered in the groves of superstition, were placed in the front of the battle; and the hostile army was devoted with dire execrations to the gods of war and of thunder. In the faith of soldiers (and such were the Germans) cowardice is the most unpardonable of sins. A brave man was the worthy favourite of their martial deities; the wretch, who had lost his shield, was alike banished from the religious and the civil assemblies of his countrymen. Some tribes of the north seem to have embraced the doctrine of transmigration, others imagined a gross paradise of immortal drunkenness.* All agreed that a life spent in arms, and a glorious death in battle, were the best preparations for a happy futurity either in this or in another world.

The immortality so vainly promised by the priests was in some degree conferred by the bards. That singular order of men has most deservedly attracted the notice of all who have attempted to investigate the antiquities of the Celts, the Scandinavians, and the Germans. Their genius and character, as well as the reverence paid to that important office, have been sufficiently illustrated. But we cannot so easily express, or even conceive, the enthusiasm of arms and glory, which they kindled in the breast of their audience. Among a polished people, a taste for poetry is rather an amusement of the fancy than a passion of the soul. And yet, when in calm retirement we peruse the combats described by Homer or Tasso, we are insensibly seduced by the fiction, and feel a momentary glow of martial ardour. But how faint, how cold is the sensation which a peaceful mind can receive from solitary study! It was in the hour of battle, or in the feast of victory, that the bards celebrated the glory of heroes of ancient days, the ancestors of those warlike chieftains who listened with transport to their artless but animated strains. The view of arms and of danger heightened the effect of the military song; and the passions which it tended to excite, the desire of fame and the contempt of death, were the habitual sentiments of a German mind.†

Such was the situation, and such were the manners, of the ancient Germans. Their climate, their want of learning, of arts, and of laws, their notions of honour, of gallantry, and of religion, their sense of freedom, impatience of peace, and thirst of enterprise, all contributed to form a people of military heroes. And yet we find that, during more than two hundred and fifty years that elapsed from the defeat of Varus to the reign of Decius, these formidable barbarians made few considerable attempts, and not any material impression on the luxurious and enslaved provinces of the empire. Their progress was checked by their want of arms and discipline, and their fury was diverted by the intestine divisions of ancient Germany.

* Concerning this gross but alluring doctrine of the Edda, see Fable xx in the curious version of that book, published by M. Mallet, in his *Introduction to the History of Denmark*.

† The classical reader may remember the rank of Demodocus in the Phaeacian court, and the ardour infused by Tyrtaeus into the fainting Spartans. Yet there is little probability that the Greeks and the Germans were the same people. Much learned trifling might be spared if our antiquarians would condescend to reflect, that similar manners will naturally be produced by similar situations.

I. It has been observed, with ingenuity, and not without truth, that command of iron soon gives a nation the command of gold. But the rude tribes of Germany, alike destitute of both these valuable metals, were reduced slowly to acquire, by their unassisted strength, the possession of the one as well as the other. The face of a German army displayed their poverty of iron. Swords, and the longer kind of lances, they could seldom use. Their *frameae* (as they called them in their own language) were long spears headed with a sharp but narrow iron point, and which, as occasion required, they either darted from a distance or pushed in close onset. With this spear, and with a shield, their cavalry was contented. A multitude of darts, scattered with incredible force, were an additional resource of the infantry. Their military dress, when they wore any, was nothing more than a loose mantle. A variety of colours was the only ornament of their wooden or osier shields. Few of the chiefs were distinguished by cuirasses, scarce any by helmets. Though the horses of Germany were neither beautiful, swift, nor practised in the skilful evolutions of the Roman manege, several of the nations obtained renown by their cavalry; but, in general, the principal strength of the Germans consisted in their infantry, which was drawn up in several deep columns, according to the distinction of tribes and families. Impatient of fatigue or delay, these half-armed warriors rushed to battle with dissonant shouts and disordered ranks; and sometimes, by the effort of native valour, prevailed over the constrained and more artificial bravery of the Roman mercenaries. But as the barbarians poured forth their whole souls on the first onset, they knew not how to rally or to retire. A repulse was a sure defeat; and a defeat was most commonly total destruction. When we recollect the complete armour of the Roman soldiers, their discipline, exercises, evolutions, fortified camps, and military engines, it appears a just matter of surprise how the naked and unassisted valour of the barbarians could dare to encounter in the field the strength of the legions, and the various troops of the auxiliaries which seconded their operations. The contest was too unequal, till the introduction of luxury had enervated the vigour, and a spirit of disobedience and sedition had relaxed the discipline, of the Roman armies. The introduction of barbarian auxiliaries into those armies was a measure attended with very obvious dangers, as it might gradually instruct the Germans in the arts of war and of policy. Although they were admitted in small numbers and with the strictest precaution, the example of Civilis was proper to convince the Romans that the danger was not imaginary, and that their precautions were not always sufficient. During

the civil wars that followed the death of Nero, that artful and intrepid
Batavian, whom his enemies condescended to compare with Hannibal
and Sertorius, formed a great design of freedom and ambition. Eight
Batavian cohorts, renowned in the wars of Britain and Italy, repaired to
his standard. He introduced an army of Germans into Gaul, prevailed
on the powerful cities of Trèves and Langres to embrace his cause,
defeated the legions, destroyed their fortified camps, and employed
against the Romans the military knowledge which he had acquired
in their service. When at length, after an obstinate struggle, he yielded
to the power of the empire, Civilis secured himself and his country
by an honourable treaty. The Batavians still continued to occupy
the islands of the Rhine, the allies not the servants of the Roman
monarchy.

II. The strength of ancient Germany appears formidable when we
consider the effects that might have been produced by its united effort.
The wide extent of country might very possibly contain a million of
warriors, as all who were of age to bear arms were of a temper to use
them. But this fierce multitude, incapable of concerting or executing any
plan of national greatness, was agitated by various and often hostile
intentions. Germany was divided into more than forty independent
states; and even in each state the union of the several tribes was extremely
loose and precarious. The barbarians were easily provoked; they knew
not how to forgive an injury, much less an insult; their resentments were
bloody and implacable. The casual disputes that so frequently happened
in their tumultuous parties of hunting or drinking were sufficient to
inflame the minds of whole nations; the private feud of any considerable
chieftains diffused itself among their followers and allies. To chastise the
insolent, or to plunder the defenceless, were alike causes of war. The
most formidable states of Germany affected to encompass their territories with a wide frontier of solitude and devastation. The awful
distance preserved by their neighbours attested the terror of their arms,
and in some measure defended them from the danger of unexpected
incursions.

'The Bructeri (it is Tacitus who now speaks) were totally exterminated by the neighbouring tribes, provoked by their insolence, allured
by the hopes of spoil, and perhaps inspired by the tutelar deities of the
empire. Above sixty thousand barbarians were destroyed; not by the
Roman arms, but in our sight, and for our entertainment. May the
nations, enemies of Rome, ever preserve this enmity to each other! We
have now attained the utmost verge of prosperity, and have nothing left

to demand of Fortune, except the discord of these barbarians.' These sentiments,* less worthy of the humanity than of the patriotism of Tacitus, express the invariable maxims of the policy of his countrymen. They deemed it a much safer expedient to divide than to combat the barbarians, from whose defeat they could derive neither honour not advantage. The money and negotiations of Rome insinuated themselves into the heart of Germany; and every art of seduction was used with dignity to conciliate those nations whom their proximity to the Rhine or Danube might render the most useful friends as well as the most troublesome enemies. Chiefs of renown and power were flattered by the most trifling presents, which they received either as marks of distinction, or as the instru- ments of luxury. In civil dissensions, the weaker faction endeavoured to strengthen its interest by entering into secret connections with the governors of the frontier provinces. Every quarrel among the Germans was fomented by the intrigues of Rome; and every plan of union and public good was defeated by the stronger bias of private jealousy and interest.

The general conspiracy which terrified the Romans under the reign of Marcus Antoninus comprehended almost all the nations of Germany, and even Sarmatia, from the mouth of the Rhine to that of the Danube. It is impossible for us to determine whether this hasty confederation was formed by necessity, by reason, or by passion; but we may rest assured that the barbarians were neither allured by the indolence, nor provoked by the ambition, of the Roman monarch. This dangerous invasion required all the firmness and vigilance of Marcus. He fixed generals of ability in the several stations of attack, and assumed in person the conduct of the most important province on the Upper Danube. After a long and doubtful conflict, the spirit of the barbarians was subdued. The Quadi and the Marcomanni, who had taken the lead in the war, were the most severely punished in its catastrophe. They were com- manded to retire five miles from their own banks of the Danube, and to deliver up the flower of the youth, who were immediately sent into Britain, a remote island, where they might be secure as hostages, and useful as soldiers. On the frequent rebellions of the Quadi and Marco- manni, the irritated emperor resolved to reduce their country into the form of a province. His designs were disappointed by death. This formidable league, however, the only one that appears in the two first centuries of the Imperial history, was entirely dissipated, without leaving any traces behind in Germany.

* The pious Abbé de la Bleterie is very angry with Tacitus, talks of the devil who was a murderer from the beginning, etc., etc.

In the course of this introductory chapter, we have confined ourselves to the general outlines of the manners of Germany, without attempting to describe or to distinguish the various tribes which filled the great country in the time of Caesar, of Tacitus, or of Ptolemy. As the ancient, or as new tribes successively present themselves in the series of this history, we shall concisely mention their origin, their situation, and their particular character. Modern nations are fixed and permanent societies, connected among themselves by laws and government, bound to their native soil by arts and agriculture. The German tribes were voluntary and fluctuating associations of soldiers, almost of savages. The same territory often changed its inhabitants in the tide of conquest and emigration. The same communities, uniting in a plan of defence or invasion, bestowed a new title on their new confederacy. The dissolution of an ancient confederacy restored to the independent tribes their peculiar but long forgotten appellation. A victorious state often communicated its own name to a vanquished people. Sometimes crowds of volunteers flocked from all parts to the standard of a favourite leader; his camp became their country, and some circumstance of the enterprise soon gave a common denomination to the mixed multitude. The distinctions of the ferocious invaders were perpetually varied by themselves, and confounded by the astonished subjects of the Roman Empire.*

Wars, and the administration of public affairs, are the principal subjects of history; but the number of persons interested in these busy scenes is very different according to the different condition of mankind. In great monarchies, millions of obedient subjects pursue their useful occupations in peace and obscurity. The attention of the writer, as well as of the reader, is solely confined to a court, a capital, a regular army, and the districts which happen to be the occasional scene of military operations. But a state of freedom and barbarism, the season of civil commotions, or the situation of petty republics, raises almost every member of the community into action, and consequently into notice. The irregular divisions, and the restless motions, of the people of Germany dazzle our imagination and seem to multiply their numbers. The profuse enumeration of kings and warriors of armies and nations inclines us to forget that the same objects are continually repeated under a variety of appellations, and that the most splendid appellations have been frequently lavished on the most inconsiderable objects.

* See an excellent dissertation on the origin and migrations of nations, in the *Memoires de l'Académie des Inscriptions*, tom. xviii. p. 48–71. It is seldom that the antiquarian and the philosopher are so happily blended.

THE EMPERORS DECIUS, GALLUS, AEMILIANUS, VALER-
IAN, AND GALLIENUS — THE GENERAL IRRUPTION OF
THE BARBARIANS — THE THIRTY TYRANTS

From the great secular games cel-
ebrated by Philip to the death of the emperor Gallienus there elapsed (AD
248–268) twenty years of shame and misfortune. During that calamitous
period every instant of time was marked, every province of the Roman
world was afflicted by barbarous invaders and military tyrants, and the
ruined empire seemed to approach the last and fatal moment of its
dissolution. The confusion of the times, and the scarcity of authentic
memorials, oppose equal difficulties to the historian, who attempts to
preserve a clear and unbroken thread of narration. Surrounded with
imperfect fragments, always concise, often obscure, and sometimes
contradictory, he is reduced to collect, to compare, and to conjecture:
and though he ought never to place his conjectures in the rank of facts,
yet the knowledge of human nature, and of the sure operation of its fierce
and unrestrained passions, might, on some occasions, supply the want of
historical materials.

There is not, for instance, any difficulty in conceiving that the
successive murders of so many emperors had loosened all the ties of
allegiance between the prince and people; that all the generals of Philip
were disposed to imitate the example of their master; and that the caprice
of armies, long since habituated to frequent and violent revolutions
might any day raise to the throne the most obscure of their fellow-
soldiers. History can only add that the rebellion against the emperor
Philip broke out in the summer of the year two hundred and forty-nine,
among the legions of Maesia; and that a subaltern officer, named
Marinus, was the object of their seditious choice. Philip was alarmed.
He dreaded lest the treason of the Maesian army should prove the first
spark of a general conflagration. Distracted with the consciousness of his
guilt and of his danger, he communicated the intelligence to the senate.
A gloomy silence prevailed, the effect of fear, and perhaps of disaffection:
till at length Decius, one of the assembly, assuming a spirit worthy of his
noble extraction, ventured to discover more intrepidity than the emperor

seemed to possess. He treated the whole business with contempt, as a hasty and inconsiderate tumult, and Philip's rival as a phantom of royalty, who in a very few days would be destroyed by the same inconstancy that had created him. The speedy completion of the prophecy inspired Philip with a just esteem for so able a counsellor: and Decius appeared to him the only person capable of restoring peace and discipline to an army whose tumultuous spirit did not immediately subside after the murder of Marinus. Decius, who long resisted his own nomination, seems to have insinuated the danger of presenting a leader of merit to the angry and apprehensive minds of the soldiers; and his prediction was again confirmed by the event. The legions of Maesia forced their judge to become (AD 249) their accomplice. They left him only the alternative of death or the purple. His subsequent conduct, after that decisive measure, was unavoidable. He conducted or followed his army to the confines of Italy, whither Philip, collecting all his force to repel the formidable competitor whom he had raised up, advanced to meet him. The Imperial troops were superior in number; but the rebels formed an army of veterans, commanded by an able and experienced leader. Philip was either killed in the battle or put to death a few days afterwards at Verona. His son and associate in the empire was massacred at Rome by the Praetorian Guards; and the victorious Decius, with more favourable circumstances than the ambition of that age can usually plead, was universally acknowledged by the senate and provinces. It is reported that, immediately after his reluctant acceptance of the title of Augustus, he had assured Philip, by a private message, of his innocence and loyalty, solemnly protesting that, on his arrival in Italy, he would resign the imperial ornaments and return to the condition of an obedient subject. His professions might be sincere. But in the situation where fortune had placed him it was scarcely possible that he could either forgive or be forgiven.

The emperor Decius had employed a few months in the works of peace and the administration of justice, when (AD 250) he was sum/ moned to the banks of the Danube by the invasion of the Goths. This is the first considerable occasion in which history mentions that great people, who afterwards broke the Roman power, sacked the Capitol, and reigned in Gaul, Spain, and Italy. So memorable was the part which they acted in the subversion of the Western empire that the name of Goths is frequently but improperly used as a general appellation of rude and warlike barbarism.

In the beginning of the sixth century, and after the conquest of Italy, the Goths, in possession of present greatness, very naturally indulged themselves in the prospect of past and of future glory. They wished to preserve the memory of their ancestors, and to transmit to posterity their own achievements. The principal minister of the court of Ravenna, the learned Cassiodorus, gratified the inclination of the conquerors in a Gothic history, which consisted of twelve books, now reduced to the imperfect abridgment of Jornandes. These writers passed with the most artful conciseness over the misfortunes of the nation, celebrated its successful valour, and adorned the triumph with many Asiatic trophies that more properly belonged to the people of Scythia. On the faith of ancient songs, the uncertain, but the only, memorials of barbarians, they deduced the first origin of the Goths from the vast island, or peninsula, of Scandinavia. That extreme country of the north was not unknown to the conquerors of Italy: the ties of ancient consanguinity had been strengthened by recent offices of friendship; and a Scandinavian king had cheerfully abdicated his savage greatness that he might pass the remainder of his days in the peaceful and polished court of Ravenna. Many vestiges, which cannot be ascribed to the arts of popular vanity, attest the ancient residence of the Goths in the countries beyond the Baltic. From the time of the geographer Ptolemy, the southern part of Sweden seems to have continued in the possession of the less enterprising remnant of the nation, and a large territory is even at present divided into east and west Gothland. During the middle ages (from the ninth to the twelfth century), while Christianity was advancing with a slow progress into the north, the Goths and the Swedes composed two distinct and sometimes hostile members of the same monarchy. The latter of these two names has prevailed without extinguishing the former. The Swedes, who might well be satisfied with their own fame in arms, have in every age claimed the kindred glory of the Goths. In a moment of discontent against the court of Rome, Charles the Twelfth insinuated that his victorious troops were not degenerated from their brave ancestors who had already subdued the mistress of the world.*

Till the end of the eleventh century, a celebrated temple subsisted at Upsal, the most considerable town of the Swedes and Goths. It was enriched with the gold which the Scandinavians had acquired in their piratical adventures, and sanctified by the uncouth representations of the three principal deities, the god of war, the goddess of generation, and the

* Voltaire, *Histoire de Charles XII*. When the Austrians desired the aid of the court of Rome against Gustavus Adolphus, they always represented that conqueror as the lineal successor of Alaric.

god of thunder. In the general festival that was solemnised every ninth year, nine animals of every species (without excepting the human) were sacrificed, and their bleeding bodies suspended in the sacred grove adjacent to the temple. The only traces that now subsist of this barbaric superstition are contained in the Edda, a system of mythology compiled in Iceland about the thirteenth century, and studied by the learned of Denmark and Sweden as the most valuable remains of their ancient traditions.

Notwithstanding the mysterious obscurity of the Edda, we can easily distinguish two persons confounded under the name of Odin, the god of war, and the great legislator of Scandinavia. The latter, the Mahomet of the North, instituted a religion adapted to the climate and to the people. Numerous tribes on either side of the Baltic were subdued by the invincible valour of Odin, by his persuasive eloquence, and by the fame, which he acquired, of a most skilful magician. The faith that he had propagated during a long and prosperous life he confirmed by a voluntary death. Apprehensive of the ignominious approach of disease and infirmity, he resolved to expire as became a warrior. In a solemn assembly of the Swedes and Goths, he wounded himself in nine mortal places, hastening away (as he asserted with his dying voice) to prepare the feast of heroes in the palace of the god of war.

The native and proper habitation of Odin is distinguished by the appellation of As-gard. The happy resemblance of that name with As-burg, or As-of, words of a similar signification, has given rise to an historical system of so pleasing a contexture that we could almost wish to persuade ourselves of its truth. It is supposed that Odin was the chief of a tribe of barbarians which dwelt on the banks of the lake Maeotis, till the fall of Mithridates and the arms of Pompey menaced the North with servitude. That Odin, yielding, with indignant fury to a power which he was unable to resist, conducted his tribe from the frontiers of the Asiatic Sarmatia into Sweden, with the great design of forming, in that inaccessible retreat of freedom, a religion and a people which, in some remote age, might be subservient to his immortal revenge; when his invincible Goths, armed with martial fanaticism, should issue in numerous swarms from the neighbourhood of the Polar circle, to chastise the oppressors of mankind.*

* This wonderful expedition of Odin, which, by deducing the enmity of the Goths and Romans from so memorable a cause, might supply the noble groundwork of an epic poem, cannot safely be received as authentic history. According to the obvious sense of the Edda, and the interpretation of the most skilful critics, As-gard, instead of denoting a real city of the Asiatic Sarmatia, is the fictitious appellation of the mystic

If so many successive generations of Goths were capable of preserving a faint tradition of their Scandinavian origin, we must not expect, from such unlettered barbarians, any distinct account of the time and circumstances of the emigration. To cross the Baltic was an easy and natural attempt. The inhabitants of Sweden were masters of a sufficient number of large vessels, with oars, and the distance is little more than one hundred miles from Carlscrona to the nearest ports of Pomerania and Prussia. Here, at length, we land on firm and historic ground. At least as early as the Christian era, and as late as the age of the Antonines, the Goths were established towards the mouth of the Vistula, and in that fertile province where the commercial cities of Thorn, Elbing, Koningsberg, and Dantzic were long afterwards founded. Westward of the Goths, the numerous tribes of the Vandals were spread along the banks of the Oder, and the seacoast of Pomerania and Mecklenburg. A striking resemblance of manners, complexion, religion, and language, seemed to indicate that the Vandals and the Goths were originally one great people. The latter appear to have been subdivided into Ostrogoths, Visigoths, and Gepidae. The distinction among the Vandals was more strongly marked by the independent names of Heruli, Burgundians, Lombards, and a variety of other petty states, many of which, in a future age, expanded themselves into powerful monarchies.

In the age of the Antonines, the Goths were still seated in Prussia. About the reign of Alexander Severus, the Roman province of Dacia had already experienced their proximity by frequent and destructive inroads. In this interval, therefore, of about seventy years, we must place the second migration of the Goths from the Baltic to the Euxine; but the cause that produced it lies concealed among the various motives which actuate the conduct of unsettled barbarians. Either a pestilence or a famine, a victory or a defeat, an oracle of the gods or the eloquence of a daring leader, were sufficient to impel the Gothic arms on the milder climates of the south. Besides the influence of a martial religion, the numbers and spirit of the Goths were equal to the most dangerous adventures. The use of round bucklers and short swords rendered them formidable in a close engagement; the manly obedience which they yielded to hereditary kings gave uncommon union and stability to their councils; and the renowned Amala, the hero of that age, and the tenth ancestor of Theodoric, king of Italy, enforced, by the ascendant of

abode of the gods, the Olympus of Scandinavia: from whence the prophet was supposed to descend, when he announced his new religion to the Gothic nations, who were already seated in the southern parts of Sweden.

personal merit, the prerogative of his birth, which he derived from the *Anses*, or demigods of the Gothic nation.

The fame of a great enterprise excited the bravest warriors from all the Vandalic states of Germany, many of whom are seen a few years afterwards combating under the common standard of the Goths. The first motions of the emigrants carried them to the banks of the Prypec, a river universally conceived by the ancients to be the southern branch of the Borysthenes.* The windings of that great stream through the plains of Poland and Russia gave a direction to their line of march, and a constant supply of fresh water and pasturage to their numerous herds of cattle. They followed the unknown course of the river, confident in their valour, and careless of whatever power might oppose their progress. The Bastarnae and the Venedi were the first who presented themselves; and the flower of their youth, either from choice or compulsion, increased the Gothic army. The Bastarnae dwelt on the northern side of the Carpath-ian mountains; the immense tract of land that separated the Bastarnae from the savages of Finland was possessed, or rather wasted, by the Venedi; we have some reason to believe that the first of these nations, which distinguished itself in the Macedonian war, and was afterwards divided into the formidable tribes of the Peucini, the Borani, the Carpi, etc., derived its origin from the Germans. With better authority, a Sarmatian extraction may be assigned to the Venedi, who rendered themselves so famous in the middle ages. But the confusion of blood and manners on that doubtful frontier often perplexed the most accurate observers.† As the Goths advanced near the Euxine Sea, they encoun-tered a purer race of Sarmatians, the Jazyges, the Alani, and the Roxolani; and they were probably the first Germans who saw the mouths of the Borysthenes and of the Tanais. If we inquire into the characteristic marks of the people of Germany and of Sarmatia, we shall discover that those two great portions of human kind were principally distinguished by fixed huts or movable tents, by a close dress or flowing garments, by the marriage of one or of several wives, by a military force consisting, for the most part, either of infantry or cavalry; and above all by the use of the Teutonic or of the Sclavonian language; the last of which has been diffused by conquest from the confines of Italy to the neighbourhood of Japan.

* D'Anville, *Géographie ancienne*, and the third part of his incomparable map of Europe.
† Tacitus most assuredly deserves that title, and even his cautious suspense is a proof of his diligent inquiries.

The Goths were now in possession of the Ukraine, a country of considerable extent and uncommon fertility, intersected with navigable rivers, which, from either side, discharge themselves into the Borys- thenes; and interspersed with large and lofty forests of oaks. The plenty of game and fish, the innumerable bee-hives, deposited in the hollows of old trees, and in the cavities of rocks, and forming, even in that rude age, a valuable branch of commerce, the size of the cattle, the temperature of the air, the aptness of the soil for every species of grain, and the luxuriancy of the vegetation, all displayed the liberality of Nature, and tempted the industry of man.* But the Goths withstood all these temptations, and still adhered to a life of idleness, of poverty, and of rapine.

The Scythian hordes, which, towards the east, bordered on the new settlements of the Goths, presented nothing to their arms except the doubtful chance of an unprofitable victory. But the prospect of the Roman territories was far more alluring; and the fields of Dacia were covered with rich harvests, sown by the hands of an industrious, and exposed to be gathered by those of a warlike, people. It is probable that the conquests of Trajan maintained by his successors, less for any real advantage than for ideal dignity, had contributed to weaken the empire on that side. The new and unsettled province of Dacia was neither strong enough to resist, nor rich enough to satiate, the rapaciousness of the barbarians. As long as the remote banks of the Dniester were considered as the boundary of the Roman power, the fortifications of the Lower Danube were more carelessly guarded, and the inhabitants of Maesia lived in supine security, fondly conceiving themselves at an inaccessible distance from any barbarian invaders. The irruptions of the Goths, under the reign of Philip, fatally convinced them of their mistake. The king, or leader, of that fierce nation traversed with contempt the province of Dacia, and passed both the Dniester and the Danube without encountering any opposition capable of retarding his progress. The relaxed discipline of the Roman troops betrayed the most important posts where they were stationed, and the fear of deserved punishment induced great numbers of them to enlist under the Gothic standard. The various multitude of barbarians appeared, at length, under the walls of Marcianopolis, a city built by Trajan in honour of his sister, and at that time the capital of the second Maesia. The inhabitants

* *Genealogical History of the Tartars.* Bell traversed the Ukraine in his journey from Petersburgh to Constantinople. The modern face of the country is a just representation of the ancient, since, in the hands of the Cossacks, it still remains in a state of nature.

consented to ransom their lives and property by the payment of a large sum of money, and the invaders retreated back into their deserts, animated, rather than satisfied, with the first success of their arms against an opulent but feeble country. Intelligence was soon transmitted to the emperor Decius that Cniva, king of the Goths, had passed the Danube a second time, with more considerable forces; that his numerous detachments scattered devastation over the province of Maesia, whilst the main body of the army, consisting of seventy thousand Germans and Sarmatians, a force equal to the most daring achievements, required the presence of the Roman monarch, and the exertion of his military power.

Decius found (AD 250) the Goths engaged before Nicopolis, on the Jatrus, one of the many monuments of Trajan's victories. On his approach they raised the siege, but with a design only of marching away to a conquest of greater importance, the siege of Philippopolis, a city of Thrace, founded by the father of Alexander, near the foot of mount Haemus. Decius followed them through a difficult country, and by forced marches; but when he imagined himself at a considerable distance from the rear of the Goths, Cniva turned with rapid fury on his pursuers. The camp of the Romans was surprised and pillaged, and, for the first time, their emperor fled in disorder before a troop of halfarmed barbarians. After a long resistance, Philippopolis, destitute of succour, was taken by storm. A hundred thousand persons are reported to have been massacred in the sack of that great city. Many prisoners of consequence became a valuable accession to the spoil; and Priscus, a brother of the late emperor Philip, blushed not to assume the purple under the protection of the barbarous enemies of Rome. The time, however, consumed in that tedious siege enabled Decius to revive the courage, restore the discipline, and recruit the numbers of his troops. He intercepted several parties of Carpi, and other Germans, who were hastening to share the victory of their countrymen, intrusted the passes of the mountains to officers of approved valour and fidelity; repaired and strengthened the fortifications of the Danube, and exerted his utmost vigilance to oppose either the progress or the retreat of the Goths. Encouraged by the return of fortune, he anxiously waited for an opportunity to retrieve, by a great and decisive blow, his own glory and that of the Roman arms.

At the same time when Decius was struggling with the violence of the tempest, his mind, calm and deliberate amidst the tumult of war, investigated the more general causes that, since the age of the Antonines, had so impetuously urged the decline of the Roman greatness. He soon discovered that it was impossible to replace that greatness on a permanent basis without restoring public virtue, ancient principles and manners, and the oppressed majesty of the laws. To execute this noble but arduous design, he first resolved to revive the obsolete officer of censor; an office which, as long as it had subsisted in its pristine integrity, had so much contributed to the perpetuity of the state,* till it was usurped and gradually neglected by the Caesars. Conscious that the favour of the sovereign may confer power, but that the esteem of the people can alone bestow authority, he submitted the choice of the censor to the unbiassed voice of the senate. By their unanimous votes, or rather acclamations, Valerian, who was afterwards emperor, and who then served with distinction in the army of Decius, was (AD 251, 27 October) declared the most worthy of that exalted honour. As soon as the decree of the senate was transmitted to the emperor, he assembled a great council in his camp, and, before the investiture of the censor elect, he apprised him of the difficulty and importance of his great office. 'Happy Valerian,' said the prince to his distinguished subject, 'happy in the general approbation of the senate and of the Roman republic! Accept the censorship of mankind; and judge of our manners. You will select those who deserve to continue members of the senate; you will restore the equestrian order to its ancient splendour; you will improve the revenue, yet moderate the public burdens. You will distinguish into regular classes the various and infinite multitude of citizens, and accurately review the military strength, the wealth, the virtue, and the resources of Rome. Your decisions shall obtain the force of laws. The army, the palace, the ministers of justice, and the great officers of the empire, are all subject to your tribunal. None are exempted, excepting only the ordinary consuls, the prefect of the city, the king of the sacrifices, and (as long as she preserves her chastity inviolate) the eldest of the vestal virgins. Even these few, who may not dread the severity, will anxiously solicit the esteem, of the Roman censor.'

A magistrate, invested with such extensive powers, would have appeared not so much the minister as the colleague of his sovereign. Valerian justly dreaded an elevation so full of envy and of suspicion. He modestly urged the alarming greatness of the trust, his own insufficiency, and the incurable corruption of the times. He artfully insinuated that the office of censor was inseparable from the Imperial dignity, and that the feeble hands of a subject were unequal to the support of such an immense

* Montesquieu, *Grandeur et décadence des Romains*. He illustrates the nature and use of the censorship with his usual ingenuity, and with uncommon precision.

weight of cares and of power. The approaching event of war soon put an end to the prosecution of a project so specious but so impracticable; and whilst it preserved Valerian from the danger, saved the Emperor Decius from the disappointment which would most probably have attended it. A censor may maintain, he can never restore, the morals of a state. It is impossible for such a magistrate to exert his authority with benefit, or even with effect, unless he is supported by a quick sense of honour and virtue in the minds of the people, by a decent reverence for the public opinion, and by a train of useful prejudices combating on the side of national manners. In a period when these principles are annihilated, the censorial jurisdiction must either sink into empty pageantry, or be converted into a partial instrument of vexatious oppression. It was easier to vanquish the Goths than to eradicate the public vices; yet even in the first of these enterprises Decius lost his army and his life.

The Goths were now, on every side, surrounded and pursued by the Roman arms. The flower of their troops had perished in the long siege of Philippopolis, and the exhausted country could no longer afford subsis- tence for the remaining multitude of licentious barbarians. Reduced to this extremity, the Goths would gladly have purchased, by the surrender of all their booty and prisoners, the permission of an undisturbed retreat. But the emperor, confident of victory, and resolving, by the chastisement of these invaders, to strike a salutary terror into the nations of the North, refused to listen to any terms of accommodation. The high-spirited barbarians preferred death to slavery. An obscure town of Maesia, called Forum Terebronii, was the scene of the battle. The Gothic army was drawn up in three lines, and, either from choice or accident, the front of the third line was covered by a morass. In the beginning of the action, the son of Decius, a youth of the fairest hopes, and already associated to the honours of the purple, was slain by an arrow, in the sight of his afflicted father; who, summoning all his fortitude, admonished the dismayed troops that the loss of a single soldier was of little importance to the republic. The conflict was terrible; it was the combat of despair against grief and rage. The first line of the Goths at length gave way in disorder; the second, advancing to sustain it, shared its fate; and the third only remained entire, prepared to dispute the passage of the morass, which was imprudently attempted by the presumption of the enemy. 'Here the fortune of the day turned, and all things became adverse to the Romans: the place deep with ooze, sinking under those who stood, slippery to such as advanced; their armour heavy, the waters deep; nor could they wield, in that uneasy situation, their weighty javelins. The barbarians,

The Monument of Philopappus

A view of the west end of the Temple of Minerva Polias, and of the Pandrosium

on the contrary, were inured to encounters in the bogs, their persons tall, their spears long, such as could wound at a distance.'* In this morass the Roman army, after an ineffectual struggle, was irrecoverably lost; nor could the body of the emperor ever be found. Such was the fate of Decius, in the fiftieth year of his age; an accomplished prince, active in war, and affable in peace; who, together with his son, has deserved to be compared, both in life and death, with the brightest examples of ancient virtue.†

This fatal blow humbled, for a very little time, the insolence of the legions. They appear to have patiently expected, and submissively obeyed, the decree of the senate, which regulated the succession to the throne. From a just regard for the memory of Decius, the Imperial title was (AD 251, December) conferred on Hostilianus, his only surviving son; but an equal rank, with more effectual power, was granted to Gallus, whose experience and ability seemed equal to the great trust of guardian to the young prince and the distressed empire. The first care of the new emperor was to deliver the Illyrian provinces from the intolerable weight of the victorious Goths. He (AD 252) consented to leave in their hands the rich fruits of their invasion, an immense booty, and, what was still more disgraceful, a great number of prisoners of the highest merit and quality. He plentifully supplied their camp with every conveniency that could assuage their angry spirits, or facilitate their so much wishedfor departure; and he even promised to pay them annually a large sum of gold, on condition they should never afterwards infest the Roman territories by their incursions.

In the age of Scipios, the most opulent kings of the earth, who courted the protection of the victorious commonwealth, were gratified with such trifling presents as could only derive a value from the hand that bestowed them; an ivory chair, a coarse garment of purple, an inconsiderable piece of plate, or a quantity of copper coin. After the wealth of nations had centred in Rome, the emperors displayed their greatness, and even their policy, by the regular exercise of a steady and moderate liberality towards the allies of the state. They relieved the poverty of the barbarians, honoured their merit, and recompensed their fidelity. These voluntary marks of bounty were understood to flow not from the fears, but merely from the generosity or the gratitude of the Romans; and whilst presents

* I have ventured to copy from Tacitus the picture of a similar engagement between a Roman army and a German tribe.
† *The Historia Augusta* gives them a very honourable place among the small number of good emperors who reigned between Augustus and Diocletian.

and subsidies were liberally distributed among friends and suppliants, they were sternly refused to such as claimed them as a debt. But this stipulation of an annual payment to a victorious enemy appeared without disguise in the light of an ignominious tribute; the minds of the Romans were not yet accustomed to accept such unequal laws from a tribe of barbarians; and the prince, who by a necessary concession had probably saved his country, became the object of the general contempt and aversion. The death of Hostilianus, though it happened in the midst of a raging pestilence, was interpreted as the personal crime of Gallus; and even the defeat of the late emperor was ascribed by the voice of suspicion to the perfidious counsels of his hated successor. The tranquil-lity which the empire enjoyed during the first year of his administration served rather to inflame than to appease the public discontent; and, as soon as the apprehensions of war were removed, the infamy of the peace was more deeply and more sensibly felt.

But the Romans were irritated to a still higher degree when they discovered that they had not even secured their repose, though at the expense of their honour. The dangerous secret of the wealth and weakness of the empire had been revealed to the world. New swarms of barbarians, encouraged (AD 253) by the success, and not conceiving themselves bound by the obligation, of their brethren, spread devastation through the Illyrian provinces, and terror as far as the gates of Rome. The defence of the monarchy, which seemed abandoned by the pusillani-mous emperor, was assumed by Aemilianus, governor of Pannonia and Maesia; who rallied the scattered forces, and revived the fainting spirits of the troops. The barbarians were unexpectedly attacked, routed, chased, and pursued beyond the Danube. The victorious leader distributed as a donative the money collected for the tribute, and the acclamations of the soldiers proclaimed him emperor on the field of battle. Gallus, who, careless of the general welfare, indulged himself in the pleasures of Italy, was almost in the same instant informed of the success of the revolt and of the rapid approach of his aspiring lieutenant. He advanced to meet him as far as the plains of Spoleto. When the armies came in sight of each other, the soldiers of Gallus compared the ignominious conduct of their sovereign with the glory of his rival. They admired the valour of Aemilianus; they were attracted by his liberality, for he offered a considerable increase of pay to all deserters. The murder of Gallus, and of his son Volusianus, put an end to the civil war; and the senate (AD 253, May) gave a legal sanction to the rights of conquest. The letters of Aemilianus to that assembly displayed a mixture of moderation and vanity. He assured them that he should resign to their wisdom the civil administration; and, contenting himself with the quality of their general, would in a short time assert the glory of Rome, and deliver the empire from all the barbarians both of the North and of the East. His pride was flattered by the applause of the senate; and medals are still extant representing him with the name and attributes of Hercules the Victor and of Mars the Avenger.

If the new monarch possessed the abilities, he wanted the time necessary to fulfil these splendid promises. Less than four months intervened between his victory and his fall. He had vanquished Gallus: he sunk under the weight of a competitor more formidable than Gallus. That unfortunate prince had sent Valerian, already distinguished by the honourable title of censor, to bring the legions of Gaul and Germany to his aid. Valerian executed that commission with zeal and fidelity; and as he arrived too late to save his sovereign, he resolved to revenge him. The troops of Aemilianus, who still lay encamped in the plains of Spoleto, were awed by the sanctity of his character, but much more by the superior strength of his army; and as they were now becoming as incapable of personal attachment as they had always been of constitu-tional principle, they (AD 253, August) readily imbrued their hands in the blood of a prince who had so lately been the object of their partial choice. The guilt was theirs, but the advantage of it was Valerian's; who obtained the possession of the throne by the means indeed of a civil war, but with a degree of innocence singular in that age of revolutions; since he owed neither gratitude nor allegiance to his predecessor whom he dethroned.

Valerian was about sixty years of age when he was invested with the purple, not by the caprice of the populace, or the clamours of the army, but by the unanimous voice of the Roman world. In his gradual ascent through the honours of the state, he had deserved the favour of virtuous princes, and had declared himself the enemy of tyrants. His noble birth, his mild but unblemished manners, his learning, prudence, and experi-ence, were revered by the senate and people; and if mankind (according to the observation of an ancient writer) had been left at liberty to choose a master, their choice would most assuredly have fallen on Valerian. Perhaps the merit of this emperor was inadequate to his reputation; perhaps his abilities, or at least his spirit, were affected by the languor and coldness of old age. The consciousness of his decline engaged him to share the throne with a younger and more active associate: the emergency of the times demanded a general no less than a prince; and the experience of the Roman censor might have directed him where to bestow the Imperial purple, as the reward of military merit. But instead of making a judicious choice, which would have confirmed his reign and endeared his memory, Valerian, consulting only the dictates of affection or vanity, immediately invested with the supreme honours his son Gallienus, a youth whose effeminate vices had been hitherto concealed by the obscurity of a private station. The joint government of the father and the son subsisted about seven, and the sole administration of Gallienus continued about eight years (AD 253–268). But the whole period was one uninterrupted series of confusion and calamity. As the Roman Empire was at the same time, and on every side, attacked by the blind fury of foreign invaders, and the wild ambition of domestic usurpers, we shall consult order and perspicuity by pursuing not so much the doubtful arrangement of dates as the more natural distribution of subjects. The most dangerous enemies of Rome, during the reigns of Valerian and Gallienus, were, 1. The Franks; 2. The Alemanni; 3. The Goths; and 4. The Persians. Under these general appellations we may comprehend the adventures of less considerable tribes, whose obscure and uncouth names would only serve to oppress the memory and perplex the attention of the reader.

I. As the posterity of the Franks compose one of the greatest and most enlightened nations of Europe, the powers of learning and ingenuity have been exhausted in the discovery of their unlettered ancestors. To the tales of credulity have succeeded the systems of fancy. Every passage has been sifted, every spot has been surveyed, that might possibly reveal some faint traces of their origin. It has been supposed that Pannonia, that Gaul, that the northern parts of Germany, gave birth to that celebrated colony of warriors. At length the most rational critics, rejecting the fictitious emigrations of ideal conquerors, have acquiesced in a sentiment whose simplicity persuades us of its truth. They suppose that, about the year 240, a new confederacy was formed under the name of Franks, by the old inhabitants of the Lower Rhine and the Weser. The present circle of Westphalia, the Landgraviate of Hesse, and the duchies of Brunswick and Luneburg, were the ancient seat of the Chauci, who, in their inaccessible morasses, defied the Roman arms; of the Cherusci, proud of the fame of Arminius; of the Catti, formidable by their firm and intrepid infantry; and of several other tribes of inferior power and renown. The love of liberty was the ruling passion of these Germans; the enjoyment of it their best treasure; the word that expressed that enjoyment the most pleasing to their ear. They deserved, they assumed, they

maintained the honourable epithet of Franks or Freemen, which concealed, though it did not extinguish, the peculiar names of the several
states of the confederacy. Tacit consent, and mutual advantage, dictated
the first laws of the union; it was gradually cemented by habit and
experience. The league of the Franks may admit of some comparison
with the Helvetic body; in which every canton, retaining its independent
sovereignty, consults with its brethren in the common cause, without
acknowledging the authority of any supreme head or representative
assembly. But the principle of the two confederacies was extremely
different. A peace of two hundred years has rewarded the wise and
honest policy of the Swiss. An inconstant spirit, the thirst of rapine, and
a disregard to the most solemn treaties, disgraced the character of the
Franks.

The Romans had long experienced the daring valour of the people of
Lower Germany. The union of their strength threatened Gaul with a
more formidable invasion, and required the presence of Gallienus, the
heir and colleague of imperial power. Whilst that prince, and his infant
son Salonius, displayed, in the court of Trèves, the majesty of the empire,
its armies were ably conducted by their general Posthumus, who,
though he afterwards betrayed the family of Valerian, was ever faithful
for the great interest of the monarchy. The treacherous language of
panegyrics and medals darkly announces a long series of victories.
Trophies and titles attest (if such evidence can attest) the fame of
Posthumus, who is repeatedly styled the conqueror of the Germans, and
the saviour of Gaul.

But a single fact, the only one indeed of which we have any distinct
knowledge, erases, in a great measure, these monuments of vanity and
adulation. The Rhine, though dignified with the title of Safeguard of the
Provinces, was an imperfect barrier against the daring spirit of enterprise
with which the Franks were actuated. Their rapid devastations stretched
from the river to the foot of the Pyrennees: nor were they stopped by those
mountains. Spain, which had never dreaded, was unable to resist, the
inroads of the Germans. During twelve years, the greatest part of the
reign of Gallienus, that opulent country was the theatre of unequal and
destructive hostilities. Tarragona, the flourishing capital of a peaceful
province, was sacked and almost destroyed, and so late as the days of
Orosius, who wrote in the fifth century, wretched cottages, scattered
amidst the ruins of magnificent cities, still recorded the rage of the
barbarians. When the exhausted country no longer supplied a variety of
plunder, the Franks seized on some vessels in the ports of Spain, and

transported themselves into Mauritania. The distant province was astonished with the fury of these barbarians, who seemed to fall from a new world, as their name, manners, and complexion were equally unknown on the coast of Africa.

II. In that part of Upper Saxony beyond the Elbe, which is at present called the Marquisate of Lusace, there existed, in ancient times, a sacred wood, the awful seat of the superstition of the Suevi. None were permitted to enter the holy precincts without confessing, by their servile bonds and suppliant posture, the immediate presence of the sovereign Deity. Patriotism contributed as well as devotion to consecrate the Sonnenwald, or wood of the Semnones. It was universally believed that the nation had received its first existence on that sacred spot. At stated periods, the numerous tribes who gloried in the Suevic blood resorted thither by their ambassadors; and the memory of their common extrac-tion was perpetuated by barbaric rites and human sacrifices. The wide extended name of Suevi filled the interior countries of Germany from the banks of the Oder to those of the Danube. They were distinguished from the other Germans by their peculiar mode of dressing their long hair, which they gathered into a rude knot on the crown of the head; and they delighted in an ornament that showed their ranks more lofty and terrible in the eyes of the enemy. Jealous as the Germans were of military renown, they all confessed the superior valour of the Suevi; and the tribes of the Usipetes and Tencteri, who, with a vast army, encountered the dictator Caesar, declared that they esteemed it not a disgrace to have fled before a people to whose arms the immortal gods themselves were unequal.

In the reign of the emperor Caracalla, an innumerable swarm of Suevi appeared on the banks of the Main, and in the neighbourhood of the Roman provinces, in quest either of food, of plunder, or of glory. The hasty army of volunteers gradually coalesced into a great and permanent nation, and as it was composed from so many different tribes, assumed the name of Alemanni, or All-men; to denote at once their various lineage and their common bravery. The latter was soon felt by the Romans in many a hostile inroad. The Alemanni fought chiefly on horseback; but their cavalry was rendered still more formidable by a mixture of light infantry, selected from the bravest and most active of the youth, whom frequent exercise had enured to accompany the horsemen in the longest march, the most rapid charge, or the most precipitate retreat.

This warlike people of Germans had been astonished by the immense preparations of Alexander Severus; they were dismayed by the arms of his successor, a barbarian equal in valour and fierceness to themselves. But still hovering on the frontiers of the empire, they increased the general disorder that ensued after the death of Decius. They inflicted severe wounds on the rich provinces of Gaul; they were the first who removed the veil that covered the feeble majesty of Italy. A numerous body of the Alemanni penetrated across the Danube, and through the Rhaetian Alps, into the plains of Lombardy, advanced as far as Ravenna, and displayed the victorious banners of barbarians almost in sight of Rome. The insult and the danger rekindled in the senate some sparks of their ancient virtue. Both the emperors were engaged in far distant wars, Valerian in the East and Gallienus on the Rhine. All the hopes and resources of the Romans were in themselves. In this emergency, the senators resumed the defence of the republic, drew out the Praetorian Guards, who had been left to garrison the capital, and filled up their numbers by enlisting into the public service the stoutest and most willing of the Plebeians. The Alemanni, astonished with the sudden appearance of an army more numerous than their own, retired into Germany laden with spoil; and their retreat was esteemed as a victory by the unwarlike Romans.

When Gallienus received the intelligence that his capital was delivered from the barbarians, he was much less delighted than alarmed with the courage of the senate, since it might one day prompt them to rescue the public from domestic tyranny as well as from foreign invasion. His timid ingratitude was published to his subjects in an edict which prohibited the senators from exercising any military employment, and even from approaching the camps of the legions. But his fears were groundless. The rich and luxurious nobles, sinking into their natural character, accepted, as a favour, this disgraceful exemption from military service; and as long as they were indulged in the enjoyment of their baths, their theatres, and their villas, they cheerfully resigned the more dangerous cares of empire to the rough hands of peasants and soldiers.

Another invasion of the Alemanni, of a more formidable aspect, but more glorious event, is mentioned by a writer of the later empire. Three hundred thousand of that warlike people are said to have been vanquished, in a battle near Milan, by Gallienus in person at the head of only ten thousand Romans. We may, however, with great probability, ascribe this incredible victory either to the credulity of the historian or to some exaggerated exploits of one of the emperor's lieutenants. It was by arms of a very different nature that Gallienus endeavoured to protect Italy from the fury of the Germans. He espoused Pipa, the daughter of a king of the Marcomanni, a Suevic tribe, which was often confounded with the Alemanni in their wars and conquests. To the father, as the price of his alliance, he granted an ample settlement in Pannonia. The native charms of unpolished beauty seem to have fixed the daughter in the affections of the inconstant emperor, and the bands of policy were more firmly connected by those of love. But the haughty prejudice of Rome still refused the name of marriage to the profane mixture of a citizen and a barbarian; and has stigmatised the German princess with the oppro-brious title of concubine of Gallienus.

III. We have already traced the emigration of the Goths from Scandinavia, or at least from Prussia, to the mouth of the Borysthenes, and have followed their victorious arms from the Borysthenes to the Danube. Under the reigns of Valerian and Gallienus, the frontier of the last-mentioned river was perpetually infested by the inroads of Germans and Sarmatians; but it was defended by the Romans with more than usual firmness and success. The provinces that were the seat of war recruited the armies of Rome with an inexhaustible supply of hardy soldiers and more than one of these Illyrian peasants attained the station and displayed the abilities of a general. Though flying parties of the barbarians, who incessantly hovered on the banks of the Danube, penetrated sometimes to the confines of Italy and Macedonia; their progress was commonly checked, or their return intercepted, by the Imperial lieutenants. But the great stream of the Gothic hostilities was diverted into a very different channel. The Goths, in their new settlement of the Ukraine, soon became masters of the northern coast of the Euxine: to the south of that inland sea were situated the soft and wealthy provinces of Asia Minor, which possessed all that could attract, and nothing that could resist, a barbarian conqueror.

The banks of the Borysthenes are only sixty miles distant from the narrow entrance of the peninsula of Crim Tartary, known to the ancients under the name of Chersonesus Taurica.* On that inhospi-table shore, Euripides, embellishing with exquisite art the tales of antiquity, has placed the scene of one of his most affecting tragedies.† The bloody sacrifices of Diana, the arrival of Orestes and Pylades, and the triumph of virtue and religion over savage fierceness, serve to represent an historical truth, that the Tauri, the original inhabitants of the peninsula, were, in some degree, reclaimed from their brutal manners

* M. de Peyssonel, who had been French consul at Caffa, in his *Observations sur les peuples barbares, qui ont habité les bords du Danube.*
† Euripides in *Iphigenia in Tauris.*

by a gradual intercourse with the Grecian colonies which settled along the maritime coast. The little kingdom of Bosphorus, whose capital was situated on the Straits, through which the Maeotis communicates itself to the Euxine, was composed of degenerate Greeks and half-civilised barbarians. It subsisted, as an independent state, from the time of the Peloponnesian war, was at last swallowed up by the ambition of Mithridates, and, with the rest of his dominions, sunk under the weight of the Roman arms. From the reign of Augustus, the kings of Bosphorus were the humble, but not useless, allies of the empire. By presents, by arms, and by a slight fortification drawn across the Isthmus, they effectually guarded against the roving plunderers of Sarmatia the access of a country which, from its peculiar situation and convenient harbours, commanded the Euxine Sea and Asia Minor. As long as the sceptre was possessed by a lineal succession of kings, they acquitted themselves of their important charge with vigilance and success. Domestic factions, and the fears, or private interest, of obscure usurpers, who seized on the vacant throne, admitted the Goths into the heart of Bosphorus. With the acquisition of a superfluous waste of fertile soil, the conquerors obtained the command of a naval force, sufficient to transport their armies to the coast of Asia. The ships used in the navigation of the Euxine were of a very singular construction. They were slight flat-bottomed barks framed of timber only, without the least mixture of iron, and occasionally covered with a shelving roof on the appearance of a tempest. In these floating houses, the Goths carelessly trusted themselves to the mercy of an unknown sea, under the conduct of sailors pressed into the service, and whose skill and fidelity were equally suspicious. But the hopes of plunder had banished every idea of danger, and a natural fearlessness of temper supplied in their minds the more rational confidence which is the just result of knowledge and experience. Warriors of such a daring spirit must have often murmured against the cowardice of their guides, who required the strongest assurances of a settled calm before they would venture to embark; and would scarcely ever be tempted to lose sight of the land. Such, at least, is the practice of the modern Turks, and they are probably not inferior in the art of navigation to the ancient inhabitants of Bosphorus.

The fleet of the Goths, leaving the coast of Circassia on the left hand, first appeared before Pityus, the utmost limits of the Roman provinces; a city provided with a convenient port and fortified with a strong wall. Here they met with a resistance more obstinate than they had reason to expect from the feeble garrison of a distant fortress. They were repulsed;

and their disappointment seemed to diminish the terror of the Gothic name. As long as Successianus, an officer of superior rank and merit, defended that frontier, all their efforts were ineffectual; but as soon as he was removed by Valerian to a more honourable but less important station, they resumed the attack of Pityus; and, by the destruction of that city, obliterated the memory of their former disgrace.

Circling round the eastern extremity of the Euxine Sea, the naviga~ tion from Pityus to Trebizond is about three hundred miles. The course of the Goths carried them in sight of the country of Colchis, so famous by the expedition of the Argonauts, and they even attempted, though without success, to pillage a rich temple at the mouth of the river Phasis. Trebizond, celebrated in the retreat of the Ten Thousand as an ancient colony of Greeks, derived its wealth and splendour from the munifi~ cence of the Emperor Hadrian, who had constructed an artificial port on a coast left destitute by nature of secure harbours. The city was large and populous; a double enclosure of walls seemed to defy the fury of the Goths, and the usual garrison had been strengthened by a reinforcement of ten thousand men. But there are not any advantages capable of supplying the absence of discipline and vigilance. The numerous garrison of Trebizond, dissolved in riot and luxury, disdained to guard their impregnable fortifications. The Goths soon discovered the supine negligence of the besieged, erected a lofty pile of fascines, ascended the walls in the silence of the night, and entered the defenceless city sword in hand. A general massacre of the people ensued, whilst the affrighted soldiers escaped through the opposite gates of the town. The most holy temples, and the most splendid edifices, were involved in a common destruction. The booty that fell into the hands of the Goths was immense: the wealth of the adjacent countries had been deposited in Trebizond, as in a secure place of refuge. The number of captives was incredible, as the victorious barbarians ranged without opposition through the extensive province of Pontus. The rich spoils of Trebizond filled a great fleet of ships that had been found in the port. The robust youth of the sea~coast were chained to the oar; and the Goths, satisfied with the success of their first naval expedition, returned in triumph to their new establishments in the kingdom of Bosphorus.

The second expedition of the Goths was undertaken with greater powers of men and ships; but they steered a different course, and, disdaining the exhausted provinces of Pontus, followed the western coast of the Euxine, passed before the wide mouths of the Borysthenes, the Dniester, and the Danube, and increasing their fleet by the capture of a great number of fishing barks, they approached the narrow outlet through which the Euxine Sea pours its waters into the Mediterranean, and divides the continents of Europe and Asia. The garrison of Chalcedon was encamped near the temple of Jupiter Urius, on a promontory that commanded the entrance of the Strait; and so dreaded were the invasions of the barbarians, that this body of troops surpassed in number the Gothic army. But it was in numbers alone that they surpassed it. They deserted with precipitation their advantageous post, and abandoned the town of Chalcedon, most plentifully stored with arms and money, to the discretion of the conquerors. Whilst they hesitated whether they should prefer the sea or land, Europe or Asia, for the scene of their hostilities, a perfidious fugitive pointed out Nicomedia, once the capital of the kings of Bithynia, as a rich and easy conquest. He guided the march, which was only sixty miles from the camp of Chalcedon, directed the resistless attack, and partook of the booty; for the Goths had learned sufficient policy to reward the traitor whom they detested. Nice, Prusa, Apamaea, Cius, cities that had sometimes rivalled, or imitated, the splendour of Nicomedia, were involved in the same calamity, which, in a few weeks, raged without control through the whole province of Bithynia. Three hundred years of peace, enjoyed by the soft inhabitants of Asia, had abolished the exercise of arms and removed the apprehension of danger. The ancient walls were suffered to moulder away, and all the revenue of the most opulent cities was reserved for the construction of baths, temples, and theatres.

When the city of Cyzicus withstood the utmost effort of Mithridates, it was distinguished by wise laws, a naval power of two hundred galleys, and three arsenals; of arms, of military engines, and of corn. It was still the seat of wealth and luxury; but of its ancient strength nothing remained except the situation, in a little island of the Propontis, connected with the continent of Asia only by two bridges. From the recent sack of Prusa, the Goths advanced within eighteen miles of the city, which they had devoted to destruction; but the ruin of Cyzicus was delayed by a fortunate accident. The season was rainy, and the lake Apolloniates, the reservoir of all the springs of Mount Olympus, rose to an uncommon height. The little river of Rhyndacus, which issues from the lake, swelled into a broad and rapid stream, and stopped the progress of the Goths. Their retreat to the maritime city of Heraclea, where the fleet had probably been stationed, was attended by a long train of waggons, laden with the spoils of Bithynia, and was marked by the flames of Nice and Nicomedia, which they wantonly burnt. Some obscure hints are mentioned of a doubtful combat that secured their retreat. But even a complete victory would have been of little moment, as the approach of the autumnal equinox summoned them to hasten their return. To navigate the Euxine before the month of May, or after that of September, is esteemed by the modern Turks the most unquestionable instance of rashness and folly.

When we are informed that the third fleet, equipped by the Goths in the ports of Bosphorus, consisted of five hundred sail of ships, our ready imagination instantly computes and multiplies the formidable armament; but as we are assured, by the judicious Strabo, that the piratical vessels used by the barbarians of Pontus and the Lesser Scythia were not capable of containing more than twenty-five or thirty men, we may safely affirm that fifteen thousand warriors, at the most, embarked in this great expedition. Impatient of the limits of the Euxine, they steered their destructive course from the Cimmerian to the Thracian Bosphorus. When they had almost gained the middle of the Straits, they were suddenly driven back to the entrance of them, till a favourable wind springing up the next day carried them in a few hours into the placid sea, or rather lake, of the Propontis. Their landing on the little island of Cyzicus was attended with the ruin of that ancient and noble city. From thence issuing again through the narrow passage of the Hellespont, they pursued their winding navigation amidst the numerous islands scattered over the Archipelago, or the Aegean Sea. The assistance of captives and deserters must have been very necessary to pilot their vessels and to direct their various incursions, as well on the coast of Greece as on that of Asia. At length the Gothic fleet anchored in the port of Piraeus, five miles distant from Athens, which had attempted to make some preparations for a vigorous defence. Cleodamus, one of the engineers employed by the emperor's orders to fortify the maritime cities against the Goths, had already begun to repair the ancient walls fallen to decay since the time of Sylla. The efforts of his skill were ineffectual, and the barbarians became masters of the native seat of the muses and the arts. But while the conquerors abandoned themselves to the licence of plunder and intemperance, their fleet, that lay with a slender guard in the harbour of Piraeus, was unexpectedly attacked by the brave Dexippus, who, flying with the engineer Cleodamus from the sack of Athens, collected a hasty band of volunteers, peasants as well as soldiers, and in some measure avenged the calamities of his country.

But this exploit, whatever lustre it might shed on the declining age of Athens, served rather to irritate than to subdue the undaunted spirit of the northern invaders. A general conflagration blazed out at the same time in every district of Greece. Thebes and Argos, Corinth and Sparta, which had formerly waged such memorable wars against each other, were now unable to bring an army into the field, or even to defend their ruined fortifications. The rage of war, both by land and by sea, spread from the eastern point of Sunium to the western coast of Epirus. The Goths had already advanced within sight of Italy, when the approach of such imminent danger awakened the indolent Gallienus from his dreams of pleasure. The emperor appeared in arms; and his presence seems to have checked the ardour, and to have divided the strength, of the enemy. Naulobatus, a chief of the Heruli, accepted an honourable capitulation, entered with a large body of his countrymen into the service of Rome, and was invested with the ornaments of the consular dignity, which had never before been profaned by the hands of a barbarian. Great numbers of the Goths, disgusted with the perils and hardships of a tedious voyage, broke into Maesia, with a design of forcing their way over the Danube to their settlements in the Ukraine. This wild attempt would have proved inevitable destruction if the discord of the Roman generals had not opened to the barbarians the means of an escape. The small remainder of this destroying host returned on board their vessels; and measuring back their way through the Hellespont and the Bosphorus, ravaged in their passage the shores of Troy, whose fame, immortalised by Homer, will probably survive the memory of the Gothic conquests. As soon as they found themselves in safety within the basin of the Euxine, they landed at Anchialus in Thrace, near the foot of Mount Haemus; and, after all their toils, indulged themselves in the use of those pleasant and salutary hot baths. What remained of the voyage was a short and easy navigation. Such was the various fate of this third and greatest of their naval enterprises. It may seem difficult to conceive how the original body of fifteen thousand warriors could sustain the losses and divisions of so bold an adventure. But as their numbers were gradually wasted by the sword, by shipwrecks, and by the influence of a warm climate, they were perpetually renewed by troops of banditti and deserters, who flocked to the standard of plunder, and by a crowd of fugitive slaves, often of German or Sarmatian extraction, who eagerly seized the glorious opportunity of freedom and revenge. In these expeditions, the Gothic nation claimed a superior share of honour and danger; but the tribes that fought under the Gothic banners are sometimes distinguished and sometimes confounded in the imperfect histories of that age; and as the barbarian fleets seemed to issue from the mouth of the

Tanais, the vague but familiar appellation of Scythians was frequently bestowed on the mixed multitude.

In the general calamities of mankind the death of an individual, however exalted, the ruin of an edifice, however famous, are passed over with careless inattention. Yet we cannot forget that the temple of Diana at Ephesus, after having risen with increasing splendour from seven repeated misfortunes, was finally burnt by the Goths in their third naval invasion. The arts of Greece, and the wealth of Asia, had conspired to erect that sacred and magnificent structure. It was supported by an hundred and twenty-seven marble columns of the Ionic order. They were the gifts of devout monarchs, and each was sixty feet high. The altar was adorned with the masterly sculptures of Praxiteles, who had, perhaps, selected from the favourite legends of the place the birth of the divine children of Latona, the concealment of Apollo after the slaughter of the Cyclops, and the clemency of Bacchus to the vanquished Amazons. Yet the length of the temple of Ephesus was only four hundred and twenty-five feet, about two-thirds of the measure of the church of St Peter's at Rome. In the other dimensions it was still more inferior to that sublime production of modern architecture. The spreading arms of a Christian cross require a much greater breadth than the oblong temples of the pagans; and the boldest artists of antiquity would have been startled at the proposal of raising in the air a dome of the size and proportions of the Pantheon. The temple of Diana was, however, admired as one of the wonders of the world. Successive empires, the Persian, the Macedonian, and the Roman, had revered its sanctity and enriched its splendour. But the rude savages of the Baltic were destitute of a taste for the elegant arts, and they despised the ideal terrors of a foreign superstition.

Another circumstance is related of these invasions, which might deserve our notice, were it not justly to be suspected as the fanciful conceit of a recent sophist. We are told that in the sack of Athens the Goths had collected all the libraries, and were on the point of setting fire to this funeral pile of Grecian learning, had not one of their chiefs, of more refined policy than his brethren, dissuaded them from the design; by the profound observation that as long as the Greeks were addicted to the study of books, they would never apply themselves to the exercise of arms.* The sagacious counsellor (should the truth of the fact be admitted) reasoned like an ignorant barbarian. In the most polite and

* Such an anecdote was perfectly suited to the taste of Montaigne. He makes use of it in his agreeable Essay on Pedantry.

A view of the eastern Portico of the Temple of Minerva, called the Parthenon

A view of a Doric Portico at Athens generally supposed to be the remains of a Temple dedicated to Rome and Augustus

powerful nations, genius of every kind has displayed itself about the same period; and the age of science has generally been the age of military virtue and success.

IV. The new sovereigns of Persia, Artaxerxes and his son Sapor, had triumphed over the house of Arsaces. Of the many princes of that ancient race, Chosroes, king of Armenia, had alone preserved both his life and his independence. He defended himself by the natural strength of his country; by the perpetual resort of fugitives and malcontents; by the alliance of the Romans, and, above all, by his own courage. Invincible in arms, during a thirty years' war, he was at length assassinated by the emissaries of Sapor, king of Persia. The patriotic satraps of Armenia, who asserted the freedom and dignity of the crown, implored the protection of Rome in favour of Tiridates the lawful heir. But the son of Chosroes was an infant, the allies were at a distance, and the Persian monarch advanced towards the frontier at the head of an irresistible force. Young Tiridates, the future hope of his country, was saved by the fidelity of a servant, and Armenia continued above twenty-seven years a reluctant province of the great monarchy of Persia. Elated with this easy conquest, and presuming on the distresses or the degeneracy of the Romans, Sapor obliged the strong garrisons of Carrhae and Nisibis to surrender, and spread devastation and terror on either side of the Euphrates.

The loss of an important frontier, the ruin of a faithful and natural ally, and the rapid success of Sapor's ambition, affected Rome with a deep sense of the insult as well as of the danger. Valerian flattered himself that the vigilance of his lieutenants would sufficiently provide for the safety of the Rhine and of the Danube; but he resolved, notwithstanding his advanced age, to march in person to the defence of the Euphrates. During his progress through Asia Minor, the naval enterprises of the Goths were suspended, and the afflicted province enjoyed a transient and fallacious calm. He passed the Euphrates, encountered the Persian monarch near the walls of Edessa, was (AD 260) vanquished and taken prisoner by Sapor. The particulars of this great event are darkly and imperfectly represented; yet by the glimmering light which is afforded us, we may discover a long series of imprudence, of error, and of deserved misfortunes on the side of the Roman emperor. He reposed an implicit confidence in Macrinus, his Praetorian prefect. That worthless minister rendered his master formidable only to the oppressed subjects, and contemptible to the enemies of Rome. By his weak or wicked counsels, the Imperial army was betrayed into a situation where valour and military skill were equally unavailing. The vigorous attempt of the Romans to cut their way through the Persian host was repulsed with great slaughter; and Sapor, who encompassed the camp with superior numbers, patiently waited till the increasing rage of famine and pesti- lence had ensured his victory. The licentious murmurs of the legions soon accused Valerian as the cause of their calamities; their seditious clamours demanded an instant capitulation. An immense sum of gold was offered to purchase the permission of a disgraceful retreat. But the Persian, conscious of his superiority, refused the money with disdain; and detaining the deputies, advanced in order of battle to the foot of the Roman rampart, and insisted on a personal conference with the emperor. Valerian was reduced to the necessity of intrusting his life and dignity to the faith of an enemy. The interview ended as it was natural to expect. The emperor was made a prisoner, and his astonished troops laid down their arms. In such a moment of triumph, the pride and policy of Sapor prompted him to fill the vacant throne with a successor entirely dependent on his pleasure. Cyriades, an obscure fugitive of Antioch, stained with every vice, was chosen to dishonour the Roman purple; and the will of the Persian victor could not fail of being ratified by the acclamations, however reluctant, of the captive army.

The Imperial slave was eager to secure the favour of his master by an act of treason to his native country. He conducted Sapor over the Euphrates, and by the way of Chalcis to the metropolis of the East. So rapid were the motions of the Persian cavalry that, if we may credit a very judicious historian,* the city of Antioch was surprised when the idle multitude was fondly gazing on the amusements of the theatre. The splendid buildings of Antioch, private as well as public, were either pillaged or destroyed; and the numerous inhabitants were put to the sword, or led away into captivity. The tide of devastation was stopped for a moment by the resolution of the high priest of Emesa. Arrayed in his sacerdotal robes, he appeared at the head of a great body of fanatic peasants, armed only with slings, and defended his god and his property from the sacrilegious hands of the followers of Zoroaster. But the ruin of Tarsus, and many other cities, furnishes a melancholy proof that, except in this single instance, the conquest of Syria and Cilicia scarcely interrupted the progress of the Persian arms. The advantages of the narrow passes of mount Taurus were abandoned, in which an invader, whose principal force consisted in his cavalry, would have been engaged

* The sack of Antioch, anticipated by some historians, is assigned, by the decisive testimony of Ammianus Marcellinus, to the reign of Gallienus.

in a very unequal combat: and Sapor was permitted to form the siege of
Caesarea, the capital of Cappadocia; a city, though of the second rank,
which was supposed to contain four hundred thousand inhabitants.
Demosthenes commanded in the place, not so much by the commission
of the emperor, as in the voluntary defence of his country. For a long time
he deferred its fate; and, when at last Caesarea was betrayed by the
perfidy of a physician, he cut his way through the Persians, who had
been ordered to exert their utmost diligence to take him alive. This heroic
chief escaped the power of a foe, who might either have honoured or
punished his obstinate valour; but many thousands of his fellow-citizens
were involved in a general massacre, and Sapor is accused of treating his
prisoners with wanton and unrelenting cruelty. Much should undoubtedly be allowed for national animosity, much for humbled pride and
impotent revenge; yet, upon the whole, it is certain that the same prince,
who, in Armenia, had displayed the mild aspect of a legislator, showed
himself to the Romans under the stern features of a conqueror. He
despaired of making any permanent establishment in the empire, and
sought only to leave behind him a wasted desert, whilst he transported
into Persia the people and the treasures of the provinces.

At the time when the East trembled at the name of Sapor, he received
a present not unworthy of the greatest kings; a long train of camels laden
with the most rare and valuable merchandises. The rich offering was
accompanied with an epistle, respectful but not servile, from
Odenathus, one of the noblest and most opulent senators of Palmyra.
'Who is this Odenathus' (said the haughty victor, and he commanded
that the presents should be cast into the Euphrates), 'that he thus
insolently presumes to write to his lord? If he entertains a hope of
mitigating his punishment let him fall prostrate before the foot of our
throne with his hands bound behind his back. Should he hesitate, swift
destruction shall be poured on his head, on his whole race, and on his
country.' The desperate extremity to which the Palmyrenian was
reduced called into action all the latent powers of his soul. He met Sapor;
but he met him in arms. Infusing his own spirit into a little army
collected from the villages of Syria and the tents of the desert, he hovered
round the Persian host, harassed their retreat, carried off part of the
treasure, and, what was dearer than any treasure, several of the women of
the Great King; who was at last obliged to repass the Euphrates with
some marks of haste and confusion. By this exploit, Odenathus laid the
foundations of his future fame and fortunes. The majesty of Rome,
oppressed by a Persian, was protected by a Syrian or Arab of Palmyra.

The voice of history, which is often little more than the organ of hatred or flattery, reproaches Sapor with a proud abuse of the rights of conquest. We are told that Valerian, in chains, but invested with the Imperial purple, was exposed to the multitude, a constant spectacle of fallen greatness; and that whenever the Persian monarch mounted on horseback, he placed his foot on the neck of a Roman emperor. Notwithstanding all the remonstrances of his allies, who repeatedly advised him to remember the vicissitude of fortune, to dread the returning power of Rome, and to make his illustrious captive the pledge of peace, not the object of insult, Sapor still remained inflexible. When Valerian sunk under the weight of shame and grief, his skin, stuffed with straw, and formed into the likeness of a human figure, was preserved for ages in the most celebrated temple of Persia; a more real monument of triumph than the fancied trophies of brass and marble so often erected by Roman vanity.* The tale is moral and pathetic, but the truth of it may very fairly be called in question. The letters still extant from the princes of the East to Sapor are manifest forgeries; nor is it natural to suppose that a jealous monarch should, even in the person of a rival, thus publicly degrade the majesty of kings. Whatever treatment the unfortunate Valerian might experience in Persia, it is at least certain that the only emperor of Rome who had ever fallen into the hands of the enemy languished away his life in hopeless captivity.

The emperor Gallienus, who had long supported with impatience the censorial severity of his father and colleague, received the intelligence of his misfortunes with secret pleasure and avowed indifference. 'I knew that my father was a mortal' said he, 'and since he has acted as becomes a brave man, I am satisfied.' Whilst Rome lamented the fate of her sovereign, the savage coldness of his son was extolled by the servile courtiers as the perfect firmness of a hero and a stoic. It is difficult to paint the light, the various, the inconstant character of Gallienus, which he displayed without constraint, as soon as he became sole possessor of the empire. In every art that he attempted his lively genius enabled him to succeed; and as his genius was destitute of judgment, he attempted every art except the important ones of war and government. He was a master of several curious but useless sciences, a ready orator and elegant poet, a skilful gardener, an excellent cook, and most contemptible prince.

* The pagan writers lament, the Christian insult, the misfortunes of Valerian. Their various testimonies are accurately collected by Tillemont. So little has been preserved of eastern history before Mahomet, that the modern Persians are totally ignorant of the victory of Sapor, an event so glorious to their nation.

When the great emergencies of the state required his presence and attention, he was engaged in conversation with the philosopher Plotinus, wasting his time in trifling or licentious pleasures, preparing his initiation to the Grecian mysteries, or soliciting a place in the Areopagus of Athens. His profuse magnificence insulted the general poverty; the solemn ridicule of his triumphs impressed a deeper sense of the public disgrace. The repeated intelligence of invasions, defeats, and rebellions, he received with a careless smile; and singling out, with affected contempt, some particular production of the lost province, he carelessly asked whether Rome must be ruined unless it was supplied with linen from Egypt and Arras cloth from Gaul? There were, however, a few short moments in the life of Gallienus when, exasperated by some recent injury, he suddenly appeared the intrepid soldier and the cruel tyrant; till satiated with blood, or fatigued by resistance, he insensibly sunk into the natural mildness and indolence of his character.*

At a time when the reins of government were held with so loose a hand, it is not surprising that a crowd of usurpers should start up in every province of the empire against the son of Valerian. It was probably some ingenious fancy, of comparing the thirty tyrants of Rome with the thirty tyrants of Athens, that induced the writers of the Augustan History to select that celebrated number, which has been gradually received into a popular appellation. But in every light the parallel is idle and defective. What resemblance can we discover between a council of thirty persons, the united oppressors of a single city, and an uncertain list of independent rivals, who rose and fell in irregular succession through the extent of a vast empire? Nor can the number of thirty be completed, unless we include in the account the women and children who were honoured with the Imperial title. The reign of Gallienus, distracted as it was, produced only nineteen pretenders to the throne; Cyriades, Macrianus, Balista, Odenathus, and Zenobia in the East; in Gaul, and the Western Provinces, Posthumus, Lollianus, Victorinus and his mother Victoria, Marius, and Tetricus. In Illyricum and the confines of the Danube, Ingenuus, Regillianus, and Aureolus; in Pontus, Saturninus; in Isauria, Trebellianus; Piso in Thessaly; Valens in Achaia; Aemilianus in Egypt; and Celsus in Africa. To illustrate the obscure monuments of the life and death of each individual would prove a laborious task, alike

---

* This singular character has, I believe, been fairly transmitted to us. The reign of his immediate successor was short and busy; and the historians who wrote before the elevation of the family of Constantine could not have the most remote interest to misrepresent the character of Gallienus.

barren of instruction and of amusement. We may content ourselves with investigating some general characters that most strongly mark the condi-tion of the times and the manners of the men, their pretensions, their motives, their fate, and the destructive consequences of their usurpation.

It is sufficiently known that the odious appellation of *Tyrant* was often employed by the ancients to express the illegal seizure of supreme power, without any reference to the abuse of it. Several of the pretenders, who raised the standard of rebellion against the emperor Gallienus, were shining models of virtue, and almost all possessed a considerable share of vigour and ability. Their merit had recommended them to the favour of Valerian, and gradually promoted them to the most important com-mands of the empire. The generals, who assumed the title of Augustus, were either respected by their troops for their able conduct and severe discipline, or admired for valour and success in war, or beloved for frankness and generosity. The field of victory was often the scene of their election; and even the armourer Marius, the most contemptible of all the candidates for the purple, was distinguished however by intrepid cour-age, matchless strength, and blunt honesty. His mean and recent trade cast indeed an air of ridicule on his elevation; but his birth could not be more obscure than was that of the greater part of his rivals, who were born of peasants and inlisted in the army as private soldiers. In times of confusion, every active genius finds the place assigned him by Nature: in a general state of war, military merit is the road to glory and to greatness. Of the nineteen tyrants, Tetricus only was a senator; Piso alone was a noble. The blood of Numa, through twenty-eight successive gene-rations, ran in the veins of Calphurnius Piso, who, by female alliances, claimed a right of exhibiting, in his house, the images of Crassus and of the great Pompey. His ancestors had been repeatedly dignified with all the honours which the commonwealth could bestow; and of all the ancient families of Rome, the Calphurnian alone had survived the tyranny of the Caesars. The personal qualities of Piso added new lustre to his race. The usurper Valens, by whose order he was killed, confessed, with deep remorse, that even an enemy ought to have respected the sanctity of Piso; and although he died in arms against Gallienus, the senate, with the emperor's generous permission, decreed the triumphal ornaments to the memory of so virtuous a rebel.

The lieutenants of Valerian were grateful to the father, whom they esteemed. They disdained to serve the luxurious indolence of his unworthy son. The throne of the Roman world was unsupported by any principle of loyalty; and treason against such a prince might easily be considered as patriotism to the state. Yet if we examine with candour the conduct of these usurpers, it will appear that they were much oftener driven into rebellion by their fears than urged to it by their ambition. They dreaded the cruel suspicions of Gallienus; they equally dreaded the capricious violence of their troops. If the dangerous favour of the army had imprudently declared them deserving of the purple, they were marked for sure destruction; and even prudence would counsel them to secure a short enjoyment of empire, and rather to try the fortune of war than to expect the hand of an executioner. When the clamour of the soldiers invested the reluctant victims with the ensigns of sovereign authority, they sometimes mourned in secret their approaching fate. 'You have lost,' said Saturninus on the day of his elevation, 'you have lost a useful commander, and you have made a very wretched emperor.'

The apprehensions of Saturninus were justified by the repeated experience of revolutions. Of the nineteen tyrants who started up under the reign of Gallienus, there was not one who enjoyed a life of peace or a natural death. As soon as they were invested with the bloody purple, they inspired their adherents with the same fears and ambition which had occasioned their own revolt. Encompassed with domestic conspir-acy, military sedition, and civil war, they trembled on the edge of precipices, in which, after a longer or shorter term of anxiety, they were inevitably lost. The precarious monarchs received, however, such honours as the flattery of their respective armies and provinces could bestow; but their claim, founded on rebellion, could never obtain the sanction of law or history. Italy, Rome, and the senate constantly adhered to the cause of Gallienus, and he alone was considered as the sovereign of the empire. That prince condescended indeed to acknow-ledge the victorious arms of Odenathus, who deserved the honourable distinction by the respectful conduct which he always maintained towards the son of Valerian. With the general applause of the Romans, and the consent of Gallienus, the senate conferred the title of Augustus on the brave Palmyrenian; and seemed to intrust him with the govern-ment of the East, which he already possessed, in so independent a manner, that, like a private succession, he bequeathed it to his illustrious widow Zenobia.

The rapid and perpetual transitions from the cottage to the throne, and from the throne to the grave, might have amused an indifferent philosopher; were it possible for a philosopher to remain indifferent amidst the general calamities of human kind. The election of these pre-carious emperors, their power and their death, were equally destructive to their subjects and adherents. The price of their fatal elevation was instantly discharged to the troops, by an immense donative, drawn from the bowels of the exhausted people. However virtuous was their charac- ter, however pure their intentions, they found themselves reduced to the hard necessity of supporting their usurpation by frequent acts of rapine and cruelty. When they fell, they involved armies and provinces in their fall. There is still extant a most savage mandate from Gallienus to one of his ministers, after the suppression of Ingenuus, who had assumed the purple in Illyricum. 'It is not enough,' says that soft but inhuman prince, 'that you exterminate such as have appeared in arms: the chance of battle might have served me as effectually. The male sex of every age must be extirpated; provided that, in the execution of the children and old men, you can contrive means to save our reputation. Let every one die who has dropped an expression, who has entertained a thought against me, against *me*, the son of Valerian, the father and brother of so many princes. Remember that Ingenuus was made emperor: tear, kill, hew in pieces. I write to you with my own hand, and would inspire you with my own feelings.' Whilst the public forces of the state were dissipated in private quarrels, the defenceless provinces lay exposed to every invader. The bravest usurpers were compelled, by the perplexity of their situation, to conclude ignominious treaties with the common enemy, to purchase with oppressive tributes the neutrality or services of the barbarians, and to introduce hostile and independent nations into the heart of the Roman monarchy.

Such were the barbarians, and such the tyrants, who, under the reigns of Valerian and Gallienus, dismembered the provinces, and reduced the empire to the lowest pitch of disgrace and ruin, from whence it seemed impossible that it should ever emerge. As far as the barrenness of materials would permit, we have attempted to trace, with order and perspicuity, the general events of that calamitous period. There still remain some particular facts; 1. The disorders of Sicily; 2. The tumults of Alexandria; and, 3. The rebellion of the Isaurians, which may serve to reflect a strong light on the horrid picture.

I. Whenever numerous troops of banditti, multiplied by success and impunity, publicly defy, instead of eluding the justice of their country, we may safely infer that the excessive weakness of the government is felt and abused by the lowest ranks of the community. The situation of Sicily preserved it from the barbarians; nor could the disarmed province have supported an usurper. The sufferings of that once flourishing and still fertile island were inflicted by baser hands. A licentious crowd of slaves and peasants reigned for a while over the plundered country, and renewed the memory of the servile wars of more ancient times. Devas-tations, of which the husbandman was either the victim or the accom-plice, must have ruined the agriculture of Sicily; and as the principal estates were the property of the opulent senators of Rome, who often enclosed within a farm the territory of an old republic, it is not improbable that this private injury might affect the capital more deeply than all the conquests of the Goths or the Persians.

II. The foundation of Alexandria was a noble design, at once conceived and executed by the son of Philip. The beautiful and regular form of that great city, second only to Rome itself, comprehended a circumference of fifteen miles; it was peopled by three hundred thousand free inhabitants, besides at least an equal number of slaves. The lucrative trade of Arabia and India flowed through the port of Alexandria to the capital and provinces of the empire. Idleness was unknown. Some were employed in blowing of glass, others in weaving of linen, others again manufacturing the papyrus. Either sex, and every age, was engaged in the pursuits of industry, nor did even the blind or the lame want occupations suited to their condition. But the people of Alexandria, a various mixture of nations, united the vanity and inconstancy of the Greeks with the superstition and obstinacy of the Egyptians. The most trifling occasion, a transient scarcity of flesh or lentils, the neglect of an accustomed salutation, a mistake of precedency in the public baths, or a religious dispute,* were at any time sufficient to kindle a sedition among that vast multitude, whose resentments were furious and implacable. After the captivity of Valerian and the insolence of his son had relaxed the authority of the laws, the Alexandrians abandoned themselves to the ungoverned rage of their passions, and their unhappy country was the theatre of a civil war, which continued (with a few short and suspicious truces) above twelve years.† All intercourse was cut off between the several quarters of the afflicted city, every street was polluted with blood, every building of strength converted into a citadel; nor did the tumults subside, till a considerable part of Alexandria was irretrievably ruined. The spacious and magnificent district of Bruchion, with its palaces and museum, the residence of the kings and philosophers of Egypt, is described above a century afterwards as already reduced to its present state of dreary solitude.

* Such as the sacrilegious murder of a divine cat.
† This long and terrible sedition was first occasioned by a dispute between a soldier and a townsman about a pair of shoes.

III. The obscure rebellion of Trebellianus, who assumed the purple in Isauria, a petty province of Asia Minor, was attended with strange and memorable consequences. The pageant of royalty was soon destroyed by an officer of Gallienus; but his followers, despairing of mercy, resolved to shake off their allegiance, not only to the emperor, but to the empire, and suddenly returned to the savage manners, from which they had never perfectly been reclaimed. Their craggy rocks, a branch of the wide-extended Taurus, protected their inaccessible retreat. The tillage of some fertile valleys supplied them with necessaries, and a habit of rapine with the luxuries of life. In the heart of the Roman monarchy, the Isaurians long continued a nation of wild barbarians. Succeeding princes, unable to reduce them to obedience either by arms or policy, were compelled to acknowledge their weakness by surrounding the hostile and independent spot with a strong chain of fortifications, which often proved insufficient to restrain the incursions of these domestic foes. The Isaurians, gradually extending their territory to the sea-coast, subdued the western and mountainous part of Cilicia, formerly the nest of those daring pirates, against whom the republic had once been obliged to exert its utmost force, under the conduct of the great Pompey.

Our habits of thinking so fondly connect the order of the universe with the fate of man, that this gloomy period of history has been decorated with inundations, earthquakes, uncommon meteors, preternatural darkness, and a crowd of prodigies fictitious or exaggerated. But a long and general famine was a calamity of a more serious kind. It was the inevitable consequence of rapine and oppression, which extirpated the produce of the present, and the hope of future harvests. Famine is almost always followed by epidemical diseases, the effect of scanty and unwholesome food. Other causes must however have contributed to the furious plague, which, from the year two hundred and fifty to the year two hundred and sixty-five, raged without interruption in every province, every city, and almost every family, of the Roman Empire. During some time five thousand persons died daily in Rome; and many towns, that had escaped the hands of the barbarians, were entirely depopulated.

We have the knowledge of a very curious circumstance, of some use perhaps in the melancholy calculation of human calamities. An exact register was kept at Alexandria, of all the citizens entitled to receive the distribution of corn. It was found that the ancient number of those comprised between the ages of forty and seventy had been equal to the whole sum of claimants, from fourteen to fourscore years of age, who remained alive after the reign of Gallienus. Applying this authentic fact to the most correct tables of mortality, it evidently proves that above half the people of Alexandria had perished; and could we venture to extend the analogy to the other provinces, we might suspect that war, pestilence, and famine had consumed, in a few years, the moiety of the human species.

I I

REIGN OF CLAUDIUS — DEFEAT OF THE GOTHS —
VICTORIES, TRIUMPH, AND DEATH OF AURELIAN

UNDER THE DEPLORABLE REIGNS OF
Valerian and Gallienus the empire was oppressed and almost destroyed
by the soldiers, the tyrants, and the barbarians. It was saved by a series of
great princes, who derived their obscure origin from the martial provinces of Illyricum. Within a period of about thirty years, Claudius,
Aurelian, Probus, Diocletian and his colleagues, triumphed over the
foreign and domestic enemies of the state, re-established, with the
military discipline, the strength of the frontiers, and deserved the glorious
title of Restorers of the Roman world.

The removal of an effeminate tyrant made way for a succession of
heroes. The indignation of the people imputed all their calamities to
Gallienus, and the far greater part were, indeed, the consequence of his
dissolute manners and careless administration. He was even destitute of a
sense of honour, which so frequently supplies the absence of public
virtue; and as long as he was permitted to enjoy the possession of Italy, a
victory of the barbarians, the loss of a province, or the rebellion of a
general, seldom disturbed the tranquil course of his pleasures. At length
a considerable army, stationed on the Upper Danube, invested with the
Imperial purple their leader Aureolus, who, disdaining a confined and
barren reign over the mountains of Rhaetia, passed the Alps, occupied
Milan, threatened Rome, and challenged Gallienus to dispute in the
field the sovereignty of Italy. The emperor, provoked by the insult, and
alarmed by the instant danger, suddenly exerted that latent vigour which
sometimes broke through the indolence of his temper. Forcing himself
from the luxury of the palace, he appeared in arms at the head of his
legions, and advanced beyond the Po to encounter his competitor. The
corrupted name of Pontirolo* still preserves the memory of a bridge over
the Adda, which, during the action, must have proved an object of the

* *Pons Aureoli*, thirteen miles from Bergamo, and thirty-two from Milan. Near this
place, in the year 1703, the obstinate battle of Cassano was fought between the French
and Austrians. The excellent relation of the Chevalier de Folard, who was present,
gives a very distinct idea of the ground.

utmost importance to both armies. The Rhaetian usurper, after receiving a total defeat and a dangerous wound, retired into Milan. The siege of that great city was immediately formed; the walls were battered with every engine in use among the ancients; and Aureolus, doubtful of his internal strength and hopeless of foreign succours, already anticipated the fatal consequences of unsuccessful rebellion.

His last resource was an attempt to seduce the loyalty of the besiegers. He scattered libels through their camp, inviting the troops to desert an unworthy master, who sacrificed the public happiness to his luxury, and the lives of his most valuable subjects to the slightest suspicions. The arts of Aureolus diffused fears and discontent among the principal officers of his rival. A conspiracy was formed by Heraclianus, the Praetorian prefect, by Marcian, a general of rank and reputation, and by Cecrops, who commanded a numerous body of Dalmatian guards. The death of Gallienus was resolved, and, notwithstanding their desire of first ter-minating the siege of Milan, the extreme danger which accompanied every moment's delay obliged them to hasten the execution of their daring purpose. At a late hour of the night, but while the emperor still protracted the pleasures of the table, an alarm was suddenly given that Aureolus, at the head of all his forces, had made a desperate sally from the town; Gallienus, who was never deficient in personal bravery, started from his silken couch, and, without allowing himself time either to put on his armour or to assemble his guards, he mounted on horseback and rode full speed towards the supposed place of the attack. Encompassed by his declared or concealed enemies, he soon, amidst the nocturnal tumult, received a mortal dart from an uncertain hand. Before he expired, a patriotic sentiment rising in the mind of Gallienus induced him to name a deserving successor, and it was his last request that the Imperial ornaments should be delivered to Claudius, who then com-manded a detached army in the neighbourhood of Pavia. The report at least was diligently propagated, and the order cheerfully obeyed by the conspirators, who had already agreed to place Claudius on the throne. On the first news of the emperor's death the troops expressed some suspicion and resentment, till the one was removed and other assuaged by a donative of twenty pieces of gold to each soldier. They then ratified the election and acknowledged the merit of their new sovereign.

The obscurity which covered the origin of Claudius, though it was afterwards embellished by some flattering fictions, sufficiently betrays the meanness of his birth. We can only discover that he was a native of one of the provinces bordering on the Danube, that his youth was spent in arms, and that his modest valour attracted the favour and confidence of Decius. The senate and people already considered him as an excellent officer, equal to the most important trusts, and censured the inattention of Valerian, who suffered him to remain in the subordinate station of a tribune. But it was not long before that emperor distinguished the merit of Claudius, by declaring him general and chief of the Illyrian frontier, with the command of all the troops in Thrace, Maesia, Dacia, Pan-nonia, and Dalmatia, the appointments of the prefect of Egypt, the establishment of the proconsul of Africa, and the sure prospect of the consulship. By his victories over the Goths he deserved from the senate the honour of a statue, and excited the jealous apprehensions of Gal-lienus. It was impossible that a soldier could esteem so dissolute a sovereign, nor is it easy to conceal a just contempt. Some unguarded expressions which dropped from Claudius were officiously transmitted to the royal ear. The emperor's answer to an officer of confidence describes in very lively colours his own character and that of the times. 'There is not anything capable of giving me more serious concern than the intelligence contained in your last despatch, that some malicious suggestions have indisposed towards us the mind of our friend and *parent* Claudius. As you regard your allegiance, use every means to appease his resentment, but conduct your negotiation with secrecy; let it not reach the knowledge of the Dacian troops; they are already provoked, and it might inflame their fury. I myself have sent him some presents: be it your care that he accepts them with pleasure. Above all, let him not suspect that I am made acquainted with his imprudence. The fear of my anger might urge him to desperate counsels.' The presents which accompanied this humble epistle, in which the monarch solicited a reconciliation with his discontented subject, consisted of a considerable sum of money, a splendid wardrobe, and a valuable service of silver and gold plate. By such arts Gallienus softened the indignation and dispelled the fears of his Illyrian general, and during the remainder of that reign the formidable sword of Claudius was always drawn in the cause of a master whom he despised. At last, indeed, he received from the conspirators the bloody purple of Gallienus; but he had been absent from their camp and counsels; and however he might applaud the deed, we may candidly presume that he was innocent of the knowledge of it. When Claudius ascended the throne he was about fifty-four years of age.

The siege of Milan was still continued, and Aureolus soon discovered that the success of his artifices had only raised up a more determined adversary. He attempted to negotiate with Claudius a treaty of alliance and partition. 'Tell him,' replied the intrepid emperor, 'that such proposals should have been made to Gallienus; *he*, perhaps, might have listened to them with patience, and accepted a colleague as despicable as himself.' This stern refusal, and a last unsuccessful effort, obliged Aureolus to yield the city and himself to the discretion of the conqueror. The judgment of the army pronounced him worthy of death, and Claudius, after a feeble resistance, consented to the execution of the sentence. Nor was the zeal of the senate less ardent in the cause of their new sovereign. They ratified, perhaps with a sincere transport of zeal, the election of Claudius; and as his predecessor had shown himself the personal enemy of their order, they exercised, under the name of justice, a severe revenge against his friends and family. The senate was permitted to discharge the ungrateful office of punishment, and the emperor reserved for himself the pleasure and merit of obtaining by his intercession a general act of indemnity.

Such ostentatious clemency discovers less of the real character of Claudius than a trifling circumstance in which he seems to have consulted only the dictates of his heart. The frequent rebellions of the provinces had involved almost every person in the guilt of treason, almost every estate in the case of confiscation; and Gallienus often displayed his liberality by distributing among his officers the property of his subjects. On the accession of Claudius, an old woman threw herself at his feet and complained that a general of the late emperor had obtained an arbitrary grant of her patrimoney. This general was Claudius himself, who had not entirely escaped the contagion of the times. The emperor blushed at the reproach, but deserved the confidence which she had reposed in his equity. The confession of his fault was accompanied with immediate and ample restitution.

In the arduous task which Claudius had undertaken of restoring the empire to its ancient splendour, it was first necessary to revive among his troops a sense of order and obedience. With the authority of a veteran commander, he represented to them that the relaxation of discipline had introduced a long train of disorders, the effects of which were at length experienced by the soldiers themselves; that a people ruined by oppres-sion, and indolent from despair, could no longer supply a numerous army with means of luxury, or even of subsistence; that the danger of each individual had increased with the despotism of the military order, since princes who tremble on the throne will guard their safety by the instant sacrifice of every obnoxious subject. The emperor expatiated on the mischiefs of a lawless caprice, which the soldiers could only gratify at the expense of their own blood, as their seditious elections had so frequently been followed by civil wars, which consumed the flower of the legions either in the field of battle or in the cruel abuse of victory. He painted in the most lively colours the exhausted state of the treasury, the desolation of the provinces, the disgrace of the Roman name, and the insolent triumph of rapacious barbarians. It was against those barbar-ians, he declared, that he intended to point the first effort of their arms. Tetricus might reign for a while over the West, and even Zenobia might preserve the dominion of the East. These usurpers were his personal adversaries, nor could he think of indulging any private resentment till he had saved an empire whose impending ruin would, unless it was timely prevented, crush both the army and the people.

The various nations of Germany and Sarmatia who fought under the Gothic standard had already collected an armament more formidable than any which had yet issued from the Euxine. On the banks of the Dniester, one of the great rivers that discharge themselves into that sea, they constructed a fleet of two thousand, or even of six thousand vessels;* numbers which, however incredible they may seem, would have been insufficient to transport their pretended army of three hundred and twenty thousand barbarians. Whatever might be the real strength of the Goths, the vigour and success of the expedition were not adequate to the greatness of the preparations. In their passage through the Bosphorus the unskilful pilots were overpowered by the violence of the current; and while the multitude of their ships were crowded in a narrow channel, many were dashed against each other or against the shore. The barbar-ians made several descents on the coasts both of Europe and Asia; but the open country was already plundered, and they were repulsed with shame and loss from the fortified cities which they assaulted. A spirit of discouragement and division arose in the fleet, and some of their chiefs sailed away towards the islands of Crete and Cyprus; but the main body, pursuing a more steady course, anchored at length near the foot of Mount Athos, and assaulted the city of Thessalonica, the wealthy capital of all the Macedonian provinces. Their attacks, in which they displayed a fierce but artless bravery, were soon interrupted by the rapid approach of Claudius, hastening to a scene of action that deserved the presence of a warlike prince at the head of the remaining powers of the empire. Impatient for battle, the Goths immediately broke up their camp, relinquished the siege of Thessalonica, left their navy at the foot of

* The Augustan History mentions the smaller, Zonaras the larger, number; the lively fancy of Montesquieu induced him to prefer the latter.

Mount Athos, traversed the hills of Macedonia, and pressed forwards to engage the last defence of Italy.

We still possess an original letter addressed by Claudius to the senate and people on this memorable occasion. 'Conscript fathers,' says the emperor, 'know that three hundred and twenty thousand Goths have invaded the Roman territory. If I vanquish them, your gratitude will reward my services. Should I fall, remember that I am the successor of Gallienus. The whole republic is fatigued and exhausted. We shall fight after Valerian, after Ingenuus, Regillianus, Lollianus, Posthumus, Celsus, and a thousand others, whom a just contempt for Gallienus provoked into rebellion. We are in want of darts, of spears, and of shields. The strength of the empire, Gaul, and Spain, are usurped by Tetricus; and we blush to acknowledge that the archers of the East serve under the banners of Zenobia. Whatever we shall perform will be sufficiently great.' The melancholy firmness of this epistle announces a hero careless of his fate, conscious of his danger, but still deriving a well-grounded hope from the resources of his own mind.

The event surpassed his own expectations and those of the world. By the most signal victories he delivered the empire from this host of barbarians, and was distinguished by posterity under the glorious appellation of the Gothic Claudius. The imperfect historians of an irregular war do not enable us to describe the order and circumstances of his exploits; but, if we could be indulged in the allusion, we might distribute into three acts this memorable tragedy. 1. The decisive battle was fought near Naissus, a city of Dardania. The legions at first gave way, oppressed by numbers and dismayed by misfortunes. Their ruin was inevitable, had not the abilities of their emperor prepared a season-able relief. A large detachment, rising out of the secret and difficult passes of the mountains, which by his order they had occupied, suddenly assailed the rear of the victorious Goths. The favourable instant was improved by the activity of Claudius. He revived the courage of his troops, restored their ranks, and pressed the barbarians on every side. Fifty thousand men are reported to have been slain in the battle of Naissus. Several large bodies of barbarians, covering their retreat with a movable fortification of waggons, retired, or rather escaped, from the field of slaughter. 2. We may presume that some insurmountable difficulty – the fatigue, perhaps, or the disobedience, of the conquer-ors – prevented Claudius from completing in one day the destruction of the Goths. The war was diffused over the provinces of Maesia, Thrace, and Macedonia, and its operations drawn out into a variety of marches, surprises, and tumultuary engagements, as well by sea as by land. When the Romans suffered any loss, it was commonly occasioned by their own cowardice or rashness; but the superior talents of the emperor, his perfect knowledge of the country, and his judicious choice of measures as well as officers, assured on most occasions the success of his arms. The immense booty, the fruit of so many victories, consisted for the greater part of cattle and slaves. A select body of the Gothic youth was received among the Imperial troops; the remainder was sold into servitude; and so considerable was the number of female captives that every soldier obtained as his share two or three women: a circumstance from which we may conclude that the invaders entertained some designs of settlement as well as of plunder; since even in a naval expedition they were accompanied by their families. 3. The loss of their fleet, which was either taken or sunk, had intercepted the retreat of the Goths. A vast circle of Roman posts, distributed with skill, supported with firmness, and gradually closing towards a common centre, forced the barbarians into the most inaccessible parts of Mount Haemus, where they found a safe refuge, but a very scanty subsistence. During the course of a rigorous winter, in which they were besieged by the emperor's troops, famine and pestilence, desertion and the sword, continually diminished the impri-soned multitude. On the return of spring nothing appeared in arms except a hardy and desperate band, the remnant of that mighty host which had embarked at the mouth of the Dniester.

The pestilence which swept away such numbers of the barbarians at length proved fatal to their conqueror. After a short but glorious reign of two years, Claudius expired at Sirmium, amidst the tears and acclama-tions of his subjects. In his last illness he convened the principal officers of the state and army, and in their presence recommended Aurelian, one of his generals, as the most deserving of the throne, and the best qualified to execute the great design which he himself had been permitted only to undertake. The virtues of Claudius, his valour, affability, justice, and temperance, his love of fame and of his country, place him in that short list of emperors who added lustre to the Roman purple. Those virtues, however, were celebrated with peculiar zeal and complacency by the courtly writers of the age of Constantine, who was the great-grandson of Crispus, the elder brother of Claudius. The voice of flattery was soon taught to repeat that the gods, who so hastily had snatched Claudius from the earth, rewarded his merit and piety by the perpetual establish-ment of the empire in his family.

Notwithstanding these oracles, the greatness of the Flavian family (a name which it had pleased them to assume) was deferred above twenty years, and the elevation of Claudius occasioned the immediate ruin of his brother Quintilius, who possessed not sufficient moderation or courage to descend into the private station to which the patriotism of the late emperor had condemned him. Without delay or reflection he assumed the purple at Aquileia, where he commanded a considerable force; and though his reign lasted only seventeen days, he had time to obtain the sanction of the senate and to experience a mutiny of the troops. As soon as he was informed that the great army of the Danube had invested the well-known valour of Aurelian with Imperial power, he sunk under the fame and merit of his rival; and, ordering his veins to be opened, prudently withdrew himself from the unequal contest.

The general design of this work will not permit us minutely to relate the actions of every emperor after he ascended the throne, much less to deduce the various fortunes of his private life. We shall only observe that the father of Aurelian was a peasant of the territory of Sirmium, who occupied a small farm, the property of Aurelius, a rich senator. His warlike son enlisted in the troops as a common soldier, successively rose to the rank of a centurion, a tribune, the prefect of a legion, the inspector of the camp, the general, or, as it was then called, the duke of a frontier; and at length, during the Gothic war, exercised the important office of commander-in-chief of the cavalry. In every station he distinguished himself by matchless valour, rigid discipline, and successful conduct. He was invested with the consulship by the emperor Valerian, who styles him, in the pompous language of that age, the Deliverer of Illyricum, the Restorer of Gaul, and the Rival of the Scipios. At the recommendation of Valerian, a senator of the highest rank and merit, Ulpius Crinitus, whose blood was derived from the same source as that of Trajan, adopted the Pannonian peasant, gave him his daughter in marriage, and relieved with his ample fortune the honourable poverty which Aurelian had preserved inviolate.

The reign of Aurelian lasted only four years and about nine months; but every instant of that short period was filled by some memorable achievement. He put an end to the Gothic war, chastised the Germans who invaded Italy, recovered Gaul, Spain, and Britain out of the hands of Tetricus, and destroyed the proud monarchy which Zenobia had erected in the East on the ruins of the afflicted empire.

It was the rigid attention of Aurelian even to the minutest articles of discipline which bestowed such uninterrupted success on his arms. His military regulations are contained in a very concise epistle to one of his inferior officers, who is commanded to enforce them, as he wishes to become a tribune, or as he is desirous to live. Gaming, drinking, and the arts of divination were severely prohibited. Aurelian expected that his soldiers should be modest, frugal, and laborious; that their armour should be constantly kept bright, their weapons sharp, their clothing and horses ready for immediate service; that they should live in their quarters with chastity and sobriety, without damaging the corn-fields, without stealing even a sheep, a fowl, or a bunch of grapes, without exacting from their landlords either salt, or oil, or wood. 'The public allowance,' continues the emperor, 'is sufficient for their support; their wealth should be collected from the spoil of the enemy, not from the tears of the provincials.' A single instance will serve to display the rigour, and even cruelty, of Aurelian. One of the soldiers had seduced the wife of his host. The guilty wretch was fastened to two trees forcibly drawn towards each other, and his limbs were torn asunder by their sudden separation. A few such examples impressed a salutary consternation. The punish- ments of Aurelian were terrible; but he had seldom occasion to punish more than once the same offence. His own conduct gave a sanction to his laws, and the seditious legions dreaded a chief who had learned to obey, and who was worthy to command.

The death of Claudius had revived the fainting spirit of the Goths. The troops which guarded the passes of Mount Haemus and the banks of the Danube had been drawn away by the apprehension of a civil war; and it seems probable that the remaining body of the Gothic and Vandalic tribes embraced the favourable opportunity, abandoned their settlements of the Ukraine, traversed the rivers, and swelled with new multitudes the destroying host of their countrymen. Their united numbers were at length encountered by Aurelian, and the bloody and doubtful conflict ended only with the approach of night. Exhausted by so many calamities, which they had mutually endured and inflicted during a twenty years' war, the Goths and the Romans consented to a lasting and beneficial treaty. It was earnestly solicited by the barbarians, and cheerfully ratified by the legions, to whose suffrage the prudence of Aurelian referred the decision of that important question. The Gothic nation engaged to supply the armies of Rome with a body of two thousand auxiliaries, consisting entirely of cavalry, and stipulated in return an undisturbed retreat, with a regular market as far as the Danube, provided by the emperor's care, but at their own expense. The treaty was observed with such religious fidelity that, when a party of five hundred men straggled from the camp in quest of plunder, the king or general of the barbarians commanded that the guilty leader should be apprehended and shot to death with darts, as a victim devoted to the sanctity of their engagements. It is, however, not unlikely that the precaution of Aurelian, who had exacted as hostages the sons and daughters of the Gothic chiefs, contributed something to this pacific temper. The youths he trained in the exercise of arms, and near his own person; to the damsels he gave a liberal and Roman education, and, by bestowing them in marriage on some of his principal officers, gradually introduced between the two nations the closest and most endearing connections.

But the most important condition of peace was understood rather than expressed in the treaty. Aurelian withdrew the Roman forces from Dacia, and tacitly relinquished that great province to the Goths and Vandals. His manly judgment convinced him of the solid advantages, and taught him to despise the seeming disgrace, of thus contracting the frontiers of the monarchy. The Dacian subjects, removed from those distant possessions which they were unable to cultivate or defend, added strength and populousness to the southern side of the Danube. A fertile territory, which the repetition of barbarous inroads had changed into a desert, was yielded to their industry, and a new province of Dacia still preserved the memory of Trajan's conquests. The old country of that name detained, however, a considerable number of its inhabitants, who dreaded exile more than a Gothic master.* These degenerate Romans continued to serve the empire, whose allegiance they had renounced, by introducing among their conquerors the first notions of agriculture, the useful arts, and the conveniences of civilised life. An intercourse of commerce and language was gradually established between the opposite banks of the Danube; and, after Dacia became an independent state, it often proved the firmest barrier of the empire against the invasions of the savages of the North. A sense of interest attached these more settled barbarians to the alliance of Rome, and permanent interest very frequently ripens into sincere and useful friendship. This various colony, which filled the ancient province, and was insensibly blended into one great people, still acknowledged the superior renown and authority of the Gothic tribe, and claimed the fancied honour of a Scandinavian origin. At the same time the lucky, though accidental, resemblance of

* The Wallachians still preserve many traces of the Latin language, and have boasted, in every age, of their Roman descent. They are surrounded by, but not mixed with, the barbarians. See a Memoir of M. d'Anville on ancient Dacia, in the Academy of Inscriptions.

the name of Getae infused among the credulous Goths a vain persuasion that, in a remote age, their own ancestors, already seated in the Dacian provinces, had received the instructions of Zamolxis, and checked the victorious arms of Sesostris and Darius.

While the vigorous and moderate conduct of Aurelian restored the Illyrian frontier, the nation of the Alemanni violated the conditions of peace which either Gallienus had purchased, or Claudius had imposed, and, inflamed by their impatient youth, suddenly flew to arms. Forty thousand horse appeared in the field,* and the numbers of the infantry doubled those of the cavalry. The first objects of their avarice were a few cities of the Rhaetian frontier; but their hopes soon rising with success, the rapid march of the Alemanni traced a line of devastation from the Danube to the Po.

The emperor was almost at the same time informed of the irruption, and of the retreat, of the barbarians. Collecting an active body of troops, he marched with silence and celerity along the skirts of the Hercynian forest; and the Alemanni, laden with the spoils of Italy, arrived at the Danube, without suspecting that on the opposite bank, and in an advantageous post, a Roman army lay concealed and prepared to intercept their return. Aurelian indulged the fatal security of the barbar-ians, and permitted about half their forces to pass the river without disturbance and without precaution. Their situation and astonishment gave him an easy victory; his skilful conduct improved the advantage. Disposing the legions in a semicircular form, he advanced the two horns of the crescent across the Danube, and, wheeling them on a sudden towards the centre, enclosed the rear of the German host. The dismayed barbarians, on whatsoever side they cast their eyes, beheld with despair a wasted country, a deep and rapid stream, a victorious and implacable enemy.

Reduced to this distressed condition, the Alemanni no longer dis-dained to sue for peace. Aurelian received their ambassadors at the head of his camp, and with every circumstance of martial pomp that could display the greatness and discipline of Rome. The legions stood to their arms in well-ordered ranks and awful silence. The principal com-manders, distinguished by the ensigns of the rank, appeared on horse-back on either side of the Imperial throne. Behind the throne the consecrated images of the emperor and his predecessors,† the golden

* Cantoclarus, with his usual accuracy, chooses to translate three hundred thousand; his version is equally repugnant to sense and to grammar.

† The emperor Claudius was certainly of the number; but we are ignorant how far this

eagles, and the various titles of the legions, engraved in letters of gold, were exalted in the air on lofty pikes covered with silver. When Aurelian assumed his seat, his manly grace and majestic figure taught the barbarians to revere the person as well as the purple of the conqueror. The ambassadors fell prostrate on the ground in silence. They were commanded to rise, and permitted to speak. By the assistance of interpreters they extenuated their perfidy, magnified their exploits, expatiated on the vicissitudes of fortune and the advantages of peace, and, with an ill-timed confidence, demanded a large subsidy as the price of the alliance which they offered to the Romans. The answer of the emperor was stern and imperious. He treated their offer with contempt, and their demand with indignation; reproached the barbarians that they were as ignorant of the arts of war as of the laws of peace; and finally dismissed them with the choice only of submitting to his unconditioned mercy, or awaiting the utmost severity of his resentment. Aurelian had resigned a distant province to the Goths; but it was dangerous to trust or to pardon these perfidious barbarians, whose formidable power kept Italy itself in perpetual alarms.

Immediately after this conference it should seem that some unexpected emergency required the emperor's presence in Pannonia. He devolved on his lieutenants the care of finishing the destruction of the Alemanni, either by the sword, or by the surer operation of famine. But an active despair has often triumphed over the indolent assurance of success. The barbarians, finding it impossible to traverse the Danube and the Roman camp, broke through the posts in their rear, which were more feebly or less carefully guarded; and with incredible diligence, but by a different road, returned towards the mountains of Italy. Aurelian, who considered the war as totally extinguished, received the mortifying intelligence of the escape of the Alemanni, and of the ravage which they already committed in the territory of Milan. The legions were commanded to follow, with as much expedition as those heavy bodies were capable of exerting, the rapid flight of an enemy, whose infantry and cavalry moved with almost equal swiftness. A few days afterwards the emperor himself marched to the relief of Italy, at the head of a chosen body of auxiliaries (among whom were the hostages and cavalry of the Vandals), and of all the Praetorian Guards who had served in the wars on the Danube.

As the light troops of the Alemanni had spread themselves from the

mark of respect was extended; if to Caesar and Augustus, it must have produced a very awful spectacle; a long line of the masters of the world.

Alps to the Apennine, the incessant vigilance of Aurelian and his officers was exercised in the discovery, the attack, and the pursuit of the numerous detachments. Nothwithstanding this desultory war, three considerable battles are mentioned, in which the principal force of both armies was obstinately engaged. The success was various. In the first, fought near Placentia, the Romans received so severe a blow that, according to the expression of a writer extremely partial to Aurelian, the immediate dissolution of the empire was apprehended. The crafty barbarians, who had lined the woods, suddenly attacked the legions in the dusk of the evening, and, it is most probable, after the fatigue and disorder of a long march. The fury of their charge was irresistible; but at length, after a dreadful slaughter, the patient firmness of the emperor rallied his troop, and restored, in some degree, the honour of his arms. The second battle was fought near Fano in Umbria; on the spot which, five hundred years before, had been fatal to the brother of Hannibal.* Thus far the successful Germans had advanced along the Aemilian and Flaminian way, with a design of sacking the defenceless mistress of the world. But Aurelian, who, watchful for the safety of Rome, still hung on their rear, found in this place the decisive moment of giving them a total and irretrievable defeat.† The flying remnant of their host was exterminated in a third and last battle near Pavia; and Italy was delivered from the inroads of the Alemanni.

Fear has been the original parent of superstition, and every new calamity urges trembling mortals to deprecate the wrath of their invisible enemies. Though the best hope of the republic was in the valour and conduct of Aurelian, yet such was the public consternation, when the barbarians were hourly expected at the gates of Rome, that, by a decree of the senate, the Sibylline books were consulted. Even the emperor himself, from a motive either of religion or of policy, recommended this salutary measure, chided the tardiness of the senate,‡ and offered to supply whatever expense, whatever animals, whatever captives of any nation, the gods should require. Notwithstanding this liberal offer, it does not appear that any human victims expiated with their blood the sins of the Roman people. The Sibylline books enjoined ceremonies of a more harmless nature – processions of priests in white robes, attended by

* The little river, or rather torrent, of Metaurus, near Fano, has been immortalised by finding such an historian as Livy, and such a poet at Horace.

† It is recorded by an inscription found at Pesaro. See Gruter, cclxxvi. 3.

‡ One should imagine, he said, that you were assembled in a Christian church, not in the temple of all the gods.

a chorus of youths and virgins; lustration of the city and adjacent country; and sacrifices, whose powerful influence disabled the barbar, ians from passing the mystic ground on which they had been celebrated. However puerile in themselves, these superstitious arts were subservient to the success of the war; and if, in the decisive battle of Fano, the Alemanni fancied they saw an army of spectres combating on the side of Aurelian, he received a real and effectual aid from this imaginary reinforcement.

But whatever confidence might be placed in ideal ramparts, the experience of the past, and the dread of the future, induced the Romans to construct fortifications of a grosser and more substantial kind. The seven hills of Rome had been surrounded, by the successors of Romulus, with an ancient wall of more than thirteen miles.* The vast enclosure may seem disproportioned to the strength and numbers of the infant state. But it was necessary to secure an ample extent of pasture and arable land against the frequent and sudden incursions of the tribes of Latium, the perpetual enemies of the republic. With the progress of Roman greatness, the city and its inhabitants gradually increased, filled up the vacant space, pierced through the useless walls, covered the field of Mars, and, on every side, followed the public highways in long and beautiful suburbs. The extent of the new walls, erected by Aurelian, and finished in the reign of Probus, was magnified by popular estimation to near fifty, but is reduced by accurate measurement to about twenty-one miles. It was a great but a melancholy labour, since the defence of the capital betrayed the decline of the monarchy. The Romans of a more prosper, ous age, who trusted to the arms of the legions the safety of the frontier camps, were very far from entertaining a suspicion that it would ever become necessary to fortify the seat of empire against the inroads of the barbarians.

The victory of Claudius over the Goths, and the success of Aurelian against the Alemanni, had already restored to the arms of Rome their ancient superiority over the barbarous nations of the North. To chastise domestic tyrants, and to reunite the dismembered parts of the empire,

* To confirm our idea, we may observe that for a long time mount Caelius was a grove of oaks, and mount Viminal was overrun with osiers; that in the fourth century the Aventine was a vacant and solitary retirement; that till the time of Augustus the Esquiline was an unwholesome burying-ground; and that the numerous inequalities remarked by the ancients in the Quirinal sufficiently prove that it was not covered with buildings. Of the seven hills, the Capitoline and Palatine only, with the adjacent valleys, were the primitive habitation of the Roman people. But this subject would require a dissertation.

was a task reserved for the second of those warlike emperors. Though he was acknowledged by the senate and people, the frontiers of Italy, Africa, Illyricum, and Thrace, confined the limits of his reign. Gaul, Spain, and Britain, Egypt, Syria, and Asia Minor, were still possessed by two rebels, who alone, out of so numerous a list, had hitherto escaped the dangers of their situation; and to complete the ignominy of Rome, these rival thrones had been unsurped by women.

A rapid succession of monarchs had arisen and fallen in the pro-vinces of Gaul. The rigid virtues of Posthumus served only to hasten his destruction. After suppressing a competitor who had assumed the purple at Metz, he refused to gratify his troops with the plunder of the rebellious city; and, in the seventh year of his reign, became the victim of their disappointed avarice. The death of Victorinus, his friend and associate, was occasioned by a less worthy cause. The shining accom-plishments of that prince were stained by a licentious passion, which he indulged in acts of violence, with too little regard to the laws of society, or even to those of love. He was slain at Cologne, by a conspiracy of jealous husbands, whose revenge would have appeared more justifiable had they spared the innocence of his son. After the murder of so many valiant princes, it is somewhat remarkable that a female for a long time controlled the fierce legions of Gaul, and still more singular that she was the mother of the unfortunate Victorinus. The arts and treasures of Victoria enabled her successively to place Marius and Tetricus on the throne, and to reign with a manly vigour under the name of those dependent emperors. Money of copper, of silver, and of gold, was coined in her name, she assumed the titles of Augusta and Mother of the Camps: her power ended only with her life; but her life was perhaps shortened by the ingratitude of Tetricus.

When, at the instigation of his ambitious patroness, Tetricus assumed the ensigns of royalty, he was governor of the peaceful province of Aquitaine, an employment suited to his character and education. He reigned four or five years over Gaul, Spain, and Britain, the slave and sovereign of a licentious army, whom he dreaded, and by whom he was despised. The valour and fortune of Aurelian at length opened the prospect of a deliverance. He ventured to disclose his melancholy situation, and conjured the emperor to hasten to the relief of his unhappy rival. Had this secret correspondence reached the ears of the soldiers, it would most probably have cost Tetricus his life; nor could he resign the sceptre of the West without committing an act of treason against himself. He affected the appearances of a civil war, led his forces into the field against Aurelian, posted them in the most disadvantageous manner, betrayed his own counsels to the enemy, and with a few chosen friends deserted in the beginning of the action. The rebel legions, though disordered and dismayed by the unexpected treachery of their chief, defended themselves with desperate valour, till they were cut in pieces almost to a man, in this bloody and memorable battle, which was fought near Châlons in Champagne. The retreat of the irregular auxiliaries, Franks and Batavians, whom the conqueror soon compelled or per- suaded to repass the Rhine, restored the general tranquillity, and the power of Aurelian was acknowledged from the wall of Antoninus to the columns of Hercules.

As early as the reign of Claudius, the city of Autun, alone and unassisted, had ventured to declare against the legions of Gaul. After a siege of seven months they stormed and plundered that unfortunate city, already wasted by famine. Lyons, on the contrary, had resisted with obstinate disaffection the arms of Aurelian. We read of the punishment of Lyons, but there is not any mention of the rewards of Autun. Such, indeed, is the policy of civil war: severely to remember injuries, and to forget the most important services. Revenge is profitable, gratitude is expensive.

Aurelian had no sooner secured the person and provinces of Tetricus than he turned his arms against Zenobia, the celebrated queen of Palmyra and the East. Modern Europe has produced several illustrious women who have sustained with glory the weight of empire; nor is our own age destitute of such distinguished characters. But if we except the doubtful achievements of Semiramis, Zenobia is perhaps the only female whose superior genius broke through the servile indolence imposed on her sex by the climate and manners of Asia. She claimed her descent from the Macedonian kings of Egypt, equalled in beauty her ancestor Cleopatra, and far surpassed that princess in chastity* and valour. Zenobia was esteemed the most lovely as well as the most heroic of her sex. She was of a dark complexion (for in speaking of a lady these trifles become important). Her teeth were of a pearly whiteness, and her large black eyes sparkled with uncommon fire, tempered by the most attractive sweetness. Her voice was strong and harmonious. Her manly under- standing was strengthened and adorned by study. She was not ignorant of the Latin tongue, but possessed in equal perfection the Greek, the Syriac, and the Egyptian languages. She had drawn up for her own use

* She never admitted her husband's embraces but for the sake of posterity. If her hopes were baffled, in the ensuing *month* she reiterated the experiment.

an epitome of oriental history, and familiarly compared the beauties of Homer and Plato under the tuition of the sublime Longinus.

This accomplished woman gave her hand to Odenathus, who, from a private station, raised himself to the dominion of the East. She soon became the friend and companion of a hero. In the intervals of war Odenathus passionately delighted in the exercise of hunting; he pursued with ardour the wild beasts of the desert, lions, panthers, and bears; and the ardour of Zenobia in that dangerous amusement was not inferior to his own. She had inured her constitution to fatigue, disdained the use of a covered carriage, generally appeared on horseback in a military habit, and sometimes marched several miles on foot at the head of the troops. The success of Odenathus was in a great measure ascribed to her incomparable prudence and fortitude. Their splendid victories over the Great King, whom they twice pursued as far as the gates of Ctesiphon, laid the foundations of their united fame and power. The armies which they commanded, and the provinces which they had saved, acknow-ledged not any other sovereigns than their invincible chiefs. The senate and people of Rome revered a stranger who had avenged their captive emperor, and even the insensible son of Valerian accepted Odenathus for his legitimate colleague.

After a successful expedition against the Gothic plunderers of Asia, the Palmyrenian prince returned to the city of Emesa in Syria. Invincible in war, he was there cut off by domestic treason, and his favourite amusement of hunting was the cause, or at least the occasion, of his death. His nephew, Maeonius, presumed to dart his javelin before that of his uncle; and, though admonished of his error, repeated the same insolence. As a monarch, and as a sportsman, Odenathus was pro-voked, took away his horse, a mark of ignominy among the barbarians, and chastised the rash youth by a short confinement. The offence was soon forgot, but the punishment was remembered; and Maeonius, with a few daring associates, assassinated his uncle in the midst of a great entertainment. Herod, the son of Odenathus, though not of Zenobia, a young man of a soft and effeminate temper, was killed with his father. But Maeonius obtained only the pleasure of revenge by this bloody deed. He had scarcely time to assume the title of Augustus before he was sacrificed by Zenobia to the memory of her husband.

With the assistance of his most faithful friends, she immediately filled the vacant throne, and governed with manly counsels Palmyra, Syria, and the East, above five years. By the death of Odenathus, that authority was at an end which the senate had granted him only as a personal distinction; but his martial widow, disdaining both the senate and Gallienus, obliged one of the Roman generals who was sent against her to retreat into Europe, with the loss of his army and his reputation. Instead of the little passions which so frequently perplex a female reign, the steady administration of Zenobia was guided by the most judicious maxims of policy. If it was expedient to pardon, she could calm her resentment; if it was necessary to punish, she could impose silence on the voice of pity. Her strict economy was accused of avarice; yet on every proper occasion she appeared magnificent and liberal. The neighbour-ing states of Arabia, Armenia, and Persia, dreaded her enmity, and solicited her alliance. To the dominions of Odenathus, which extended from the Euphrates to the frontiers of Bithynia, his widow added the inheritance of her ancestors, the populous and fertile kingdom of Egypt. The emperor Claudius acknowledged her merit, and was content that, while *he* pursued the Gothic war, *she* should assert the dignity of the empire in the East. The conduct, however, of Zenobia was attended with some ambiguity; nor is it unlikely that she had conceived the design of erecting an independent and hostile monarchy. She blended with the popular manners of Roman princes the stately pomp of the courts of Asia, and exacted from her subjects the same adoration that was paid to the successors of Cyrus. She bestowed on her three sons a Latin education, and often showed them to the troops adorned with the Imperial purple. For herself she reserved the diadem, with the spendid but doubtful title of Queen of the East.

When Aurelian passed over into Asia, against an adversary whose sex alone could render her an object of contempt, his presence restored obedience to the province of Bithynia, already shaken by the arms and intrigues of Zenobia. Advancing at the head of his legions, he accepted the submission of Ancyra, and was admitted into Tyana, after an obstinate siege, by the help of a perfidious citizen. The generous though fierce temper of Aurelian abandoned the traitor to the rage of the soldiers: a superstitious reverence induced him to treat with lenity the countrymen of Apollonius the philosopher.* Antioch was deserted on his approach, till the emperor, by his salutary edicts, recalled the fugitives, and granted a general pardon to all who, from necessity rather than choice, had been engaged in the service of the Palmyrenian queen. The unexpected mildness of such a conduct reconciled the minds of the Syrians, and, as

* Apollonius of Tyana was born about the same times as Jesus Christ. His life (that of the former) is related in so fabulous a manner by his disciples, that we are at a loss to discover whether he was a sage, an impostor, or a fanatic.

far as the gates of Emesa, the wishes of the people seconded the terror of his arms.

Zenobia would have ill deserved her reputation had she indolently permitted the emperor of the West to approach within an hundred miles of her capital. The fate of the East was decided in two great battles; so similar in almost every circumstance, that we can scarcely distinguish them from each other, except by observing that the first was fought near Antioch, and the second near Emesa. In both the queen of Palmyra animated the armies by her presence, and devolved the execution of her orders on Zabdas, who had already signalised his military talents by the conquest of Egypt. The numerous forces of Zenobia consisted for the most part of light archers, and of heavy cavalry clothed in complete steel. The Moorish and Illyrian horse of Aurelian were unable to sustain the ponderous charge of their antagonists. They fled in real or affected disorder, engaged the Palmyrenians in a laborious pursuit, harassed them by a desultory combat, and at length discomfited this impenetrable but unwieldy body of cavalry. The light infantry, in the meantime, when they had exhausted their quivers, remaining without protection against a closer onset, exposed their naked sides to the swords of the legions. Aurelian had chosen those veteran troops who were usually stationed on the Upper Danube, and whose valour had been severely tried in the Alemannic war. After the defeat of Emesa, Zenobia found it impossible to collect a third army. As far as the frontier of Egypt, the nations subject to her empire had joined the standard of the conqueror, who detached Probus, the bravest of his generals, to possess himself of the Egyptian provinces. Palmyra was the last resource of the widow of Odenathus. She retired within the walls of her capital, made every preparation for a vigorous resistance, and declared, with the intrepidity of a heroine, that the last moment of her reign and of her life should be the same.

Amid the barren deserts of Arabia a few cultivated spots rise like islands out of the sandy ocean. Even the name of Tadmor, or Palmyra, by its signification in the Syriac as well as in the Latin language, denoted the multitude of palm-trees which afforded shade and verdure to that temperate region. The air was pure, and the soil, watered by some invaluable springs, was capable of producing fruits as well as corn. A place possessed of such singular advantages, and situated at a convenient distance between the Gulf of Persia and the Mediterranean, was soon frequented by the caravans which conveyed to the nations of Europe a considerable part of the rich commodities of India. Palmyra insensibly increased into an opulent and independent city, and, connecting the Roman and the Parthian monarchies by the mutual benefits of commerce, was suffered to observe an humble neutrality, till at length, after the victories of Trajan, the little republic sunk into the bosom of Rome, and flourished more than one hundred and fifty years in the subordinate though honourable rank of a colony. It was during that peaceful period, if we may judge from a few remaining inscriptions, that the wealthy Palmyrenians constructed those temples, palaces, and porticos of Grecian architecture, whose ruins, scattered over an extent of several miles, have deserved the curiosity of our travellers. The elevation of Odenathus and Zenobia appeared to reflect new splendour on their country, and Palmyra, for a while, stood forth the rival of Rome; but the competition was fatal, and ages of prosperity were sacrificed to a moment of glory.*

In his march over the sandy desert between Emesa and Palmyra, the emperor Aurelian was perpetually harassed by the Arabs; nor could he always defend his army, and especially his baggage, from those flying troops of active and daring robbers, who watched the moment of surprise, and eluded the slow pursuit of the legions. The siege of Palmyra was an object far more difficult and important, and the emperor, who, with incessant vigour, pressed the attacks in person, was himself wounded with a dart. 'The Roman people,' says Aurelian, in an original letter, 'speak with contempt of the war which I am waging against a woman. They are ignorant both of the character and of the power of Zenobia. It is impossible to enumerate her warlike preparations, of stones, of arrows, and of every species of missile weapons. Every part of the walls is provided with two or three *balistae*, and artificial fires are thrown from her military engines. The fear of punishment has armed her with a desperate courage. Yet still I trust in the protecting deities of Rome, who have hitherto been favourable to all my undertakings.' Doubtful, however, of the protection of the gods, and of the event of the siege, Aurelian judged it more prudent to offer terms of an advantageous capitulation; to the queen, a splendid retreat; to the citizens, their ancient privileges. His proposals were obstinately rejected, and the refusal was accompanied with insult.

The firmness of Zenobia was supported by the hope that in a very

* Some English travellers from Aleppo *discovered* the ruins of Palmyra about the end of the last century. Our curiosity has since been gratified in a more splendid manner by Messieurs Wood and Dawkins. For the history of Palmyra we may consult the masterly dissertation of Dr Halley in the *Philosophical Transactions*: Lowthorp's *Abridgment*.

short time famine would compel the Roman army to repass the desert; and by the reasonable expectation that the kings of the East, and particularly the Persian monarch, would arm in the defence of their most natural ally. But fortune and the perseverance of Aurelian overcame every obstacle. The death of Sapor, which happened about this time, distracted the councils of Persia, and the inconsiderable succours that attempted to relieve Palmyra were easily intercepted either by the arms or the liberality of the emperor. From every part of Syria a regular succession of convoys safely arrived in the camp, which was increased by the return of Probus with his victorious troops from the conquest of Egypt. It was then that Zenobia resolved to fly. She mounted the fleetest of her dromedaries,* and had already reached the banks of the Euph-rates, about sixty miles from Palmyra, when she was overtaken by the pursuit of Aurelian's light horse, seized and brought back a captive to the feet of the emperor. Her capital soon afterwards surrendered, and was treated with unexpected lenity. The arms, horses, and camels, with an immense treasure of gold, silver, silk, and precious stones, were all delivered to the conqueror, who, leaving only a garrison of six hundred archers, returned to Emesa, and employed some time in the distribution of rewards and punishments at the end of so memorable a war, which restored to the obedience of Rome those provinces that had renounced their allegiance since the captivity of Valerian.

When the Syrian queen was brought into the presence of Aurelian, he sternly asked her, how she had presumed to rise in arms against the emperors of Rome? The answer of Zenobia was a prudent mixture of respect and firmness. 'Because I disdained to consider as Roman emperors an Aureolus or a Gallienus. You alone I acknowledge as my conqueror and my sovereign.' But as female fortitude is commonly artificial, so it is seldom steady or consistent. The courage of Zenobia deserted her in the hour of trial; she trembled at the angry clamours of the soldiers, who called aloud for her immediate execution, forgot the generous despair of Cleopatra, which she had proposed as her model, and ignominiously purchased life by the sacrifice of her fame and her friends. It was to their counsels, which governed the weakness of her sex, that she imputed the guilt of her obstinate resistance; it was on their heads

---

* Though the camel is a heavy beast of burden, the dromedary, which is either of the same or of a kindred species, is used by the natives of Asia and Africa on all occasions which require celerity. The Arabs affirm that he will run over as much ground in one day as their fleetest horses can perform in eight or ten. See Buffon, *Histoire naturelle*, and Shaw's *Travels*.

These three engravings make up a panoramic view of the ruined city of Palmyra

that she directed the vengeance of the cruel Aurelian. The fame of Longinus, who was included among the numerous and perhaps inno-cent victims of her fear, will survive that of the queen who betrayed, or the tyrant who condemned him. Genius and learning were incapable of moving a fierce unlettered soldier, but they had served to elevate and harmonise the soul of Longinus. Without uttering a complaint, he calmly followed the executioner, pitying his unhappy mistress, and bestowing comfort on his afflicted friends.

Returning from the conquest of the East, Aurelian had already crossed the Straits which divide Europe from Asia, when he was provoked by the intelligence that the Palmyrenians had massacred the governor and garrison which he had left among them, and again erected the standard of revolt. Without a moment's deliberation, he once more turned his face towards Syria. Antioch was alarmed by his rapid approach, and the helpless city of Palmyra felt the irresistible weight of his resentment. We have a letter of Aurelian himself, in which he acknowledges that old men, women, children, and peasants, had been involved in that dreadful execution, which should have been confined to armed rebellion; and although his principal concern seems directed to the re-establishment of a temple of the Sun, he discovers some pity for the remnant of the Palmyrenians, to whom he grants the permission of re-building and inhabiting their city. But it is easier to destroy than to restore. The seat of commerce, of arts, and of Zenobia, gradually sunk into an ob-scure town, a trifling fortress, and at length a miserable village. The present citizens of Palmyra, consisting of thirty or forty families, have erected their mud-cottages within the spacious court of a magnificent temple.

Another and a last labour still awaited the indefatigable Aurelian; to suppress a dangerous though obscure rebel, who, during the revolt of Palmyra, had arisen on the banks of the Nile. Firmus, the friend and ally, as he proudly styled himself, of Odenathus and Zenobia, was no more than a wealthy merchant of Egypt. In the course of his trade to India he had formed very intimate connections with the Saracens and the Blemmyes, whose situation, on either coast of the Red Sea, gave them an easy introduction into the Upper Egypt. The Egyptians he inflamed with the hope of freedom, and, at the head of their furious multitude, broke into the city of Alexandria, where he assumed the Imperial purple, coined money, published edicts, and raised an army, which, as he vainly boasted, he was capable of maintaining from the sole profits of his paper trade. Such troops were a feeble defence against the approach of Aurelian; and it seems almost unnecessary to relate that Firmus was routed, taken, tortured, and put to death. Aurelian might now con-gratulate the senate, the people, and himself, that, in little more than three years, he had restored universal peace and order to the Roman world.

Since the foundation of Rome no general had more nobly deserved a triumph than Aurelian; nor was a triumph ever celebrated with superior pride and magnificence. The pomp was opened by twenty elephants, four royal tigers, and above two hundred of the most curious animals from every climate of the North, the East, and the South. They were followed by sixteen hundred gladiators, devoted to the cruel amusement of the amphitheatre. The wealth of Asia, the arms and ensigns of so many conquered nations, and the magnificent plate and wardrobe of the Syrian queen, were disposed in exact symmetry or artful disorder. The ambassadors of the most remote parts of the earth, of Ethiopia, Arabia, Persia, Bactriana, India, and China, all remarkable by their rich or singular dresses, displayed the fame and power of the Roman emperor, who exposed likewise to the public view the presents that he had received, and particularly a great number of crowns of gold, the offerings of grateful cities. The victories of Aurelian were attested by the long train of captives who reluctantly attended his triumph – Goths, Vandals, Sarmatians, Alemanni, Franks, Gauls, Syrians, and Egyptians. Each people was distinguished by its peculiar inscription, and the title of Amazons was bestowed on ten martial heroines of the Gothic nation who had been taken in arms.* But every eye, disregarding the crowd of captives, was fixed on the emperor Tetricus and the queen of the East. The former, as well as his son, whom he had created Augustus, was dressed in Gallic trousers,† a saffron tunic, and a robe of purple. The beauteous figure of Zenobia was confined by fetters of gold; a slave supported the gold chain which encircled her neck, and she almost fainted under the intolerable weight of jewels. She preceded on foot the magnificent chariot in which she once hoped to enter the gates of Rome. It was followed by two other chariots, still more sumptuous, of Odenathus and of the Persian monarch. The triumphal car of Aurelian

* Among barbarous nations women have often combated by the side of their husbands. But it is *almost* impossible that a society of Amazons should ever have existed either in the old or new world.

† The use of *braccae*, breeches, or trousers, was still considered in Italy as a Gallic and barbarian fashion. The Romans, however, had made great advances towards it. To encircle the legs and thighs with *fasciae*, or bands, was understood, in the time of Pompey and Horace, to be a proof of ill health or effeminacy. In the age of Trajan the custom was confined to the rich and luxurious. It gradually was adopted by the meanest of the people.

(it had formerly been used by a Gothic king) was drawn, on this memorable occasion, either by four stags or by four elephants. The most illustrious of the senate, the people, and the army closed the solemn procession. Unfeigned joy, wonder, and gratitude swelled the acclama-tions of the multitude; but the satisfaction of the senate was clouded by the appearance of Tetricus; nor could they suppress a rising murmur that the haughty emperor should thus expose to public ignominy the person of a Roman and a magistrate.

But, however in the treatment of his unfortunate rivals Aurelian might indulge his pride, he behaved towards them with a generous clemency which was seldom exercised by the ancient conquerors. Princes who, without success, had defended their throne or freedom, were frequently strangled in prison as soon as the triumphal pomp ascended the Capitol. These usurpers, whom their defeat had convicted of the crime of treason, were permitted to spend their lives in affluence and honourable repose. The emperor presented Zenobia with an elegant villa at Tibur or Tivoli, about twenty miles from the capital; the Syrian queen insensibly sunk into a Roman matron, her daughters married into noble families, and her race was not yet extinct in the fifth century. Tetricus and his son were reinstated in their rank and fortunes. They erected on the Caelian hill a magnificent palace, and, as soon as it was finished, invited Aurelian to supper. On his entrance he was agreeably surprised with a picture which represented their singular history. They were delineated offering to the emperor a civic crown and the sceptre of Gaul, and again receiving at his hands the ornaments of the senatorial dignity. The father was afterwards invested with the government of Lucania, and Aurelian, who soon admitted the abdicated monarch to his friendship and conversation, familiarly asked him, whether it were not more desirable to administer a province of Italy than to reign beyond the Alps? The son long continued a respectable member of the senate; nor was there any one of the Roman nobility more esteemed by Aurelian, as well as by his successors.

So long and so various was the pomp of Aurelian's triumph, that, although it opened with the dawn of day, the slow majesty of the procession ascended not the Capitol before the ninth hour; and it was already dark when the emperor returned to the palace. The festival was protracted by theatrical representations, the games of the circus, the hunting of wild beasts, combats of gladiators, and naval engagements. Liberal donatives were distributed to the army and people, and several institutions, agreeable or beneficial to the city, contributed to perpetuate the glory of Aurelian. A considerable portion of his oriental spoils was consecrated to the gods of Rome; the Capitol, and every other temple, glittered with the offerings of his ostentatious piety; and the temple of the Sun alone received above fifteen thousand pounds of gold. This last was a magnificent structure, erected by the emperor on the side of the Quirinal hill, and dedicated, soon after the triumph, to that deity whom Aurelian adored as the parent of his life and fortunes. His mother had been an inferior priestess in a chapel of the Sun; a peculiar devotion to the god of Light was a sentiment which the fortunate peasant imbibed in his infancy; and every step of his elevation, every victory of his reign, fortified superstition by gratitude.

The arms of Aurelian had vanquished the foreign and domestic foes of the republic. We are assured that, by his salutary rigour, crimes and factions, mischievous arts and pernicious connivance, the luxuriant growth of a feeble and oppressive government, were eradicated through-out the Roman world. But if we attentively reflect how much swifter is the progress of corruption than its cure, and if we remember that the years abandoned to public disorders exceeded the months allotted to the martial reign of Aurelian, we must confess that a few short intervals of peace were insufficient for the arduous work of reformation. Even his attempt to restore the integrity of the coin was opposed by a formidable insurrection. The emperor's vexation breaks out in one of his private letters: 'Surely,' says he, 'the gods have decreed that my life should be a perpetual warfare. A sedition within the walls has just now given birth to a very serious civil war. The workmen of the mint, at the instigation of Felicissimus, a slave to whom I had intrusted an employment in the finances, have risen in rebellion. They are at length suppressed; but seven thousand of my soldiers have been slain in the contest, of those troops whose ordinary station is in Dacia and the camps along the Danube.' Other writers, who confirm the same fact, add likewise, that it happened soon after Aurelian's triumph; that the decisive engagement was fought on the Caelian hill; that the workmen of the mint had adulterated the coin; and that the emperor restored the public credit, by delivering out good money in exchange for the bad, which the people were com-manded to bring into the treasury.

We might content ourselves with relating this extraordinary trans-action, but we cannot dissemble how much, in its present form, it appears to us inconsistent and incredible. The debasement of the coin is indeed well suited to the administration of Gallienus; nor is it unlikely that the instruments of the corruption might dread the inflexible justice

of Aurelian. But the guilt, as well as the profit, must have been confined
to a few; nor is it easy to conceive by what arts they could arm a people
whom they had injured against a monarch whom they had betrayed.
We might naturally expect that such miscreants should have shared the
public detestation with the informers and the other ministers of oppression; and that the reformation of the coin should have been an action
equally popular with the destruction of those obsolete accounts which,
by the emperor's order, were burnt in the forum of Trajan. In an age
when the principles of commerce were so imperfectly understood, the
most desirable end might perhaps be effected by harsh and injudicious
means; but a temporary grievance of such a nature can scarcely excite
and support a serious civil war. The repetition of intolerable taxes,
imposed either on the land or on the necessaries of life, may at last
provoke those who will not, or who cannot, relinquish their country.
But the case is far otherwise in every operation which, by whatsoever
expedients, restores the just value of money. The transient evil is soon
obliterated by the permanent benefit, the loss is divided among multitudes; and if a few wealthy individuals experience a sensible diminution
of treasure, with their riches, they at the same time lose the degree of
weight and importance which they derived from the possession of them.
However Aurelian might choose to disguise the real cause of the insurrection, his reformation of the coin could furnish only a faint pretence
to a party already powerful and discontented. Rome, though deprived of
freedom, was distracted by faction. The people, towards whom the
emperor, himself a plebeian, always expressed a peculiar fondness, lived in
perpetual dissension with the senate, the equestrian order, and the
Praetorian Guards. Nothing less than the firm though secret conspiracy of
those orders, of the authority of the first, the wealth of the second, and the
arms of the third, could have displayed a strength capable of contending in
battle with the veteran legions of the Danube, which, under the conduct of
a martial sovereign, had achieved the conquest of the West and of the East.

Whatever was the cause or the object of this rebellion, imputed with
so little probability to the workmen of the mint, Aurelian used his
victory with unrelenting rigour. He was naturally of a severe disposition.
A peasant and a soldier, his nerves yielded not easily to the impression of
sympathy, and he could sustain without emotion the sight of tortures and
death. Trained from his earliest youth in the exercise of arms, he set too
small a value on the life of a citizen, chastised by military execution the
slightest offences, and transferred the stern discipline of the camp into the
civil administration of the laws. His love of justice often became a blind

and furious passion; and, whenever he deemed his own or the public safety endangered, he disregarded the rules of evidence and the propor, tion of punishments. The unprovoked rebellion with which the Romans rewarded his services exasperated his haughty spirit. The noblest families of the capital were involved in the guilt or suspicion of this dark conspiracy. A hasty spirit of revenge urged the bloody prosecution, and it proved fatal to one of the nephews of the emperor. The executioners (if we may use the expression of a contemporary poet) were fatigued, the prisons were crowded, and the unhappy senate lamented the death or absence of its most illustrious members. Nor was the pride of Aurelian less offensive to that assembly than his cruelty. Ignorant or impatient of the restraints of civil institutions, he disdained to hold his power by any other title than that of the sword, and governed by right of conquest an empire which he had saved and subdued.

It was observed by one of the most sagacious of the Roman princes, that the talents of his predecessor Aurelian were better suited to the command of an army than to the government of an empire.* Conscious of the character in which nature and experience had enabled him to excel, he again took the field a few months after his triumph. It was expedient to exercise the restless temper of the legions in some foreign war, and the Persian monarch, exulting in the shame of Valerian, still braved with impunity the offended majesty of Rome. At the head of an army, less formidable by its numbers than by its discipline and valour, the emperor advanced as far as the Straits which divide Europe from Asia. He there experienced that the most absolute power is a weak defence against the effects of despair. He had threatened one of his secretaries who was accused of extortion, and it was known that he seldom threatened in vain. The last hope which remained for the criminal was to involve some of the principal officers of the army in his danger, or at least in his fears. Artfully counterfeiting his master's hand, he showed them, in a long and bloody list, their own names devoted to death. Without suspecting or examining the fraud, they resolved to secure their lives by the murder of the emperor. On his march, between Byzantium and Heraclea, Aurelian was suddenly attacked by the conspirators, whose stations gave them a right to surround his person, and, after a short resistance, fell by the hand of Mucapor, a general whom he had always loved and trusted. He died regretted by the army, detested by the senate, but universally acknowledged as a warlike and fortunate prince, the useful though severe reformer of a degenerate state.

* It was the observation of Diocletian. See Vopiscus in *Historia Augusta*.

CONDUCT OF THE ARMY AND SENATE AFTER THE DEATH
OF AURELIAN — REIGNS OF TACITUS, PROBUS, CARUS,
AND HIS SONS

SUCH WAS THE UNHAPPY CONDITION OF
the Roman emperors, that, whatever might be their conduct, their fate
was commonly the same. A life of pleasure or virtue, of severity or
mildness, of indolence or glory, alike led to an untimely grave; and
almost every reign is closed by the same disgusting repetition of treason
and murder. The death of Aurelian, however, is remarkable by its
extraordinary consequences. The legions admired, lamented, and
revenged their victorious chief. The artifice of his perfidious secretary was
discovered and punished. The deluded conspirators attended the funeral
of their injured sovereign with sincere or well-feigned contrition, and
submitted to the unanimous resolution of the military order, which was
signified by the following epistle: 'The brave and fortunate armies to the
senate and people of Rome: The crime of one man, and the error of
many, have deprived us of the last emperor Aurelian. May it please you,
venerable lords and fathers! to place him in the number of the gods, and
to appoint a successor whom your judgment shall declare worthy of the
Imperial purple! None of those whose guilt or misfortune have contributed to our loss shall ever reign over us.' The Roman senators heard,
without surprise, that another emperor had been assassinated in his
camp; they secretly rejoiced in the fall of Aurelian; but the modest and
dutiful address of the legions, when it was communicated in full
assembly by the consul, diffused the most pleasing astonishment. Such
honours as fear and perhaps esteem could extort they liberally poured
forth on the memory of their deceased sovereign. Such acknowledg-
ments as gratitude could inspire they returned to the faithful armies of the
republic, who entertained so just a sense of the legal authority of the
senate in the choice of an emperor. Yet, notwithstanding this flattering
appeal, the most prudent of the assembly declined exposing their safety
and dignity to the caprice of an armed multitude. The strength of the
legions was, indeed, a pledge of their sincerity, since those who may
command are seldom reduced to the necessity of dissembling; but could

it naturally be expected that a hasty repentance would correct the inveterate habits of fourscore years? Should the soldiers relapse into their accustomed seditions, their insolence might disgrace the majesty of the senate and prove fatal to the object of its choice. Motives like these dic- tated a decree by which the election of a new emperor was referred to the suffrage of the military order.

The contention that ensued is one of the best attested but most improbable events in the history of mankind.* The troops, as if satiated with the exercise of power, again conjured the senate to invest one of its own body with the Imperial purple. The senate still persisted in its refusal; the army in its request. The reciprocal offer was pressed and rejected at least three times, and, whilst the obstinate modesty of either party was resolved to receive a master from the hands of the other, eight months insensibly elapsed; an amazing period of tranquil anarchy, during which the Roman world remained without a sovereign, without an usurper, and without a sedition. The generals and magistrates appointed by Aurelian continued to execute their ordinary functions; and it is observed that a proconsul of Asia was the only considerable person removed from his office in the whole course of the interregnum.

An event somewhat similar but much less authentic is supposed to have happened after the death of Romulus, who, in his life and character, bore some affinity with Aurelian. The throne was vacant during twelve months till the election of a Sabine philosopher, and the public peace was guarded in the same manner by the union of the several orders of the state. But, in the time of Numa and Romulus, the arms of the people were controlled by the authority of the patricians; and the balance of freedom was easily preserved in a small and virtuous com- munity. The decline of the Roman state, far different from its infancy, was attended with every circumstance that could banish from an interregnum the prospect of obedience and harmony: an immense and tumultuous capital, a wide extent of empire, the servile equality of despotism, an army of four hundred thousand mercenaries, and the experience of frequent revolutions. Yet, notwithstanding all these temp- tations, the discipline and memory of Aurelian still restrained the seditious temper of the troops, as well as the fatal ambition of their

* Vopiscus, our principal authority, wrote at Rome sixteen years only after the death of Aurelian; and, besides the recent notoriety of the facts, constantly draws his materials from the Journals of the Senate and the original papers of the Ulpian library. Zosimus and Zonaras appear as ignorant of this transaction as they were in general of the Roman constitution.

leaders. The flower of the legions maintained their stations on the banks of the Bosphorus, and the Imperial standard awed the less powerful camps of Rome and of the provinces. A generous though transient enthusiasm seemed to animate the military order; and we may hope that a few real patriots cultivated the returning friendship of the army and the senate as the only expedient capable of restoring the republic to its ancient beauty and vigour.

On the twenty-fifth of September, near eight months after the murder of Aurelian, the consul convoked an assembly of the senate, and reported the doubtful and dangerous situation of the empire. He slightly insinuated that the precarious loyalty of the soldiers depended on the chance of every hour and of every accident; but he represented, with the most convincing eloquence, the various dangers that might attend any farther delay in the choice of an emperor. Intelligence, he said, was already received that the Germans had passed the Rhine and occupied some of the strongest and most opulent cities of Gaul. The ambition of the Persian king kept the East in perpetual alarms; Egypt, Africa, and Illyricum were exposed to foreign and domestic arms; and the levity of Syria would prefer even a female sceptre to the sanctity of the Roman laws. The consul then, addressing himself to Tacitus, the first of the senators, required his opinion on the important subject of a proper candidate for the vacant throne.

If we can prefer personal merit to accidental greatness, we shall esteem the birth of Tacitus more truly noble than that of kings. He claimed his descent from the philosophic historian whose writings will instruct the last generations of mankind. The senator Tacitus was then seventy-five years of age. The long period of his innocent life was adorned with wealth and honours. He had twice been invested with the consular dignity, and enjoyed with elegance and sobriety his ample patrimony of between two and three millions sterling. The experience of so many princes, whom he had esteemed or endured, from the vain follies of Elagabalus to the useful rigour of Aurelian, taught him to form a just estimate of the duties, the dangers, and the temptations of their sublime station. From the assiduous study of his immortal ancestor he derived the knowledge of the Roman constitution and of human nature.* The voice of the people had already named Tacitus as the citizen the most worthy

* After his accession he gave orders that ten copies of the historian should be annually transcribed and placed in the public libraries. The Roman libraries have long since perished, and the most valuable part of Tacitus was preserved in a single MS, and discovered in a monastery of Westphalia. See Bayle, *Dictionnaire*, Art. *Tacite*.

of empire. The ungrateful rumour reached his ears, and induced him to seek the retirement of one of his villas in Campania. He had passed two months in the delightful privacy of Baiae, when he reluctantly obeyed the summons of the consul to resume his honourable place in the senate, and to assist the republic with his counsels on this important occasion.

He arose to speak, when, from every quarter of the house, he was saluted with the names of Augustus and emperor. 'Tacitus Augustus, the gods preserve thee! we choose thee for our sovereign, to thy care we intrust the republic and the world. Accept the empire from the authority of the senate. It is due to thy rank, to thy conduct, to thy manners.' As soon as the tumult of acclamations subsided, Tacitus attempted to decline the dangerous honour, and to express his wonder that they should elect his age and infirmities to succeed the martial vigour of Aurelian. 'Are these limbs, conscript fathers! fitted to sustain the weight of armour, or to practise the exercises of the camp? The variety of climates, and the hardships of a military life, would soon oppress a feeble constitution, which subsists only by the most tender management. My exhausted strength scarcely enables me to discharge the duty of a senator; how insufficient would it prove to the arduous labours of war and government! Can you hope that the legions will respect a weak old man, whose days have been spent in the shade of peace and retirement? Can you desire that I should ever find reason to regret the favourable opinion of the senate?'

The reluctance of Tacitus, and it might possibly be sincere, was encountered by the affectionate obstinacy of the senate. Five hundred voices repeated at once, in eloquent confusion, that the greatest of the Roman princes, Numa, Trajan, Hadrian, and the Antonines, had ascended the throne in a very advanced season of life; that the mind, not the body, a sovereign, not a soldier, was the object of their choice; and that they expected from him no more than to guide by his wisdom the valour of the legions. These pressing though tumultuary instances were seconded by a more regular oration of Metius Falconius, the next on the consular bench to Tacitus himself. He reminded the assembly of the evils which Rome had endured from the vices of headstrong and capricious youths, congratulated them on the election of a virtuous and experienced senator, and with a manly, though perhaps a selfish, freedom, exhorted Tacitus to remember the reasons of his elevation, and to seek a successor, not in his own family, but in the republic. The speech of Falconius was enforced by a general acclamation. The emperor elect submitted to the authority of his country, and received the voluntary homage of his equals. The judgment of the senate was confirmed by the consent of the Roman people and of the Praetorian Guards.

The administration of Tacitus was not unworthy of his life and principles. A grateful servant of the senate, he considered that national council as the author, and himself as the subject, of the laws. He studied to heal the wounds which Imperial pride, civil discord, and military violence had inflicted on the constitution, and to restore, at least, the image of the ancient republic as it had been preserved by the policy of Augustus and the virtues of Trajan and the Antonines. It may not be useless to recapitulate some of the most important prerogatives which the senate appeared to have regained by the election of Tacitus. 1. To invest one of their body, under the title of emperor, with the general command of the armies and the government of the frontier provinces. 2. To determine the list, or, as it was then styled, the College of Consuls. They were twelve in number, who, in successive pairs, each during the space of two months, filled the year, and represented the dignity of that ancient office. The authority of the senate, in the nomination of the consuls, was exercised with such independent freedom, that no regard was paid to an irregular request of the emperor in favour of his brother Florianus. 'The senate,' exclaimed Tacitus, with the honest transport of a patriot, 'understand the character of a prince whom they have chosen.' 3. To appoint the proconsuls and presidents of the provinces, and to confer on all the magistrates their civil jurisdiction. 4. To receive appeals through the intermediate office of the prefect of the city from all the tribunals of the empire. 5. To give force and validity, by their decrees, to such as they should approve of the emperor's edicts. 6. To these several branches of authority we may add some inspection over the finances, since, even in the stern reign of Aurelian, it was in their power to divert a part of the revenue from the public service.

Circular epistles were sent, without delay, to all the principal cities of the empire – Trèves, Milan, Aquileia, Thessalonica, Corinth, Athens, Antioch, Alexandria, and Carthage – to claim their obedience, and to inform them of the happy revolution which had restored the Roman senate to its ancient dignity. Two of these epistles are still extant. We likewise possess two very singular fragments of the private correspon‑ dence of the senators on this occasion. They discover the most excessive joy and the most unbounded hopes. 'Cast away your indolence,' it is thus that one of the senators addresses his friend, 'emerge from your retirements of Baiae and Puteoli. Give yourself to the city, to the senate. Rome flourishes, the whole republic flourishes. Thanks to the Roman army, to an army truly Roman, at length we have recovered our just authority, the end of all our desires. We hear appeals, we appoint proconsuls, we create emperors; perhaps, too, we may restrain them – to the wise a word is sufficient.' These lofty expectations were, however, soon disappointed; nor, indeed, was it possible that the armies and the provinces should long obey the luxurious and unwarlike nobles of Rome. On the slightest touch the unsupported fabric of their pride and power fell to the ground. The expiring senate displayed a sudden lustre, blazed for a moment, and was extinguished for ever.

All that had yet passed at Rome was no more than a theatrical representation, unless it was ratified by the more substantial power of the legions. Leaving the senators to enjoy their dream of freedom and ambition, Tacitus proceeded to the Thracian camp, and was there, by the Praetorian prefect, presented to the assembled troops as the prince whom they themselves had demanded, and whom the senate had bestowed. As soon as the prefect was silent the emperor addressed himself to the soldiers with eloquence and propriety. He gratified their avarice by a liberal distribution of treasure under the names of pay and donative. He engaged their esteem by a spirited declaration that, although his age might disable him from the performance of military exploits, his counsels should never be unworthy of a Roman general, the successor of the brave Aurelian.

Whilst the deceased emperor was making preparations for a second expedition into the East, he had negotiated with the Alani, a Scythian people, who pitched their tents in the neighbourhood of the lake Maeotis. Those barbarians, allured by presents and subsidies, had promised to invade Persia with a numerous body of light cavalry. They were faithful to their engagements; but when they arrived on the Roman frontier Aurelian was already dead, the design of the Persian war was at least suspended, and the generals who, during the interregnum, exer-cised a doubtful authority, were unprepared either to receive or to oppose them. Provoked by such treatment, which they considered as trifling and perfidious, the Alani had recourse to their own valour for their payment and revenge; and as they moved with the usual swiftness of Tartars, they had soon spread themselves over the provinces of Pontus, Cappadocia, Cilicia, and Galatia. The legions who, from the opposite shores of the Bosphorus, could almost distinguish the flames of the cities and villages, impatiently urged their general to lead them against the invaders. The conduct of Tacitus was suitable to his age and station. He convinced the barbarians of the faith, as well as of the power, of the empire. Great numbers of the Alani, appeased by the punctual discharge of the engagements which Aurelian had contracted with them, relinquished their booty and captives, and quietly retreated to their own deserts beyond the Phasis. Against the remainder, who refused peace, the Roman emperor waged, in person, a successful war. Seconded by an army of brave and experienced veterans, in a few weeks he delivered the provinces of Asia from the terror of the Scythian invasion.

But the glory and life of Tacitus were of short duration. Transported in the depth of winter from the soft retirement of Campania to the foot of Mount Caucasus, he sunk under the unaccustomed hardships of a military life. The fatigues of the body were aggravated by the cares of the mind. For a while the angry and selfish passions of the soldiers had been suspended by the enthusiasm of public virtue. They soon broke out with redoubled violence, and raged in the camp, and even in the tent of the aged emperor. His mild and amiable character served only to inspire contempt, and he was incessantly tormented with factions which he could not assuage, and by demands which it was impossible to satisfy. Whatever flattering expectations he had conceived of reconciling the public disorders, Tacitus soon was convinced that the licentiousness of the army disdained the feeble restraint of laws, and his last hour was hastened by anguish and disappointment. It may be doubtful whether the soldiers imbrued their hands in the blood of this innocent prince. It is certain that their insolence was the cause of his death. He expired at Tyana in Cappadocia, after a reign of only six months and about twenty days.

The eyes of Tacitus were scarcely closed before his brother Florianus showed himself unworthy to reign by the hasty usurpation of the purple, without expecting the approbation of the senate. The reverence of the Roman constitution, which yet influenced the camp and the provinces, was sufficiently strong to dispose them to censure, but not to provoke them to oppose, the precipitate ambition of Florianus. The discontent would have evaporated in idle murmurs, had not the general of the East, the heroic Probus, boldly declared himself the avenger of the senate. The contest, however, was still unequal; nor could the most able leader, at the head of the effeminate troops of Egypt and Syria, encounter, with any hopes of victory, the legions of Europe, whose irresistible strength appeared to support the brother of Tacitus. But the fortune and activity of Probus triumphed over every obstacle. The hardy veterans of his rival, accustomed to cold climates, sickened and consumed away in the sultry heats of Cilicia, where the summer proved remarkably unwholesome.

Their numbers were diminished by frequent desertion, the passes of the mountains were feebly defended; Tarsus opened its gates; and the soldiers of Florianus, when they had permitted him to enjoy the Imperial title about three months, delivered the empire from civil war by the easy sacrifice of a prince whom they despised.

The perpetual revolutions of the throne had so perfectly erased every notion of hereditary right, that the family of an unfortunate emperor was incapable of exciting the jealousy of his successors. The children of Tacitus and Florianus were permitted to descend into a private station, and to mingle with the general mass of the people. Their poverty indeed became an additional safeguard to their innocence. When Tacitus was elected by the senate he resigned his ample patrimony to the public service, an act of generosity specious in appearance, but which evidently disclosed his intention of transmitting the empire to his descendants. The only consolation of their fallen state was the remembrance of transient greatness, and a distant hope, the child of a flattering prophecy, that, at the end of a thousand years, a monarch of the race of Tacitus should arise, the protector of the senate, the restorer of Rome, and the conqueror of the whole earth.*

The peasants of Illyricum, who had already given Claudius and Aurelian to the sinking empire, had an equal right to glory in the elevation of Probus. Above twenty years before, the emperor Valerian, with his usual penetration, had discovered the rising merit of the young soldier, on whom he conferred the rank of tribune long before the age prescribed by the military regulations. The tribune soon justified his choice by a victory over a great body of Sarmatians, in which he saved the life of a near relation of Valerian; and deserved to receive from the emperor's hand the collars, bracelets, spears, and banners, the mural and the civic crown, and all the honourable rewards reserved by ancient Rome for successful valour. The third, and afterwards, the tenth, legion were intrusted to the command of Probus, who, in every step of his promotion, showed himself superior to the station which he filled. Africa and Pontus, the Rhine, the Danube, the Euphrates, and the Nile, by turns afforded him the most splendid occasions of displaying his personal prowess and his conduct in war. Aurelian was indebted to him for the conquest of Egypt, and still more indebted for the honest courage

* He was to send judges to the Parthians, Persians, and Sarmatians, a president to Taprobana, and a proconsul to the Roman island (supposed by Casaubon and Salmasius to mean Britain). Such a history as mine (says Vopiscus with proper modesty) will not subsist a thousand years to expose or justify the prediction.

with which he often checked the cruelty of his master. Tacitus, who desired by the abilities of his generals to supply his own deficiency of military talents, named him commander-in-chief of all the eastern provinces, with five times the usual salary, the promise of the consulship, and the hope of a triumph. When Probus ascended the Imperial throne he was about forty-four years of age; in the full possession of his fame, of the love of the army, and of a mature vigour of mind and body.

His acknowledged merit, and the success of his arms against Florianus, left him without an enemy or a competitor. Yet, if we may credit his own professions, very far from being desirous of the empire, he had accepted it with the most sincere reluctance. 'But it is no longer in my power,' says Probus in a private letter, 'to lay down a title so full of envy and of danger. I must continue to personate the character which the soldiers have imposed upon me.' His dutiful address to the senate displayed the sentiments, or at least the language, of a Roman patriot: 'When you elected one of your order, conscript fathers! to succeed the emperor Aurelian, you acted in a manner suitable to your justice and wisdom. For you are the legal sovereigns of the world, and the power which you derive from your ancestors will descend to your posterity. Happy would it have been if Florianus, instead of usurping the purple of his brother, like a private inheritance, had expected what your majesty might determine, either in his favour, or in that of any other person. The prudent soldiers have punished his rashness. To me they have offered the title of Augustus; but I submit to your clemency my pretensions and my merits.' When this respectful epistle was read by the consul, the senators were unable to disguise their satisfaction that Probus should condescend thus humbly to solicit a sceptre which he already possessed. They celebrated with the warmest gratitude his virtues, his exploits, and above all his moderation. A decree immediately passed, without a dissenting voice, to ratify the election of the eastern armies, and to confer on their chief all the several branches of the Imperial dignity: the names of Caesar and Augustus, the title of Father of his country, the right of making in the same day three motions in the senate, the office of Pontifex Maximus, the tribunitian power, and the proconsular command; a mode of investiture which, though it seemed to multiply the authority of the emperor, expressed the constitution of the ancient republic. The reign of Probus corresponded with this fair beginning. The senate was permitted to direct the civil administration of the empire. Their faithful general asserted the honour of the Roman arms, and often laid at their feet crowns of gold and barbaric trophies, the fruits of his numerous victories. Yet, whilst he gratified their vanity, he must secretly have despised their indolence and weakness. Though it was every moment in their power to repeal the disgraceful edict of Gallienus, the proud successors of the Scipios patiently acquiesced in their exclusion from all military employments. They soon experienced that those who refuse the sword must renounce the sceptre.

The strength of Aurelian had crushed on every side the enemies of Rome. After his death they seemed to revive with an increase of fury and of numbers. They were again vanquished by the active vigour of Probus, who, in a short reign of about six years, equalled the fame of ancient heroes, and restored peace and order to every province of the Roman world. The dangerous frontier of Rhaetia he so firmly secured that he left it without the suspicion of an enemy. He broke the wandering power of the Sarmatian tribes, and by the terror of his arms compelled those barbarians to relinquish their spoil. The Gothic nation courted the alliance of so warlike an emperor. He attacked the Isaurians in their mountains, besieged and took several of their strongest castles, and flattered himself that he had for ever suppressed a domestic foe whose independence so deeply wounded the majesty of the empire. The troubles excited by the usurper Firmus in the Upper Egypt had never been perfectly appeased, and the cities of Ptolemais and Coptos, fortified by the alliance of the Blemmyes, still maintained an obscure rebellion. The chastisement of those cities, and of their auxiliaries the savages of the South, is said to have alarmed the court of Persia, and the Great King sued in vain for the friendship of Probus. Most of the exploits which distinguished his reign were achieved by the personal valour and conduct of the emperor, insomuch that the writer of his Life expresses some amazement how, in so short a time, a single man could be present in so many distant wars. The remaining actions he intrusted to the case of his lieutenants, the judicious choice of whom forms no inconsiderable part of his glory. Carus, Diocletian, Maximian, Constantius, Galerius, Asclepiodatus, Annibalianus, and a crowd of other chiefs, who after-wards ascended or supported the throne were trained to arms in the severe school of Aurelian and Probus.

But the most important service which Probus rendered to the republic was the deliverance of Gaul, and the recovery of seventy flourishing cities oppressed by the barbarians of Germany, who, since the death of Aurelian, had ravaged that great province with impunity. Among the various multitude of those fierce invaders, we may distinguish, with some degree of clearness, three great armies, or rather nations, successively vanquished by the valour of Probus. He drove back the Franks into their morasses; a descriptive circumstance from whence we may infer that the confederacy known by the manly appellation of *Free* already occupied the flat maritime country, intersected and almost overflown by the stagnating waters of the Rhine, and that several tribes of the Frisians and Batavians had acceded to their alliance. He vanquished the Burgun-dians, a considerable people of the Vandalic race. They had wandered in quest of booty from the banks of the Oder to those of the Seine. They esteemed themselves sufficiently fortunate to purchase, by the restitution of all their booty, the permission of an undisturbed retreat. They attempted to elude that article of the treaty. Their punishment was immediate and terrible. But of all the invaders of Gaul, the most formidable were the Lygians, a distant people who reigned over a wide domain on the frontiers of Poland and Silesia. In the Lygian nation the Arii held the first rank by their numbers and fierceness. 'The Arii' (it is thus that they are described by the energy of Tacitus) 'study to improve by art and circumstances the innate terrors of their barbarism. Their shields are black, their bodies are painted black. They choose for the combat the darkest hour of the night. Their host advances, covered as it were with a funeral shade; nor do they often find an enemy capable of sustaining so strange and infernal an aspect. Of all our senses, the eyes are the first vanquished in battle.' Yet the arms and discipline of the Romans easily discomfited these horrid phantoms. The Lygii were defeated in a general engagement, and Semno, the most renowned of their chiefs, fell alive into the hands of Probus. That prudent emperor, unwilling to reduce a brave people to despair, granted them an honourable capitula-tion, and permitted them to return in safety to their native country. But the losses which they suffered in the march, the battle, and the retreat, broke the power of the nation: nor is the Lygian name ever repeated in the history either of Germany or of the empire. The deliverance of Gaul is reported to have cost the lives of four hundred thousand of the invaders; a work of labour to the Romans, and of expense to the emperor, who gave a piece of gold for the head of every barbarian. But as the fame of warriors is built on the destruction of human kind, we may naturally suspect that the sanguinary account was multiplied by the avarice of the soldiers, and accepted without any very severe examination by the liberal vanity of Probus.

Since the expedition of Maximin, the Roman generals had confined their ambition to a defensive war against the nations of Germany, who perpetually pressed on the frontiers of the empire. The more daring

Probus pursued his Gallic victories, passed the Rhine, and displayed his invincible eagles on the banks of the Elbe and the Neckar. He was fully convinced that nothing could reconcile the minds of the barbarians to peace, unless they experienced in their own country the calamities of war. Germany, exhausted by the ill success of the last emigration, was astonished by his presence. Nine of the most considerable princes repaired to his camp, and fell prostrate at his feet. Such a treaty was humbly received by the Germans as it pleased the conqueror to dictate. He exacted a strict restitution of the effects and captives which they had carried away from the provinces; and obliged their own magistrates to punish the more obstinate robbers who presumed to detain any part of the spoil. A considerable tribute of corn, cattle, and horses, the only wealth of barbarians, was reserved for the use of the garrisons which Probus established on the limits of their territory. He even entertained some thoughts of compelling the Germans to relinquish the exercise of arms, and to trust their differences to the justice, their safety to the power, of Rome. To accomplish these salutary ends, the constant residence of an Imperial governor, supported by a numerous army, was indispensably requisite. Probus therefore judged it more expedient to defer the execu-tion of so great a design; which was indeed rather of specious than solid utility. Had Germany been reduced into the state of a province, the Romans, with immense labour and expense, would have acquired only a more extensive boundary to defend against the fiercer and more active barbarians of Scythia.

Instead of reducing the warlike natives of Germany to the condition of subjects, Probus contented himself with the humble expedient of raising a bulwark against their inroads. The country which now forms the circle of Swabia had been left desert in the age of Augustus by the emigration of its ancient inhabitants. The fertility of the soil soon attracted a new colony from the adjacent provinces of Gaul. Crowds of adventurers, of a roving temper and of desperate fortunes, occupied the doubtful possession, and acknowledged, by the payment of tithes, the majesty of the empire. To protect these new subjects, a line of frontier garrisons was gradually extended from the Rhine to the Danube. About the reign of Hadrian, when that mode of defence began to be practised, these garrisons were connected and covered by a strong entrenchment of trees and palisades. In the place of so rude a bulwark, the emperor Probus constructed a stone wall of a considerable height and streng-thened it by towers at convenient distances. From the neighbourhood of Neustadt and Ratisbon on the Danube, it stretched across hills, valleys,

The Temple of Rome and Augustus at Pola in the Province of Istria. A view of the front of the Temple

A view of the Incantada of c. AD 300 taken in the courtyard of a Spanish-speaking Jewish merchant on whose premises it stood at Thessalonica

rivers, and morasses, as far as Wimpfen on the Neckar, and at length terminated on the banks of the Rhine, after a winding course of near two hundred miles. This important barrier, uniting the two mighty streams that protected the provinces of Europe, seemed to fill up the vacant space through which the barbarians, and particularly the Alemanni, could penetrate with the greatest facility into the heart of the empire. But the experience of the world, from China to Britain, has exposed the vain attempt of fortifying any extensive tract of country.* An active enemy, who can select and vary his points of attack, must in the end discover some feeble spot, or some unguarded moment. The strength, as well as the attention, of the defenders is divided; and such are the blind effects of terror on the firmest troops that a line broken in a single place is almost instantly deserted. The fate of the wall which Probus erected may confirm the general observation. Within a few years after his death it was overthrown by the Alemanni. Its scattered ruins, universally ascribed to the power of the Daemon, now serve only to excite the wonder of the Swabian peasant.

Among the useful conditions of peace imposed by Probus on the vanquished nations of Germany was the obligation of supplying the Roman army with sixteen thousand recruits, the bravest and most robust of their youth. The emperor dispersed them through all the provinces, and distributed this dangerous reinforcement, in small bands of fifty or sixty each, among the national troops; judiciously observing that the aid which the republic derived from the barbarians should be felt but not seen. Their aid was now become necessary. The feeble elegance of Italy and the internal provinces could no longer support the weight of arms. The hardy frontier of the Rhine and Danube still produced minds and bodies equal to the labours of the camp; but a perpetual series of wars had gradually diminished their numbers. The infrequency of marriage, and the ruin of agriculture, affected the principles of population, and not only destroyed the strength of the present, but intercepted the hope of future generations. The wisdom of Probus embraced a great and beneficial plan of replenishing the exhausted frontiers by new colonies of captive or fugitive barbarians, on whom he bestowed lands, cattle, instruments of husbandry, and every encouragement that might engage

* See *Récherches sur les Chinois et les Egyptiens*. The anonymous author is well acquainted with the globe in general, and with Germany in particular: with regard to the latter, he quotes a work of M. Hanselman; but he seems to confound the wall of Probus, designed against the Alemanni, with the fortification of the Mattiaci, constructed in the neighbourhood of Frankfort against the Catti.

them to educate a race of soldiers for the service of the republic. Into Britain, and most probably into Cambridgeshire, he transported a considerable body of Vandals. The impossibility of an escape reconciled them to their situation, and in the subsequent troubles of that island they approved themselves the most faithful servants of the state. Great numbers of Franks and Gepidae were settled on the banks of the Danube and the Rhine. An hundred thousand Bastarnae, expelled from their own country, cheerfully accepted an establishment in Thrace, and soon imbibed the manners and sentiments of Roman subjects. But the expectations of Probus were too often disappointed. The impatience and idleness of the barbarians could ill brook the slow labours of agriculture. Their unconquerable love of freedom, rising against despotism, provoked them into hasty rebellions, alike fatal to themselves and to the provinces, nor could these artificial supplies, however repeated by succeeding emperors, restore the important limit of Gaul and Illyricum to its ancient and native vigour.

Of all the barbarians who abandoned their new settlements, and disturbed the public tranquillity, a very small number returned to their own country. For a short season they might wander in arms through the empire, but in the end they were surely destroyed by the power of a warlike emperor. The successful rashness of a party of Franks was attended, however, with such memorable consequences that it ought not to be passed unnoticed. They had been established by Probus on the sea-coast of Pontus, with a view of strengthening the frontier against the inroads of the Alani. A fleet stationed in one of the harbours of the Euxine fell into the hands of the Franks; and they resolved, through unknown seas, to explore their way from the mouth of the Phasis to that of the Rhine. They easily escaped through the Bosphorus and the Hellespont, and, cruising along the Mediterranean, indulged their appetite for revenge and plunder by frequent descents on the unsuspecting shores of Asia, Greece, and Africa. The opulent city of Syracuse, in whose port the navies of Athens and Carthage had formerly been sunk, was sacked by a handful of barbarians, who massacred the greatest part of the trembling inhabitants. From the island of Sicily the Franks proceeded to the columns of Hercules, trusted themselves to the ocean, coasted round Spain and Gaul, and, steering their triumphant course through the British Channel, at length finished their surprising voyage by landing in safety on the Batavian or Frisian shores. The example of their success, instructing their countrymen to conceive the advantages and to despise the dangers of the sea, pointed out to their enterprising spirit a new road to wealth and glory.

Notwithstanding the vigilance and activity of Probus, it was almost impossible that he could at once contain in obedience every part of his wide-extended dominions. The barbarians who broke their chains had seized the favourable opportunity of a domestic war. When the emperor marched to the relief of Gaul, he devolved the command of the East on Saturninus. That general, a man of merit and experience, was driven into rebellion by the absence of his sovereign, the levity of the Alexan-drian people, the pressing instances of his friends, and his own fears; but from the moment of elevation he never entertained a hope of empire or even of life. 'Alas!' he said, 'the republic has a lost a useful servant, and the rashness of an hour has destroyed the services of many years. You know not,' continued he, 'the misery of sovereign power: a sword is perpetually suspended over our head. We dread our very guards, we distrust our companions. The choice of action or of repose is no longer in our disposition, nor is there any age, or character, or conduct, that can protect us from the censure of envy. In thus exalting me to the throne, you have doomed me to a life of cares, and to an untimely fate. The only consolation which remains is the assurance that I shall not fall alone.' But as the former part of his prediction was verified by the victory, so the latter was disappointed by the clemency, of Probus. That amiable prince attempted even to save the unhappy Saturninus from the fury of the soldiers. He had more than once solicited the usurper himself to place some confidence in the mercy of a sovereign who so highly esteemed his character that he had punished as a malicious informer the first who related the improbable news of his defection. Saturninus might perhaps have embraced the generous offer had he not been restrained by the obstinate distrust of his adherents. Their guilt was deeper, and their hopes more sanguine, than those of their experienced leader.

The revolt of Saturninus was scarcely extinguished in the East before new troubles were excited in the West by the rebellion of Bonosus and Proculus in Gaul. The most distinguished merit of those two officers was their respective prowess, of the one in the combats of Bacchus, of the other in those of Venus,* yet neither of them were destitute of courage and capacity, and both sustained with honour the august character which the fear of punishment had engaged them to assume, till they sunk at length beneath the superior genius of Probus. He used the victory with

---

* A very surprising instance is recorded of the prowess of Proculus. He had taken one hundred Sarmatian virgins. The rest of the story he must relate in his own language: *Ex his unâ nocte decem inivi; omnes tamen, quod in me erat, mulieres intra dies quindecim reddidi.*

his accustomed moderation, and spared the fortunes as well as the lives of their innocent families.

The arms of Probus had now suppressed all the foreign and domestic enemies of the state. His mild but steady administration confirmed the re-establishment of the public tranquillity; nor was there left in the provinces a hostile barbarian, a tyrant, or even a robber, to revive the memory of past disorders. It was time that the emperor should revisit Rome, and celebrate his own glory and the general happiness. The triumph due to the valour of Probus was conducted with a magnificence suitable to his fortune; and the people, who had so lately admired the trophies of Aurelian, gazed with equal pleasure on those of his heroic successor. We cannot on this occasion forget the desperate courage of about fourscore gladiators, reserved, with near six hundred others, for the inhuman sports of the amphitheatre. Disdaining to shed their blood for the amusement of the populace, they killed their keepers, broke from the place of their confinement, and filled the streets of Rome with blood and confusion. After an obstinate resistance, they were overpowered and cut in pieces by the regular forces; but they obtained at least an honourable death, and the satisfaction of a just revenge.

The military discipline which reigned in the camps of Probus was less cruel than that of Aurelian, but it was equally rigid and exact. The latter had punished the irregularities of the soldiers with unrelenting severity, the former prevented them by employing the legions in constant and useful labours. When Probus commanded in Egypt, he executed many considerable works for the splendour and benefit of that rich country. The navigation of the Nile, so important to Rome itself, was improved; the temples, bridges, porticoes, and palaces, were constructed by the hands of the soldiers, who acted by turns as architects, as engineers, and as husbandmen. It was reported of Hannibal that, in order to preserve his troops from the dangerous temptations of idleness, he had obliged them to form large plantations of olive-trees along the coast of Africa. From a similar principle, Probus exercised his legions in covering with rich vineyards the hills of Gaul and Pannonia, and two considerable spots are described which were entirely dug and planted by military labour. One of these, known under the name of Mount Alma, was situated near Sirmium, the country where Probus was born, for which he ever retained a partial affection, and whose gratitude he endeavoured to secure, by converting into tillage a large and unhealthy tract of marshy ground. An army thus employed constituted perhaps the most useful as well as the bravest portion of Roman subjects.

But, in the prosecution of a favourite scheme, the best of men, satisfied with the rectitude of their intentions, are subject to forget the bounds of moderation; nor did Probus himself sufficiently consult the patience and disposition of his fierce legionaries. The dangers of the military profession seem only to be compensated by a life of pleasure and idleness; but if the duties of the soldier are incessantly aggravated by the labours of the peasant, he will at last sink under the intolerable burden or shake it off with indignation. The imprudence of Probus is said to have inflamed the discontent of his troops. More attentive to the interests of mankind than to those of the army, he expressed the vain hope that, by the establishment of universal peace, he should soon abolish the necessity of a standing and mercenary force. The unguarded expression proved fatal to him. In one of the hottest days of summer, as he severely urged the unwholesome labour of draining the marshes of Sirmium, the soldiers, impatient of fatigue, on a sudden threw down their tools, grasped their arms, and broke out into a furious mutiny. The emperor, conscious of his danger, took refuge in a lofty tower constructed for the purpose of surveying the progress of the work. The tower was instantly forced, and a thousand swords were plunged at once into the bosom of the unfortunate Probus. The rage of the troops subsided as soon as it had been gratified. They then lamented their fatal rashness, forgot the severity of the emperor whom they had massacred, and hastened to perpetuate, by an honourable monument, the memory of his virtues and victories.

When the legions had indulged their grief and repentance for the death of Probus, their unanimous consent declared Carus, his Praetorian prefect, the most deserving of the Imperial throne. Every circumstance that relates to this prince appears of a mixed and doubtful nature. He gloried in the title of Roman Citizen; and affected to compare the purity of *his* blood with the foreign, and even barbarous, origin of the preceding emperors; yet the most inquisitive of his contemporaries, very far from admitting his claim, have variously deduced his own birth, or that of his parents, from Illyricum, from Gaul, or from Africa. Though a soldier, he had received a learned education; though a senator, he was invested with the first dignity of the army; and in an age when the civil and military professions began to be irrecoverably separated from each other, they were united in the person of Carus. Notwithstanding the severe justice which he exercised against the assassins of Probus, to whose favour and esteem he was highly indebted, he could not escape the suspicion of being accessory to a deed from whence he derived the principal advantage. He enjoyed, at least before his elevation, an acknowledged character of virtue and abilities; but his austere temper insensibly degenerated into moroseness and cruelty; and the imperfect writers of his life almost hesitate whether they shall not rank him in the number of Roman tyrants. When Carus assumed the purple he was about sixty years of age, and his two sons, Carinus and Numerian, had already attained the season of manhood.

The authority of the senate expired with Probus; nor was the repentance of the soldiers displayed by the same dutiful regard for the civil power which they had testified after the unfortunate death of Aurelian. The election of Carus was decided without expecting the approbation of the senate, and the new emperor contented himself with announcing, in a cold and stately epistle, that he had ascended the vacant throne. A behaviour so very opposite to that of his amiable predecessor afforded no favourable presage of the new reign: and the Romans, deprived of power and freedom, asserted their privilege of licentious murmurs. The voice of congratulation and flattery was not however silent; and we may still peruse, with pleasure and contempt, an eclogue which was composed on the accession of the emperor Carus. Two shepherds, avoiding the noontide heat, retire into the cave of Faunus. On a spreading beech they discover some recent characters. The rural deity had described, in prophetic verses, the felicity promised to the empire under the reign of so great a prince. Faunus hails the approach of that hero, who, receiving on his shoulders the sinking weight of the Roman world, shall extinguish war and faction, and once again restore the innocence and security of the golden age.

It is more than probable that these elegant trifles never reached the ears of a veteran general who, with the consent of the legions, was preparing to execute the long-suspended design of the Persian war. Before his departure for this distant expedition, Carus conferred on his two sons, Carinus and Numerian, the title of Caesar, and, investing the former with almost an equal share of the Imperial power, directed the young prince first to suppress some troubles which had arisen in Gaul, and afterwards to fix the seat of his residence at Rome, and to assume the government of the Western Provinces. The safety of Illyricum was confirmed by a memorable defeat of the Sarmatians; sixteen thousand of those barbarians remained on the field of battle, and the number of captives amounted to twenty thousand. The old emperor, animated with the fame and prospect of victory, pursued his march, in the midst of winter, through the countries of Thrace and Asia Minor, and at length, with his younger son Numerian, arrived on the confines of the Persian monarchy. There, encamping on the summit of a lofty mountain, he pointed out to his troops the opulence and luxury of the enemy whom they were about to invade.

The successor of Artaxerxes, Varanes, or Bahram, though he had subdued the Segestans, one of the most warlike nations of Upper Asia, was alarmed at the approach of the Romans, and endeavoured to retard their progress by a negotiation of peace. His ambassadors entered the camp about sunset, at the time when the troops were satisfying their hunger with a frugal repast. The Persians expressed their desire of being introduced to the presence of the Roman emperor. They were at length conducted to a soldier who was seated on the grass. A piece of stale bacon and a few hard peas composed his supper. A coarse woollen garment of purple was the only circumstance that announced his dignity. The conference was conducted with the same disregard of courtly elegance. Carus, taking off a cap which he wore to conceal his baldness, assured the ambassadors that, unless their master acknow/ ledged the superiority of Rome, he would speedily render Persia as naked of trees as his own head was destitute of hair. Notwithstanding some traces of art and preparation, we may discover in this scene the manners of Carus, and the severe simplicity which the martial princes who succeeded Gallienus had already restored in the Roman camps. The ministers of the Great King trembled and retired.

The threats of Carus were not without effect. He ravaged Mesopota/ mia, cut in pieces whatever opposed his passage, made himself master of the great cities of Seleucia and Ctesiphon (which seem to have surren/ dered without resistance), and carried his victorious arms beyond the Tigris. He had seized the favourable moment for an invasion. The Persian councils were distracted by domestic factions, and the greater part of their forces were detained on the frontiers of India. Rome and the East received with transport the news of such important advantages. Flattery and hope painted in the most lively colours the fall of Persia, the conquest of Arabia, the submission of Egypt, and a lasting deliverance from the inroads of the Scythian nations. But the reign of Carus was destined to expose the vanity of predictions. They were scarcely uttered before they were contradicted by his death; an event attended with such ambiguous circumstances that it may be related in a letter from his own secretary to the prefect of the city. 'Carus,' says he, 'our dearest emperor, was confined by sickness to his bed, when a furious tempest arose in the camp. The darkness which overspread the sky was so thick that we could no longer distinguish each other; and the incessant flashes of lightning took from us the knowledge of all that passed in the general confusion. Immediately after the most violent clap of thunder we heard a sudden cry that the emperor was dead; and it soon appeared that his chamberlains, in a rage of grief, had set fire to the royal pavilion, a circumstance which gave rise to the report that Carus was killed by lightning. But, as far as we have been able to investigate the truth, his death was the natural effect of his disorder.'

The vacancy of the throne was not productive of any disturbance. The ambition of the aspiring generals was checked by their mutual fears; and young Numerian, with his absent brother Carinus, were unani⁄ mously acknowledged as Roman emperors. The public expected that the successor of Carus would pursue his father's footsteps, and, without allowing the Persians to recover from their consternation, would advance sword in hand to the palaces of Susa and Ecbatana. But the legions, however strong in numbers and discipline, were dismayed by the most abject superstition. Notwithstanding all the arts that were practised to disguise the manner of the late emperor's death, it was found impossible to remove the opinion of the multitude, and the power of opinion is irresistible. Places or persons struck with lightning were considered by the ancients with pious horror, as singularly devoted to the wrath of Heaven. An oracle was remembered which marked the river Tigris as the fatal boundary of the Roman arms. The troops, terrified with the fate of Carus and with their own danger, called aloud on young Numerian to obey the will of the gods, and to lead them away from this inauspicious scene of war. The feeble emperor was unable to subdue their obstinate prejudice, and the Persians wondered at the unexpected retreat of a victorious enemy.

The intelligence of the mysterious fate of the late emperor was soon carried from the frontiers of Persia to Rome; and the senate, as well as the provinces, congratulated the accession of the sons of Carus. These fortunate youths were strangers, however, to that conscious superiority, either of birth or of merit, which can alone render the possession of a throne easy, and as it were natural. Born and educated in a private station, the election of their father raised them at once to the rank of princes; and his death, which happened about sixteen months after⁄ wards, left them the unexpected legacy of a vast empire. To sustain with temper this rapid elevation, an uncommon share of virtue and prudence was requisite; and Carinus, the elder of the brothers, was more than commonly deficient in those qualities. In the Gallic war he discovered some degree of personal courage; but from the moment of his arrival at

Rome he abandoned himself to the luxury of the capital, and to the abuse of his fortune. He was soft, yet cruel; devoted to pleasure, but destitute of taste; and, though exquisitely susceptible of vanity, indiffer-ent to the public esteem. In the course of a few months he successively married and divorced nine wives, most of whom he left pregnant; and, notwithstanding this legal inconstancy, found time to indulge such a variety of irregular appetites as brought dishonour on himself and on the noblest houses of Rome. He beheld with inveterate hatred all those who might remember his former obscurity, or censure his present conduct. He banished or put to death the friends and counsellors whom his father had placed about him to guide his inexperienced youth; and he persecuted with the meanest revenge his schoolfellows and companions who had not sufficiently respected the latent majesty of the emperor. With the senators Carinus affected a lofty and regal demeanour, frequently declaring that he designed to distribute their estates among the populace of Rome. From the dregs of that populace he selected his favourites, and even his ministers. The palace, and even the Imperial table, was filled with singers, dancers, prostitutes, and all the various retinue of vice and folly. One of his doorkeepers* he intrusted with the government of the city. In the room of the Praetorian prefect, whom he put to death, Carinus substituted one of the ministers of his looser pleasures. Another, who possessed the same or even a more infamous title to favour, was invested with the consulship. A confidential secre-tary, who had acquired uncommon skill in the art of forgery, delivered the indolent emperor, with his own consent, from the irksome duty of signing his name.

When the emperor Carus undertook the Persian war, he was induced, by motives of affection as well as policy, to secure the fortunes of his family by leaving in the hands of his eldest son the armies and provinces of the West. The intelligence which he soon received of the conduct of Carinus filled him with shame and regret; nor had he concealed his resolution of satisfying the republic by a severe act of justice, and of adopting, in the place of an unworthy son, the brave and virtuous Constantius, who at that time was governor of Dalmatia. But the elevation of Constantius was for a while deferred; and as soon as the father's death had released Carinus from the control of fear or decency, he displayed to the Romans the extravagancies of Elagabalus, aggra-vated by the cruelty of Domitian.

* *Cancellarius.* This word, so humble in its origin, has by a singular fortune risen into the title of the first great office of state in the monarchies of Europe.

The only merit of the administration of Carinus that history could record, or poetry celebrate, was the uncommon splendour with which, in his own and his brother's name, he exhibited the Roman games of the theatre, ·the circus, and the amphitheatre. More than twenty years afterwards, when the courtiers of Diocletian represented to their frugal sovereign the fame and popularity of his munificent predecessor, he acknowledged that the reign of Carinus had indeed been a reign of pleasure. But this vain prodigality, which the prudence of Diocletian might justly despise, was enjoyed with surprise and transport by the Roman people. The oldest of the citizens, recollecting the spectacles of former days, the triumphal pomp of Probus or Aurelian, and the secular games of the emperor Philip, acknowledged that they were all surpassed by the superior magnificence of Carinus.

The spectacles of Carinus may therefore be best illustrated by the observation of some particulars which history has condescended to relate concerning those of his predecessors. If we confine ourselves solely to the hunting of wild beasts, however we may censure the vanity of the design or the cruelty of the execution, we are obliged to confess that neither before nor since the time of the Romans so much art and expense have ever been lavished for the amusement of the people. By the order of Probus, a great quantity of large trees, torn up by the roots, were transplanted into the midst of the circus. The spacious and shady forest was immediately filled with a thousand ostriches, a thousand stags, a thousand fallow-deer, and a thousand wild boars; and all this variety of game was abandoned to the riotous impetuosity of the multitude. The tragedy of the succeeding day consisted in the massacre of an hundred lions, an equal number of lionesses, two hundred leopards, and three hundred bears. The collection prepared by the younger Gordian for his triumph, and which his successor exhibited in the secular games, was less remarkable by the number than by the singularity of the animals. Twenty zebras displayed their elegant forms and variegated beauty to the eyes of the Roman people.* Ten elks, and as many camelopards, the loftiest and most harmless creatures that wander over the plains of Sarmatia and Ethiopia, were contrasted with thirty African hyaenas and ten Indian tigers, the most implacable savages of the torrid zone. The unoffending strength with which Nature has endowed the greater

* They are called *Onagri*; but the number is too inconsiderable for mere wild asses. Cuper has proved from Oppian, Dion, and an anonymous Greek, that zebras had been seen at Rome. They were brought from some island of the ocean, perhaps Madagascar.

quadrupeds was admired in the rhinoceros, the hippopotamus of the Nile,* and a majestic troop of thirty-two elephants. While the populace gazed with stupid wonder on the splendid show, the naturalist might indeed observe the figure and properties of so many different species, transported from every part of the ancient world into the amphitheatre of Rome. But this accidental benefit which science might derive from folly is surely insufficient to justify such a wanton abuse of the public riches. There occurs, however, a single instance in the first Punic war in which the senate wisely connected this amusement of the multitude with the interest of the state. A considerable number of elephants, taken in the defeat of the Carthaginian army, were driven through the circus by a few slaves, armed only with blunt javelins. The useful spectacle served to impress the Roman soldier with a just contempt for those unwieldy animals; and he no longer dreaded to encounter them in the ranks of war.

The hunting or exhibition of wild beasts was conducted with a magnificence suitable to a people who styled themselves the masters of the world; nor was the edifice appropriated to that entertainment less expressive of Roman greatness. Posterity admires, and will long admire, the awful remains of the amphitheatre of Titus, which so well deserved the epithet of Colossal. It was a building of an elliptic figure, five hundred and sixty-four feet in length, and four hundred and sixty-seven in breadth, founded on fourscore arches, and rising, with four successive orders of architecture, to the height of one hundred and forty feet.† The outside of the edifice was encrusted with marble and decorated with statues. The slopes of the vast concave, which formed the inside, were filled and surrounded with sixty or eighty rows of seats, of marble likewise, covered with cushions, and capable of receiving with ease above four-score thousand spectators. Sixty-four *vomitories* (for by that name the doors were very aptly distinguished) poured forth the immense multitude; and the entrances, passages, and staircases were contrived with such exquisite skill, that each person, whether of the senatorial, the equestrian, or the plebeian order, arrived at his destined place without trouble or confusion. Nothing was omitted which, in any respect, could

* Carinus gave an hippopotamus. In the latter spectacles I do not recollect any crocodiles, of which Augustus once exhibited thirty-six.
† The height was very much exaggerated by the ancients. It reached almost to the heavens, according to Calpurnius; and surpassed the ken of human sight, according to Ammianus Marcellinus. Yet how trifling to the great pyramid of Egypt, which rises 500 feet perpendicular!

be subservient to the convenience and pleasure of the spectators. They were protected from the sun and rain by an ample canopy, occasionally drawn over their heads. The air was continually refreshed by the playing of fountains, and profusely impregnated by the grateful scent of aro-matics. In the centre of the edifice, the *arena*, or stage, was strewed with the finest sand, and successively assumed the most different forms. At one moment it seemed to rise out of the earth, like the garden of the Hesperides, and was afterwards broken into the rocks and caverns of Thrace. The subterraneous pipes conveyed an inexhaustible supply of water; and what had just before appeared a level plain might be suddenly converted into a wide lake, covered with armed vessels, and replenished with the monsters of the deep. In the decoration of these scenes the Roman emperors displayed their wealth and liberality; and we read on various occasions that the whole furniture of the amphitheatre consisted either of silver, or of gold, or of amber. The poet who describes the games of Carinus, in the character of a shepherd attracted to the capital by the fame of their magnificence, affirms that the nets designed as a defence against the wild beasts were of gold wire; that the porticoes were gilded; and that the *belt* or circle which divided the several ranks of spectators from each other was studded with a precious mosaic of beautiful stones.

In the midst of this glittering pageantry, the emperor Carinus, secure of his fortune, enjoyed the acclamations of the people, the flattery of his courtiers, and the songs of the poets, who, for want of a more essential merit, were reduced to celebrate the divine graces of his person. In the same hour, but at the distance of nine hundred miles from Rome, his brother expired; and a sudden revolution transferred into the hands of a stranger the sceptre of the house of Carus.*

The sons of Carus never saw each other after their father's death. The arrangements which their new situation required were probably deferred till the return of the younger brother to Rome, where a triumph was decreed to the young emperors for the glorious success of the Persian war. It is uncertain whether they intended to divide between them the administration or the provinces of the empire; but it is very unlikely that their union would have proved of any long duration. The jealousy of power must have been inflamed by the opposition of characters. In the most corrupt of times Carinus was unworthy to live: Numerian deserved

* With regard to the time when these Roman games were celebrated, Scaliger, Salmasius, and Cuper have given themselves a great deal of trouble to perplex a very clear subject.

to reign in a happier period. His affable manners and gentle virtues secured him, as soon as they became known, the regard and affections of the public. He possessed the elegant accomplishments of a poet and orator, which dignify as well as adorn the humblest and the most exalted station. His eloquence, however it was applauded by the senate, was formed not so much on the model of Cicero as on that of the modern declaimers; but in an age very far from being destitute of poetical merit, he contended for the prize with the most celebrated of his contemporaries, and still remained the friend of his rivals; a circumstance which evinces either the goodness of his heart, or the superiority of his genius. But the talents of Numerian were rather of the contemplative than of the active kind. When his father's elevation reluctantly forced him from the shade of retirement, neither his temper nor his pursuits had qualified him for the command of armies. His constitution was destroyed by the hardships of the Persian war; and he had contracted, from the heat of the climate, such a weakness in his eyes, as obliged him, in the course of a long retreat, to confine himself to the solitude and darkness of a tent or litter. The administration of all affairs, civil as well as military, was devolved on Arrius Aper, the Praetorian prefect, who, to the power of his important office, added the honour of being father-in-law to Numerian. The Imperial pavilion was strictly guarded by his most trusty adherents; and during many days Aper delivered to the army the supposed mandates of their invisible sovereign.

It was not till eight months after the death of Carus that the Roman army, returning by slow marches from the banks of the Tigris, arrived on those of the Thracian Bosphorus. The legions halted at Chalcedon in Asia, while the court passed over to Heraclea, on the European side of the Propontis. But a report soon circulated through the camp, at first in secret whispers, and at length in loud clamours, of the emperor's death, and of the presumption of his ambitious minister, who still exercised the sovereign power in the name of a prince who was no more. The impatience of the soldiers could not long support a state of suspense. With rude curiosity they broke into the imperial tent, and discovered only the corpse of Numerian. The gradual decline of his health might have induced them to believe that his death was natural; but the concealment was interpreted as an evidence of guilt, and the measures which Aper had taken to secure his election became the immediate occasion of his ruin. Yet, even in the transport of their rage and grief, the troops observed a regular proceeding, which proves how firmly discipline had been re-established by the martial successors of Gallienus. A general assembly of the army was appointed to be held at Chalcedon, whither Aper was transported in chains, as a prisoner and a criminal. A vacant tribunal was erected in the midst of the camp, and the generals and tribunes formed a great military council. They soon announced to the multitude that their choice had fallen on Diocletian, commander of the domestics or body-guards, as the person the most capable of revenging and succeeding their beloved emperor. The future fortunes of the candidate depended on the chance or conduct of the present hour. Conscious that the station which he had filled exposed him to some suspicion, Diocletian ascended the tribunal, and, raising his eyes towards the sun, made a solemn profession of his own innocence, in the presence of that all-seeing Deity. Then, assuming the tone of a sovereign and a judge, he commanded that Aper should be brought in chains to the foot of the tribunal. 'This man,' said he, 'is the murderer of Numerian;' and without giving him time to enter on a dangerous justification, drew his sword, and buried it in the breast of the unfortunate prefect. A charge supported by such decisive proof was admitted without contradiction, and the legions, with repeated acclamations, acknowledged the justice and authority of the emperor Diocletian.

Before we enter upon the memorable reign of that prince, it will be proper to punish and dismiss the unworthy brother of Numerian. Carinus possessed arms and treasures sufficient to support his legal title to the empire. But his personal vices over-balanced every advantage of birth and situation. The most faithful servants of the father despised the incapacity, and dreaded the cruel arrogance of the son. The hearts of the people were engaged in favour of his rival, and even the senate was inclined to prefer an usurper to a tyrant. The arts of Diocletian inflamed the general discontent; and the winter was employed in secret intrigues and open preparations for a civil war. In the spring the forces of the East and of the West encountered each other in the plains of Margus, a small city of Maesia, in the neighbourhood of the Danube. The troops, so lately returned from the Persian war, had acquired their glory at the expense of health and numbers, nor were they in a condition to contend with the unexhausted strength of the legions of Europe. Their ranks were broken, and, for a moment, Diocletian despaired of the purple and of life. But the advantage which Carinus had obtained by the valour of his soldiers he quickly lost by the infidelity of his officers. A tribune, whose wife he had seduced, seized the opportunity of revenge, and by a single blow extinguished civil discord in the blood of the adulterer.

INDEX

Scotland

Wall of Antoninus

Hadrian's Wall

Ireland

York

Lincoln

BRITAIN

Bath   London

ATLANTIC OCEAN

Lower Germany

GERMAN

Celtic Gaul

Belgic Gaul

R. Seine

R. Rhine

Upper Germany

Lyonnese Gaul

R. Loire

G A U L

Aquitania

R. Rhone

Maritime Alps

Rhaetic

Noricum

PANNONI

Verona

I T A L Y

Venice

Narbonnese Gaul

Liguria

Genoa

Dalmatia

Tarraconensis

Pyrenees Mts.

Lusitania

SPAIN

Corsica

Apennine Mts.

R. Tiber

ROME

Apulia

Naples

Minorca

Majorca

Sardinia

M E D I T E R R A

MAURETANIA

Carthage

Sicily

Tingitana

Numidia   Zama

Atlas   Mts.

A F R I C A

L   I   B

——-——-—   Roman Empire Frontier A.D. 14

· · · · · · · · · ·   Roman Empire Frontier A.D. 117